ESL SMART!

Ready-to-Use Life Skills & Academic Activities for Grades K-8

MARGARET BOUCHARD

Illustrations by Shelley Freese

THE CENTER FOR APPLIED
RESEARCH IN EDUCATION
West Nyack, New York 10994

Library of Congress Cataloging-in-Publication Data

Bouchard, Margaret.
    ESL smart! : a ready-to-use life & content skills activities
program for ESL students / Margaret Bouchard ; illustrations
by Shelley Freese.
        p.   cm
    ISBN 0-13-017481-5 (spiral wire)   ISBN 0-13-092573-X (paper)
    1. English language—Textbooks for foreign speakers.
    2. Life skills—Problems, excercises, etc.   I. Title.
PE1128 .B64 2000
428.2′4—dc21

                                                00-064331

Printed in the United States of America

10 9 8 7 6 5 4 3 2 1   10 9 8 7 6 5 4 3 2 1

ISBN 0-13-017481-5 (spiral wire)   ISBN 0-13-092573-X (paper)

ATTENTION: CORPORATIONS AND SCHOOLS

The Center for Applied Research in Education books are available at quantity discounts with bulk purchase for educational, business, or sales promotional use. For information, please write to: Prentice Hall Special Sales, 240 Frisch Court, Paramus, NJ 07652. Please supply: title of book, ISBN, quantity, how the book will be used, date needed.

**THE CENTER FOR APPLIED RESEARCH
IN EDUCATION**
West Nyack, NY 10994

www.phdirect.com

Dedication

To my husband, Emerson, for his neverending patience, support, and sense of humor. And to my children, Marc, Rob, and Nicole. I can be the person I am because of you.

Over the years, I have never stopped learning from my students and their families, who are the strongest individuals I have ever met. This book is for you and the thousands of people who will follow in your footsteps. You are the past and future of America. You are what makes us strong. God bless you.

About the Author

MARGIE MAX BOUCHARD received her Bachelor of Science, Ed. from Valparaiso University and her Master of Education/Reading from National College of Education, Evanston, Illinois. She received a TESOL endorsement from Eastern Michigan University and an ESL endorsement from the University of Kansas. Mrs. Bouchard is a doctoral student at Walden University, Minneapolis, and is focusing her studies in the area of ESL/Early Literacy.

Mrs. Bouchard has served as a member of the Oakland County Bilingual Directors Board, an ESL Teacher/Coordinator for the Lamphere School District, and presented staff development and professional workshops for Title I and MITESOL. She is currently an instructor at the Applied Language Institute, University of Missouri, Kansas City.

In addition to her work in the field of ESL education, Mrs. Bouchard is also a Reading Specialist with expertise in the area of early literacy. She is the author of an early literacy program entitled, *I'm a Letter A, B, C, D, I'm a Number 1, 2, 3*. She has also worked in the field of reading literacy as an Educational Consultant for the Oakland Schools Intermediate School District, Child Development Center.

Acknowledgments

This book became a reality because of the initial encouragement of Winfield Huppuch, and the patient, insightful guidance of my editor, Susan Kolwicz. Thank you both for believing in this project and for your support.

I would like to honor the following educators who have devoted their lives to the children of this world and from whom I have learned so much: Jackie Moase-Burke, Fida Shaya, Rafid Jarbo, Dr. Nancy Campbell, Dr. Donna Ogle, Dr. Nat Peters, Nita Peters, Dr. Liz England, Dr. Kathy Day, Doris Rentner, Jeannie Sill, Susan Edgar, Judy Crain, Sharon Stephens, James McCann, Bobbie Labriola, Carol Domrose, Denise Jenkins, Kathy Riehle, Linda Lange, Monica Mingucci, Stella Green, and Leah Pearl. You are very special people.

Also Lewis Deugood, editor at the *Kansas City Star,* who fights for the rights of all human beings. Yours is the voice of wisdom and truth.

About This Resource

Educators have become increasingly aware of the changing ethnic and racial make-up of the typical American classroom for some time now. A total of approximately 4.1 million Limited English Proficient (LEP) students presently attend public schools. This number is increasing every year and is expected to grow by 20 percent in the next two decades! It is also a fact that these students will enter American schools with varied educational backgrounds and little or no knowledge of American culture. The implications for the ESL professional and mainstream classroom teacher are staggering. These professionals will not only be responsible for teaching grade-level curriculum, but also for laying a solid foundation of entry-level life skills for the ESL student.

The first experiences an ESL student has in American schools is crucial to the future success of cultural assimilation, language development, and creating a positive attitude toward him-/herself in this new environment. *In order to survive in his/her new country, the newcomer must learn essential, entry-level life skills.* However, in many school districts across the country, ESL teachers find themselves overwhelmed by large numbers of students and staff, and mainstream classroom teachers can find themselves with little or no support. This makes the task of teaching basic life skills difficult to accomplish. In addition, locating, organizing, and managing information that teaches entry-level life skills is a time consuming, often frustrating task. The purpose of this book is to serve as a comprehensive, all-inclusive resource that organizes basic information and life skills into one convenient resource.

ESL Smart is divided into two main categories of life skills. Part 1, **Personal Life Skills,** includes the life skills necessary to succeed and function in the everyday world of American society. Part 2, **School and Academic Skills,** provides the newcomer with information about life in American schools and includes basic academic content that contains an extensive literacy section. These lessons can be invaluable for "filling-in" information gaps.

ESL Smart provides over 175 detailed lesson plans accompanied by convenient ready-to-use activity sheets and suggested extension activities. Vocabulary is included with each lesson and highlights important conceptual language. ESL students enter your classroom at varying stages of competency, so a Pretest–Posttest accompanies each academic section of Part 2.

Although each lesson in *ESL Smart* is designed as part of a larger unit, the lessons can also be used independently. The lessons should be introduced according to student need. (You may also find that the lessons are appropriate for your American students.) *ESL Smart* is intended to provide practical and focused information for teachers of varying levels of expertise and experience.

The joys of teaching ESL students can be endless. It can be a life-changing experience for both teacher and student. The sharing of cultures and the nurturing of mutual respect and friendship are life skills that we all must learn in order to make this world a more positive and peaceful place in which to live.

Margie Bouchard

Contents

Section 4: Personal Hygiene and Health   124

Section 5: Safety   166

Part 2: SCHOOL AND ACADEMIC SKILLS   221

Section 10: Time, Calendar, and Weather   495

Section 11: Colors and Shapes   545

Section 12: Spatial Concepts, Direction, & World Geography   556

Part 1

PERSONAL LIFE SKILLS

In order for ESL students to function efficiently, safely, and socially in their new environment, specific information and social skills must be understood and practiced. Over the years, different cultures and societies have developed social behaviors and rules that are viewed as accepted practice. When these parameters are crossed, negative reaction will soon follow. It is crucial, therefore, for the newcomer to know appropriate behavior and responses in routine social and life situations. Becoming acquainted with their new country's social parameters can help the newcomer avoid many embarrassing situations that may result in resentful reactions against him/her. Finally, understanding the rules for safety and how to get emergency help will keep the student safe in his/her new environment.

The following information will give brief descriptions of each section and the lessons that are presented.

Personal Information: Almost on a daily basis, situations will arise in which the student must provide personal information, both written and verbal. The lessons in this section teach the important information of name, age, gender, address, and phone number and how to provide it correctly. Also included are lessons in which the student can effectively express personal information about him-/herself. This information can help the teacher and others know the newcomer in a more personal manner.

Personal Communication: Learning how to communicate is the essence of functioning successfully in a new culture. The areas of communication that are presented in this section include using the telephone, culturally accepted guidelines for speaking and listening, and understanding nonverbal communication (gestures, body talk, noises, and pictures).

Manners and Social Interaction: Understanding the social rules of a new culture can pave the way for a smooth transition and acceptance of the newcomer. Basic manners as well as socially accepted interactions are taught in this section.

Personal Hygiene and Health: Guidelines for culturally accepted hygiene and health practices are taught. This can often be an uncomfortable subject to address; however, when presented in lesson format, these issues become less embarrassing for both student and instructor. Lessons include hygiene, parts of the body, how to communicate when you are sick, and how to keep your body physically and emotionally healthy.

Safety: These lessons teach the newcomer to recognize dangerous situations, how to respond to them, and how to get emergency help for them. Safety rules for pedestrians, bikes, railroad, water, strangers, drugs, and guns are addressed. International safety signs are also included.

Section 1

Personal Information

"Remember that a person's name is to that person the sweetest and most important sound in any language."

—Dale Carnegie

These words of Dale Carnegie should be placed indelibly in our minds and hearts. One of the first English words to which a new ESL student will respond is his/her name. It makes that person unique among all others. Therefore, it is very important for you to use the correct pronunciation and spelling of the student's name and to relate it to other staff members and classmates. This creates an atmosphere of acceptance and respect. Take a few minutes to practice any difficult pronunciations or spellings; the time will be well spent and appreciated.

When many newcomers arrive in our country, they seek to be as "Americanized" as possible. One way to assimilate into this new society is to choose an American or English name to replace an obvious or difficult ethnic one. This is particularly common among adolescents and teenagers who have a very strong desire to "belong." Also, many parents will choose an American name for a younger child thinking this will help the child's transition into the new cultural environment. This is a valid coping skill and should be accepted by the school community. It is helpful for you or the contact person to inquire if the student has a preference in names. If so, this name can be used informally at school. However, on any legal documents, tests, or official information, the student's legal name must be used. Knowing this in advance can save much time and confusion.

Very often, after a period of assimilation, many children will choose to revert back to their birth names. It is truly their identity and should be encouraged, but never forced.

When asking a student or family member to supply personal information, always explain why the information is needed. This helps relieve any suspicions on the part of those who have immigrated from oppressive governments.

By using Lesson 1–8, "Getting to Know You," as a whole group activity, the entire class can become acquainted with their new classmate. It also gives the newcomer an opportunity to feel part of the group and share interesting information about him-/herself.

Lesson 1-1: What Is Your Name?

. . . .

Objectives: The student will understand the concept of first, middle, last, and full name. The student will respond appropriately to the question, "What is your name?" The student will spell and write his/her full name.

Vocabulary: name; first; middle; last; full name

Materials: Activity Sheet 1–1; Pencil; Picture of the student (*optional*)

Teaching Notes:

1. Know how to correctly pronounce the name of the student.

2. Check for any irregular or special spellings.

3. Many Hispanic students will use two last names (their mother's and father's). In this case, use the father's last name; it is usually the one that is used for legal purposes.

4. If a student has more than one middle name, use the first one listed on the school enrollment form. If a student does not have a middle name, explain the concept and adapt the lesson for first name, last name.

Directions:

1. Point to yourself and say, "My *name* is <u>your name</u>. What is your name?" (Point to student.) If possible, the student should respond with a full sentence, "My name is _____." If the student does not respond, point to other students and say, "His *name* is _____. Her *name* is _____." Then point to the student again and ask, "What is your name?" If the student still does not understand the concept of "name," use a picture of the student as a visual aid.

2. Give the student a copy of Activity Sheet 1–1. Read #1. Point to the illustration and say, "Her name is Rosa Maria Garza." Ask the student to repeat. Then say, "She has three names." (Hold up three fingers.) Now, point to each name as you say it. "Her first name is Rosa, her middle name is Maria, her last name is Garza."

3. Point to #2 and say, "You have three names. (**Gesture:** Point to the student and hold up three fingers.) Your first name is _____." Point to the box, student says his/her first name. Then ask the student to write his/her first name, saying each letter name. If necessary, write the letters and ask the student to trace. Continue with the same procedure for "a middle name" and "a last name."

4. Direct the student to point to his/her first name, then middle name, then last name. If correct, ask for a verbal response, "What is your first name?" (Student

5

says name, then spells it.) "What is your middle name? What is your last name?" Ask the student to write his/her first, middle, and last names in the correct boxes provided in #3. Check for accuracy.

5. With your finger, trace a continuous line under each name as you say them in order. Ask the student to do the same. Then say, "When we say all three names in order, it is called your *full name*. What is your full name?" Student responds by saying his/her full name in the correct order.

6. After that task is completed, ask the student to practice writing his/her full name on the lines provided in #4.

7. For reinforcement, cut out the three name cards in #2. Turn them face down and mix them up. Have the student turn them face up and put them in correct order. Or, ask the student to turn over a name card and identify it as his/her first, middle, or last name.

8. Play "Conversation." This activity is done with a partner. Tell the student that when he/she tells another person his/her name, use the first and last names. (**Gesture:** Point to the student and his/her partner. Make the talking gesture with your hands [fingers touch the thumb and go up and down].) Then say, "First name, last name." Ask the student to practice the following conversation with his/her partner. Model.

PERSON 1: "Hi, my name is <u>first name, last name.</u>"
PERSON 2: "Hi, I'm <u>first name, last name.</u>"

Extension Activities:

1. Choose a student's first, middle, or last name. Then give that student a direction, such as "If your last name is _____, jump up and down."

2. Play "The Name Game." Say a student's name and toss a foam ball to him/her. Then that student must say the name of a student and toss the ball to that person. You may want to make a rule that the student can't throw the ball back to the person who threw it to him/her, or that he/she must choose a different person for each turn.

3. For older or more advanced students, teach the following:

   • Teach the meaning of personal initials.
   • Explain the meaning or general use of first, middle, and last names:

   <u>First name</u>—used primarily by friends, used informally
   <u>Middle name</u>—generally a name given in honor of someone, or the last name of the mother's family
   <u>Last name</u>—your "family" name

4. Explain the meaning of the word *signature.* Have the student practice writing his/her signature.

Name_____ Date_____

Your First, Middle, and Last Names

1.

"My name is

Rosa Maria Garza."

1   2   3

2. **Write your name in the boxes. Cut out the cards and mix them up.**

First Name	Middle Name	Last Name

3. **Write the correct name in the box.**

4. **Write your full name three times.**

_____ _____ _____

_____ _____ _____

_____ _____ _____

Lesson 1-2: Address

• • • • • • • • • • • • • • • • •

Objectives: The student will understand the concept of the word "address." The student will correctly respond to the question, "What is your address?" The student will correctly verbalize and write his/her personal address.

Vocabulary: address; live; house number; apartment number; street name; city; state; ZIP Code

Materials: Activity Sheet 1–2; Examples of items that have an address written on them (envelopes, packages, magazines, etc.); Pencil; Scissors; Pictures of various kinds of houses (*optional*)

Teaching Notes:

1. Before beginning the lesson, obtain the student's current address and keep it in a convenient place (e.g., index card). Many newcomers have frequent changes of address.

2. Many ESL students do not understand the significance of the various parts of an address and omit important information. This is an essential part of the lesson.

3. The student needs to review this information frequently.

Directions:

1. Give the student a copy of Activity Sheet 1–2. Say, "People live in different kinds of homes." Show the student pictures of homes or use the illustrations on the activity sheet. Say the name of each type of home. Ask the student to say and point to the kind of home in which he/she lives and then place an X on the appropriate illustration.

2. Next show the student a letter/envelope on which an address has been printed and say, "This is an address." (Point to address.) "Each home has an address." (**Gesture:** Point to the homes on the activity sheet, then point to the address on the envelope.) Say, "An address tells people where the home is (located)." Display other items that need an address to be delivered: packages, newspapers, magazines, etc. Point to the address on each example. If possible, discuss the reasons a home needs an address and why it is important to know your address (safety, visitors, legal and school forms, etc.).

3. Point to the address boxes in Part One on the activity sheet. Then point to the student and say, "Your address is _____." Say the student's address. Then help the student write the correct information in each box. Use the illustrations to explain what each part of the address means. (For *state*, draw an illustration that represents your state.)

8

4. Ask the student, "What is your address?" Student responds verbally. Explain that another way to ask for an address is, "Where do you live?"

5. Ask the student to copy his/her address in Part Two on the activity sheet. Check for accuracy.

6. For further reinforcement, ask the student to cut out the boxes in Part Two. Then mix them up and put them in the correct order.

7. Ask the student to recite his/her address from memory. (Younger students may require several sessions, and should review this information frequently. An older student should be asked to write his/her address from memory.)

Extension Activities:

1. The student draws a picture of his/her home and writes the address under it.

2. Write the student's address on a strip of paper, omitting some parts. The student must supply the missing items.

Name _____

Date _____

Address

Put an X on the kind of home you live in.

Apartment Building	House	Mobile Home (Trailer)	Townhouse

Part One: Write your address in the boxes. Cut out the boxes, mix them up, and put them in order.

House/building #	Direction: N, S, E, W	Street Name	Apartment #
City	State	ZIP Code	

Part Two: Write and say your address.

_____

_____

Lesson 1-3: Telephone Number

•••••••••••••••••••••••••••

Objectives: The student will learn to say/write his/her telephone number from memory. The student will understand the question, "What is your telephone number?"

Vocabulary: telephone number; area code; home telephone number

Materials: Activity Sheet 1–3; Pencil; Scissors; Practice phone (real or toy) (*optional*)

Teaching Note:

Obtain the student's current telephone number and keep it in a convenient place.

Directions:

Copy the student's telephone number in #1 on the activity sheet.

1. Give the student a copy of Activity Sheet 1–3 and say, "Today you are going to learn your telephone number." To clarify, point to the student and then to the illustration of the telephone. Point to the student's telephone number in #1 and repeat the numbers. Ask the student to point to each number and repeat.

2. Point to the *area code* and say, "These three numbers (repeat numbers) are called your *area code*." Ask the student to repeat, "My area code is _____." Explain that an area code is given to a certain neighborhood, town, or city. Say, "People and businesses in your neighborhood (town, city) have the same area code." Refer to the illustration in #2 on the activity sheet.

3. Ask the student to write the area code on the telephone provided in #2 on the activity sheet.

4. Point to and say the *home telephone* number. Ask the student to repeat. Say, "These numbers are for your telephone only. They are called your *home telephone number*." Refer to the illustration.

5. Ask the student to write his/her home telephone number on the telephone in #2.

6. Ask the student, "What is your whole telephone number?" This should include the area code and home number.

7. Ask the student to write his/her telephone number in the boxes provided in #3 on the activity sheet.

8. Ask the student to write his/her telephone number in #4.

9. Ask the student to recite his/her telephone number from memory.

11

10. Ask the student to write his/her telephone number from memory.

11. For further reinforcement, ask the student to cut out the number boxes in #3. Mix them up. The student then puts them in the correct order.

12. This information should be reviewed frequently.

Extension Activities:

1. Write the student's telephone number on a card, leaving some spaces blank. Ask the student to fill in the correct numbers.

2. Ask the student to dial his/her correct telephone number on a practice telephone.

Name_____ Date_____

Telephone Number

1. **My telephone number is:** (Fill in the blanks.)

____ ____ ____ — ____ ____ ____ ____ ____ ____ ____

Area code   Home Telephone Number

2.

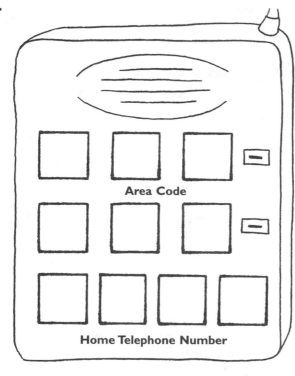

Area Code = Neighborhood, town, or city

Home Telephone Number = Only Me!

3. **Write your telephone number in the boxes. Cut them out and put in correct order.**

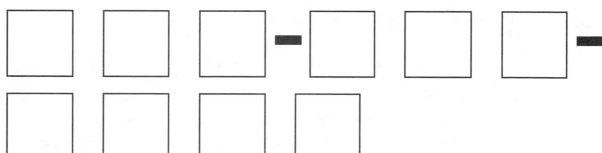

4. **Write your telephone number.**

____ ____ ____ — ____ ____ ____ — ____ ____ ____ ____

Lesson 1-4: Emergency Information

Objectives: The student will understand the concept of "emergency information." The student will learn the important information placed on the Emergency Information Card.

Vocabulary: emergency; contact person; medicine; allergy

Materials: Activity Sheet 1–4; Pencil; Scissors

Teaching Notes:

1. Make a copy of the student's current emergency information from school records.

2. Check for medications or allergies.

Directions:

Before beginning the lesson, have a copy of the student's emergency information with you.

1. Give the student a copy of Activity Sheet 1–4. Point to the illustrations in #1 and say, "Sometime, you may become sick or hurt at school. Then your mother or father or another adult (relative, friend of the family) must be called."

2. Point to the illustrations in #2 on the activity sheet, and tell the student it is very important to know where his/her parents are while he/she is in school. (Refer to the student's emergency information.) Read the sentences in #2. Ask the student to put an X next to the correct location. Ask the student to repeat in a complete sentence, "My mother is at (home, work). My father is at (home, work)." If the parent is at work, recite the work information and ask the student to repeat. Then have the student write the work information in the blanks. (NOTE: For younger students, it is enough for them to know the name of the workplace. For more advanced students, the telephone number should be learned.)

3. Point to the illustrations in #1 and say, "If Father or Mother can't be called (**gesture:** point to the pictures of Father and Mother and shake your head "no"), we can call another adult for help, a family member or a friend of your family. This person is called your *emergency contact person*."

4. Point to the illustration in #3 and say, "Your *emergency contact person* is _____. The phone number is _____." Ask the student to repeat and write the correct information in the blanks.

5. **If applicable:** Next, point to the illustrations in #4 and say, "Some people take medicine and some people are allergic to things. This is your medicine

14

_____, or you are allergic to _____." (**Gesture:** For medicine, pretend to take a pill and drink water. For allergy, itch vigorously.)

6. Ask the student to copy the correct information on the Emergency Information Card. The student can cut this out and carry it in his/her backpack, wallet, or purse.

7. Review this information periodically.

Extension Activities:

1. Role Play: Ask a student to pretend he/she is sick or hurt. Another student plays the teacher or nurse and asks, "Who do we call?" The student must give the location and phone number of at least one parent.

2. Use a practice telephone. Ask the student to dial the parent at work or home. Pretend no one answers. The student must then give the name and number of the emergency contact person.

Name_____ Date_____

Emergency Information

1.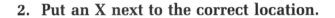

   sick   hurt   Mother   Father   Relative or Friend

2. **Put an X next to the correct location.**

   I am at school.   My mother is at: home _____ work _____

      My father is at: home _____ work _____

   Fill in the blanks.

    Mother's work: _____ Telephone # _____

    Father's work: _____  Telephone # _____

3. **Fill in the blanks.**

    Emergency Contact Person: _____ Telephone # _____

4. **Fill in the blanks.**

   Medication _____   Allergies: _____

5. **Fill in the correct information. Cut out and keep in backpack, wallet, or purse.**

   Emergency Information Card

   Name: _____
   In case of emergency, call:
   Mother's name: _____ Telephone # _____
   Workplace: _____ Telephone # _____
   Father's name: _____ Telephone # _____
   Workplace: _____ Telephone # _____
   Contact person: _____ Telephone # _____
   Medications: _____ Allergies: _____

Lesson 1-5: Birthday/Age

• •

Objectives: The student will memorize the month, day, and year of his/her birthday. The student will correctly identify his/her chronological age. The student will understand and correctly respond to the questions: "When is your birthday?" "What is your age?" and "How old are you?" The student will write his/her birthdate and age.

Vocabulary: birthday; age; old

Materials: Activity Sheet 1–5; Pencil; Crayons, colored pencils; Examples of the following—a birthday party invitation, a box wrapped as a gift, a birthday card, gift wrap, a party hat, candles, streamers, ribbon/bow, balloons, "Pin the Tail on the Donkey" game, other party items (*optional*)

Teaching Notes:

1. In some cultures, the child is considered one year old at birth. Therefore, there will be a one-year discrepancy between the native age and the American age.

2. When saying the date, many cultures use the following order: the number of the day, the name of the month, then the year. This may cause some confusion for the student. If this occurs, explain that in America the order in which we say the date is: name of the month, number of the day, then the year.

Directions:

Before beginning the lesson, write the student's birthday in #1 on the activity sheet.

1. Give the student a copy of Activity Sheet 1–5 and say, "Today we are going to talk about your birthday and age." Sing the universal "Happy Birthday" song. Most students will recognize the tune immediately. Ask the students to sing along with you.

2. (If you haven't yet done so, write the student's birthday in #1.) Point to the student and ask, "When is your birthday?" Point to the information in #1 and model for the student, "My birthday is _____." Ask the student to repeat the sentence, "My birthday is _____." Then ask the student again, "When is your birthday?" If possible, the response should be in a complete sentence.

3. Point to #2 and ask the student to circle the correct month, day, and year of his/her birthday. Check for accuracy. Then ask the student to write his/her birthday in the spaces provided. Ask the student again, "When is your birthday?" The student should respond with the complete sentence.

4. Point to the birthday cake in #3. Tell the student, "Your age tells how many years you have lived. Your age is _____. Draw a candle on the cake for

each year." Have the student draw the correct number of candles on the birthday cake. Ask the student to count the candles and then say the number. Now ask the student again, "What is your age?" If possible, the student should respond in a complete sentence, "My age is _____."

5. Explain to the student that another way to ask a person's age is to say "How old are you?" Ask the student to respond with the sentence, "I am _____ years old." Complete #4 on the activity sheet.

6. Review the information frequently.

Extension Activities:

1. Create a "Birthday Box." Decorate a cardboard box. Place assorted birthday items in it. (See optional materials for this lesson.) Ask the student to close his/her eyes, choose an item from the box, and identify it.

2. Draw a picture of My Favorite Birthday or a picture of how birthdays are celebrated in the student's native land. Let the student share.

3. Play some popular birthday party games, such as "Pin the Tail on the Donkey," "Fish and Straw," "Musical Chairs."

4. Practice singing the song "Happy Birthday" in English. Ask the student to sing it in his/her native language or share any other ethnic birthday songs.

Name_____ Date_____

 **Birthday/Age**

1. **Teacher: Supply the correct information. Ask the student to repeat the sentence.**

    "My birthday is _____ _____ _____."
    Month Day Year

2. **Circle the correct answer.**   **Write the correct number.**

Month		Day	Year
1 January	7 July	1,2,3,4,5,6,7,8,9,10,	
2 February	8 August		19_____
3 March	9 September	11,12,13,14,15,16,17,	
4 April	10 October	18,19,20,21,22,23,24,	
5 May	11 November		
6 June	12 December	25,26,27,28,29,30,31	20_____

   Fill in the blanks and repeat the sentence.

    "My birthday is _____ _____ _____."
    Month Day Year

   Write your birthday the "quick way." Use only numbers (numerical date).

    _____ / _____ / _____
    Month Day Year

3. **How old are you? Draw the correct number of candles on the cake.**

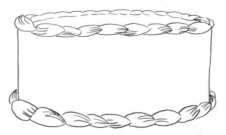

4. **Count the number of candles on the cake and fill in the blanks. Repeat the sentences.**

    "I am _____ years old."   "My age is _____."

Lesson 1-6: Gender

• • • • • • • • • • • • • • • •

Objectives: The student will identify the correct gender for him-/herself. The student will understand the meaning of boy, girl, man, woman, male, and female.

Vocabulary: boy; girl; man; woman; male; female

Materials: Activity Sheet 1–6; Pencil; Scissors; Glue; Catalogs and magazines

Directions:

1. Give the student a copy of Activity Sheet 1–6. Point to illustrations in #1 and say, "This is a boy. This is a girl." Then point to the student and ask, "Are you a boy or a girl?" The student should respond with a complete sentence, "I am a boy/girl." Ask the student to circle the correct answer in #1.

2. Point to the illustrations in #2 and say, "This is a man. This is a woman. When a boy grows up, he is a man. When a girl grows up, she is a woman." (**Gesture:** Use your hand and raise it in a growing manner over your head.) Point to the student and ask, "When you grow up, will you be a man or a woman?" The student should circle the correct response in #2.

3. Point to the illustrations in #3 and say, "A boy and a man are male. A girl and a woman are female." Ask the student to repeat. Point to the student and ask, "Are you a male or a female?" Check response. Read the sentences in #3. Ask the student to circle the correct answers.

4. For reinforcement, have the student cut out pictures from catalogs and magazines of a boy, man, girl, and woman. These should be glued in the correct spaces provided in #4.

Extension Activity:

If there is more than one student in the room, play a game in which the boys and girls are each given a different activity. For example, tell all the girls (or females) to jump. Then tell all the boys (or males) to stand up, etc. The children can take turns giving directions to each group.

Name_____ Date_____

Are You a Boy or a Girl?

1.

Circle the correct answer and repeat the sentence.

"I am a: Boy   Girl ."

Boy   Girl

2.

Boy  Man   Girl Woman

Man   Woman   **Circle the correct answer and repeat the sentence.**

"When I grow up, I will be a: Man   Woman ."

---

3. Boy + Man = Male   Girl + Woman = Female

Circle the correct answer.

 John is a: Male   Female   Sally is a: Male   Female

I am a: Male   Female

---

4. Cut out pictures from catalogs and magazines. Glue them in the correct box.

Girl	Boy	Woman	Man

Lesson 1-7: Completing a Form

Objective: The student will understand the format and correctly complete a simple personal information form.

Vocabulary: form; fill out

Materials: Activity Sheet 1–7; Pencil; Examples of various (school, contests, sports, etc.) forms (*optional*)

Teaching Notes:

1. This lesson is an excellent opportunity for the student to review his/her personal information.

2. Use this as a tool to measure how much the student has retained from previous personal information lessons.

3. This lesson is designed for the older student.

4. Inform the student that for male and female, a **M or F** is frequently used. Explain that *sex* means "gender."

Directions:

1. If possible, show the student various types of forms and explain that he/she will be asked to give personal information for many reasons. Discuss the different forms and for what purpose they are used (e.g., school, sports, contests, organizations, etc.). Give the student a copy of Activity Sheet 1–7 and say, "Today you are going to practice completing a form. This form will ask you for personal information about yourself. Look at the form. What items do you know?" For help, the student should use the small illustrations on Practice Form #1. (These illustrations coincide with the ones used in previous lessons.)

2. Review the practice form item by item. Ask the student to fill in the blanks for each item. If needed, make note of the illustrations.

3. After the student has successfully completed the practice form, ask him/her to independently complete Practice Form #2. The student may refer to Form #1 for help. Explain that sometimes this is called "filling out" a form.

4. As an evaluation, make a copy of Practice Form #2 and ask the student to complete it without assistance.

Extension Activity:

Get copies of various types of forms (for example, forms for school, forms to enter a contest, forms for a sport team, etc.). Let the students practice completing these forms.

Name_____ Date_____

Completing a Form

1. **Write the correct information on Practice Form #1. Use the pictures for help.**

Name:

_____

1. First Name   2. Middle Name   3. Last Name

Address: 🏠

_____

House/building # 🏠   N,S,E,W ✛   Street Name 🔨   🏠 Apartment #

_____

City 🏢   State   ZIP Code 🏤

Telephone Number: 📱   🎂 Birthday: Numbers Only!   M = Male   F = Female

___ — ___ — _____   _____/_____/_____   Sex: Circle **M** or **F**
                                Month Day   Year

Emergency: 😊 🏃

_____

Name 😊   💊 Telephone Number   Relationship

Medications: 🧴 💊 💉   Allergies: 🐝 🥜 🦞

_____   _____

2. **Write the correct information on Practice Form #2.**

Name:

_____

1. First Name   2. Middle Name   3. Last Name

Address:

_____

House/building #   N,S,E,W   Street Name   Apartment #

_____

City   State   ZIP Code

Telephone Number: Birthday: M = Male   F = Female

___ — ___ — _____   _____/_____/_____   Sex: Circle **M** or **F**
                                Month Day   Year

Emergency:

_____

Name   Telephone Number   Relationship

Medications: Allergies:

_____   _____

Lesson 1-8: Getting to Know You!

• •

Objective: The student will have an opportunity to share personal information about him-/herself in regard to family, native country, favorite things, and friends.

Vocabulary: family; native country; favorite things; friends

Materials: Activity Sheets 1–8A, 1–8B, 1–8C, 1–8D, 1–8E, 1–8F; Crayons, colored pencils, or markers; Scissors; Glue; Magazines and catalogs; *Optional*: Student may bring photographs/pictures to share, and/or pictures of the student's native country (*National Geographic* is a helpful resource)

Teaching Notes:

1. This is an excellent activity for the whole class. It gives the children a chance to learn about one another and for the ESL child to participate in a classroom activity.

2. If done as a class activity, be sure American students complete Activity Sheet 1–8C, "My Native Country." It is an opportunity for them to focus on the United States, what is here, and our way of life.

3. To provide variety, allow the student to cut out pictures from magazines and catalogs.

Directions:

1. Give the student a copy of the activity sheet you have chosen to teach. If clarification for a concept is needed, use pictures cut from magazines, photographs, or the illustrations provided on the activity sheet.

2. Give the student an opportunity to share.

3. The following are suggestions for teaching the concepts found in the Activity Sheets.

1–8A, "Miguel's Birthday Party," and 1–8B, "My Family"—Give the student a copy of Activity Sheet 1–8A. Read the introduction about Miguel's birthday party. Point to the illustrations of the various family members and say each name. Ask the student to repeat. Explain to the student that families are different. Some children have stepfathers or stepmothers, stepsiblings, or half brothers and sisters, etc. For the older or more advanced student, discuss the lineage of each family member. On Activity Sheet 1–8B, the student can draw his/her family. Encourage the student to include members of the extended family. Ask the student to write the names of his/her family members. Help with spelling, if necessary.

1–8C, "My Native Country"—Write and say the name of the student's native country. Locate it on a map or globe in the classroom and have the student draw the geographical shape. The student may wish to include some interesting things found in his/her native country.

1–8D, "My Favorite Things"—Point to each illustration in each category and read the name to the student. The beginning student may need to dictate the answer and have someone else write the words. The more advanced student should attempt to write the words independently.

1–8E, "My Friends" (in the U.S. and my native country)—To clarify, point to the illustrations of the friends on the activity sheet. Ask the student to name his/her friends. The student can include what he/she likes to do with friends. If necessary, give the student help with the spelling of names.

1–8F, "Story Frame"—The student should write the information on the lines. Help with reading may be necessary. This is a wonderful activity for the beginning of the school year or for a school Open House. Take a picture of each student and put it with his/her story frame to make a wonderful bulletin board.

Extension Activities:

1. Make a classroom notebook. Put all of these sheets in a notebook, and keep it in an accessible spot for the students to enjoy during free time.

2. Choose a student page at random. Read it to the class and ask the children to guess to whom that page belongs.

Name_____ Date_____

Miguel's Birthday Party

It is Miguel's birthday. Many of his family members are here to help him celebrate. Who has come to his party?

Stepmother: Lenora

Mother

Grandmother

Half-brother: Luis

Father

Uncle Jose

Miguel

Grandfather

Brother: Josh

Aunt Maria

Cousin: Caleb

Pet: Woof

Sister: Carmen

Name_____ Date_____

My Family

Draw a picture of your family. Write each name and then tell about your family.

Name_____ Date_____

My Native Country

Write the name of your native country. Draw its shape.
(Teacher: Help, if needed.)

Draw some interesting things about your native country.

Name_____ Date_____

 ## My Favorite Things

Draw a picture and write the name of your favorite things.
(Teacher: Help, if necessary.)

Food    Color    Sport

Book   Drink   Game

TV Show   Animal    Clothes

Car   Movie   Class (reading, math, gym, etc.)

Name_____ Date_____

My Friends

Draw a picture of your friends. Write their names.
(Teacher: Help, if necessary.)

Name_____ Date_____

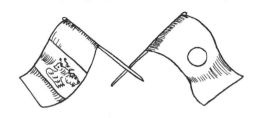

(Picture of student)

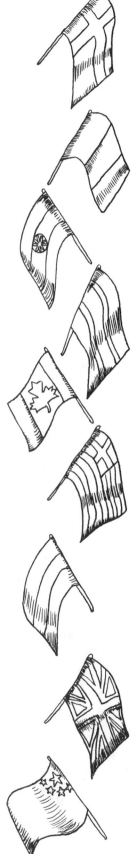

My name is _____.

My native country is _____.

I came to America when I was _____

years old. There are _____ people in my

family. I have _____ sisters and

_____ brothers.

Some interesting things about me are: I like to

play _____. My favorite food is

_____. The subject I like most

is _____. I am very happy

when _____.

When I grow up, I want to be _____

_____. The best thing about me is

_____.

Section 2

Personal Communication

Communication is the soul of language. People communicate for many reasons, ranging from a simple wave or "hello," to holding a lengthy conversation. In order for the newcomer to successfully function in a new cultural environment, he/she must be able to communicate with others.

Over the centuries, cultures have developed unspoken guidelines to follow when communicating with another person. These guidelines differ from culture to culture, and what may be perfectly acceptable in one may be the height of rudeness in another. Often, a person who does not observe these culturally accepted rules is perceived as ill mannered and uninformed. Also, crossing the lines of these communication boundaries can cause other participants to feel uncomfortable, irritated, and uneasy. Therefore, it is essential for the ESL student to understand and put into practice these culturally appropriate guidelines for communication.

Different situations dictate specific behaviors involving both the verbal and physical elements of delivery. In America, these guidelines revolve around the following fundamental concepts:

> *Verbal*: volume, rate, and expression of voice
> *Physical*: personal space, eye contact, and touching

Understanding nonverbal communication—gestures, facial expression, and body language—is also a crucial element in the process of communication.

Spending some time teaching and practicing the accepted behaviors involving personal communication will be well worth your effort. It can help the newcomer avoid embarrassing situations and negative reaction.

Pattern: Practice Telephone

Make a copy of this pattern and glue it onto stiff paper or cardboard.
(*Optional:* Connect the base and the receiver with a piece of yarn.) You will
use this cardboard phone if a real telephone is not available.

Lesson 2-1: Dialing the Telephone

• •

Objectives: The student will become familiar with the dial of a telephone and how to dial a telephone number. The student will understand the word *dial*, both as a noun and as a verb.

Vocabulary: dial; push; button; listen; telephone; dial tone; busy signal; star key; pound sign

Materials: Activity Sheet 2–1; Working telephone (to hear dial tone and busy signal); Practice telephone (a toy or real telephone that is disconnected); NOTE: If a practice telephone is not available, make one from cardboard or construction paper using the pattern given on page 33.

Teaching Note:

It is very helpful to have a real telephone that has been disconnected to use as a practice phone. These can be found very cheaply at garage sales or thrift shops. Also, many toy stores carry play phones that are reasonable and resemble real phones.

Directions:

1. Give the student a copy of Activity Sheet 2–1. Say, "Today we are going to practice 'dialing' the telephone." Point to the buttons on a practice phone or use the illustration in #1 on the activity sheet, and say, "This is called the dial of the telephone." (Point to the entire dial.) Ask the student to point and repeat the word "dial."

2. Point to the buttons on the dial and say, "These are called buttons. They have numbers and small letters on them. We push the button for the number we want." Demonstrate by saying a certain number and then pushing the button. Give the student a number to push. Next, explain that when we dial a telephone number, we push the buttons in a certain order to reach that number. This is called "dialing" the telephone number. Write a telephone number on the chalkboard or slip of paper, and demonstrate dialing that number. Also remind the student that he/she does not want to dial too quickly or push the buttons too hard. (Demonstrate.) Give the student a telephone number to dial.

3. Explain to the student that there are two buttons that do not have numbers or letters. Point to the star (*) and the pound (#) and tell the student the name of each. Then ask the student to push the star and the pound.

4. Get a dial tone on a working telephone and let the student listen. Say, "This is called a 'dial tone.' You must hear this sound before you dial the number. Listen, then dial." See #2 on the activity sheet. (**Gesture:** Point to your ear, then push the buttons.) Ask the student to repeat. (If you do not have access

to a working telephone, pretend to hold the telephone to your ear and hum a single tone, then dial.) Ask the student to circle the correct number under each picture in #2.

5. Give the student a telephone number to dial on a practice telephone. Make sure the student models listening first by holding the receiver up to his/her ear, then he/she dials the number.

6. Tell the student that several things can happen after he/she dials a number: (1.) Someone will answer. (2.) He/She will hear a busy signal. This means that someone at that number is using the telephone. (If possible, let the student hear a busy signal. This can be done by dialing the number of the telephone from which you are calling.) Remind the student that if a busy signal is heard, he/she should hang up and try again in a few minutes. (3.) A recording will ask that he/she leave a message. (4.) No one will answer. Try again later.

7. Ask the student to complete #3 and #4 on the activity sheet. You will be asked to supply telephone numbers for #4. Be sure to use important numbers relevant to the student.

Extension Activities:

1. Using different colored paper for each button, make a telephone dial large enough to be used as a foot dial. Laminate. Put the dial on the floor and give the student a telephone number. The student then "dials" the number by stepping or jumping on each number. (This activity can also be used when the student needs to practice his/her home telephone number.)

2. Older students can practice dialing when letters are substituted for numbers. Explain that some businesses use this method. Show the students examples from the Yellow Pages and have them practice a few (e.g., 345-RUGS, 222-HAIR).

3. Find telephone numbers for the weather, current news, or sports updates in your local newspaper. Allow the student to dial these numbers and make a report.

4. Appoint a different student each day to dial the weather and make a weather report.

Name_____ Date_____

Dialing the Telephone

1. Use this as a practice dial.

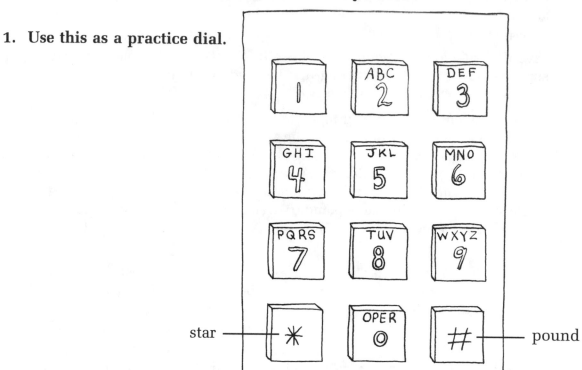

star — ✳   OPER   # — pound

2. **Which comes first? Circle the correct number under each picture.**

Listen   Dial

1   2   1   2

3. **Circle the ✳ star. Put an X on the # pound.**

4. **Practice dialing these telephone numbers. (Teacher: Help supply numbers.)**

Home: _____ School: _____ Other: _____

9-1-1 Emergency: _____ Friend:_____ Other: _____

Lesson 2-2: Answering the Telephone and Taking a Message

Objective: The student will learn how to politely answer the telephone and take a message.

Vocabulary: hello; repeat; "Just a minute, please."; "May I take a message?"

Materials: Activity Sheet 2–2; Pen/pencil; Plain paper; 2 practice telephones (toy or real); NOTE: If practice phones are not available, make them from construction paper or cardboard using the pattern on page 33.

Teaching Note:

Be sure to remind the student that when taking a message, *never* tell that he/she is home alone.

Directions:

1. Give the student a copy of Activity Sheet 2–2. Say, "Today you are going to practice answering the telephone." Say, "Ring! Ring!" Then hold the receiver of a practice telephone to your ear and say, "Hello." Give the student a telephone and you say, "Ring! Ring!" The student picks up the receiver and responds with "Hello."

2. Practice the following role play. (See Activity Sheet 2–2, #1.)

   TEACHER: (Holds receiver to ear, dials number) "Ring! Ring!"
   STUDENT: (Holds receiver to ear) "Hello."
   TEACHER: "May I speak to your (Mother, Father)?"
   STUDENT: "Just a minute, please."

   Repeat as necessary.

3. Tell the student that when his/her father/mother is not home, the student needs to take a message. (**Gesture:** Pretend to write on a pad of paper.) Inform the student that when taking a message, the three pieces of information he/she needs to get are: (1.) The caller's name. (2.) The caller's telephone number. (3.) The reason for the call. Ask the student to repeat. For illustrations, see #2 on the activity sheet.

4. Practice the following role play. (See #2 on the activity sheet.)

   TEACHER: (Holds receiver to ear, dials phone) "Ring! Ring!"
   STUDENT: (Holds receiver to ear) "Hello."
   TEACHER: "May I speak to your father?"
   STUDENT: "He can't come to the phone. May I take a message?"
   TEACHER: "Yes. Please ask him to call Dave Anderson. My telephone number is 913-567-2234. The car is fixed."

STUDENT: "Can you repeat that please?" (*Options*: "Can you spell your
name please?" or "Repeat, please.")

TEACHER: "Dave Anderson. 913-567-2234. The car is fixed." (Student
writes the message in #2 on the activity sheet. If possible, have
the student write one or two important words about the message
or draw a picture of the message, e.g., "The car is fixed." Words:
car, okay, fixed. Picture: car.)

STUDENT: "Thank you. I will give him the message."

TEACHER: "Thank you. Goodbye."

STUDENT: "Goodbye."

Remind the student to say "goodbye" at the end of the conversation.

5. Give the student a pad of paper and a pencil. Ask him/her to take different
messages. Change the name, telephone number, and reason for the call. If
someone is selling something, the student should say, "You will have to talk
to my mother or father about that." They should not give out any more information. Model this situation.

6. Tell the student that sometimes people dial the wrong number. Explain that if
someone calls and asks for a name the student doesn't know, it's usually a
wrong number. If that happens, the student should say, "I'm sorry, you must
have the wrong number." Then hang up. Use the practice telephones to model
this situation.

7. Ask the student to complete #3 on the activity sheet.

Extension Activities:

1. Write names, telephone numbers, and messages on slips of paper. Ask the
student to choose one. Then read the information as the student takes the
message.

2. Have the student create a "message center" for the family. Include pens, pencils, and a container in which to keep them.

Name_____ Date_____

Answering the Telephone and Taking a Message

1. **Practice the following role play:**

   TEACHER: (Holds receiver to ear, dials number) "Ring! Ring!"
   STUDENT: (Holds receiver to ear) "Hello."
   TEACHER: May I speak to your (mother, father), please?"
   STUDENT: "Just a minute, please."

2. **Practice the following role play. Write the message at the bottom.**

   TEACHER: (Holds receiver to ear, dials number) "Ring! Ring!"
   STUDENT: (Holds receiver to ear) "Hello."
   TEACHER: "May I speak to your father?"
   STUDENT: "He can't come to the phone. May I take a message?"
   TEACHER: "Yes. Please ask him to call Dave Anderson. My telephone number is 913-567-2234. The car is fixed."
   STUDENT: "Can you repeat that, please?"
   TEACHER: "Dave Anderson. 913-567-2234. The car is fixed." (Student writes message.)
   STUDENT: "Thank you. I will give him the message."
   TEACHER: "Thank you. Goodbye."
   STUDENT: "Goodbye."

Write the message here.

 Name   Telephone number   Reason

3. **Match the correct response to the picture.**

 Ring! Ring!

Jane?

"Hello."

"I'm sorry, you must have the wrong number."

"He can't come to the phone. May I take a message?"

Lesson 2-3: Leaving a Message

· ·

Objective: The student will learn to leave a message with a person and on a recording.

Vocabulary: message; recorded message

Materials: Activity Sheet 2–3; 2 practice telephones (toy or real); NOTE: If practice telephones are not available, make them from cardboard or construction paper using the pattern on page 33.

Directions:

1. Give the student a copy of Activity Sheet 2–3. Point to the illustrations in #1 and say, "When you make a telephone call and the person you are calling isn't home, you may want to leave a message. Today, we will practice two ways to leave a message: with another person and on a recording."

2. Point to #2 and say, "When you leave a message, you need to give three items: Your name, your telephone number, and the reason you called." Ask the student to repeat.

3. Practice the following role play. Tell the student that he/she must call a classmate, Mary, to get a homework assignment. Mary is not home.

   TEACHER: Write Mary's name, phone number, and reason on a sheet of paper. Give it to the student.
   STUDENT: Holds practice phone to ear and dials the number.
   TEACHER: "Ring! Ring!" (Holds receiver to ear) "Hello."
   STUDENT: May I speak to Mary, please?"
   TEACHER: "No, I'm sorry Mary isn't home. May I take a message?"
   STUDENT: "Please ask her to call (student's name) (student's phone number) and (reason)."
   TEACHER: "Okay, I'll give her the message."
   STUDENT: "Thank you. Goodbye."
   TEACHER: "Goodbye."

4. Role play as necessary using different names, telephone numbers, and reasons. See #3 on the activity sheet.

5. Say, "When no one is home, you may be asked to leave a recorded message." Point to the illustration in #1. Tell the student a recorded message may sound like this: "Hello. We can't come to the phone right now. Please leave your name, telephone number, and a short message. Thank you." (If possible, arrange to call someone with an answering machine and let the student listen to the recorded message.) Remind the student again of the three important pieces of information in a message: your name, your telephone number, and reason. Role play the following:

TEACHER: Give the student a name to call, a telephone number to dial, along with a short message; e.g., Susan. 345-6780. I'm sick. I can't come to the party.

STUDENT: Holds (practice) telephone to ear and dials.

TEACHER: "Ring, Ring, Ring, Ring! Hello. We can't come to the phone right now. Please leave your name, telephone number, and a short message. Thank you."

STUDENT: Says his/her name, telephone number, and the message.

6. Review the role play as necessary. Substitute different names, phone numbers, and reasons.

7. Read the situation in #4. Ask the student to write the information needed in the Message Box. Check for accuracy. If the student is unable to write the message, ask for a verbal response.

Extension Activity:

Make up different "recorded" messages. Each one should ask for different types of information (e.g., date, time, etc.). The student should repeat the information requested.

Name_____ Date_____

Leaving a Message

1. "May I speak to John, please?"   "John isn't home. May I take a message?"

Person

or

"We can't come to the phone right now . . ."   Recording

2. **Message   =   Your Name   +   Your Telephone Number   +   Reason**

3. **Role Play: Create different messages. Then practice.**

   STUDENT: Holds receiver to ear and dials.
   TEACHER: "Ring! Ring!" (Picks up receiver) "Hello."
   STUDENT: "May I speak to _____, please?"
   TEACHER: "No, I'm sorry _____ isn't home. May I take a message?"
   STUDENT: "Please ask him/her to call . . . (Message)_____
   _____."
   TEACHER: "Okay, I'll give him/her the message."
   STUDENT: "Thank you. Goodbye."
   TEACHER: "Goodbye."

4. **Write the correct information in the Message Box. Situation: You call Peter to ask him for a ride to the football game. This is what you hear: "We can't come to the phone right now. Please leave your name, telephone number, and a short message. Thank you."**

Message Box

 Your Name   Your Telephone Number   Reason

Lesson 2-4: Using the Telephone Book

• •

Objective: The student will understand how the telephone book is organized and how to locate the information it contains.

Vocabulary: telephone book; White Pages; Yellow Pages; alphabetical/ABC order

Materials: Activity Sheet 2–4; Pencil; Yellow Pages (as many as needed); White Pages (as many as needed)

Teaching Notes:

1. If multiple copies are needed, you may want to copy a few pages of the telephone book for student use.

2. You can divide this lesson into two sessions.

3. NOTE: In larger urban areas, two separate telephone books are usually used for White and Yellow Pages.

Directions: The White Pages

1. Give the student a copy of Activity Sheet 2–4. Then show the student a copy of the telephone book and say, "If you need to find a person's telephone number or address, you can look in this telephone book." Explain that the telephone book has two parts: the White Pages and the Yellow Pages. Show examples of each. Now show the White Pages to the student and explain that it contains the names, addresses, and telephone numbers of people who live in the area. Discuss whose numbers would be included: neighbors, friends, relatives, etc.

2. Point to the illustrations in #1 on the activity sheet and say, "The information is given in this order: (1.) Name, (2.) Address, (3.) Telephone Number." Ask the student to repeat and match the illustrations to the correct number.

3. Have the student look at the telephone book (or copies of pages), and point to examples of a name, address, and telephone number. For additional practice, give the student a name and ask him/her to say the address, or phone number, or both.

4. Show the student that the names are organized in alphabetical/ABC order by last name. Have the students find a page with the "A" names, then the "B" names, then "C" and "D." Point out that if people have the same last name, such as "Brown," the alphabetical order then goes to the first name, then the middle initial. Ask the student to complete #2 on the activity sheet by finding names in certain letter groups.

5. Ask the student to complete #3. In #3, you will be asked to supply names for the student to locate in the telephone book.

Directions: The Yellow Pages

1. Show the student a copy of the Yellow Pages and say, "There are many businesses and services in the community. This part of the telephone book is called the Yellow Pages. It gives the names, address, and telephone number of these businesses." Ask the student to look through the Yellow Pages and share some businesses he/she found.

2. Tell the students that the businesses are grouped together according to what they do. These groups are put in alphabetical order. Use automobile, bakery, carpet, and furniture as examples. Help the student find these catagories in the phone book. Point out that the names of the businesses are put in alphabetical order within the group.

3. Ask the student to complete #4 on the activity sheet. Check for accuracy.

Extension Activities:

1. Show the student how to keep a personal address/telephone book.

2. Write various situations on pieces of paper, e.g., "You need new furniture. Where can you find it?" Students pick a piece of paper and must find the correct heading in the phone book, then write the name, address, and telephone number of a business in that category.

3. If you have more than one student, divide into teams. Give a name that is listed in the telephone book, and ask for either the telephone number or address of that person. The first team to say the correct answer is given a point.

Activity Sheet 2-4

Name_____ Date_____

Using the Telephone Book

The White Pages

1. Put the pictures in order. Match them to the correct number.

Name   Address   Telephone Number

1	Telephone Number
2	Name
3	Address

2. Look in the telephone book. Find a name for each letter group and write it on the line.

A _____ B _____ C _____

3. Find each name in the telephone book. Write the correct address and telephone number. (Teacher: Supply the names.)

Name   Address   Telephone Number

_____   _____   _____

_____   _____   _____

_____   _____   _____

_____   _____   _____

The Yellow Pages

4. Look in the telephone book. Find a name, address, and telephone number for each business.

Name   Address   Telephone number

Florist: _____ _____ _____

Pizza: _____ _____ _____

Dentist: _____ _____ _____

Pet Shop: _____ _____ _____

Music Store: _____ _____ _____

Lesson 2-5: Using a Pay Phone

· ·

Objective: The student will understand how to use a pay phone, using coins or a pre-paid calling card.

Vocabulary: pay phone; coins; coin return box; receiver; dial; coin slot; coin return lever; pre-paid calling card; PIN; 800 number

Materials: Activity Sheets 2–5A and 2–5B; Nickel, dime, quarter; Pre-paid calling card (if presenting this part of the lesson) (*optional*)

Teaching Note:

Due to the common use of pre-paid calling cards, this method will also be taught. This portion of the lesson relates to the older student.

Directions:

1. Give the student a copy of Activity Sheet 2–5A. Say, "When you are not at home and need to make a telephone call, you can use a pay phone." Point to the illustration in #1. Point to the different parts of the telephone and discuss each function. Discuss the situations when the student would use a pay phone: need a ride home from the shopping mall, movie theater, sports event, pool, or park, or to ask permission to go to a friend's home. Brainstorm other ideas with the student. Also discuss where pay phones might be located, e.g., near restroom areas, lobbies, school gym area, etc. It would be helpful to show the students where the pay phones are located in the school.

2. Tell the student he/she can make a call from a pay phone by using coins. For clarification, point to the illustrations in #1 on Activity Sheet 2–5A.

3. Discuss the types of coins that can be used: nickels, dimes, quarters. Show the student an example of each coin. Tell the student that the amount of money he/she needs is usually written on the front of the telephone. Ask the student to complete #2. **Answer Key:** *nickel*, *dime*, *quarter* are circled.

4. Give the student a copy of Activity Sheet 2–5B. Explain to the student the steps for using a pay phone. (See the illustrations in #1.)

    (1.) Pick up the receiver on the telephone.

    (2.) Listen for the dial tone.

    (3.) Put in the coins.

    (4.) Dial the number.

    (5.) Talk or hang up.

(6.) Hang up if no one answers or you hear a busy signal. Push the lever and take your money from the coin return.

It would be helpful for the students to practice these steps using a real pay phone. You may want to inform the student that if the call is not to a location nearby, he/she may be asked to deposit more money.

5. Ask the student to complete #2 on Activity Sheet 2–5B. The student will be asked to put the correct number next to the steps for using a telephone. **Answer Key:** 4, 3, 5, 6, 2, 1.

Using a Pre-paid Calling Card:

6. Appropriate for older students: Practice the procedure for making a telephone call using a pre-paid calling card.

7. Show the student a pre-paid calling card. Say, "You can buy a card that will let you make phone calls from a pay phone. It is called a calling card. You can buy them in many stores: grocery stores, drug stores, discount stores, convenience stores, etc. Depending on how much you pay, this card will give you a certain amount of phone time to use."

8. Explain the following procedure for using a pre-paid calling card. NOTE: Before you begin, show the student how to locate the 800 number and PIN on the calling card.

(1.) Locate the 800 number and PIN on the card.

(2.) Pick up the receiver.

(3.) Listen for the dial tone.

(4.) Dial the 800 number.

(5.) Listen. Then dial the PIN.

(6.) Listen. You will be told how much time remains on the card.

(7.) Dial the number you want to call.

(8.) Talk or hang up.

Extension Activity:

If school funding is available, let each student make a phone call using coins and using a pre-paid calling card.

Name_____ Date_____

Using a Pay Phone

1. A pay phone

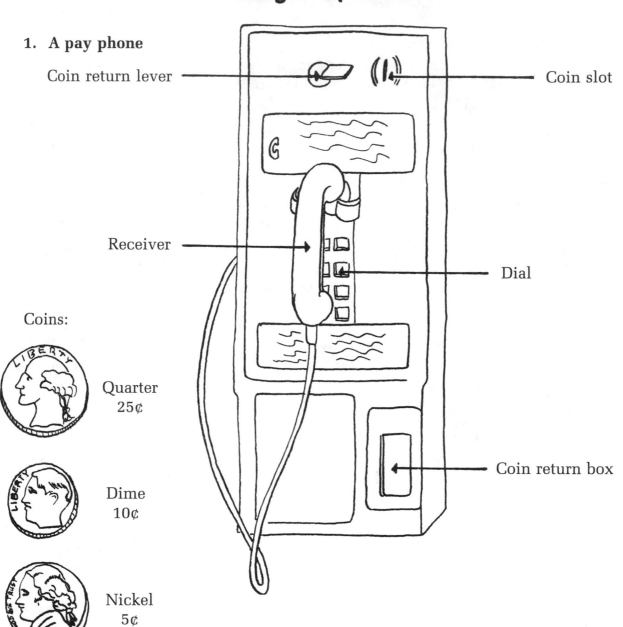

Coin return lever —————————   ————————— Coin slot

Receiver ————————————→

————————— Dial

Coins:

Quarter
25¢

Dime
10¢

Nickel
5¢

Coin return box

2. Circle the money that can be used in a pay phone.

Name_____ Date_____

Using a Pay Phone

Part One: Read and Practice:

(1.) Pick up the receiver.

(2.) Listen for the dial tone.

(3.) Put in the coins.

(4.) Dial the number.

(5.) Talk or hang up.

(6.) Hang up if no one answers or you hear a busy signal. Push the lever and take your money from the coin return.

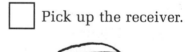

Part Two: Put the correct number next to each step.

☐ Put in the coins.

☐ Talk or hang up.

☐ Pick up the receiver.

☐ Hang up if no one answers or you hear a busy signal. Push the lever and take your money from the coin return.

☐ Dial the number.

☐ Listen for the dial tone.

Lesson 2-6: Dialing the Operator

Objective: The student will understand that dialing "O" OPER (zero) will connect them with the operator. The operator is a person who can help in special situations.

Vocabulary: operator; collect call

Materials: Activity Sheet 2–6; Pencil; Practice telephone (toy or real); NOTE: If you do not have a practice telephone, make one from cardboard or construction paper using the pattern on page 33.

Teaching Note:

Be sure to refer to the number "zero" OPER when dialing the operator. This will eliminate any confusion with the letter "O."

Directions:

1. Give the student a copy of Activity Sheet 2–6. Point to the illustrations in #1 and say, "When you need help reaching a telephone number or getting help for a phone problem, you can dial zero. This let's you speak to a person called an operator. An operator works for the telephone company." On a practice telephone (or use the illustration), demonstrate and push "O" once. Explain that the letters "OPER" on the button mean Operator. Ask the student to push the "O" button once.

2. Tell the student that the operator is to be called only for important reasons. Then share some reasons for which the student might call the operator: the number you call always has a busy signal, a number you need isn't listed in the phone book, you want to place a collect call. Complete #2 on the activity sheet. Discuss the reasons.

3. Explain to the student that the operator can help him/her make a special kind of telephone call, the "collect" call. A collect call means the person you are calling agrees to pay for the telephone call. Explain that if the student doesn't have any money to use in a pay phone, he/she can make a collect call. Discuss the reasons why a student might need to make a collect call (e.g., need a ride home, permission to do something, you will be late, etc.). Stress the fact that collect calls are made for important reasons. Also, inform the student that a collect call can be made from either a private phone or a pay phone.

4. Explain the procedure for making a collect call. See #3 on the activity sheet.

   (1.) Pick up the receiver.

   (2.) Listen for the dial tone.

   (3.) Dial "O" OPER.

50

(4.) Say, "I would like to make a collect call."

(5.) Give the operator the telephone number you are calling and your name.

(6.) Wait for the operator to tell you it's okay to talk.

5. Ask the student to complete #4 on the sheet. Check for accuracy.

Extension Activity:

Write various situations on slips of paper to role play. The student chooses one and decides if he/she should call the operator. If so, on a practice telephone, he/she must dial "O" and relate the message.

Name_____ Date_____

Dialing the Operator

Part One:

Push

"I can help."

Part Two: Put an O next to a good reason to call the operator:

_____ The number you call is always busy.

_____ You want to know what shop makes a good pizza.

_____ You want to make a collect call.

_____ A telephone number you need isn't listed in the telephone book.

_____ You don't want to use the telephone book.

Part Three: Follow these steps to make a collect call:

(1.) Pick up the receiver.

(2.) Listen for the dial tone.

(3.) Dial "O" OPER.

(4.) Say, "I would like to make a collect call."

(5.) Give the operator the number you are calling and your name.

(6.) Wait for the operator to tell you it's okay to talk.

Part Four: Put the steps in order. Write the correct number next to each one.

1 _____ Wait for the operator to tell you it's okay to talk.

2 _____ Dial "O" OPER.

3 _____ Pick up the receiver.

4 _____ Give the operator the number you are calling and your name.

5 _____ Say, "I would like to make a collect call."

6 _____ Listen for the dial tone.

Lesson 2-7: Guidelines for Speaking–Volume, Speed, and Tone of Voice

• •

Objective: The student will understand and practice the culturally accepted guidelines for speaking in regard to volume, speed, and tone of voice.

Vocabulary: volume; loud; soft; "just right"; speed; fast; slow; tone; yell; shout; whisper

Materials: Activity Sheet 2–7; Small radio (or classroom TV); Small toy car (Matchbox™); Pencil

Teaching Note:

Many ESL students come from cultures in which the accepted volume of voice is much louder than the American culture is willing to tolerate. It is very important that the ESL student use the appropriate volume of voice for specific situations. (This lesson is divided into three parts: volume, speed, and tone of voice. Activity Sheet 2–7 relates to volume.)

Directions:

Volume of Voice

1. (Radio or TV will be needed.) Say, "Today we are going to talk about how 'loud' or 'soft' our voices should be when we speak. That is called 'volume.'" Ask the student if he/she has seen or heard of the word *volume.* (Responses: radio, stereo, TV.) To clarify, point to the knob on the radio (or TV).

2. Say, "This volume is 'loud.'" Ask the student to repeat. Now turn the volume on the radio (TV) very high. Cover your ears and frown. Turn the volume off.

3. Say, "You can do the same thing with your voice. I am going to speak in a very loud voice." Say very loudly, "I like to read!" Ask the student to repeat the sentence in a loud voice. Explain that this volume is too loud for indoor use in the classroom or for conversation with another person. Say, "We call this *yelling* or *shouting.*" Ask, "How does it make you feel when someone you are speaking with yells or shouts?" (Responses: nervous, angry, afraid.) **(Gestures:** Frown, shake.)

4. Explain that sometimes it's okay to yell and shout. Brainstorm the situations where this is acceptable: cheering for your team, playing certain sports (calling for the ball in basketball or baseball), in an emergency, outdoors on the playground, when you need to speak above a loud noise.

5. Say, "This volume is soft." Ask the student to repeat. Then turn the volume on the radio (TV) very low, cup your ear, bend close, and listen.

6. Say, "You can do the same thing with your voice. I am going to speak in a very soft voice." Say softly, "I likc to read." Ask the student to repeat the sentence in a soft voice. Then explain that when we use a very soft voice, it is called a *whisper*. Cup your ears and tell the student that if someone whispers, it is often difficult for others to hear what is being said.

7. Explain that sometimes a person needs to whisper. Brainstorm the situations where it is expected: movie, religious service, funeral, when someone is sleeping, a ballet, etc.

8. Say, "This volume is 'just right.'" Ask the student to repeat. Turn the radio (TV) to a moderate volume, smile, and nod your head "yes."

9. Say, "We can do the same thing with our voices." Say in a moderate voice, "I like to read." Ask the student to repeat in a moderate voice. Evaluate.

10. Explain that this voice is used for classroom use and for face-to-face conversations. Brainstorm other places when a "just right" voice should be used: shopping, telephone conversations, riding on the bus, etc. (Some teachers refer to this as an "indoor" voice.)

11. Complete Activity Sheet 2–7 and discuss.

Speed of Voice

1. (A toy car will be needed.) Say, "Now we are going to talk about how fast or slow we should speak. This is called 'speed.'"

2. Say, "This speed is fast." Take the toy car and move it very quickly on a desk or floor. Ask the student to repeat the sentence while moving the car quickly.

3. Say, "You can do the same thing with your voice. I am going to speak very fast." Say very quickly, "I like to play soccer." Ask the student to repeat the same sentence (very quickly). Discuss the fact that if we speak too fast, it is difficult for another person to understand the words. (**Gesture:** Scratch your head and look puzzled.)

4. Give the student a number of commands to perform but say them *very quickly* (i.e., "Stand up and open the door," "Write your name at the top of the paper," etc.). This will model the difficulty others experience when we speak too fast.

5. Say, "This speed is slow." Take the car and move it very slowly across a desk or floor. Ask the student to repeat the sentence, while moving the car very slowly.

6. Say, "You can do the same thing with your voice. I am going to speak very slowly." Say, very slowly, "I like to play soccer." Ask the student to repeat the sentence very slowly.

7. Explain that when we speak too slowly, people can become bored and disinterested. (**Gesture:** Yawn, look around like you are not paying attention.)

8. Say, "This speed is 'just right.'" Move the car at a moderate speed across a desk or floor. Ask the student to repeat the sentence, while moving the car at a moderate speed.

9. Say, "You can do the same thing with your voice. I am going to speak at a 'just right' speed." Say at a moderate speed, "I like to play soccer." Ask the student to repeat. Check. (**Gesture:** Nod your head "yes" and make the okay sign with your fingers.)

10. Give the student several sentences to practice using a "just right" speed (e.g., "May I have a pencil?" "I like your shoes," etc.).

Tone of Voice (The teaching strategy used for this lesson will be teacher modeling.)

1. Say, "We are going to talk about 'how' you say words when you speak. This is called the 'tone' of your voice. The tone you use can give meaning to words."

2. Set up the following role play: Ask the student to play the role of the teacher. He/she will ask you if you have done your homework. The teacher will play the role of the student.

   STUDENT: "Have you done your homework?"
   TEACHER: (say very politely) "No, I didn't have time."

   Repeat the role play:

   STUDENT: "Have you done your homework?"
   TEACHER: (very sarcastically, snotty) "No. I didn't have time!"

3. Discuss the difference in tone and what it conveys about the person.

4. Demonstrate and role play the following situations. Change the tone for each.

   • Call the student's name—nicely, in anger, whiny.

   • Say "Hurry"—nicely, impatiently.

   • Say "Thank you"—politely, sarcastically.

   • Say "No"—nicely, in anger, command, surprise.

   • Say "I don't want to play"—nicely, whiny, mean.

   • Say "Yes"—excited, as a question, statement.

   Discuss the differences in meaning and what each conveys about the person speaking.

Name_____ Date_____

Guidelines for Speaking—Volume

Draw a line from the picture to the correct volume of voice.

Classroom

Loud Voice
- **shout**
- **yell**

Movie

Playground

"Just Right" Voice

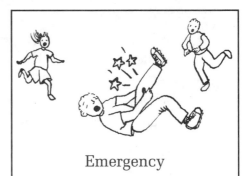

Emergency

Telephone Conversation

Sleeping—Do Not Disturb!

GO BEARS!

Cheer

Soft Voice
- **whisper**

Church

Lesson 2-8: Personal Space

• •

Objective: The student will understand the acceptable guidelines for observing personal space, eye contact, and touching, and relate these concepts to personal communication.

Vocabulary: close; near; far; space; "just right"

Materials: Activity Sheet 2–8; Bench or sofa

Teaching Note:

Many cultures have developed specific parameters for what is termed "personal space." Personal space is the amount of distance an individual requires between him-/herself and another person. It is a comfort level. When an individual's personal space is invaded, it can cause discomfort and irritation. As a general rule, for face-to-face conversation, most Americans are comfortable with a personal space of about 36 inches (one arm's length).

Directions:

1. Say, "It is important to know where to stand when you speak with another person." Ask the student to stand. Then stand face-to-face with the student and say, "There is space between us." (**Gesture:** Move your hand back and forth through the "space.")

2. Now stand very close (facing the student) and say, "This is near." Ask the student to repeat. Tell the student that another word for near is "close." Say, "I am standing too close (near) to you. There is too little space between us." (**Gesture:** Hold thumb and index finger apart to indicate little, then move your hand back and forth through the space.) Explain that standing too close can make the person you are speaking with feel uncomfortable and nervous. (**Gesture:** Look around in a nervous way, frown.) Also, inform the student that sometimes a person will take a few steps back in order to create a more comfortable space for him-/herself. Say, "If this happens, **don't follow!** Allow the person more space."

3. Walk away (about 6–8 feet), face the student, and say, "This is far." Ask the student to repeat. Say, "I am standing too far from you. There is too much space between us." (**Gesture:** Hold your hands far apart to indicate "far," and move your hand back and forth through the space.) Explain that a person might have trouble hearing the words and lose interest. (**Gesture:** Cup ear, look around.)

4. Stand about 36 inches (one arm's length), face the student, and say, "This is 'just right.' There is the right amount of space between us." (**Gesture:** With

57

your thumb and index finger, make the 'okay' sign, and move your hands back and forth between the space.) Ask the student to model the correct distance.

5. Explain that in America most people like about 36 inches or one arm's length between themselves and the person with whom they are speaking. Move away from the student and ask him/her to model the "accepted" distance.

Sitting—Personal Space

6. (A bench, sofa, or several chairs will be needed.) Explain to the student that it is important to leave enough space when he/she sits next to a person. Ask the student to sit down. Now, sit right next to the student (shoulders touching) and say, "I am sitting too close." (**Gesture:** Shake your head "no.") Explain that sitting too close can make another person uncomfortable and nervous. (**Gesture:** Edge away, frown.)

7. Now move over and sit at an appropriate distance (about 8–12 inches) and say, "This is 'just right.'" (**Gesture:** Shake your head "yes.")

8. Sit down on a bench or sofa. Ask the student to sit next to you, demonstrating the appropriate distance.

Standing in Line—Personal Space

9. Tell the student that he/she will probably spend a lot of time standing in line. Say, "When you stand in line, it is polite to leave enough space between you and the person standing in front of you." (Model.) Ask the student to stand. Stand in front of the student and model the appropriate distance (12–18 inches). Ask the student to model. If you have more than one student, ask them to make a line and model the correct personal space for standing in line. Check for accuracy.

10. Explain that in some situations, the boundaries for personal space cannot be observed. Brainstorm these situations: crowded buses, trains, lobbies, elevators, sitting on bleachers at a sports event, concerts, etc.

11. Complete Activity Sheet 2–8. Discuss.

Name_____ Date_____

Personal Space

1. Circle the 🙂 for the appropriate personal space.

   Circle the ☹ for uncomfortable personal space.

Speaking:

Sitting:

Standing in Line:

2. **Circle the situations where it would be difficult to give personal space.**

Crowded Bus   Sports Event   Classroom

Lesson 2-9: Eye Contact and Touching

Objective: The student will understand the culturally accepted practice of eye contact and touching when speaking with another person.

Vocabulary: eye; look; touch

Materials: Activity Sheet 2–9; Pencil

Teaching Note:

In America, the practice of having direct eye contact while speaking to another person is considered polite and respectful. However, for some cultures (particularly Asian), it is considered rude and disrespectful to initiate eye contact, especially with someone in authority. This can become a difficult issue for the ESL student. It is important for you to recognize that, for these students, the practice of using direct eye contact is in conflict with the student's native culture. The transition may take time and should be approached with patience.

Directions:

Eye Contact

1. Give the student a copy of activity sheet 2–9. Say, "Today you are going to learn what to do with your eyes when you speak to another person." (**Gesture:** Point to your eyes.)

2. Point to Illustration A in #1 on the activity sheet. Explain to the student that in America, people want the person speaking to them to look directly at their eyes. This is called "eye contact."

3. Model good eye contact by facing the student and pointing from your eyes to the student's eyes. **Be sure the student is comfortable with the procedure.** Then say, "How are you?" Ask the student to repeat and use direct eye contact while speaking to you.

4. Point to Illustration B in #1 on the activity sheet. Explain to the student that if good eye contact is not used, the other person may feel offended and confused.

5. Complete #2 on the activity sheet. Discuss.

Touching

In many cultures touching is widely used and accepted as part of everyday communication. In other cultures, it is used only as a sign of affection, reserved for close friends and family. In America, we are generally reserved and regard touching as a matter of personal preference. The best policy for the ESL student to follow is *not* to touch others when engaged in general conversation.

1. Explain to the student that many people do not want to be touched by others, especially by people they don't know well. Point to Illustration C in #3 on the activity sheet. Discuss the fact that touching can often be misinterpreted and cause problems.

2. Point to Illustration D in #3. Explain to the student that keeping his/her hands to him-/herself is best.

3. Explain that a simple handshake is one form of touching that is generally accepted by everyone. (Practice.) Say, "Hello!" Hold out your hand and indicate that the student should shake it. Ask the student to repeat.

4. Complete #4 on Activity Sheet 2–9.

Name_____ Date_____

Eye Contact and Touching

1.   Illustration A   Illustration B

   OK   **X**

2. **Draw a line to show good eye contact.**

3.   Illustration C   Illustration D

   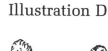

                                                    Handshake

   X   **OK**

4. **You are talking with a classmate. Circle the correct behavior for "touching."**

   Arm Around Shoulder   Hands at Your Side   Pat on the Back

Lesson 2-10: Interrupting

• •

Objectives: The student will understand the polite behaviors associated with interrupting a conversation. The student will understand when it is appropriate and when it is not appropriate to interrupt.

Vocabulary: interrupt; "Excuse me."; "This is an emergency!"

Materials: 2 puppets or finger puppets; Activity Sheet 2–10; Pencil

Teaching Note:

Before you start the lesson, you will need two puppets. Position one in front of you and one behind your back.

Directions:

1. Pretend to be having a conversation with one of the puppets. Suddenly, bring the other puppet from behind your back and have it abruptly interrupt your conversation, calling your name and asking a trivial question (e.g., "<u>Your Name!</u> <u>Your Name!</u> I'm done with my work. Can I play a game?")

2. Explain to the student that the puppet started talking while you were speaking with someone else. This is called *interrupting.* Tell the student that interrupting can be considered rude and if he/she needs to interrupt, there is a polite way to do it.

3. Give the student a copy of Activity Sheet 2–10 and point to #1. Read through and discuss the steps for interrupting politely. Use the illustrations for clarification.

    Step 1: Think. Ask yourself the question, Do I need to interrupt? Is this a question or problem I can solve myself?

    Step 2: Walk. Approach the person you want to speak with.

    Step 3: Stop and wait. Discuss the importance of waiting until the person you want to speak with makes eye contact and stops talking (or other activity).

    Step 4: Say, "Excuse me." Explain that after saying "Excuse me," it is okay to talk.

4. Brainstorm (with the student's input) good reasons for interrupting: you don't understand an assignment, you need help with a procedure or reading instructions, etc. Use the puppets for practice or role-play with the student.

5. Discuss poor reasons for interrupting: you are bored, you want to play, you want to get a drink of water, tattling for unimportant reasons, etc. Use the puppets for practice or role-play with the student.

6. Explain that in an emergency, interrupting is necessary. Practice the steps for interrupting for an emergency. See #2 on the activity sheet.

   Step 1: Find an Adult. Hurry to the person who can help.

   Step 2: Say, "This is an emergency." Stress the fact that the student should *not* wait to speak in an emergency situation.

7. Brainstorm (with the student) emergency situations: someone is hurt, sick, bathroom emergency, etc. Use the puppets for practice or role-play with the student.

8. Complete #3 and #4 on the activity sheet.

9. Discuss the fact that interrupting can also occur when the person you want to speak with is busy with an activity or work, such as when the teacher is correcting papers, the custodian is fixing a faucet, the teacher is writing on the chalkboard, etc. Remind the student to use the same guidelines as interrupting a conversation. Practice with puppets or role-play.

Extension Activity:

Create different situations for which the student might need to interrupt. With puppets, or as a role-play, practice the following:

- Your mother or father is talking on the telephone and you want permission to go to a friend's house.

- Your teacher is talking with another teacher, and a classmate has fallen and hit his head.

- You have an urgent need to use the bathroom.

- Your teacher is helping another student and you need help, too.

- You have a message from your teacher for the school secretary, but she is on the phone.

Name_____ Date_____

Interrupting

1. **Practice these steps:**

   1. Think! Do I need to interrupt? Can I answer this myself? Discuss when it is appropriate to interrupt, e.g., help with an assignment, an emergency, delivering a message, etc. Discuss when not to interrupt, e.g., you are bored, tattling for an unimportant reason, telling a joke, etc.

   2. Walk. Find the person (adult) you need.

   3. Stop and wait! Wait for the person to stop talking (or working) and make eye contact with you.

   4. Say, "Excuse me." Then speak.

2. **Follow these steps in an emergency.**

   1. Find an adult. Hurry to an adult who can help.

   2. Say, "This is an emergency!" Don't wait to speak.

3. **Put the steps in order. Label them 1, 2, 3, 4.**

_____ Say, "Excuse Me."   _____ Think!   _____Walk.   _____Stop and wait!

4. **Put an X next to a good reason to interrupt.**

_____ You are bored.

_____ You need help reading instructions.

_____ A classmate has fallen and hit his head.

_____ You need a pencil.

_____ You have a bathroom emergency.

_____ You want to tell a joke.

Lesson 2-11: How to Be a Good Listener

Objective: The student will learn the qualities and practices of good listening.

Vocabulary: look; listen; think; daydream; quiet

Materials: Activity Sheet 2–11; Pencil

Teaching Note:

Receptive language is the first step in the process of learning a new language. Therefore, developing effective listening skills is an essential part of the language learning process. The "Look, Listen, and Think" strategy presented in this lesson is an easy and effective method to teach good listening skills.

Directions:

1. Say, "Today we are going to talk about being a good listener." (**Gesture:** Point to your ears.) Discuss the reasons why it is important to be a good listener—get information, polite behavior, enjoyment (music, theater), etc.

2. Give the student a copy of Activity Sheet 2–11. Point to the illustrations in #1 and say, "A good listener does three important things:

    "1. 'Look'—Look at the eyes of the person who is speaking. Use 'direct eye contact.'

    "2. 'Listen'—Stay quiet and still. Don't talk.

    "3. 'Think'—Think about what the person is saying. Draw mental pictures in your mind to help you remember. Repeat important words silently in your mind."

3. Now say, "Sometimes other thoughts come into a person's mind when he/she should be thinking about what the speaker is saying. This is called 'daydreaming.'" (Point to the illustration in #2 on the activity sheet.) Discuss what the student might daydream about and the times it is easy to daydream (bored, tired, excited about something else).

4. Discuss the reasons it is not a good idea to daydream, e.g., miss parts of information, considered impolite, embarrassing if asked a question, etc.

5. Tell the student that if he/she finds him-/herself daydreaming, say silently in his/her mind: **Look, Listen, Think!** Explain that after the person has stopped speaking, ask someone for any information that was missed.

6. Complete #3 on the activity sheet.

Extension Activities:

1. Play various listening games, such as "Whisper Game." Ask the students to sit in a group. Begin by whispering a sentence in one student's ear; then that student must whisper the same message to the person sitting next to him/her. Go around the circle until the last person is told the message. He/she must repeat the message. Compare that message with the original one and discuss the differences.

2. Play "Simon Says."

3. Play "Mother, May I?"

4. Put **Look! Listen! Think!** on a poster and display it in the room as a reminder.

Name_____ Date_____

How to Be a Good Listener

1. **Discuss the following steps for good listening:**

    1. Look! Look at the eyes of the person who is speaking. Use direct eye contact.

    2. Listen! Be quiet and still. Don't talk.

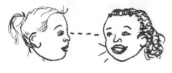

    3. Think! Make pictures in your mind to help you remember. Repeat important words silently in your mind.

2. **This is what happens when you daydream. Draw some things you daydream about.**

3. **Draw a line to the Happy Face for good listening.**
   Draw a line to the Sad Face for poor listening.

    Look!   Wiggle   

   Think   Quiet

   Daydream   Look away

Lesson 2-12: Body Language, Gestures, and Noises

Objective: The student will learn the various types of nonverbal communication and the meaning associated with them.

Vocabulary: gestures; noises; body language

Materials: Activity Sheets 2–12A, 2–12B, 2–12C; Pencil

Teaching Note:

The activity sheets present illustrations of the various examples of nonverbal communication. The primary teaching method will be modeling. The concepts of body language, gestures, and noises can be taught as one lesson or separately.

Directions:

Body Language

1. Say, "You do not always have to use words to tell what you are thinking or how you are feeling. Sometimes your body sends these messages. This is called 'body language.'"

2. Give the student a copy of Activity Sheet 2–12A. Model the types of body language and discuss what they mean. Ask the student to model and repeat.

Gestures

3. Say, "You do not have to use words to give information to another person. You can move your body. These are called 'gestures.'"

4. Give the student a copy of Activity Sheet 2–12B. Model the different gestures and discuss what they mean. Ask the student to model and repeat.

Noises

5. Say, "You can make noises to give another person information or show how you are feeling."

6. Give the student a copy of Activity Sheet 2–12C. Model the noises and discuss each meaning. Ask the student to model and repeat. **Answer Key:** 3, 7, 1, 11, 6, 5, 4, 10, 2, 9, 8.

Name_____ Date_____

Body Language

Model the body language and discuss their meanings. Put more ideas in the empty boxes.

(Head resting on arm)	(Yawn or stretch)	(Frown)
Bored	Tired	Unhappy/Sad
(Hunched shoulders)	(Tapping feet or fingers)	(Smile)
Depressed or feeling low	Nervous	Happy
(Hands on hip)	(Standing tall)	(Clenched teeth)
Disgust	Proud	Anger
(Body trembling)	(Holding head in hands)	(Wringing hands)
Fear	Despair or Worry	Anxiety

Name_____ Date_____

Gestures

Practice the gestures and discuss their meanings. Think of other gestures and draw them in the empty boxes.

(Wave)	(Thumb up!)	(Crooked finger)	(Scratch head)
Hello or Goodbye	Good job!	Come here.	Puzzled
(Shaking fist)	(Looking at watch)	(Raised palm)	(Shaking head) Yes! No!
Angry	Impatient/Hurry!	Stop!	Yes or No
(Hands over ears)	(Hold nose)	(Index finger raised)	(Raised hand)
Too loud	Smells bad	"We're No. 1!"	"May I speak?"
(Shrug shoulders)	(Hug/Kiss)		
"I don't know."	Affection		

Name_____ Date_____

Noises

Put the number of the noise next to the correct meaning.

Noises	Meaning
1. Tsk! Tsk!	_____ Tastes good
2. Clap	_____ Question
3. M-M-M-M	_____ Shame, shame
4. Scream	_____ Get someone's attention
5. Hum	_____ Sadness
6. Sob, cry	_____ Content
7. H-M-M-M-M?	_____ Fear
8. UH-UH	_____ Bored melancholy
9. Laugh	_____ Approval
10. Sigh	_____ Happy
11. Whistle	_____ No

Can you think of more noises that have meaning? Make the noise and ask others to guess the meaning.

_____

_____

_____

_____

_____

Section 3

Manners and Social Interaction

One of the most difficult challenges an ESL student faces in a new culture is understanding and learning the guidelines for manners and social interaction. What may be perfectly acceptable behavior in one culture may be viewed as taboo in another culture.

Often, negative reaction is the result when a newcomer unknowingly crosses the barrier of what is considered socially acceptable behavior. That negativity not only reflects upon the individual but often upon his/her culture as a whole. It is a challenge for the ESL student to discern the subtleties of social interaction, particularly when language serves as a barrier.

The purpose of the lessons in this section is to help the ESL student understand what is considered admissible social behavior in the American culture. Every attempt has been made to present the lessons in a nonthreatening and positive light.

Social acceptance is key to the success of assimilating into a new cultural environment. Young people particularly yearn for acceptance and a feeling of belonging. Knowing how to relate to people on a personal level will be an invaluable skill the ESL student can carry with him-/herself for a lifetime.

Lesson 3-1: Common Greetings and Farewells

Objectives: The student will learn the common terms for greeting another person. The student will understand the common terms for bidding farewell. The nonverbal forms of each will be introduced.

Vocabulary: Hello, (Person's name); Good morning; Hi; Welcome; Goodbye (Person's name); Bye; Good night; wave; hug; kiss; handshake

Materials: Activity Sheet 3–1; Pencil

Teaching Note:

For this lesson, the most common forms of greeting and farewell have been used. If other terms are common to your specific locale or population, incorporate those in the course of the lesson.

Directions:

Greetings

1. Say, "When you first see or meet someone, it is polite to say a greeting. The words you use for your greeting depend upon who you are greeting and the situation." Stress that, whenever possible, the student should use the person's name in the greeting.

2. Relate the following situations to the student and model the appropriate greeting. Ask the student to repeat.

Situation	Greeting
• It is morning. You walk into the classroom and greet your teacher.	"Good morning, (teacher's name)."
• You see your friends on the playground.	"Hi!"
• You greet your neighbor, Mrs. Perez.	"Hello, Mrs. Perez."
• A visitor has come to your home.	"Welcome."

3. Explain to the student that "Hi" is used informally with friends and other young people and that "Hello" should be used with adults and people in authority. Stress the fact that the person's name should be used with the greeting, e.g., "Hello, Mr. Jones."

4. Complete #1 on Activity Sheet 3–1 and discuss.

Farewells

5. Tell the student that when he/she leaves someone, a farewell is said. Explain that the farewell used depends upon who you are saying it to and the situation. Stress that, whenever possible, the person's name should be used in the farewell.

6. Relate the following situations to the student and model the appropriate farewell. Ask the student to repeat.

Situation	Farewell
• You leave Uncle Jose's home at night.	"Goodnight, Uncle Jose."
• After a movie, you leave your friends.	"Bye."
• School is over. You leave your teacher, Mr. Dean.	"Goodbye, Mr. Dean."

7. Inform the student that sometimes informal farewells are used, e.g., "Take care" or "See you soon."

8. Complete #2 on the activity sheet. Discuss.

Nonverbal Greetings and Farewells

9. Inform the student that another way to give a greeting or farewell is to use our bodies. Explain that most of these gestures can be used as a greeting or a farewell. Point to the illustrations in #3 on the activity sheet. Discuss. Model the wave and the handshake.

   • Hug: Use for family and close friends as both a greeting and a farewell.

   • Kiss: Use for family and close friends as both a greeting and a farewell.

   • Wave: Use informally for both a greeting and a farewell.

   • Handshake: Use with a person of authority and more formal situations, for both a greeting and a farewell.

Extension Activity:

Write situations on slips of paper. The student chooses one and models the correct greeting or farewell.

Name_____ Date_____

Common Greetings and Farewells

1. **Match the appropriate greeting to the situation.**

Situation	Greeting
• You see your friends on the school bus.	"Good morning, Mrs. Sands."
• You walk past your neighbor, Mr. Gomez.	"Hi."
• It is morning. You see the Principal, Mrs. Sands.	"Welcome."
• A relative has come to visit your home.	"Hello, Mr. Gomez."

2. **Match the appropriate farewell to the situation.**

Situation	Farewell
• You leave Uncle Rod's home late at night.	"Goodbye, Mr. Knight."
• You leave your friends after the party.	"Goodnight, Uncle Rod."
• Class is over. You leave your teacher, Mr. Knight.	"Bye."

3. **Draw a line from the picture to the correct name.**

Hug

Handshake

Kiss

Wave

4. **How do people in your native country give greetings and farewells? Draw a picture.**

Greeting	Farewell

Lesson 3-2: Introductions

• • • • • • • • • • • • • • • • • • • •

Objectives: The student will learn how to make an introduction and how to respond when introduced. The student will learn how to make a personal introduction.

Vocabulary: introduce

Materials: Activity Sheet 3–2; Pencil; 2 puppets or finger puppets (the puppets should be gender free, so that you can assign different identities according to the introduction being presented)

Teaching Note:

Practicing introductions will help the ESL student feel more comfortable in social settings and also alleviate self-consciousness when he/she needs to respond to an introduction or make a personal introduction.

Directions:

1. Say, "Today you are going to learn how to introduce people and how to answer when you are introduced. When you are with people who have never met each other, it is polite to 'introduce' them. There are special rules to follow when you introduce someone."

2. Explain the rules to the student and use the puppets to model. After you have modeled the introduction, ask the student to repeat it.

   • **Rule #1: Young people are introduced to older people.**

      Example: "Grandmother, I'd like you to meet my friend, Maria."

      "Maria, this is my grandmother, Mrs. Pinto."

   • **Rule #2: Men (boys) are introduced to women (girls).**

      Example: "Layla, I'd like to introduce my brother, Rami."

      "Rami, this is Layla."

   • **Rule #3: A person of lower rank is introduced to a person of higher rank.**

      Example: "Senator Brown, I'd like to introduce my neighbor, Mr. Lucas."

      "Mr. Lucas, this is Senator Brown."

   • **Rule #4: People of the same age and gender can be introduced in any order.**

      Example: "Gus, this is Patrick."

      "Patrick, this is Gus."

3. Explain to the student that when he/she is the one being introduced, his/her response depends upon the person he/she is meeting and the situation. Remind the student that it is always polite to repeat the person's name in the response. Inform the student of these guidelines for responding to an introduction:

   • **An adult (informal situation):** "Hello, (person's name)" or "It's nice to meet you, (person's name)."

   Role-play: Pretend to introduce the student to Mrs. Lee. Check for appropriate response.

   • **A person of high rank (formal situation):** "It's an honor to meet you, (person's name)."

   Role-play: Pretend to introduce the student to Senator Rozinski. Check for an appropriate response.

   • **A child (student) of approximately the same age:** "Hi, (child's name)."

   Role-play: Pretend to introduce the student to another student named Paula.

4. Explain to the student that in some situations, he/she may be asked to "introduce yourself." Explain that this means that a person says his/her own name to another person or a group. Practice the following situation:

   TEACHER: "I'm going to ask you to introduce yourself."
   STUDENT: "My name is (first name and last name)."

5. Explain that in some situations the student may be asked to "introduce yourself and say a few words telling about yourself." Inform the student that "telling about yourself" could mean giving your age, grade, name of school, native country, family members, special hobbies or interests, etc. Practice the following situation:

   TEACHER: "I'd like you to introduce yourself and say a few words telling about yourself."
   STUDENT: "My name is (first name and last name). I am _____ years old. My native country is _____. I like to (special interests)."

6. Ask the student to complete Activity Sheet 3–2. The student will be asked to fill in the blanks with the proper name for various types of introductions.

7. **Answer Key:**

   1. "Grandmother/Mr. Chen"

      "Mayor Puchinski/Ms. Smith"

      "Amy/Carlos"

"Father/Ling Ye"

"Maria/Susan" or "Susan/Maria"

2. "It's an honor to meet you, Senator Black."

"It's nice to meet you, Mrs. Yoda."

"Hi, Lee."

Extension Activities:

1. If you have a group of students, ask each one to "introduce yourself" and say a few words telling about "yourself."

2. Write different situations on slips of paper. Ask the student to make the correct introduction: e.g., introduce your friend, Max, to your mother; introduce a new student to your friends; introduce your father to the principal, etc.

Name_____ Date_____

Introductions

1. **Write the correct name in the blank and complete the introduction.**

   • Introduce: Mr. Chen (a neighbor)   and   Grandmother.

   "_____, I'd like you to meet _____."

   • Introduce: Ms. Smith (a teacher)   and   Mayor Puchinski.

   "_____, I'd like you to meet _____."

   • Introduce: Amy (a friend)   and   Carlos (a friend).

   "_____, I'd like you to meet _____."

   • Introduce: Ling Ye (friend)   and   Your Father.

   "_____, I'd like you to meet _____."

   • Introduce: Maria (a friend)   and Susan   (a friend).

   "_____, I'd like you to meet _____."

2. **Draw a line to the correct response. Then write the person's name on the line.**

   • You are introduced to Senator Black.   "Hi, _____."

   • You are introduced to Mrs. Yoda.   "It's an honor to meet you, _____."

   • You are introduced to a new student, Lee.   "It's nice to meet you, _____."

3. **Pretend you are asked to introduce yourself at a school assembly. Write an introduction telling about yourself. Then share it. (This can also be an oral activity.)**

Lesson 3-3: Polite Phrases

• •

Objective: The student will learn the vocabulary and understand when to appropriately use the polite phrases.

Vocabulary: please; thank you; you're welcome; excuse me

Materials: Sheets of paper; Pencil; Box of tissues; Box of crayons; Book; Activity Sheet 3–3

Teaching Notes:

1. In order to gain acceptance into a new culture, it is essential for the ESL student to become aware of and practice polite behavior. Expressing simple, polite phrases can endear a person to his/her new neighbors. It can also pave the way for a smooth journey toward social acceptance.

2. Even the most limited speakers of English can learn to use these simple phrases appropriately. Adaptations for them are included in the lesson plan. Also, an effective method to teach these concepts is to model a situation and ask the student to role-play. This method will be used frequently throughout the lesson.

Directions:

In the first set of instructions, "please," "thank you," and "you're welcome" will be taught as a sequential unit. Separate situations for "please," "thank you," and "excuse me" will follow.

1. Have the students sit around a table or in a circle on the floor. Place a pencil, a piece of paper, a box of crayons, and a box of tissues in the middle. Then say, "Today we are going to learn to use some polite words. Other people will think well of you if you show them polite behavior."

2. Say, "We are going to learn when to say: 'please,' 'thank you,' and 'you're welcome.' We say 'please' when we ask for something." Have the students repeat the word *please*. "We say 'thank you' when someone gives us something." Have the students repeat the phrase *thank you*. "We say 'you're welcome' after someone says 'thank you.'" Have the students repeat the phrase *you're welcome*. "Let's practice."

   Choose a student to help you model this procedure:

   TEACHER: "(Student's name), may I have a pencil, please?" (point to the pencil, and hold your hand out, if necessary)
   STUDENT: Takes the pencil from the middle and hands it to the teacher.

TEACHER: "Thank you." Then point to the student and say, "Now you say, 'you're welcome.'"
STUDENT: "You're welcome."

If the students are zero level or beginning speakers of English, it is appropriate to make the following accommodation: Simplify the request to two words, such as "Pencil, please."

Practice this same procedure with the rest of the students, varying the objects. Have the students practice with each other. Monitor for accuracy.

3. Tell the students that we also use "please" and "thank you" when we ask someone to help us. Model the following situations:

TEACHER: Take several pieces of paper and drop them on the floor. Then choose a student to help you pick them up and say, "(Student's name), will you help me, please?' or "Help, please." This is an excellent opportunity to teach the beginning ESL student a simple way to ask for help. After the student has helped, respond with "thank you." Switch roles and have the student ask for help. Practice and use "please" and "thank you" with other requests for help, e.g., close the door, open the window, turn on the light, pick up a pencil.

4. Then explain to the students that they should also use "please" when they ask permission to do something. Take the students to the nearest drinking fountain. Model the sentence, "May I have a drink, please?" or "Drink, please?" Have each student repeat the request before they get a drink. You may also wish to incorporate this with restroom time. Require that the children say, "May I use the restroom, please?" or "Restroom, please?"

5. Tell the students that there are also other times when we say "thank you." When someone says something nice to us or about us (i.e., pays us a compliment), we say, "thank you." Choose a student to help you model the following conversation:

TEACHER: "(Student's name), I like your shirt." Then point to the student and say, "Now you say 'thank you.'"
STUDENT: "Thank you."

This activity is a wonderful opportunity to build self-esteem. Have the children practice by saying something nice about each other and responding with "thank you."

6. Next show the students when to say "thank you" after someone has been kind or polite to them. Model the situation in which someone holds open the door for you. Say, "Thank you." Switch roles and practice.

7. Tell the students that they are going to learn when to say "excuse me!" Explain that *excuse me* is used when a person does something that seems to be impolite. Dramatize the following situations and ask the students to respond with "excuse me."

   • Bump into someone accidentally

   • Cut in front of a person

   • Need to interrupt a conversation (refer to Lesson 2–10)

   • Walk between two people who are talking

   • Reach across someone for an object

   • Sneeze

   • Belch (teacher's discretion)

8. Always insist that the students use these polite phrases in class. This will develop automatically and the students will more readily use them in situations outside of the classroom.

9. For reinforcement, complete Activity Sheet 3–3 as a class or independently. **Answer Key:** (column 1) "Thank you." "Excuse me!" "please?"; (column 2) "You're welcome." "Thank you." "Excuse me!"

Name_____ Date_____

Polite Phrases

Look at the pictures and decide how each person should respond. Write the correct words in the speech bubbles.

"Please?"

"Thank you."

"You're welcome."

"Excuse me!"

Lesson 3-4: May I?

• • • • • • • • • • • • • • • • •

Objective: The student will learn to use "May I?" when asking for permission.

Vocabulary: "May I . . .?"; permission

Materials: Activity Sheet 3–4; Symbol for a restroom (see Lesson 4–5); Pencil; Piece of paper; Book (any kind)

Teaching Note:

This lesson teaches basic vocabulary when asking for permission. The primary teaching method is that of role play.

Directions:

1. Ask the student to sit on the floor or at a table. Place familiar classroom objects in front of the student. Say the name of each item and ask the student to repeat. Next, ask the student to hand you a specific item. Say, "May I have the pencil, please?" (**Gesture:** Hold out your hand. [Place the object in the student's hand, if necessary.]) Student hands you the pencil. Say, "Thank you." Continue with the other objects.

2. Next, hold an object in your hand and have the student ask, "May I have the _____, please?" If needed, break the request into smaller units until the student can repeat it, e.g., "May I," "May I have," "May I have the pencil," "May I have the pencil, please?" Give the student the object. Student says, "Thank you." *Variation*: Students ask each other for objects.

3. Hold up the International sign for the restroom. Say, "May I use the restroom, please?" Ask the student to repeat. Then say, "Yes, you may." Student says, "Thank you." Give each student an opportunity to practice this dialogue.

4. Next, walk to the drinking fountain and say, "May I get a drink, please?" Ask the student to repeat. Then say, "Yes, you may." Student says, "Thank you," and takes a drink.

5. For fun you may want to get a bag of treats and have each student ask for one using the "May I . . . please?" pattern.

6. Give the student a copy of Activity Sheet 3–4. The student will be asked to complete sentences by choosing words and writing "May I." Responses are included. Help with reading when needed. You may want to do this as a directed activity.

Name_____ Date_____

May I?

Write "May I" on the line. Read the sentence. Use the pictures to help you. Find a partner to read the response.

May I   **Response**

1. _____ use the restroom, please? Yes, you may.

2. _____ get a drink of water, please? Yes, you may.

3. _____ go to Jose's house, please? Yes, you may.

4. _____ go first, please? No, you may not.

5. _____ have a pencil, please? Yes, you may.

6. _____ watch TV, please? No, you may not.

7. _____ read a book, please? Yes, you may.

8. _____ chew gum, please? No, you may not.

9. _____ go outside, please? Yes, you may.

10. _____ have some candy, please? Yes, you may.

Lesson 3-5: Mr., Mrs., Miss, Ms., Sir, and Ma'am

• •

Objective: The student will understand and correctly use the terms: Mr., Mrs., Miss, Ms., Sir, and Ma'am.

Vocabulary: Mr.; Mrs.; Miss; Ms.; Sir; Ma'am

Materials: Activity Sheet 3–5; Chalkboard and chalk; Pencil

Directions:

1. Say, "There is a polite way to say the name of an adult. You use the words *Mr.*, *Mrs.*, *Miss*, or *Ms.* before the last name." Write each term on the chalkboard.

2. Ask the student to brainstorm names of people for whom these terms are used (teachers, custodians, parents, neighbors, etc.). As the student says each name, write it under the correct term. Then ask the student if the people in each category have something in common (same), e.g., man, woman, etc.

3. Give the student a copy of Activity Sheet 3–5. In #1, point to the illustration and the abbreviation **Mr.** Tell the student that Mister is used before a man's last name. Explain that most of the time the word Mister is written a short way, "Mr." Ask the student to trace the letters. Remind the student that **Mr.** begins with a capital letter and ends with a period.

4. Next, point to the illustration and the abbreviation **Mrs.** Tell the student that the abbreviation for Mistress is used before the last name of a woman who is married or who has been married. Tell the student that most of the time, the word Mistress is written a short way, "Mrs." Ask the student to trace the letters.

5. Point to the illustration and the word **Miss**. Explain that "Miss" is used before a young girl's or unmarried woman's last name. Ask the student to trace the word "Miss."

6. Now, point to the term **Ms.** Tell the student that "Ms." can be used before the last name of all women, married or unmarried. Ask the student to trace the letters.

7. Tell the student that there is another way to politely address an adult. He/she can use the terms **Sir** or **Ma'am**. Point to the illustrations in #2 on the activity sheet. Explain that "Sir" is used for a man and "Ma'am" is used for a woman. Tell the student that these terms can be helpful when speaking to a person of authority (principal, teacher, police officer, etc.), or when he/she doesn't know the adult's name ("Excuse me, Ma'am." "Sir, you dropped your keys." etc.) Practice.

8. For reinforcement, complete #3 and #4 on Activity Sheet 3–5. **Answer Key: 3.** Miss, Mr., Ms., Mrs.; 4. Sir—man, Ma'am—Woman

Extension Activities:

1. On chart paper, write Mr., Mrs., Miss, and Ms. Ask the student to write as many names as possible under each category. The student may use a newspaper or magazine to find the names.

2. Write descriptions of people on slips of paper (e.g., "woman, married, last name Brown." "Man, last name Mendes"). The student would then choose the correct term (Mr., Mrs., Miss, Ms.).

3. Write situations on pieces of paper (e.g., [1.] A man standing in front of you drops his keys, you don't know his name. [2.] The mayor of your city is a woman. She visits your school and asks, "Are you a good citizen?") The student should include "Sir" or "Ma'am" in the response.

Name_____ Date_____

Mr., Mrs., Miss, Ms., Sir, and Ma'am

1. **Repeat each term and trace the letters.**

Mr.    Mrs.    Miss    Ms.

2. **Repeat each term.**

Sir = Man   Ma'am = Woman

3. **Circle the correct term.**

Mr.	Mr.	Mr.	Mr.
Mrs.	Mrs.	Mrs.	Mrs.
Miss	Miss	Miss	Miss
Ms.	Ms.	Ms.	Ms.

4. **Draw a line to the correct person.**

   Sir

Ma'am

Lesson 3-6: Taking Turns

· ·

Objective: The student will understand the reasons for taking turns, different kinds of turns, ways to choose the order of turns, and appropriate behavior while waiting for a turn. Proper responses when a student doesn't get a turn are discussed.

Vocabulary: turn; take a turn; order; wait; choose; lose a turn

Materials: Activity Sheets #3–6A and 3–6B; Paper strips or tongue depressors on which to write student names; Container in which to put names; Various board games (Chutes and Ladders™, Candyland™, etc.); Various card games (Old Maid, Go Fish, Slapjack, etc.); Spinner from a board game; Example of a classroom job chart; Straws cut in different lengths (enough for each child); 1 coin (quarter, nickel) to toss

Teaching Note:

You may wish to divide this lesson into several sessions or choose a particular aspect you feel the children need to develop. After the lesson is completed, incorporate the concepts into authentic teaching situations in your classroom. The diagrams on Activity Sheet 3–6A can serve as visual behavior guides.

Directions:

1. Say, "Today we are going to learn about taking turns. We take turns when more than one person wants to do something." To demonstrate the concept of "turn," take a spinner from a board game, spin the arrow, and say, "I'm going to take a turn." Then hand the spinner to the student and say, "Take your turn." If there is more than one student in the class, have each student take a turn, pass the spinner to the next person, and say, "Take your turn." Continue until each student has had a turn. Ask the student to brainstorm ideas as to when he/she has to take turns.

2. Give the student a copy of Activity Sheet 3–6A. Point to #1A and say, "Taking turns lets us do things in a safe and orderly manner." (**Gesture:** *Safe:* Cross your arms across your chest. *Orderly:* Move your hand in consecutive arches ⌣⌣⌣⌣). Next, discuss the positive nature of the picture (children standing in line, hands to themselves, orderly). Say, "The children are taking turns in a safe and orderly way. Each one will be able to get a drink."

3. Point to #1B and say, "If we don't take turns, it may become dangerous and confusing." (**Gesture:** Pretend to show fright and and confusion with facial expressions and holding your hands to your face.) Encourage the student to describe what is happening in the picture (child is hurt at fountain, child falling down, children being pushed, angry teacher). Read the words of the teacher, "You lost your turn!" Explain that to "lose your turn" means that

90

your turn is taken away. Ask the student to repeat this sentence, "The children will lose their turn."

4. Next, ask the student to look at #2 and describe other situations when people need to take turns (playing games, reading in school, at the doctor's office, grocery store, movie theater).

5. Say, "Sometimes, people take turns doing the 'same' thing and sometimes they take turns doing 'different' things." Refer the student to #3 and ask him/her to name children taking turns doing the 'same' thing (reading group, cafeteria line). Brainstorm other ideas. Next, ask the student to name "different kinds of turns" (classroom jobs, cooperative groups, center work).

6. Now say, "The same person cannot always be first. That is not fair. There are many ways to decide the order of turns." Demonstrate the following methods. (During the course of the school year, incorporate a variety of these methods in authentic classroom use.)

   - **Tongue depressor:** Put each student's name on a stick. Put the sticks in a container and choose. (Variation: You choose the first stick and that child chooses the next, and so on.)

   - **Draw straws:** Cut straws in different lengths. Hold them in your hand and let the students choose. The longest straw goes first, and so on.

   - **Rhyme:** Eenie, Meenie, Miney, Moe,

      Catch a Tiger by the Toe,

      If He Hollers, Let Him Go,

      Eenie, Meenie, Miney, Moe.

   Point to each person as you say the rhyme. The person to whom you point on the word MOE goes first.

   - **Choose a number between 1 and 10 (or any other numbers that are selected):** Each person chooses a number between the numbers stated. The one who guesses correctly, or the closest, goes first. Remind the student that the first and last numbers are included.

   - **Coin Toss:** Demonstrate this method by showing the student the two sides of a coin; one called *heads*, one called *tails*. Then ask the student to choose *heads* or *tails*. Toss the coin and explain that the side that lands face up (heads) wins and that person goes first.

   - **Rock, Paper, Scissors:** Explain that a fist is a rock, a flat hand is the paper, and two pointing fingers are the scissors. Each student decides what he/she will be. Count to three and all show their hands. The rock smashes the scissors, so the rock wins if the other person has chosen the scissors. The scissors cut the paper, so the scissors win if the other person has chosen the paper. The paper covers the rock, so the paper wins if the other person has chosen the rock.

7. Explain that when people take turns, someone has to "wait." *To wait* means the time when it isn't your turn yet, or your turn is over. Tell the student that he/she needs to show good behavior while waiting. Point to the illustrations in #4 on the sheet and discuss the fact that in school students are expected to wait quietly, listen, and keep hands to themselves. Also discuss the fact that, at times, it is fine to talk while we wait, e.g., when playing a game, at the store, in the lunch line, etc. Brainstorm other ideas with the student.

8. Point to #5 and explain that it is important to be polite to the person who is taking his/her turn. Ask the student to look at the illustrations and describe the impolite behavior. If necessary, help with reading.

9. Finally, say to the student, "Sometimes, it may happen that you might not get a turn. This happens most often when there isn't enough time." Point to #6 and discuss the positive way to respond to this situation. Ask the student to practice the responses.

10. If you have a group of students, you may want to choose a game for them to play in which they have to take turns. Perhaps, they can practice one of the methods explained in this lesson to choose the order of turns.

11. Ask the student to complete Activity Sheet 3–6B. The student will choose "Do" or "Don't" for behavioral choices. **Answer Key:** (column 1) Don't, Do, Do, Don't; (column 2) Do, Don't, Do, Don't.

Name_____ Date_____

Taking Turns

1A. Safe and orderly	1B. Dangerous and confusing

2.   We take turns at different times and places.

3.   The same kind of turn   Different kinds of turns

Name_____ Date_____

Taking Turns

4. Polite behavior while waiting

5. Impolite behavior while waiting

6. If I don't get a turn:

| Do | Don't |

Name_____ Date_____

Taking Turns

Look at the pictures. If it shows what to do when taking turns, draw a line to the "Do" face. If it shows what *not* to do, draw a line to the "Don't" face.

Lesson 3-7: Dealing with Anger and Conflict Resolution

Objective: The student will learn a strategy for dealing with his/her anger and resolving conflicts in a positive manner.

Materials: Activity Sheets 3–7A and 3–7B; Pencil

Vocabulary: angry; mad; calm

Teaching Note:

Much has been written about anger management and conflict resolution. This lesson will give the ESL student two simple strategies for dealing with these issues. As the student advances, you may wish to explore these areas in greater depth.

Directions:

Dealing with Anger

1. Give the student a copy of Activity Sheet 3–7A. Point to the illustration in #1 and say, "Everyone feels angry or mad sometimes." Discuss with the student what it feels like to be angry or mad. Ask the student to draw a picture of what he/she feels like when he/she gets mad. Discuss.

2. Point to #2 on the activity sheet. Ask the student to share thoughts of what makes him/her angry and to write them here.

3. Say, "You must remember that just because you are angry, you do not have the right to hurt others or yourself or use bad language." Point to the illustrations in #3 on the activity sheet. Discuss.

4. Point to #4 on the activity sheet. Tell the student that if he/she needs to calm down, following these steps might help. Discuss each step.

   (1.) **Stop!** Don't do anything.

   (2.) **Breathe.** Take 3 deep breaths. Give yourself time to think.

   (3.) **Think.** Ask: "Can I walk away from the person or situation?" "Can I talk with the person and tell him/her how I am feeling?" "Can I get involved in another activity to get my mind thinking about something else?" Think about the consequences of physically hurting someone or yourself.

   (4.) **Action.** Put your choice into action.

5. Discuss the importance of having a plan or choices for dealing with anger. Brainstorm other options.

Conflict Resolution

6. Tell the student that it is important to have a plan when a conflict or problem arises with another person. Stress the fact that *talking* with the other person is very important. Explain that sometimes the person who has made you mad, or hurt your feelings, may not know that you are feeling that way or *why* you are angry or hurt.

7. Give the student a copy of Activity Sheet 3–7B. Explain that following the steps in #1 may help him/her solve a conflict or problem. Discuss each step.

   (1.) **Talk.** Tell the person how you feel. Tell the person what he/she did to make you feel that way.

   (2.) **Solve.** Tell the person what you want him/her to do.

   (3.) **Move on.** Don't dwell on what happened. Get involved in another activity.

8. Complete #2 and #3 on Activity Sheet 3–7B. Discuss.

Extension Activities:

1. Ask the students to share different conflict situations they have encountered. Ask them to relate how they handled it. Discuss their choices.

2. Write negative and positive responses on slips of paper. Ask the student to identify if the response was negative or positive. If negative, ask the student to give a better choice for dealing with the conflict.

Name_____ Date_____

Dealing with Anger

1.　　　**Angry! Mad!**

Draw what you feel like when you are mad.

2. **What makes you angry? Make a list.**

_____　　_____

_____　　_____

_____　　_____

3. **When I am angry, I do not have the right to:**

Hurt Others　　　　Hurt Myself　　　　Use Bad Language

4. **When I need to calm down, I can follow these steps. Read and discuss.**

1. **Stop!** Don't do anything!

2. **Breathe.** Take 3 deep breaths. Give yourself time to think.

3. **Think.** Make a choice. Ask: "Can I walk away from this person or situation?" "Can I talk with this person?" "Can I choose another activity that will get me thinking about something else?" Think about the consequences of hurting someone.

4. **Action.** Put your choice into action.

Name_____ Date_____

Conflict Resolution

1. **When I am angry with someone, I can follow these steps. Read and discuss.**

1. **Talk!** Tell the person how you feel. Tell the person what he/she did to make you feel this way.

2. **Solve.** Tell the person what you want him/her to do.

3. **Move on.** Don't dwell on what happened. Get involved in an activity.

2. **Put a ✓ by the helpful solutions:**

3. **Discuss how to solve the following situations:**

- Yousif made a mark on your art project.
- Your best friend, Maria, wouldn't play with you today.
- Lela accidentally kicked you in a soccer game.
- Your teacher canceled recess and it was your turn to be line leader.
- Ye copied the answers off your test paper.
- Oscar slammed you into the lockers.
- Marjorie called you a bad name.
- Daniel and his friends made fun of you.

Lesson 3-8: When and How to Apologize

• •

Objective: The student will understand when an apology is needed, to whom it should be given, and how to apologize.

Vocabulary: apologize; apology; mistake; "I'm sorry"

Materials: Activity Sheet 3–8; Pencil

Directions:

1. Give the student a copy of Activity Sheet 3–8, point to #1, and say, "Everyone makes mistakes." Discuss the different kinds of mistakes pictured. Brainstorm other ideas.

2. Then say, "If you make a mistake that hurts others in any way, or you show bad behavior, you need to say, 'I'm sorry.' That is called an apology." Stress that an apology makes everyone feel better.

3. Point to #2 on the activity sheet and point to the Apology section. Tell the student that these are different ways to apologize. Read the apologies in #2 and ask the student to repeat.

4. Now point to the Mistake section. Read each mistake and ask the student to identify to which person the apology should be made. Underline the name.

5. Ask the student to choose an appropriate apology for each mistake. Draw a line to connect them. Discuss.

6. Complete #3 on the sheet. The student should model an appropriate apology for each mistake.

7. Inform the student of these familiar phrases that are used in this situation and explain each one:

   "You deserve an apology."
   "Make an apology."
   "Give an apology."

Extension Activity:

Read the following books about forgiveness:

> *Glennis* by Patricia Calvert
> *The Whirligig* by Paul Fleischman
> *Green Mango Magic* by Sylvie Hoffack
> *Honor Bright* by Randal Beth Platt
> *The Fastest Car in the County* by Nancy Simpson-LeVene

Name_____ Date_____

When and How to Apologize

1. Some mistakes hurt others: **Some mistakes are bad behavior:**

Mistakes ⟶ Apology ⟶ Everyone feels better.

2. Match an appropriate apology to each mistake. Underline the name of the person to whom it is given.

Apology	**Mistake**
"I'm sorry. It was an accident."	You took a pencil from Gustavo's desk and didn't ask.
"I'm sorry. I won't do that again."	You fell down during a soccer game and kicked Athen.
"I'm sorry, (person's name)."	You and a friend made fun of Yuji, and made him cry. 
"I'm sorry I (reason for apology)."	You didn't do your chores and Mother had to do them when she came home from work. 

3. Practice an apology for these mistakes:

- You hit your little brother, Rico, and made him cry.
- You accidentally pulled up your grandmother's flowers while you were weeding.
- You made fun of Rosa's new hair style.
- You were disrupting an assembly and were sent to the Principal's office.
- You ignored your teacher, Miss Max, when she asked you to stop running.

Lesson 3-9: Early, On Time, or Late

Objectives: The student will understand the concepts of "early," "on time," and "late." The student will become aware of the relationship of these concepts to time and the social implications involved.

Vocabulary: early; on time; late; tardy

Materials: Activity Sheets 3–9A and 3–9B; Highlighter marker; Pencil; Teaching clock

Teaching Note:

Punctuality has different meanings in various cultures. It is important for the newcomer to understand that in America being "on time" means arriving at the scheduled time and that it is a valued practice.

Directions:

1. Say, "Many times you will be given a certain time for which you are expected to arrive at a certain place." Brainstorm various situations where a definite time is given: school, concerts, parent–teacher conferences, club meetings, athletic events, parties, doctor's appointments, etc.

2. Give the student a copy of Activity Sheet 3–9A. Read the conversations in #1. Explain that times for different events or situations can be given verbally: by speaking in person, over the telephone, or as an announcement on the PA system. Tell the student that if this is done, it is a good idea to write down the time so he/she won't forget. Ask the student to highlight the times that are given.

3. Explain that sometimes an invitation or letter will be sent with this information. Refer to the illustrations in #2 on the sheet. Ask the student to highlight the time given on the invitation and in the letter. Brainstorm ideas for which an invitation or letter will be sent (parties, conferences, meetings, etc.).

4. Explain that sometimes a poster or announcement is put on a wall or on the bulletin board. (Refer to #2.) Ask the student to highlight the time given on the poster. Brainstorm situations where this is likely to be the case (concerts, plays, school events, etc.). Again, remind the student that it is a good idea to write down the correct time.

5. Explain to the student that certain "regular" times are set for certain situations, for example, school, religious services, certain meetings (Boy Scouts, Girl Scouts, etc.).

6. Tell the student that in America being "on time" means to come at exactly the time that was given. Read the statements in #1 on Activity Sheet 3–9B. Ask the student to tell you what time would be "on time" for each conversation.

7. Using the teaching clock, show the student what "early" would be. Point to the illustration of the birthday invitation. Explain that you are expected to come at 4:00. If you come too early (3:45 or earlier), your host may either not be ready and will be embarrassed, or may not be there. See the illustration in #3.

8. Explain to the student that being "late" means to come after the time given. Again, point to the illustration of the invitation. Explain to the student that to come to the party late (after 4:00) is not polite. (Show on the teaching clock.) Emphasize that in America being late is considered rude and irresponsible. See the illustration in #3. (NOTE: You might explain to the student that if he/she cannot arrive at the scheduled time, it is acceptable to speak with the host and ask if it is okay to arrive a little late to the event.)

9. Stress the fact to the ESL student that school activities begin "on time." Point to the poster of the Spring Concert in #2. Ask the student to tell you what time he/she should arrive. (8:00 P.M.) Explain that in some situations (a concert, doctor's appointment, teacher's conference) it is good to be a little "early." Explain that to arrive late to these events is considered rude and inconsiderate.

10. Ask the student what time school begins. Ask him/her to show you on the teaching clock. Stress the fact that students are expected to be at school on time. Discuss why it is important to be "on time" to school. Explain that if a student is late, he/she is marked "tardy." Discuss the consequences that your school imposes if a student is tardy.

11. For reinforcement, ask the student to choose a time for a party. Then you show a time on the teaching clock and ask the student to say if you are "on time," "early," or "late." Ask the student to give the proper reaction. (See the illustration in #3.)

12. Ask the student to complete Activity Sheet 3–9B. The student will be asked to decide if a given arrival time is "early," "on time," or "late." **Answer Key:** (1.) Late; (2.) Late; (3.) On Time; (4.) Early; (5.) Late; (6.) On Time; (7.) Late.

Name_____ Date_____

Early, On Time, Late

1. **When a person wants to see you at a certain time, he/she may "speak" the words.**

"Let's meet at the mall at five o'clock."

"Okay."

"Can you come over to my house at four o'clock?"

"Sure!"

"The math club will meet at 3:30 this afternoon."

4:00 Rico

I better write that down.

2. **Sometimes, the time will be "written" on an invitation, letter, or poster.**

I'll see you at my birthday party.
Date <u>May 19</u>
Time <u>4:00 pm</u>
Place <u>Pete's Pizza</u>
<u>1701 Main Street</u>
signed <u>Mary</u>

Dear Member,
  Our first meeting will be held in the gym on Mon., Jan. 4, at 7:00 P.M. We hope to see you.
  Yours truly,
  Karen
  Karen Doe

Jane Ortega
14521 N 1st
Chicago, IL

Spring Concert
May 24
7:00 p.m.
In the gym.

3. **Socially acceptable time for 4 o'clock:**

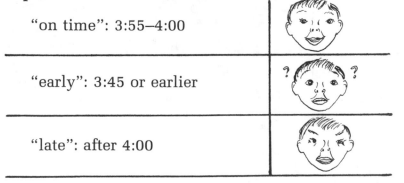

"on time": 3:55–4:00

"early": 3:45 or earlier

"late": after 4:00

Name_____ Date_____

Early, On Time, Late

Read each group of sentences. Look at the scheduled time and the arrival time. Decide if the person is "early," "on time," or "late." Write the word on the line.

1. School begins at 8:10 A.M.

   Jane arrives at 8:30 A.M.

   _____

Early

2. The choir concert is at 7:30 P.M.

   Your family arrives at 8:00 P.M.

   _____

3. Maria's birthday party is at 4 o'clock.

   Juanita arrives at 4 o'clock.

   _____

4. Sergio's friend has invited him to dinner at 5 P.M.

   He arrives at 4:15 P.M.

   _____

On Time

5. You are to meet Jan at the mall at 6:00 P.M.

   She arrives at 7:30 P.M.

   _____

6. Grandmother invites you to visit at 2:00 P.M.

   You arrive at 1:55 P.M.

   _____

Late

7. Your piano lesson is at 4:30 P.M.

   You arrive at 4:45 P.M.

   _____

Lesson 3-10: Clean Up After Yourself!

Objectives: The student will understand the importance of cleaning up after him-/herself. The student will understand that it is considerate behavior.

Vocabulary: mess; clean up

Materials: Activity Sheet 3–10; Pencil

Directions:

1. Point to #1 on Activity Sheet 3–10, and say, "Today we're going to talk about cleaning up after yourself. I'm going to read some situations about what happens when you don't clean up and how it effects others." Ask the student to listen to the situation and look at the picture. Then discuss the questions. Ask the student to circle the items that need to be cleaned up.

2. Continue with the same procedure for #2, 3, 4, 5, and 6.

Extension Activities:

1. Ask the students to be on Cafeteria Patrol for a week. If they see a mess, they are to remind the person to clean it up or clean it up themselves. Keep a log. Reward for good service.

2. Students make a list of things or places at home that need to be cleaned up. They do it and surprise their parents.

3. Appoint an Art monitor. He/she is in charge of seeing that people clean up their work areas after an art project.

4. Make thank-you notes and send them to the custodian. Thank him for his hard work keeping the school clean for everyone.

Name_____ Date_____

Clean Up!

Read the situation. Then discuss the questions. Circle the items that need to be cleaned up.

1. Carlos and Anne left to spend the night at Aunt Carol's house. When their mother comes home from work, this is the mess she finds. How do you think Mother feels? What should Carlos and Anne have done?

2. Mr. Jones's class is excited. Their basketball tournament is today! When they get to the gym, this is what they find. Is this fair?

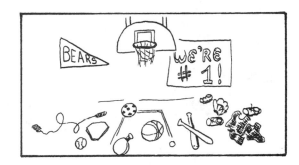

3. Maggie is at her Grandmother's house. While Grandmother worked in the garden, Maggie ate lunch. This is what she left. What is happening? What should Maggie have done?

4. Father has an important meeting today. He needs to dress and shower. Nicole used the bathroom before him. What did she forget to do? How does this make Father feel? Is this considerate?

5. Mr. Lee, the custodian, works very hard keeping the school clean. What are these students doing? Why is this unkind?

6. You and your friends go on a picnic to the park. Your friends leave this mess. What should you do? Why?

Lesson 3-11: How to Be a Gracious Guest

Objective: The student will understand the guidelines for polite behavior when he/she is an invited guest.

Vocabulary: guest; visit; polite

Materials: Activity Sheet 3–11; Pencil

Teaching Note:

This activity is helpful if the student is beginning to visit or spend the night at friends' homes.

Directions:

1. Say, "When someone invites you to visit their home, it important to be polite. These are some rules to follow if you are visiting someone's home."

2. Give the student a copy of Activity Sheet 3–11. Read each guideline and discuss.

   - **Don't complain!** Never say you don't like the food. Politely say, "No, thank you." Don't complain about the room you are in or the rules you must obey. If your host has planned a special activity and you didn't enjoy it, be grateful; don't criticize. If you are asked to help, help willingly.

   - **Obey the rules.** You may have different rules at home about bedtime, curfew, noise, etc. When you are a guest, you should obey the rules of the house.

   - **Clean up after yourself.** A polite guest always cleans up after him-/herself. For example, take your dishes to the sink and clean them. Pick up anything you have been using (toys, magazines, food). Don't drop your clothes on the floor. Keep the bathroom clean.

   - **Ask permission.** If you want to use the telephone or anything that doesn't belong to you, *ask first*.

   - **Say, "Thank you."** When you leave, always thank your friend and any adult who was with you.

3. Ask the student to complete #2 on the activity sheet. Discuss.

Extension Activity:

Role-play various situations in which the student is an invited guest. Ask him/her to respond in a polite manner. *Examples:* Your friend's mother tells you that curfew time is 8:00. You are having dinner and don't like the food.

Name_____ Date_____

Be a Gracious Guest

1. **Read the rules and discuss.**

   - **Don't complain!** Never say you don't like the food. Politely say, "No, thank you." Don't complain about the room you are in or the rules you must obey. If your host has planned a special activity and you didn't enjoy it, be grateful; don't criticize. If you are asked to help, help willingly.

   - **Obey the rules.** You may have different rules at home about bedtime, curfew, noise, etc. When you are a guest, you should obey the rules of the house.

   - **Clean up after yourself.** A polite guest always cleans up after him-/herself. For example, take your dishes to the sink and clean them. Pick up anything you have been using (toys, magazines, food). Don't drop your clothes on the floor. Keep the bathroom clean.

   - **Ask permission.** If you want to use the telephone or anything that doesn't belong to you, *ask first.*

   - **Say, "Thank you."** When you leave, always thank your friend and any adult who was with you.

2. **Meet Rude Ruthie and Polite Pierre. Match the words to each one. Who do you think will be invited back?**

Rude Ruthie

Polite Pierre

"I'm tired. I think I'll leave my clothes on the floor."

"Thank you very much. I had a nice time."

"See ya later!"

"May I use the phone to call my mother?"

"Nine o'clock is fine."

"Nine o'clock! I don't go to bed until ten!"

"I'm on the phone!"

"May I help you with the dishes?"

"No, thank you."

"I never have to set the table at home!"

"Yuk! I don't like carrots!"

Lesson 3-12: Making New Friends

Objective: The student will learn strategies for making new friends.

Vocabulary: decide; be friendly; join in

Materials: Activity Sheet 3–12; Chalkboard and chalk; Pencil

Teaching Note:

This is a valuable lesson to present to the ESL student. Many newcomers know no one when they first arrive in America. This can be a lonely time. Giving the student some strategies and hints on how to make new friends can make the transition easier.

Directions:

1. Say, "Today we are going to talk about making new friends. There are some things you can do that will help you meet new people." Ask the student if he/she has made any new friends in America. Discuss (How did he/she meet them?).

2. Write the word "Decide" on the chalkboard. Tell the student that the first thing to do is to decide who you want to be friends with. Present the following guidelines to the student and discuss.

    Decide—Who do you want to be friends with? Have you noticed someone who likes to do the same things you do? Does this person behave well?

3. Now write the words "Be Friendly" on the chalkboard. Explain to the student that when a person is new, it is helpful to act friendly. Discuss the following guidelines:

    Be Friendly—You can act friendly by greeting others first, smiling, showing a positive attitude (be happy), accepting help if offered, looking at others when you speak to them, or inviting others to do something with you.

    Brainstorm other ideas with the student. Stress that others are not comfortable around a person who acts unhappy, e.g., does not smile, complains, walks with head down, etc. Practice the following role-play:

    PERSON #1:   "Hi, my name is _____."
    PERSON #2:   "Hi, I'm _____."
    PERSON #1:   "Where do you go to school?" (or any other conversation starter)
    PERSON #2:   "I go to _____."

4. Write the words "Join In" on the chalkboard. Tell the student it is important to try and join in or be part of the group.

   Join In—Try new things.

   Tell the student that sometimes it takes some courage to join in a new group. Explain that there are different ways to "join in":

   • *A conversation*—Listen to others. Wait until there is a pause and a chance to talk.

   • *A game*—Choose a good time to join in, before the game begins or during a pause. Stand close by, and then ask if you can play or join in.

   • *An organized group*—There are many groups that meet after school. Ask your teacher about them. If you are interested in joining a group, ask how you can get information about joining. (NOTE: Inform the student about the various groups offered at your school, e.g., Girl/Boy Scouts, sports teams, clubs, etc.)

5. Give the student a copy of Activity Sheet 3–12. Discuss it with the student. Complete the activities. The student will be asked to circle the students who will make friends.

Extension Activity:

Give the student various situations and ask him/her to model how he/she could join in. *Examples*: You want to join a basketball game at recess or lunch. You want to join the after-school math club. You want to play a board game during free time.

Name_____ Date_____

Making New Friends

Think about the strategies for making new friends: Decide—Be Friendly—Join In. Look at each picture. Circle the students who will make friends.

"Miss Parker, I'd like to join the Math Club. How do I do that?"

"I don't like it here! I like France better."

(Frowning, stooped shoulders, no eye contact)

"This group likes to play soccer. So do I. I'll wait for a break and then I'll ask to play."

"I think I'll stay away from this group."

"Hi, Sammie. Can you come over after school tomorrow?"

Lesson 3-13: Being Tactful

• •

Objectives: The student will understand how to politely express him-/herself. The student will understand the difference between polite expressions and rude expressions.

Vocabulary: polite; rude; tactful

Materials: Activity Sheet 3–13; Pencil

Teaching Note:

This lesson will inform the ESL student about impolite expressions and questions. Very often the newcomer will hear these words and statements and not know that they are offensive to others.

Directions:

1. Explain to the student that there are different ways to say things. One way is "polite" or with good manners (nice), another way is "rude" or with bad manners (not nice). Ask, "Why is it better to speak politely?" (It gives people a good impression of you, avoids conflict, etc.) Discuss how it makes others feel when you are polite to them and how they feel when you are rude to them. Also discuss rude questions, e.g., asking an older person's age, asking someone's weight, asking the price of a gift, etc.

2. Give the student a copy of Activity Sheet 3–13. Point to "Tactful Tony." Tell the student that this boy speaks politely and is called "Tactful Tony." Explain that another word for speaking politely is *tactful*.

3. Read through the statements and questions on the activity sheet. Help the student decide which ones belong with Tactful Tony. Have the student write the number of the expression in the speech bubble. **Answer Key:** 2, 3, 5, 8, 13, 15, 16, 17, 18.

Extension Activity:

For an alternative game, cut out the statement boxes on Activity Sheet 3–11, "Be a Gracious Guest." Put them in a container, and have the students take turns picking strips. The student decides if the statement or question drawn is tactful (polite) or rude. Score 1 point for each polite response. The winner is the player with the most points at the end of the game.

Name_____ Date_____

Being Tactful

This is Tactful Tony. Read and discuss the sentence strips below. Decide which ones belong to Tactful Tony. Write the number in the speech bubble.

Tactful Tony

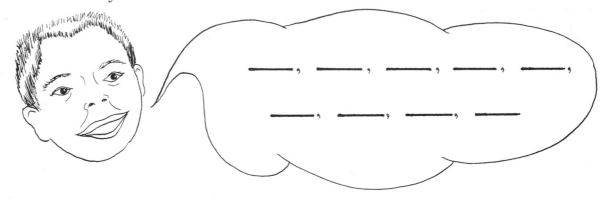

1. "How come we only get one piece of candy? I want two."	12. "Knock it off!"
2. "Excuse me, I didn't hear you."	13. "I think you made a mistake."
3. "I like it here, but I miss (native country)."	14. "How much did this gift cost?"
4. "I can't understand you when you talk."	15. "Please be quiet."
5. "Would you repeat that, please?"	16. "Please, stop that!"
6. "My country is better than America."	17. "Thank you for the gift."
7. "Huh?"	18. "I don't care for any, thank you."
8. "Thanks, but I'm busy. I can't play today."	19. "Yuk! I told you I don't like beans."
9. "I don't want to play with you."	20. "Shut up!"
10. "You're so dumb!"	21. (To an adult) "How old are you?"
11. (After opening a gift) "I already have one of these!"	22. (Pointing to a person in a wheelchair) "What's the matter with him?"

Lesson 3-14: Table Manners

• •

Objective: The student will learn appropriate table manners.

Vocabulary: good manners; bad manners

Materials: Activity Sheet 3–14 (two pages); Pencil; Scissors; Enough of the following items for entire class: paper plates, plastic forks, knives, spoons, napkins, cups; Large bowl

Teaching Note:

See Lesson 6–9 if you wish to coordinate this with school lunchroom behavior.

Directions:

1. Before you begin, you will need paper plates, napkins, forks, knives, spoons, and cups. Say, "Today you are going to learn good table manners. This means how you act while you are eating." Give each student one of the above items. Name them and ask the student to repeat. Explain and model these rules, and the student follows.

   (1.) Help set the table. (Ask the student to place his/her items on the table.)

   (2.) Put your napkin on your lap.

   (3.) Wait until everyone is sitting. Then eat. (Pretend to eat.)

   (4.) If you want something on the table that is not close to you, say: "Please pass the _____." Then say, "Thank you." (Model this using the empty bowl.)

   (5.) Chew with your mouth closed. Don't talk with a mouth full of food.

   (6.) If you have used a utensil and are finished, place it on the edge of the plate.

   (7.) Don't belch. If you must, do so quietly and say "Excuse me."

   (8.) Talk about nice (appropriate) topics. (Not "Ben threw up at school today.")

   (9.) Wipe your mouth with your napkin.

   (10.) Take your things off the table and bring to the sink or counter.

2. Give the student a copy of Activity Sheet 3–14. Play the "Manners Game." (To be played in groups of two or three people.) Read each card and discuss it. Ask the student to repeat and then cut out the cards. Mix them up and place them face down. Each student chooses a card, describes it, and decides if it shows good table manners or poor table manners. One point is scored for a good manners card; zero points for a poor manners card. The player with the most points after all the cards are drawn wins.

115

The Manners Game

Cut out the manners cards. Mix them up and turn them over. Take turns choosing a card. Score 1 point for a "Good Manners" card; 0 for a "Bad Manners" Card. The player with the most points wins. (Use the blank cards on the next page to make your own manners cards.)

When dinner is over, you take your dishes to the sink.

You burp loudly.

You tell everyone at the table that Carlos threw up in gym class.

You reach for the bowl and spill your milk.

When you are done eating, you put your knife and fork at the edge of the plate.

You help set the table.

You say, "Please pass the corn."

You put your napkin on your lap.

You use your napkin to wipe your mouth after you are done eating.

You wait until everyone is seated and then begin eating.

You take most of the potatoes before anyone else comes to the table.

You chew with your mouth closed.

You talk with food in your mouth.

You throw a meatball to the dog.

Gulp!

You loudly gulp your drink.

You kick your brother's leg under the table.

You wipe your mouth with your sleeve.

You use your fingers to push food onto your fork.

Lesson 3-15: Good Sportsmanship

• •

Objective: The student will understand the behavior associated with good sportsmanship and apply it in various situations, both as a participant and as a spectator.

Vocabulary: sportsmanship; ran; boo; a good sport; a poor sport, a sore loser; referee/official; complain; fair; coin toss; cheat

Teaching Note:

This is an excellent lesson plan to coordinate with the physical education teacher. Choose specific parts of this lesson that are appropriate for the level, age, and needs of your students. Role-play is the primary teaching method used throughout the lesson.

Materials: Ball (basketball, soccer ball, large rubber ball); Activity Sheets 3–15A and 3–15B; Pencil; Coin; Whiffle ball and bat; Deck of cards

Directions:

1. Say, "Today we are going to talk about 'good sportsmanship.' Good sportsmanship means to obey the rules, and to be courteous and fair when playing a sport or game. Good sportsmanship also means showing polite behavior when watching a game. Sometimes, a person who shows good sportsmanship is called 'a good sport.'" Next, ask the student to share some examples of the sports and games he/she likes to play. Then say, "Let's talk about some rules for good sportsmanship." Present the following rules and role-play the accompanying situations.

    Rule: Don't cheat. Explain to the student that games have rules so that everyone has a fair chance to win. Define *fair* as rules being the same for all the players. If the rules of the game are followed, everyone can have fun and enjoy playing. However, if a player tries to win by not obeying the rules, that is called *cheating*. **Role-play:** Say, "I'm going to show you what cheating means." Take a deck of cards and deal the same amount to yourself and the student. Now pretend that you and the student are playing a card game. Then model cheating by obviously trying to look at the student's cards. Say, "The rules say that I'm not supposed to look at another player's cards. I'm not following the rules. That's called cheating." Now, reverse rolls and ask the student to look at your cards. Respond by putting down your cards and angrily saying, "You're cheating! I'm not playing with you anymore!" Explain that other players can become very angry when another player cheats.

    Rule: Be a polite winner. Explain to the student that when we play a game, usually someone wins and someone loses; that is part of the fun. Explain

118

that if a person or team wins a game, it is fine to be excited and cheer, but also remember to act in a polite way to the other person or players who have lost. Now, model the behavior of a polite winner. ***Role-play:*** Pretend that you are the winner of a game and the student has lost. Write a score on the chalkboard (point to yourself and the student when you say each score): Teacher 60, Student 35. Shake hands and say, "Good game!" Or "You played very well." Now ask the student to switch roles. Reverse the score on the chalkboard. The student should shake your hand and repeat a positive remark. Next, tell the student that a polite winner never "taunts" other players. Again, pretend that you won the game and say, "I won! I'm the best!" or "Ha! Ha! You lost!" Discuss how these nasty remarks make the other person feel.

Rule: Don't be a sore loser. Explain to the student that a "sore loser" is someone who gets angry if he/she loses a game. Inform them that a sore loser can also be called a "poor sport." ***Role-play:*** Again put a score on the board: Teacher 24, Student 75. Say very angrily, "You didn't win! You cheated!" or "Who cares if you won!" Discuss the results of being a sore loser (takes the fun out of playing, others don't want to play with a poor sport). Remind the students that everyone respects a polite winner, but no one respects a sore loser.

Rule: Be fair and kind when choosing teams. ***Role-play:*** Tell the student that you and he/she are the captains of two teams. Explain that you must decide who chooses first. Suggest a coin toss. Teach the student to do a coin toss for "heads" or "tails" to see who chooses first. Now draw a picture of a girl and say, "Ericka is not a good player and she is the only one left to choose." Explain to the student that Ericka should be chosen in a nice way. "Sure, Ericka, you can be on my team." Or simply say, "I choose Ericka." Ask the student to repeat. Then instruct the student not to say unkind remarks or complain about a poorer player (e.g., "We'll lose if he's on our team!" or "I don't want her. You take her!") Remind the student how hurtful these remarks can be.

Rule: Let others play. (This is a good rule for recess games.) Explain to the student that others want to play just as much as he/she does and that everyone should be able to join into games, especially at recess time. ***Role-play:*** Use a ball and pretend to be playing a game. Have the student stand to the side and watch you. Then say, "C'mon you can play." Or "Do you want to play?" Remind the student that if a newcomer wants to play and doesn't know how, it would be kind to teach them the game or ask them to join in. Say, "Sure you can play. We'll teach you." Never refuse to let another person play. Share the fact that no one wants to be left out.

Rule: Take turns and share. Explain to the student that everyone playing in a game wants a turn. That is what makes it fun for everyone. But if one person is not sharing and is taking all the turns, then it spoils the game for the other players. *Role-play:* Dribble a ball and pretend to play basketball. Throw the ball to the student and say, "Here, you shoot." Or "I'm going to pass the ball to you." Ask the student to repeat this example. Now, ask the student to hold the ball, grab it away, and say, "I want the ball first!" or "Give me the ball!" Explain the common sports term "ball hog," which means a player who always wants the ball for him-/herself and won't share or pass it to others.

Rule: Don't try to hurt other players. Explain to the student that when two teams play against each other, it is for enjoyment and for the competition of the game. It is not good sportsmanship to try and hurt another player. *Role-play:* Pretend that you are a player from one team and the student is a player on the opposing team. Pretend to be thinking out-loud, "I think I'll trip this guy so he falls really hard." Now, ask the student to dribble/ bounce the ball, and pretend to slam into him. Stress the dangers of this kind of behavior.

Rule: Good sports don't argue with the referee/official. Explain to the student that it is the job of the referee/official to make sure that the rules of the game are followed. This keeps the game safe and fair. Inform the student that if a player disagrees with what the official has done, he/she needs to be quiet and accept the decision (or let the coach deal with the issue). *Role-play:* Ask the student to pretend to bat a baseball. (Use a whiffle and plastic bat, if possible.) You play the role of the umpire. Say, "Strike three! You're out!" Have the student quietly put down the bat and walk away. Now, you pretend to bat. Have the student say, "Strike three! You're out!" Respond with, "Are you blind?" Or "I'm not out! You need glasses!" Explain to the student that this kind of behavior can result in him/her being ejected (thrown out) of the game. Discuss the term *cry baby*.

Rule: Encourage (cheer) your teammates when you are not playing. Explain to the student that sometimes in a game not every player gets a chance to play. However, members of the same team cheer for each other. *Role-play:* Ask the student to dribble/bounce the ball as if in a basketball game. You pretend to sit on the bench (a chair) and cheer on the team. Say, "Good play!" Or "Great shot!" Next, model what *not* to do. Sit on the bench and complain, "I never get to play." Or "I'm better than him/her." Or "I'm going to quit this team." Remind the student that these reactions will only develop into a bad attitude and poor team spirit.

Rule: Be a polite fan. Explain that a part of good sportsmanship is being a polite "fan." Define the word *fan* as a person who has a favorite team, attends the games, and cheers them on. Ask the student if he/she has ever attended a game and brainstorm ideas about how to show polite behavior at a game. *Role-play:* (To simulate being at a game, you may want to take the student to the bleachers at the gym or make several rows of chairs in the classroom.) Pretend you are a fan and demonstrate the following rules:

Rules for attending a sporting event

- Don't boo, scream, or yell in a disorderly manner.

- Don't push or shove people in a crowd.

- Don't throw objects in the air or onto the field.

- Say "Excuse me" if you need to pass over people.

- Don't stand in front of or block another person's view.

- Safety first—If you find yourself in a crowd that is pushing, shoving, or running onto the field, leave as quickly as possible.

---

2. For closure, remind the student that practicing good sportsmanship allows everyone to enjoy themselves.

3. Give the student a copy of Activity Sheet 3–15A. The student must match a rule for good sportsmanship with an illustration. **Answer Key:** (by row across) 1, 7, 6, 8, 3, 4, 5, 2.

4. *Good Sportsmanship Award.* Use the award on Activity Sheet 3–15B to reinforce the rules of good sportsmanship. You may wish to give this award on a weekly basis to students who exhibit good sportsmanship. The physical education teacher may also want to participate or supply input.

Name_____ Date_____

Good Sportsmanship

Read the rules. Then look at each picture. Match the rule to the correct picture and put the number in the box.

Rules

1. Don't cheat!
2. Be a polite winner, not a sore loser.
3. Be fair and kind when choosing teams.
4. Don't throw objects into the air or onto the field.
5. Encourage your teammates.
6. Don't block another person's view.
7. Don't argue with the referee/official.
8. Take turns and share.

Good Sportsmanship Award

To: _____

For: _____

_____

Date: _____

You are a Good Sport!

Section 4

Personal Hygiene and Health

The information included in this section is designed to help the ESL student understand the vocabulary necessary to express and understand important information regarding his/her body and health. Section 4 also informs the student about the standard of personal hygiene that is expected in the American culture and shows the student how he/she can practice healthy personal hygiene.

Section 4 includes lessons to teach the student the vocabulary necessary to express how he/she is feeling and to relate any health problems that he/she may be experiencing. Knowledge of body parts is helpful not only in this situation but many others. For example, simple directions given to the student during the school day may involve the use of specific body parts, such as, "Raise your hand." Healthy sanitation practices and consideration of others' health is also presented.

Emotional health is also an integral part of the human body. Moving to another country and trying to assimilate into a new culture can be emotionally trying and stressful. It is important for the ESL student to have the ability to describe the state of his/her emotional health and seek support, if necessary.

Making healthy lifestyle choices is a decision that the student will have to make throughout life. One danger that can present itself to a new ESL student is that he/she may be tempted to make unhealthy choices in order to become an accepted member of a particular group. Knowing the dangers and harmful consequences of such choices is crucial information for the student to understand.

Personal hygiene can differ greatly from culture to culture. Cleanliness is a definite necessity in aiding assimilation into American culture. Most Americans tend to be particular about this issue and tend to be critical of those who do not meet their standard of cleanliness.

Lesson 4-1: Taking a Shower or Bath

Objectives: The student will understand the importance of cleanliness to his/her personal health and appearance. The student will understand how to take a shower or bath.

Vocabulary: bathtub; shower; soap; soap gel; clean; washcloth; towel; bubble bath; bath mat

Materials: Activity Sheet 4–1; One of each: towel, washcloth, bar soap, soap gel, bubble bath, bath mat

Teaching Note:

It is important to realize that standards of cleanliness vary from country to country. In areas where water is in short supply, people will probably not bathe often. Also, students whose families have experienced refugee camps or such difficult circumstances as war or disaster may have different habits of cleanliness than that of the average U.S. citizen. You must be sensitive to the student's background.

Directions:

1. Give the student a copy of Activity Sheet 4–1. Say, "Today we are going to talk about keeping our bodies clean. One way we can keep our bodies clean is to take a bath or shower *everyday*." Point to the illustrations in #1 on the activity sheet. Discuss the differences and similarities between a shower and a bath.

2. Discuss the reasons for cleanliness. *Health:* fewer germs, less infection, less sickness. *Social:* feels good, smells good. *Appearance:* looks good. (Refer to the illustrations in #2 on the activity sheet.)

3. Show the students examples of a towel, washcloth, bar soap, soap gel, bubble bath, and bath mat. Explain the name and use of each item.

4. Point to #3 on the activity sheet, and discuss the steps in taking a shower or bath. **Steps:** (1.) Turn on the water. Test the temperature. (2.) Get in. (3.) Wet the washcloth and rub soap on it. (4.) Wash myself–every little part. (5.) Rinse off the soap. (6.) Dry with a towel. (7.) Wipe up any water that splashed on the floor.

5. Complete #4 on the activity sheet. The student will match the picture to the correct name.

6. For the older student, this would be an excellent opportunity to discuss the use of deodorant. Bring a sample and explain its use.

7. This also may be a good time to discuss the use of fragrances: when to use and how much is appropriate.

Extension Activity: Collect samples of hygiene items from hotels and motels. Make hygiene kits for each student to take home. Or donate the kits to a local homeless shelter.

Name_____ Date_____

Taking a Shower or Bath

1. Taking a bath  **Taking a shower**

2. Why I Want to Keep Clean: (read and discuss)

I smell good.   I look good.   Keeps me healthy.   Other people like to be around me!

Look, no germs!

3. Read and discuss. Follow these steps when you take a shower or bath.

(1.) Turn on the water. TEST the temperature.

Not too hot!

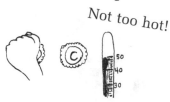

(2.) Get in.

(3.) Wet the washcloth. Rub soap on it.

(4.) Clean every little part of me.

(5.) Dry myself.

(6.) Wipe up any water that splashed on the floor.

4. Match the correct picture to the correct name.

Towel
Washcloth
Bathtub
Shower
Soap

Lesson 4-2: Washing Your Hands

• •

Objective: The student will understand the importance of washing his/her hands, and when and how to wash them.

Vocabulary: wash; hands; soap; rub; towel; dry

Materials: Activity Sheet 4–2; Bar soap or soap gel; Towel or paper towel; Access to a sink

Directions:

1. Give the student a copy of Activity Sheet 4–2, point to the illustration at the top of the page, and say, "Today you are going to learn about washing your hands." Ask, "Why is it important to keep our hands clean?" (washes away germs, won't get things dirty when we touch them, appearance)

2. Point to #1. Read and discuss the steps for washing hands. Then take the student to a sink where soap and towels are available and ask him/her to wash his/her hands following all of the steps. Have the student describe what he/she is doing.

3. Inform the student that it is very important to wash our hands at certain times. Brainstorm specific situations: before you eat, after you use the toilet, before you cook food, after you pet an animal, after you touch something unhealthy, after you sneeze.

4. Ask the student to complete #2 on the activity sheet. Discuss.

5. For older students, you may want to discuss using fingernail files and keeping the nails well groomed.

6. **Answer Key:** (1.) Wash after petting a dog. (2.) Wash before eating. (3.) Wash after sneezing or coughing into your hands. (4.) Wash before cooking. (5.) Wash after touching something unhealthy. (6.) Wash after using the restroom.

Extension Activity: Have the class make signs for the school restrooms: "Washing your hands is a healthy habit!"

Name_____ Date_____

Washing Your Hands

Part One: Follow these steps:

Step 1: Wet your hands.

Step 2: Pick up the bar of soap or squirt some liquid soap on your hands.

Step 3: Rub your hands together. Don't forget the backs!

Step 4: Rinse them in clean water until all the soap is gone.

Step 5: Dry your hands.

Part Two: Put an X on each person who needs to wash his/her hands and tell why.

(1.)

(2.)

(3.)

(4.)

(5.)

(6.)

Lesson 4-3: Taking Care of Your Teeth

Objective: The student will understand the importance of practicing good dental hygiene and caring for his/her teeth.

Vocabulary: teeth; toothbrush; toothpaste; dental floss; dentist; decay

Materials: Activity Sheet 4–3; Toothbrush; Tube of toothpaste; Container of dental floss; Cup

Directions:

1. Show the student the toothbrush, toothpaste, and dental floss. Ask the student to identify each one by name (supply help when needed). Then ask, "What are these items used for?" (brushing your teeth, cleaning your teeth) Discuss the purpose of each one: *toothpaste*—to help clean the teeth and stop decay; *toothbrush*—to brush the teeth and clean away food; *floss*—to remove tiny pieces of food from between the teeth.

2. Ask, "Why is it important to keep your teeth clean?" Brainstorm ideas: to stop decay, to look good, to have nice smelling breath. See #1 on the activity sheet.

3. Point to the steps for brushing in #2. Model and discuss each step.

   Step 1: Put toothpaste on the brush, just a small dab. Demonstrate the appropriate amount that should be used.
   Step 2: Brush up and down, over all the areas of each tooth. Don't forget the back!
   Step 3: Rinse your mouth with water. Spit it out into the sink.
   Step 4: Floss between the teeth to get small pieces of food that were missed.
   Step 5: Smile!

   Stress the fact that we need to brush at least twice a day; if possible, three times a day. Discuss the best time of the day to brush your teeth. Brainstorm with the student: in the morning after breakfast, after school in the afternoon, and at night before bed.

4. Inform the student that a person who helps us take care of our teeth is called the *Dentist.* Explain that going to the dentist for regular checkups is an important part of caring for our teeth.

5. Remind the student that eating the right food can help keep our teeth healthy. Discuss the fact that too much candy and too many snacks can be harmful to our teeth.

6. Ask the student to complete #3 and #4 on the activity sheet.

7. If the student is older, you may want to discuss the use of mouthwash.

Extension Activities:

1. Invite a dentist or health care professional to visit the class and present a dental hygiene program.

2. Collect samples of toothpaste from hotels and motels and donate them to various shelters.

Name_____ Date_____

Taking Care of Your Teeth

Part One: I brush my teeth to:

Stop decay.   Look nice.   Have nice smelling breath.

Part Two: Choose the correct word and write it in the blank.

toothpaste, 3 times, floss, up and down, smile, decay, great, dentist, checkups

(1.) I brush my teeth _____ a day.

(2.) I put _____ on my brush.

(3.) I brush _____. (direction)

(4.) _____ helps me clean between my teeth.

(5.) Regular brushing stops tooth _____.

(6.) My _____ looks _____.

(7.) I go to the _____ for regular _____.

Part Three: Choose healthy food for Mr. Molar to eat. Circle the food that is good for your teeth. Put an X on the food that is not good for your teeth.

Part Four: Help Mr. Molar get to the dentist for his checkup.

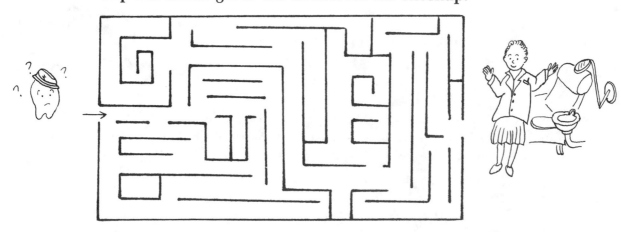

Lesson 4-4: Taking Care of Your Hair

• •

Objective: The student will understand how to care for his/her hair by washing, combing/brushing, and styling it.

Vocabulary: hair; shampoo; tangle; conditioner; comb; brush; hair dryer; towel; beauty salon; stylist; barber shop; barber

Materials: Activity Sheet 4–4; Comb, brush, hair dryer, towel, shampoo, conditioner; Doll with hair that can be washed (*optional*)

Teaching Note:

If you choose to do the optional activity with the doll, you will need a sink or access to water.

Directions:

1. Say, "Today we are going to talk about taking care of your hair." Touch your hair. Ask the student to brainstorm ideas about ways to care for his/her hair (e.g., washing, brushing everyday, styling). Discuss why we want to take care of our hair (e.g., to look good, keep it healthy).

2. Show the students the brush, comb, towel, shampoo, conditioner, and hair dryer. Encourage the student to name as many of these items as possible and explain their use. Supply help when needed.

3. Give the student a copy of Activity Sheet 4–4. Point to #1 and the illustrations. Read each step in the process of washing hair and discuss. Ask the student to repeat. (*Optional*: Ask the student to wash the hair of the doll following each step in order. To enhance vocabulary development, ask the student to tell you what he/she is doing.) Supply help when needed.

   (1.) Wet your hair.

   (2.) Put on shampoo.

   (3.) Rub all over your head.

   (4.) Rinse. Be sure to get all the soap out!

   (5.) If your hair is tangled, put on conditioner. Rinse.

   (6.) Dry your hair. Use a towel first, then the hair dryer.

   (7.) Comb and style.

4. Explain that people go to a place called the Beauty Salon (or Hair Stylist or Hair Salon) to have their hair cut, washed, and styled (makes it look nice). The person who works at a salon is called a "stylist." Discuss where Beauty

Salons are located: at the mall, in the neighborhood. Explain that another kind of shop where a person can get a haircut and style is called a Barber Shop. Inform the student that usually men go to a Barber Shop and the person who works at a Barber Shop is called a "barber."

5. Inform the student that it is not a good idea to use other people's combs or brushes. It is also not a good idea to wear another person's hat. Explain that a person can get lice from doing this.

6. Ask the student to complete #2 on the activity sheet. Check for accuracy.

Answer Key:

s	t	y	l	i	s	t	l	g	e	a	e	s	a
w	o	d	h	a	i	r	d	r	y	e	r	h	t
y	m	k	x	n	p	r	e	a	u	o	b	a	m
l	a	f	b	z	a	i	g	b	t	r	f	m	t
e	b	m	d	k	q	n	c	d	r	s	s	p	z
t	o	w	e	l	f	s	o	e	h	u	k	o	t
c	z	p	o	x	p	e	u	h	y	d	s	o	l
t	a	n	g	l	e	s	s	n	v	s	c	h	i
a	i	p	c	o	n	d	i	t	i	o	n	e	r

Extension Activities:

1. Take the students on a field trip to a beauty shop or invite a stylist to visit the class as a guest speaker.

2. Make hair care kits. Fill a plastic bag with samples of shampoo, crème rinse, and a comb. The students may take these home or make them for the shelters in the area.

Name_____ Date_____

Taking Care of Your Hair

Part One: Look at the pictures. Describe what is happening in each one.

(1.)

Wet your hair.

(2.)

Put on shampoo.

(3.)

Rub your whole head and make suds!

(4.)

Rinse with clean water. If you get tangles, put on conditioner and rinse again.

(5.)

Dry. Use a towel or a hair dryer.

(6.)

Comb and style.

Part Two: Look at the word list in the box. Find each word, circle it, then cross it off the list.

s	t	y	l	i	s	t	l	g	e	a	e	s	a
w	o	d	h	a	i	r	d	r	y	e	r	h	t
y	m	k	x	n	p	r	e	a	u	o	b	a	m
l	a	f	b	z	a	i	g	b	t	r	f	m	t
e	b	m	d	k	q	n	c	d	r	s	s	p	z
t	o	w	e	l	f	s	o	e	h	u	k	o	t
c	z	p	o	x	p	e	u	h	y	d	s	o	l
t	a	n	g	l	e	s	s	n	v	s	c	h	i
a	i	p	c	o	n	d	i	t	i	o	n	e	r

brush

shampoo

comb

towel

conditioner

hair dryer

stylist

tangles

rinse

suds

Lesson 4-5: Using a Public Restroom

• •

Objective: The student will become familiar with the use and items in a public restroom.

Vocabulary: Public Restroom; Men; Women; Unisex; Handicapped; paper towel; automatic hand dryer; toilet; toilet paper; paper toilet seat cover; hook; lever; shelf; lock; trash can; mirror; sink; soap dispenser; changing table; urinal; stall

Materials: Activity Sheet 4–5; Pencil

Teaching Note:

It is especially helpful to do this lesson before the student goes on a field trip or to a facility where he/she will need to use a public restroom. In many countries, public restrooms do not have the amenities found in American public restrooms. **For safety reasons, tell young children never to use a public restroom unless a known adult is with them.**

Directions:

1. Give the student a copy of Activity Sheet 4–5. Explain that you are going to discuss using a public restroom. Discuss the different locations at which public restrooms can be found: stores, airports, theaters, restaurants, train and bus stations, zoos, libraries, etc.

2. Point to the identifying signs in #1 on the activity sheet, and discuss the sign and meaning of each: "Men," "Women," "Unisex," and "Handicapped." Ask the student to identify which sign would be on the restroom door he/she can use.

3. Identify each item found in the restroom and discuss its use. See the illustrations on the activity sheet.

4. Discuss the following helpful information:

   • How to use the automatic hand dryer.

   • Use a paper toilet seat cover (when available) or clean the seat with toilet paper before using it. Both are found **inside the stall**.

   • In some sinks the water goes on automatically when you put your hand under the faucet.

   • The "Handicapped" stall is larger to provide room for a wheelchair. Also, a sink, towels, and soap are provided at the correct height for a person in a wheelchair.

   • Always wash your hands after you use the restroom.

5. Ask the student to complete #2 on the activity sheet. The student will be asked to identify the various items found in a public restroom and place the correct letter next to the name of the item. When necessary, help with reading.

Answer Key:

E	L	G	A
B	H	M	C
D	K	T	F
J	N	S	Q
I	O	P	
		R	

Name_____ Date_____

Using a Public Restroom

1. **Put an X on the sign for a restroom you can use.**

A

B

C

D

2. **Look at the picture of the restroom, including the signs at the top of the page. Then find the items listed below. Put the correct letter next to each word.**

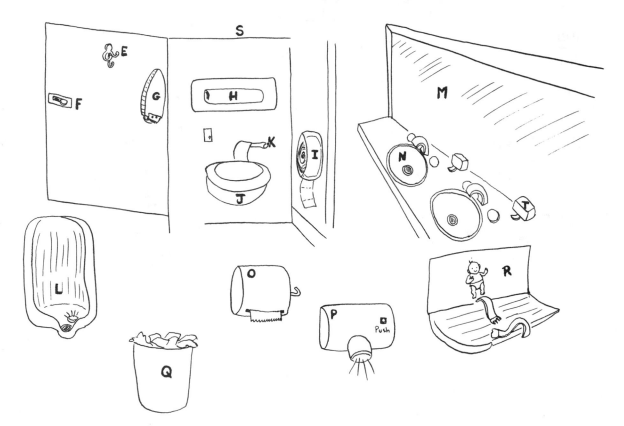

____ Hook   ____ Men's urinal   ____ Shelf   ____ Men

____ Women   ____ Paper toilet seat   ____ Mirror   ____ Unisex

____ Handicapped   ____ Lever   ____ Soap   ____ Lock

____ Toilet   ____ Sink   ____ Stall   ____ Trash can

____ Toilet paper   ____ Paper towels   ____ Automatic hand dryer

____ Baby changing table

Lesson 4-6: Body Parts—Outside and Inside

Objective: The student will learn the names and be able to identify common body parts.

Vocabulary: (*Outside*) head, hair, eye, nose, ear, mouth, neck, shoulder, chest, arm, elbow, waist, hip, wrist, hand, fingers, thigh, knee, leg, shin, ankle, toes, feet, back, buttocks, heel, elbow, skin; (*Face*) forehead, eyebrow, eyelash, eyelid, nostril, lips, chin, cheek, jaw, dimple; (*Hands*) finger, fingernail, thumb, palm, knuckle; (*Inside*) brain, teeth, tongue, heart, lungs, stomach, liver, intestine, muscle, bone, artery, vein, kidney

Materials: Activity Sheets 4–6A, 4–6B, 4–6C, 4–6D, 4–6E; Pencil; Large pieces of chart paper (long enough to trace a body); Colored markers or pencils

Teaching Note:

This lesson is divided into two basic parts: the external parts of the body and the internal parts. These should be taught in two separate sessions. Because of the detail on the face and hands, a separate illustration sheet has been done. It is helpful to staple the five activity sheets into a packet; this keeps the information organized and easily located by the student.

Directions:

1. *Outside parts.* Give each student a copy of Activity Sheet 4–6A. As you say each body part, point to it on the picture and then point to it on your body. Ask the students to repeat this sequence after you. At this point, you may want to play one of the several games suggested below. Point out to the student that the *skin* covers the entire body and protects the inside.

2. Next, have the student complete Activity Sheet 4–6B. He/she will be asked to write the correct name of the body part on the line pointing to it. You may also want to use this activity sheet as an assessment tool.

3. *Face and hands.* Give the student a copy of Activity Sheet 4–6C. Point to each feature on the face and say its name. Ask the student to identify the feature on his/her own face and repeat the name. The student will then draw a picture of a funny face, a scary face, a sad face, and a happy face. Follow the same procedure for the hands. The student will then trace his/her hands and write a list of verbs that describe what he/she can do with the hands. If necessary, help with vocabulary.

4. *Inside body parts.* Give the student a copy of Activity Sheet 4–6D. Say, point to, and discuss the "inside" body parts. For the older or more advanced student, you may want to explain the function of each inside body part (brain—

thinks; tongue—tastes, talks, chews; teeth—chews; heart—pumps blood; artery—carries blood to the parts of the body; veins—carry blood back to the heart; lungs—breathe; stomach—stores and digests food; intestine—digests food; liver—takes impurities out of body; muscle—movement; bone—structure; kidney—eliminates waste). Ask the student to complete Activity Sheet 4–6D. The student will write the correct body name next to a designated number. Supply help, if needed.

5. Brainstorm words that describe the body (e.g., strong, weak, thin, fat, tall, short, etc.). Do the same for the hair, eyes, and face. Ask the student to complete Activity Sheet 4–6E. The student will complete sentences describing parts of the body and draw a picture of him-/herself.

6. *Optional*: Give each student a piece of chart paper large enough to be able to trace his/her body onto it. Have the student lie down as you, or another student, trace around the perimeter of the body. The student cuts out his/her body form and labels the parts. Display these in the room.

Suggested Games:

- *Simon Says*. The leader gives a command prefacing it with the words "Simon Says." "Simon Says touch your (body part)." If the leader does not say "Simon Says," the others do not follow. The focus of the game is to trick the others.

- *The Yarn Game*. Cut pieces of yarn into 2- to 3-inch strips. Instruct the students to put the yarn on certain body parts, e.g., "Put the yarn on your leg."

- *The Touch and Say Game*. The intent of this game is for the student to identify and remember the body parts. The leader says "Head," for example. Everyone says and touches their head. Next, the leader adds another body part and says, "Head, Leg." Everyone says and touches "Head, Leg." Continue in this fashion until all the body parts are named, or until there are too many to remember and humorous confusion ensues.

Name_____ Date_____

This Is My Body—Outside!

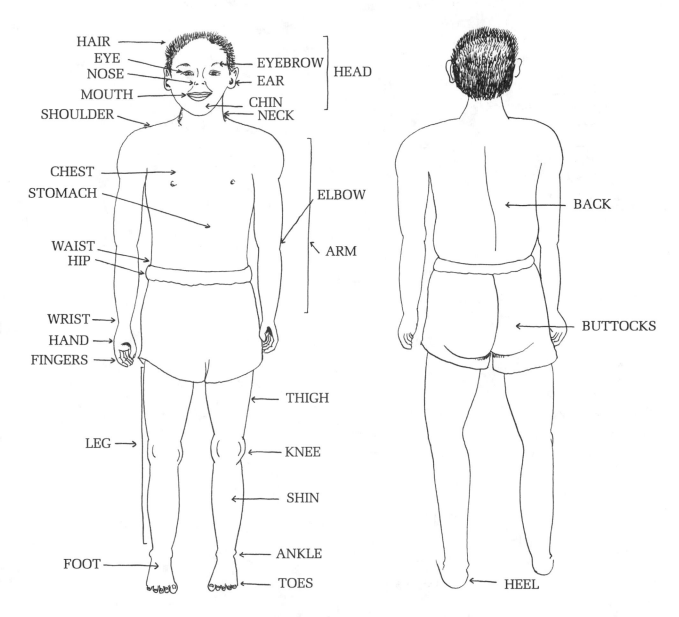

HAIR
EYE
NOSE
MOUTH
SHOULDER
EYEBROW
EAR
CHIN
NECK
HEAD
CHEST
STOMACH
ELBOW
WAIST
HIP
ARM
WRIST
HAND
FINGERS
THIGH
LEG
KNEE
SHIN
FOOT
ANKLE
TOES

BACK
BUTTOCKS
HEEL

Front   **Back**

Name_____ Date_____

This Is My Body—Outside!

Look at the arrows. Write the name of the body part on the line.

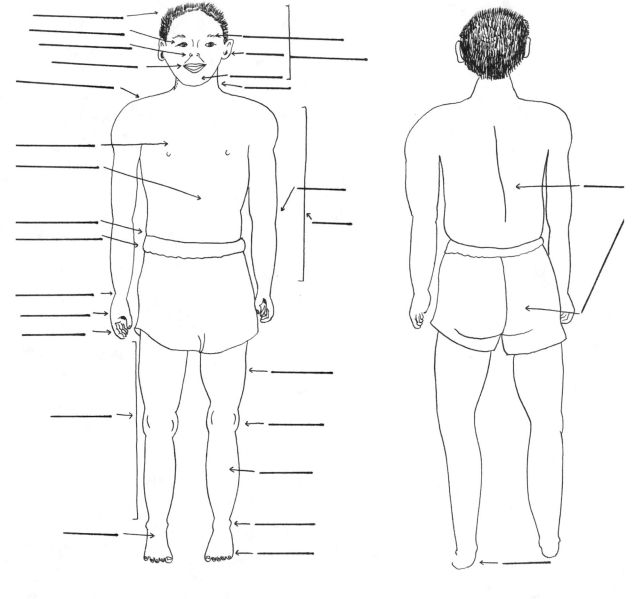

Front　　　　　　　　　　　**Back**

Name_____ Date_____

This Is My Face

All these parts together are called your "face."

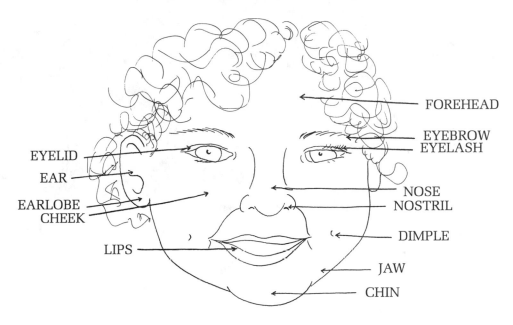

FOREHEAD

EYEBROW
EYELASH

EYELID
EAR

EARLOBE
CHEEK

NOSE
NOSTRIL

DIMPLE

LIPS

JAW
CHIN

Draw a picture of a funny face, a scary face, a sad face, a happy face.

These Are My Hands

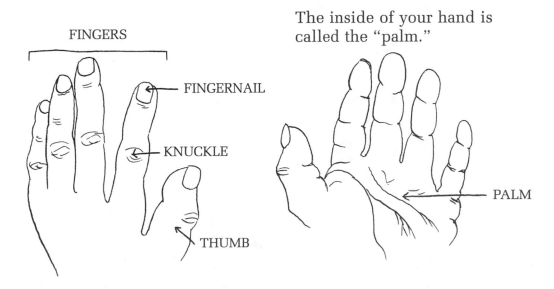

FINGERS

The inside of your hand is called the "palm."

FINGERNAIL

KNUCKLE

THUMB

PALM

Trace your hands on a sheet of paper. Now make a list of verbs that tells what you can do with your hands.

Name_____ Date_____

This Is My Body—Inside!

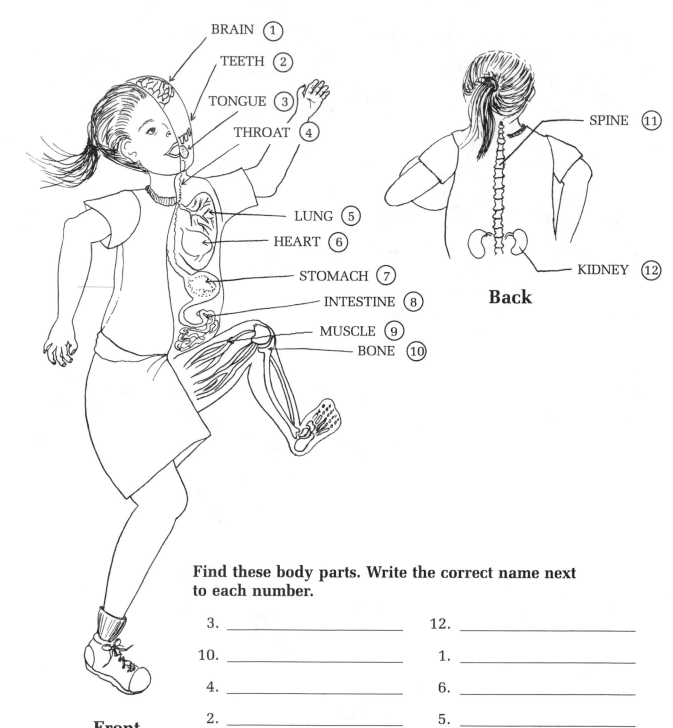

BRAIN ①
TEETH ②
TONGUE ③
THROAT ④
LUNG ⑤
HEART ⑥
STOMACH ⑦
INTESTINE ⑧
MUSCLE ⑨
BONE ⑩

SPINE ⑪
KIDNEY ⑫

Back

Front

Find these body parts. Write the correct name next to each number.

3. _____   12. _____

10. _____   1. _____

4. _____   6. _____

2. _____   5. _____

11. _____   9. _____

8. _____   7. _____

Name_____ Date_____

All My Body Parts = Me!

Brainstorm words that describe your body. Then fill in the blanks.

1. My hair is _____.

2. My eyes are _____.

3. My face is _____.

4. My body is _____.

5. The thing I like best about my body is _____.

Draw a picture of yourself.

Lesson 4-7: "How Do You Feel?"

• •

Objective: The student will understand and learn the appropriate language to describe how he/she feels.

Vocabulary: fine; hurts; headache; earache; cold; sore throat; cough; toothache; stomachache; fever; sick; tired; ill; backache; breathe; "How are you?"; How do you feel?"

Materials: Activity Sheet 4–7; Scissors

Directions:

1. Give the student a copy of the two-page Activity Sheet 4–7. Ask the student, "How are you?" (**Response:** "I'm fine.") Clarify and shake your head "yes." Use the illustration on the activity sheet, if necessary.

2. Next, hold your head and moan and explain sometimes our bodies are sick and don't feel well. Shake your head "no." Explain that is called being sick or ill.

3. Point to the illustrations on Activity Sheet 4–7. Explain that usually a person or the doctor will ask, "How do you feel?" Say each statement and use gestures to demonstrate. Then ask the student, "How do you feel?" (**Response:** Student repeats the response and does the gesture.)

4. Ask the student to cut out the picture cards and the statement cards. Mix them up and have the student match them together. If necessary, read the card to the student.

5. Now, take away the statement cards. Point to each picture card and ask the student to supply the correct statement from memory. (On the cards where two statements are given, one choice is sufficient.)

Extension Activity: Give the following situations; use gestures or illustrations to clarify. Ask the student to give the proper response:

- You hit your head on the door. ("I have a headache.")
- You carried a heavy load on your back. ("I have a backache.")
- You didn't sleep well last night. ("I'm tired.")
- You are panting after a long run. ("I can't breathe.")
- You are sneezing and your nose is stuffy. ("I have a cold.")
- Your face is flushed (red) and you feel hot. ("I have a fever.")
- Your whole body aches. ("I feel sick.")
- You bit a hard candy and broke your tooth. ("I have a toothache.")

"How Do You Feel?"

"I'm fine."

"My tooth hurts."
or
"I have a toothache."

"My throat hurts."
or
"I have a sore throat."

"I have a cough"

"I feel sick."
or
"I don't feel well."

"My stomach hurts."
or
"I have a stomachache."

"My ear hurts."
or
"I have an earache."

"How Do You Feel?"

	"My head hurts." or "I have a headache."
	"I feel hot." or "I have a fever."
	"I feel tired."
	"I have a cold."
	"My back hurts." or "I have a backache."
	"I can't breathe."

Lesson 4-8: Keep Those Germs Away

• •

Objective: The student will understand the appropriate behaviors involved to avoid spreading germs.

Vocabulary: wash; cough; sneeze; taste; utensil; rim; silverware; bite; sip

Materials: Activity Sheet 4–8; Knife, fork, spoon, and glass; Picture of a classroom; Empty soda can; Saucepan; Candy bar or cookie; Mixing spoon

Teaching Note:

Many health care professionals agree that a common way for young people to spread germs to each other is by sharing food or drinks. Stress this fact as you present the lesson.

Directions:

1. Ask the student, "Have you ever felt sick?" Discuss. Next say, "Germs make us sick. Germs are so small that we can't see them. But we can do certain things to help keep germs from our bodies and from spreading germs to others."

2. Write the following rules on the chalkboard and discuss each one. Demonstrate and use realistic items as much as possible.

   Rule 1: Always wash your hands after using the restroom. (Draw the universal sign for restrooms. Then pretend to wash your hands.)
   Rule 2: If you are offered food, use this rule: "The one you touch is the one you take." (This is a good rule especially for classroom use when treats are passed out.)
   Rule 3: Cover your mouth if you cough or sneeze. (Demonstrate).
   Rule 4: Don't take a bite of anyone else's food. (Demonstrate with candy/cookie.)
   Rule 5: Don't drink from anyone else's cup, can, or bottle. (Demonstrate with cup, can, or bottle.)
   Rule 6: Don't come to school if you are sick. (Show a picture of a classroom and pretend to be sick. Shake your head "no.")
   Rule 7: Always wash your hands before cooking or preparing food. (Demonstrate with a saucepan and spoon.)
   Rule 8: When you set the table, don't touch the parts of the silverware that touch the mouth, or the rim of a glass. (Demonstrate with silverware and a glass.)

3. Brainstorm other rules with the student. Ask the student to complete Activity Sheet 4–8. The student will be asked to identify students who practice healthy behavior. The student will also identify unhealthy behavior. Discuss. **Answer Key:** (1.) Circle—Washed hands after using the restroom. (2.) Circle—Covered nose and mouth after sneezing and coughing. (3.) X—Came to school sick. (4.) Circle—Held drinking glass at the bottom, away from rim. (5.) X—Offered a sip from the same soda can. (6.) X—Touched other food before making a choice. (7.) Circle—Washed hands before making a sandwich. (8.) X—Offered a bite of the same candy bar.

Extension Activities: Brainstorm "Keep Our Classroom Healthy" behaviors and post in the classroom.

Name_____ Date_____

Keep Those Germs Away

Circle the students who are keeping germs away from themselves and others. Put an X on those who need to improve and tell why.

1.

2.

3. "I feel sick!"

4.

5. "May I have a sip of your soda?"

6. "I can't decide which one I want."

7. "I can make you a sandwich."

8. "Take a bite of my candy bar. It's good!"

Lesson 4-9: Emotions–How Do You Feel Inside?

Objective: The student will be able to identify emotions and situations that elicit them.

Vocabulary: feelings; emotions; happy; sad; shy; excited; sorry; proud; embarrassed; angry; guilty; surprised; afraid; impatient; jealous; hopeful; hurt; loved

Materials: Activity Sheet 4–9 (2 pages); Scissors

Teaching Note:

The major teaching strategy in this lesson will be gesturing and modeling the emotion.

Directions:

1. Say, "Today we are going to talk about how you feel inside yourself, how your brain and your heart feel." (**Gesture:** Point to your head and your heart.) "These are called emotions or feelings."

2. Give the student a copy of Activity Sheet 4–9. Name and make the appropriate facial expression for each emotion. Ask the student to repeat. The following list gives some suggestions for gestures: *Happy*—smile; *Sad*—frown, look down; *Shy*—look down, fold your hands in front of you, and shuffle your feet; *Excited*—clap your hands, smile, jump up and down; *Sorry*—look down; *Proud*—stick out your chest and give the thumbs-up sign; *Embarrassed*—hide your face with your hand; *Angry*—frown, shake your fist; *Guilty*—look up and move your eyes around; *Surprised*—open your mouth and your eyes very widely; *Afraid*—shake and open your mouth and put your hand in front of it as in fear; *Impatient*—put your hands on your hips and tap your foot; *Jealous*—sneer and say, "I wanted that!"; *Hopeful*—shake your head "yes" and open your eyes widely; *Hurt*—put your hand over your heart, look down, shake your head; *Loved*—smile and hug yourself.

3. Ask the student to cut out the faces of the emotions on Activity Sheet 4–9.

4. ***Emotion Charades.*** Mix up the faces and turn them face down. The student chooses one and acts out the emotion. The others guess what emotion it is. The student who guesses correctly gets the face. The player with the most faces at the end of the game, wins. (Each student takes a turn until all the faces are used.) *Team Play:* Divide into teams. Teams take turns choosing faces and acting out the emotion. Give a certain amount of time for each team to guess the emotion. Score one point for the team that guesses correctly. The team with the most points after all the faces are used, wins.

5. Give the students the following situations and ask them to match each one to an emotion that might arise:

- You get a special present for your birthday. (happy)
- Your best friend is moving. (sad)
- You are at a new school and don't know anyone. (shy or afraid)
- You accidentally kick Jose in the soccer game. (sorry)
- You got the highest grade on the math test. (proud)
- It is your turn to sing and you forget the words to the song. (embarrassed)
- Rosa hits you for no reason. (angry)
- You get caught cheating on a test. (guilty)
- Your friends have a surprise birthday party for you. (surprised)
- You are home alone at night and the lights go out. (afraid)
- You have to wait one hour for your brother at the bus stop. (impatient)
- Your sister gets the dress you wanted to buy. (jealous)
- Your teacher is giving a special award. You want to be chosen. (hopeful)
- Your best friend won't talk to you today. (hurt)
- Your father comes home from work and gives you a big hug. (loved)

Extension Activities:

1. Cut out the faces on Activity Sheet 4–9. Then cut them in half. Mix them up and have the student put them back together, saying each emotion. OR, for two or more students, mix them up and put them face down. Each student takes turns turning over two halves to make a whole face. The student with the most complete faces, wins.

2. Ask the students to think of other words to describe a feeling or emotion, e.g., happy—glad, jealous—envious, etc.

My Emotions

Play this game with a partner. Cut out each face. Turn them face down. Choose one and act out the emotion. If your partner guesses the correct emotion, he/she gets to keep the face. The player with more faces at the end of the game, wins.

Happy

Sad

Bored

Angry

Loved

Shy

Excited

Sorry

Proud

My Emotions

Embarrassed

Guilty

Surprised

Afraid

Jealous

Hurt

Think of three more emotions you might feel. Draw them in the empty circles. Then write a word describing them.

Lesson 4-10: Beware: Cigarettes, Drugs, and Alcohol

Objective: The student will be introduced to the dangers of cigarettes, drugs, and alcohol.

Vocabulary: cigarette; drugs; alcohol; unhealthy; illegal

Materials: Activity Sheet 4–10; Pencil

Teaching Notes:

1. This lesson introduces the student to the dangers of three unhealthy substances: cigarettes, drugs, and alcohol. If you want to explore these areas in more depth, obtain extensive materials through the school counseling department, police department, or professional health care providers.

2. In many countries, children smoke and consume alcohol at an early age. It is beneficial for the students and parents (caregivers) to know the dangers involved with these substances **and that this is illegal in the United States.**

Directions:

1. Give the student a copy of Activity Sheet 4–10. Point to the illustrations in #1. Say, "Some things can hurt our bodies." Point to the illustrations and discuss the harmful effects.

   - *Cigarettes*—Causes diseases (cancer, asthma, emphysema); gives you bad breath, discolored teeth, smell on clothes, etc.

   - *Drugs*—Mind altering (don't know what you are doing); harms internal organs (heart, liver, kidneys, etc.); causes permanent damage to the brain; death; illegal

   - *Alcohol*—Causes diseases (cancer, heart disease, liver disease, brain damage); is mind altering (don't know what you are doing); illegal until you are 21

2. Next say, "People may offer you cigarettes, drugs, or alcohol. These are some answers you can give them." Then write these on the chalkboard or chart paper. (Clarify any language that may be unknown, such as "illegal," "kicked off the team," "ground.")

   "No, I'm sick. My doctor says I can't do that."
   "I'm not allowed to do that."
   "That stuff is illegal."
   "My parents will ground me forever!"
   "That's not my medicine."
   "I'll get kicked off the team."
   "No."

Remind the student that the best solution is to avoid the situation. If you see someone using cigarettes, drugs, or alcohol, leave. Also, choose friends who live a healthy lifestyle.

3. Role-play and have the student respond using one of the answers given in Direction 2.

   TEACHER: "Hey, do you want a cigarette?"
   "I've got some great pills that will make you feel really good!"
   "C'mon, try some of this stuff. Are you chicken?"
   "My parents aren't home. Let's have a beer."
   "We won't get caught. Have a drink with us."

4. Now ask the student to complete #2 on the activity sheet. The student will be asked to complete a "Crack the Code" activity. **Answer Key:**

   I will not drink alcohol.
   I will not smoke cigarettes.
   I will not do drugs.
   I will keep my body healthy!

Extension Activity: Invite police officers and health care professionals to speak to the students about the dangers of cigarettes, drugs, and alcohol, and the consequences involved with illegal behavior.

Name_____ Date_____

Beware: Cigarettes, Drugs, & Alcohol

Part One: Read these picture sentences. Discuss the unhealthy results.

Cigarettes	Unhealthy lungs and heart	Cough	Bad Breath	Yellow, stained teeth	Smells Bad

Drugs	Alcohol	Mind Altering	Harms your body	Death	Illegal

Part Two: "Crack the Code!" Use the letter chart at the bottom. Find the number, then put the letter on the line above it. Unlock the secret codes and pledge to be healthy.

___ ___ ___ ___ ___   ___ ___ ___   ___ ___ ___ ___ ___
3   11 3 4 4   7 21 23   6 13 3 7 15

___ ___ ___ ___ ___ ___ ___ .
8   4 12 21 24 21 4

___ ___ ___ ___ ___   ___ ___ ___   ___ ___ ___ ___ ___
3   11 3 4 4   7 21 23   1 25 21 15 20

___ ___ ___ ___ ___ ___ ___ ___ ___ ___ .
12 3 9 8 13 20 23 23 20 1

___ ___ ___ ___ ___   ___ ___ ___   ___ ___
3   11 3 4 4   7 21 23   6 21

___ ___ ___ ___ ___ .
6 13 2 9 1

___ ___ ___ ___ ___   ___ ___ ___ ___   ___ ___
3   11 3 4 4   15 20 20 5   25 18

___ ___ ___ ___   ___ ___ ___ ___ ___ ___ ___ !
22 21 6 18   24 20 8 4 23 24 18

S	U	I	L	P	D	N	A	G	X	W	C	R
1	2	3	4	5	6	7	8	9	10	11	12	13
F	K	V	J	Y	Q	E	O	B	T	H	M	Z
14	15	16	17	18	19	20	21	22	23	24	25	26

Lesson 4-11: Making Healthy Choices

Objective: The student will understand the general areas of a healthy lifestyle and how to make healthy choices.

Vocabulary: choices; healthy; exercise; snack; food; smoking; sleep; alcohol; drugs

Materials: Activity Sheet 4–11; Piece of candy for each student; Pencil

Directions:

1. Say, "Today we are going to talk about making a choice. A choice is when you have to pick one thing and not another. For example, I'm going to put both of my hands behind my back. I will hold a piece of candy in one hand. Then you must pick a hand. This is called making a 'choice.' If the candy is in that hand, you get to keep it." (Student chooses a hand.) Then say, "As you grow older, you will need to make choices for yourself. Some choices are healthy (good for you), and some choices are not healthy (bad for you)."

2. Continue, "One way to decide if something is healthy (good) for you is to ask these three questions:

   (1.) Is this choice healthy (good) for my body?

   (2.) Is this choice healthy (good) for my mind?

   (3.) Will this choice hurt me or someone else?

3. Give the student a copy of Activity Sheet 4–11. Discuss each situation and, using the questions, ask the student to decide which choices are healthy and which are unhealthy. **Answer Key:**

   Eating healthy food—circle   Showering or bathing daily—circle
   Fighting—X   Reading a book—circle
   Exercising—circle   Skateboarding on a crowded sidewalk—X
   Smoking—X   Wearing a seatbelt—circle
   Playing with guns—X   Eating a lot of junk food—X
   Watching TV for hours—X

Extension Activities:

1. Make a "Healthy Lifestyle" collage. Ask students to find pictures in magazines of people making healthy lifestyle choices. Cut them out and glue them to posterboard and display in the classroom.

2. Have the student keep a diary for a week and list the healthy choices he/she has made.

Name_____ Date_____

Make Healthy Choices

Before you make a choice, ask these questions:

1. "Is this choice healthy (good) for my body?"
2. "Is this choice healthy (good) for my mind?"
3. "Will this choice hurt me or someone else?"

Directions: Use the questions above to circle the healthy choices. Put an X on the unhealthy choices.

Eating healthy food

Fighting

Exercising

Smoking

Playing with guns

Watching TV for hours

Showering or bathing daily

Reading a book

Skateboarding on a crowded sidewalk

Wearing a seatbelt

Eating a lot of junk food

Lesson 4-12: The Five Senses

* *

Objectives: The student will be able to identify the five senses (sight, hearing, touch, taste, and smell). The student will understand how each sense helps a person understand the world around him/her.

Vocabulary: brain; eyes; see; ears; hear; listen; hands; fingers; touch; skin; feel; mouth; tongue; taste; nose; smell

Materials: Activity Sheet 4–12; Cotton balls; Small pieces of candy (M&M's™, Life-savers™); Red, blue, and green paper circles; Bottle of perfume or cologne; CD/cassette player or radio; Crayons or colored pencils

Directions:

1. Draw this simple illustration on the chalkboard or chart paper. Now say, "Your brain (point to the outline of the brain) and your body (point to the outline of the body) work together to help you learn and remember things in the world around you. These are called your senses. There are five senses: Sight (point to your eyes), Hearing (cup your ears), Smell (point to your nose and sniff), Touch or Feel (hold up your hand and rub your thumb and fingers together), and Taste (pretend to eat something, smack your lips and say 'M-M-M-!')."

2. Explain each sense using the following demonstrations:

   * *Sight*—Point to your eyes and say, "Sight is a sense. Your eyes help you see." Hold up different colored circles and ask the student to identify each color. Then ask, "What sense did you use to see the colors?" (sight)

   * *Hearing*—Cup your ears and say, "Hearing is a sense. Your ears help you hear." (Point to your ears.) Play a song on the CD/cassette player or the radio. Then ask, "What did you hear?" (music, song) "What sense did you use?" (hearing)

   * *Smell*—Sniff and say, "Smell is a sense. Your nose helps you smell." (Point to your nose.) Have the student smell a bottle of cologne or perfume. Then ask, "What sense did you use?" (smell)

   * *Touch/Feel*—Hold up your hand, rub your thumb and fingers together, and say, "Touch or feel is a sense. Most of the time you use your fingers and hands to touch/feel." Put a cotton ball in the student's hands. Then ask him/her to describe how it feels. (soft, nice, squishy, smooth) Next ask, "What sense did you use?" (touch/feel) Rub your arm and tell the student, "Your skin can feel, too." Ask the student to close his/her eyes. Gently touch the student's arm. Have the student open his/her eyes and ask, "Did

161

you feel something on your arm?" (yes) "What sense told you that?" (touch/feel)

- *Taste*—(Smack your lips and say "M-M-M-!") Say, "Taste is a sense." Point to your tongue and say, "Your tongue helps you taste what is in your mouth." Have the student close his/her eyes. Then give the student a piece of candy. Ask the student to describe this taste. (sweet, good) For fun, ask the student to try and identify the food. Ask, "What sense did you use?" (taste)

- *Extension of Taste*—Ask the student to predict what will happen if he/she holds his/her nose and tries to taste. Ask the student to close his/her eyes; give the student something to taste. Discuss the outcome. (Can't taste) Ask, "Can you think of a time when you had trouble tasting?" (When the student has a cold) "What does this tell you about the sense of taste and the sense of smell?" (They work together. Taste depends upon smell.) Ask, "Why do some people like the way something tastes and others do not?" Discuss.

3. Ask the student to complete Activity Sheet 4–12. The student is asked to draw pictures relating to the five senses. The student will also match a body part to its corresponding sense.

Extension Activities:

1. Brainstorm ideas when the senses work together to help you do something, e.g., enjoying a movie (sight and hearing), safely crossing the street (sight and hearing), etc.

2. Have the student pretend that he/she has lost his/her sense of sight. What would the world be like? Write a few sentences telling about it or verbally describe it.

3. Have the student pretend he/she can't feel anything. Why could this be a problem? Brainstorm ideas.

4. Ask the student to make a list of foods he/she likes and a list of foods he/she dislikes. Compare. (If this is a group activity, have students compare lists.)

5. Ask the student to close his/her eyes and identify these different smells: coffee crystals, popcorn, chocolate, banana, orange, various flavors of extracts, peanut butter.

6. Ask the student to close his/her eyes. Then ask him/her to taste various foods and identify them.

7. Ask the student to listen to a tape of nature sounds. Try to identify each one.

8. Use holograms, Hidden Pictures, and pictures that can be perceived as two different things. Ask the student to describe how he/she uses the sense of sight for each one.

9. Ask the student to draw a picture using "smelly" markers.

10. Give "smelly" stickers as a reward.

Name_____ Date_____

The Five Senses

1. Draw something that . . .

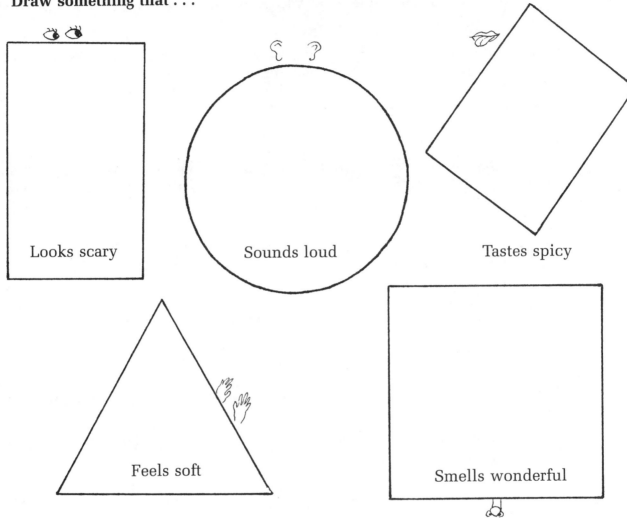

Looks scary

Sounds loud

Tastes spicy

Feels soft

Smells wonderful

2. Draw a line from the body part to the matching

 Tongue   Smell

Hands & Skin   Taste

Eyes   Hearing

 Nose   Sight

 Ears   Touch & Feeling

Lesson 4-13: A Trip to the Doctor—What to Expect

Objective: The student will learn the vocabulary and what to expect during a visit to the doctor.

Vocabulary: doctor; checkup; waiting room; nurse; weigh; blood pressure; receptionist; injection; examining room; immunization

Materials: Activity Sheet 4–13; Pencil

Teaching Note:

Ask the school nurse to speak with your class and demonstrate some of the things that will be done during an examination (weigh, blood pressure, tongue depressor, etc.).

Directions:

1. Tell the student that he/she is going to learn about going for a visit to the doctor's office. Explain that a doctor is a person who takes care of human bodies. Discuss and explain the reasons why people go to the doctor. *Checkup:* To make sure everything inside and outside our bodies is healthy. *Illness:* Person is not feeling well (sick). *Immunizations (injections)*: These are required by law for immigrants. They have medicine in them that keeps people from getting sick.

2. Give the student a copy of Activity Sheet 4–13. Read and discuss the sequence of events when going to the doctor for a visit. Allow time for the student to ask questions.

3. Ask the student to complete the activity sheet. He/she will be asked to match a word with an event.

Extension Activity: Ask the student to write or tell what it is like to visit the doctor in his/her native country.

164

Name_____ Date_____

Juan Visits the Doctor

Dr. Saran   Juan   Mother

Read the story. The pictures will help you.

 went to the doctor's office with his . He sat in the .

He read . The called his name. His 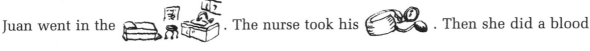 came with him. First, he stood

on the . He weighed 105 pounds. Then the nurse measured him. He was 5 feet tall.

Juan went in the 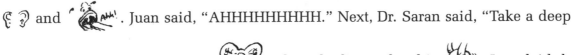. The nurse took his 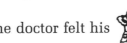. Then she did a blood

test. It only hurt a little bit.

The came into the room and said, "Hello, I'm Dr. Saran." She looked in Juan's

 and . Juan said, "AHHHHHHHHH." Next, Dr. Saran said, "Take a deep

breath." She listened to Juan's . Then she listened to his . Juan laid down

on the examining table and the doctor felt his . "You're just fine," she said. "But it

is time for you to get an . It will keep you healthy."

 was a little nervous. "Will it hurt?" he asked.

"Yes, but just for a second," said Dr. Saran. gave Juan an . Then she

smiled and gave him some . "You're a good patient, Juan."

"Thank you," he answered. and his mother walked home. His trip to

wasn't so bad afterall.

Section 5

Safety

Personal safety is a major concern for the new ESL student and his/her family. Understanding safety rules and developing personal safety strategies is essential to the welfare of the student. Dangerous situations and hazardous conditions present themselves on a daily basis. What may be a serious threat to personal safety in one country is not of concern in another. Knowing how to recognize and react to obvious and hidden dangers in a new environment is an essential life skill for the newcomer to develop.

The lessons in Section 5, Safety, are designed to teach the ESL student how to identify and handle many important safety issues. How to call 9-1-1, staying safe in traffic, reacting to hazardous weather conditions, and strategies for handling strangers are a few examples of the lessons taught in this section. It is the intent of these lessons to give you the tools and information necessary to help the ESL student learn to protect him-/herself and others from danger.

Lesson 5-1: Being Safe at Home

Objectives: The student will understand the safety rules for keeping themselves and other family members safe at home.

Vocabulary: safe; unsafe; accident; pick up; stay away; don't touch; wipe up; spills; safety plugs; ask for help

Materials: Activity Sheet 5–1; Chart paper (*optional*)

Directions:

1. Say, "Many bad accidents happen at home. An accident is when something happens and no one means for it to happen. It is not done on purpose. Sometimes, it means that someone gets hurt. Many things in our homes can be 'unsafe' or hurt us. It is very important for everyone in the family to help keep the home safe." The following are some examples of home safety rules. Share them with the student and discuss. Draw pictures for clarification. Then ask the student to think of more safety rules for his/her home.

   - Pick up toys and items from the stairs or the floor.

   - Keep emergency numbers close to the telephone.

   - Have smoke detectors on every floor of your home.

   - Wipe up any water or spills from the floor, especially after you take a shower or bath.

   - Don't touch guns, bullets, knives, fire crackers, medicine, cigarette lighters, matches, lit candles, and hot irons.

   - Stay away from electrical plugs, hot pans, hot stove, moving garage door, moving lawn mower, and strange animals.

   - Put safety plugs on electrical outlets.

   - Ask for help if you need to use the stove or sharp objects.

   - Don't play with a dog or cat while it is sleeping or eating. *Never* tease an animal.

   - Don't stand on unsteady chairs or unsafe things.

   - Don't touch, taste, or smell cleaners, floor polish, gasoline, paint, and glue. Lock these things up, especially if there are little children in your home.

2. Give the student a copy of Activity Sheet 5–1. The student will be asked to find and circle the safety hazards. **Answer Key:** Child reaching for cord on the blinds; cleaners; poisons are not locked away; child playing with matches; water on the floor; no safety plug on outlet; toys on the steps; standing on unsafe chair; teasing the dog; a gun on the table; pot handle sticking out from the stove.

Extension Activity: Ask the student to take home Activity Sheet 5–1, and conduct a home safety check. Ask him/her to share it with the adults in the home.

Name_____ Date_____

Be Safe at Home

Be a detective. Circle all the unsafe things you see in this home. Describe how they can be corrected.

Lesson 5-2: International Safety Signs and Words

Objectives: The student will be able to visually recognize and know the meaning of the most common international safety signs. The student will be able to read selected safety words.

Vocabulary: Stop; Fire; Walk; Don't Walk; RR; Railroad Crossing; Danger; Poison; (H) Hot; (C) Cold; On; Off; Hospital; Yield; Handicapped; One Way; No Smoking; Bike Route; Use Crosswalk; Watch Your Step; Do Not Enter; School Crossing; Pedestrian Crossing; No Bicycles; Telephone; Exit

Materials: Activity Sheets 5–2A, 5–2B, 5–2C, 5–2D; Scissors; Bingo markers (e.g., beans, macaroni, small pieces of paper)

Directions:

Safety Signs

1. Give the student a copy of Activity Sheet 5–2A. Say, "Today you are going to learn some signs that will keep you safe and healthy. These are called Safety Signs."

2. Discuss each of the signs and what they mean. Use gestures as needed.

   Stop—Traffic must stop. If you are on your bike, obey the Stop Sign. (red and white)

   Yield—Let the other person go first. If you are on your bike, yield to other traffic. (yellow)

   Fire—A fire alarm will be located here. Remind the students that a fire alarm is never pulled for a joke or prank. Discuss the serious issues involved.

   Handicapped—Special (restroom stall, ramps, parking space, etc.) help for handicapped people. (blue and white)

   Bicycle Crossing—A safe place to cross the street with your bicycle. (yellow and black)

   No Bicycles—Do not ride a bicycle here. (yellow and black)

   RR (Railroad Crossing)—Trains will be moving along the tracks. (yellow and black)

   One Way—Traffic can only go in the direction of the arrow. (black with a white arrow)

   Hospital—Tells that a hospital is near. (blue and white)

   Danger—Be careful! Something here can hurt you. (yellow and black)

   School Crossing—A safe spot for school children to cross the street when walking to and from school. (yellow and black)

   Pedestrian Crossing—A safe place for people to cross the street. (yellow and black)

Bike Route—A special place for people to ride their bikes. (yellow and black)
Do Not Enter—Do not go in here. (red circle, white background)
Telephone—You will find a telephone here. (blue and white)
Watch Your Step—Look out when you walk. Something here could make you fall. (yellow and black)
Use Crosswalk—Cross the street at the crosswalk (especially at busy streets). (yellow and black)
Poison—Do not touch, drink, or smell. This can make you very sick or even kill you. (black with white skull and crossbones)
No Smoking—Smoking is not allowed here. (black and white)

3. After you have discussed the signs, ask the students to cut them out. You may want the student to color them also. Colors are given in the descriptions above.

4. Put the signs in a container. Have the student close his/her eyes and choose a sign. Then the student gives the name of the sign and describes its meaning.

5. Play "Safety Bingo." Make as many copies of Activity Sheet 5–2B as you need. Cut out the Bingo cards. (Four different cards have been provided.) Give each player several bingo markers (e.g., beans, small pieces of paper, macaroni), and place the cutout Safety Signs (from Activity Sheet 5–2A) in a container. Choose a player to be the Caller. The Caller chooses Safety Signs from the container and reads them to the other players. The first player to get three signs in a row, diagonal, horizontal (across), or vertical (up and down) is the winner.

Directions:

Safety Words

1. Give the student a copy of Activity Sheet 5–2C. Read the Safety Words and use the gestures that are given here. Ask the student to repeat after you, including the gestures. Discuss the meaning of each.

2. No pneumonic (picture) has been used because in most instances the signs themselves consist only of words. It would be very helpful for the student to recognize the words by sight, without a visual aid. However, in the early stages of reading, you may want to incorporate visuals and gestures and then gradually take them away.

STOP—Hold up your hand in a stopping motion.
FIRE—Point to the picture of the fire alarm or fire alarm in the room or hallway.
WALK—Walk.
DON'T WALK—Hold up your hand in a stopping motion and stop walking.

BEWARE—Pretend to be looking around very suspiciously.
HIGH VOLTAGE—Pretend to touch something, then stiffen as if getting a shock.
CONDEMNED—Make a crashing noise.
DANGER—Look frightened and startled.
(H) HOT—Pretend to touch something, then quickly take your hand away. Then shake your hand in the air.
(C) COLD—Pretend to shiver.
POISON—Pretend to drink something, then grasp your throat and gasp.
FLAMMABLE—Draw a flame on the board.
(RR) RAILROAD—Make train noises, "Ding, Ding, Whoo! Whoo!"
EXIT—Point to the door, walk toward it, open it, and pretend to walk out.

3. Additional blank cards have been provided on Activity Sheet 5–2C. Either you or the student can use these to create more safety words.

Extension Activities:

1. Make two sets of international safety signs and play "Safety Memory." Place two sets of signs on the table or floor. The players take turns turning over two signs trying to make a pair. The players must say the name of each sign as he/she turns it over. The player with the most pairs at the end of the game is the winner. *Variation*: Play with safety words instead of signs.

2. Play "Safety Pictionary." The student chooses a safety sign and must draw it on the chalkboard or chart paper. The first player to guess it correctly gets a point. The player with the most points at the end of the game wins. *Variation*: The player chooses a safety word and must draw the sign. For each correct attempt, a point is given.

International Safety Signs

Safety Bingo

Directions: See Lesson Plan 5–2, #5.

Safety Words

STOP	EXIT
FIRE	ENTER
DON'T WALK	POISON
WALK	DANGER
RAILROAD CROSSING	H HOT C COLD
TELEPHONE	ON / OFF

Make Your Own Safety Words

CONDEMNED	**FLAMMABLE**
HIGH VOLTAGE	**BEWARE**

Lesson 5-3: Traffic Lights, Traffic Signs, and Crossing the Street

•••••••••••••••••••••••••••••••••••

Objective: The student will understand the meaning of the traffic lights and signs and how to use them to safely cross the street.

Vocabulary: face; cross; red; stop; yellow; wait; green; go; WALK; DON'T WALK; Stop sign; crosswalk; crossing guard

Materials: 2 copies of Activity Sheet 5–3 (one colored, to use as a visual, and another, not colored, for the student); Red, yellow, and green circles; Red hand (STOP); White figure (WALK); Masking tape

Teaching Notes:

1. Understanding the concept "to face" will help the student better understand this lesson. Explain to the student that "to face" means to look in front of you, or something that you look toward. Practice this concept by naming items in the room that the student must face (e.g., the door, window, chalkboard, etc.).

2. Explain that "to cross" the street means to walk from one side of the street to the other.

Directions:

1. Give the student a copy (not colored) of Activity Sheet 5–3. Point to the illustration of the traffic light (on your colored copy) and ask the student, "Where have you seen this?" (in the street, riding in the car, crossing the street, etc.) Then ask, "What is it called?" (traffic light) Ask, "How can it help you?" (tells us when it is safe to cross the street, tells cars when to stop and go)

2. Point to the red light on the colored activity sheet and say, "The red light means STOP." (Hold up your hand in a stopping motion.) Ask the student to repeat. Then say, "If you want to cross the street and the light you face is red, it means STOP, don't walk across the street. If you are riding your bike, you must also stop."

3. Point to the red hand on the traffic light. Tell the student that on most traffic lights, this sign is seen with the red light. It means DON'T WALK. (**Gesture:** Hold your hand up and shake your head "no," then walk in place.)

4. Point to the yellow light and say, "The yellow light means WAIT (to stop)." Ask the student to repeat. Explain that WAIT actually means to stop. Then tell the student that a yellow light means the light will soon change to red. Say, "If you want to cross the street and the light you face is yellow, stop and wait. Don't cross."

177

5. Tell the student that he/she will again see the red hand that means DON'T WALK later in the lesson.

6. Point to the green light and say, "The green light means GO." Ask the student to repeat. Say, "If you want to cross the street and the light you face is green, it is okay to walk."

7. Point to the illustration of the person walking across the street and explain that this means WALK. It is safe to cross the street. Most of the time when the light is green, this figure will be seen.

8. Discuss and practice the following rules and safety guidelines for crossing the street. (Model.)

   • Walk, don't run across the street. (Shake your head "yes" and walk in place. Shake your head "no" and run in place.)

   • Stop! Look! and Listen! for approaching and turning vehicles, especially those turning on red. (Say "Stop" and hold your hand up. Student repeats. Say "Look" and point to your eyes. Student repeats. Say "Listen" and point to your ears. Student repeats.)

   • Give yourself enough time to cross the street.

   • Look "Left–Right–Left" before you cross the street. (Gesture and say, "Left–Right–Left." The student repeats the words and the movement.)

   • Obey the school safety patrol and crossing guards.

   • Ask your parents to map out the safest route (way) to and from school.

9. Make the noise of a siren. Ask, "Have you heard this sound before?" (yes) "What makes this sound?" (police car, fire truck, ambulance) Then tell the student that when he/she hears this noise, he/she must STOP even if the light is green, because these cars and trucks do not have to stop for a red light and will keep going.

10. Make a crosswalk in the classroom by placing two long strips of masking tape on the floor parallel to each other. Make it approximately six feet wide. Explain to the student that the lines on the street are called the crosswalk and that he/she should stay between those lines when crossing the street. Stand facing the student at the opposite side of the crosswalk. Hold up the red, yellow, and green circles in random order. Ask the student to say the command that the light gives ("Stop," "Wait," or "Go") and then walk across the street within the crosswalk. Give the student an opportunity to hold up the circles as well. (NOTE: Make sure the student is using the Look Left–Right–Left rule before crossing.) Continue the procedure, only this time hold up the red hand for DON'T WALK and the person walking for WALK. (Let the student have a turn holding up the signs.) (NOTE: You may want to make the noise of a siren and have the student practice this situation, too.)

11. Point to the stop sign on Activity Sheet 5–3 and ask, "Can you read the word on this sign?" (Stop) "This sign is like a red light, only the cars or bikes stop for a little bit and then they can go ahead. It is very important to watch that a car has completely stopped before you cross the street."

12. Ask the student to color the traffic lights and the STOP sign on the activity sheet. The student will fill in the blanks for two important safety rules: *Look Left, Right, Left*, and *Stop! Look! and Listen!* before you cross the street.

Extension Activities:

1. It is always beneficial to practice crossing the street in a real situation. Take a mini field trip to a nearby street and have the students practice crossing the street safely. Try to include a crosswalk, traffic light, and STOP sign.

2. Ask the student to work with his/her parents to map out the safest route to school.

Name_____ Date_____

Traffic Signs

1. Color the traffic light.

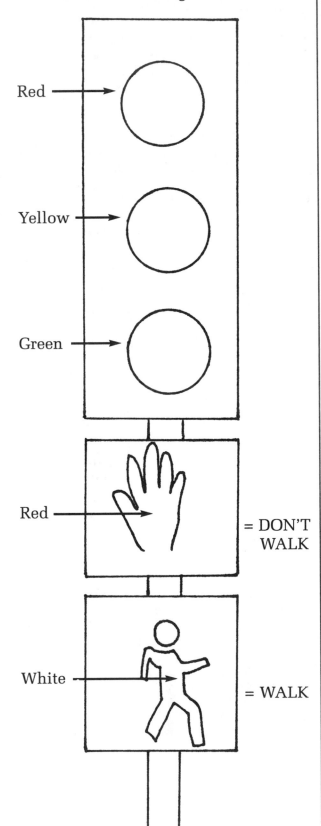

Red →

Yellow →

Green →

Red → = DON'T WALK

White → = WALK

2. Color the STOP sign.

3. What three words do you need to remember when you cross the street?

_____! _____! and _____!

4. Fill in the blanks:

Look _____, _____, _____.

LEFT   RIGHT   LEFT

Lesson 5-4: Bicycle Safety

Objective: The student will understand and know how to apply bicycle safety rules to his/her personal situation.

Vocabulary: bicycle (bike); helmet; arm signals; stop; left; right; ride with traffic; handlebars; single file; reflector

Materials: Activity Sheet 5–4; Bicycle helmet; Bicycle (for demonstration)

Teaching Note: It would be very helpful to use a bicycle to teach vocabulary and model various procedures suggested in the lesson plan, such as checking brakes.

Directions:

1. Say, "Today you are going to learn how to ride your bike safely. Many bicycle accidents happen because people don't obey the safety (traffic) rules for riding a bike." Discuss the following safety rules. Draw pictures and gestures as needed.

   - **Always wear a helmet.** This protects you from serious head injuries. Head injuries can leave you paralyzed (can't move) or brain damaged. Head injuries could also kill you.

   - **Stop and walk your bike across the street.** The safest way to cross the street is to stop, look Left–Right–Left, then walk your bike across the street.

   - **Obey traffic signs and signals.** Just like other traffic, a person riding a bicycle must obey the traffic signs and signals.

   - **Ride 'with' traffic on the right hand side of the street.** Ride your bike going the same direction as traffic. (You may want to practice this concept with the student. Pretend you are driving a car and the student is on a bike. Walk in one direction and have the student pretend to "ride" with traffic, going in the same direction. Ride single file on the street. Demonstrate single file.)

   - **Know the hand signals for Stop, Left Turn, and Right Turn.** (Practice these with the student. See the illustration.)

- **Check your brakes before riding. Make sure your bike has reflectors.** (Tell the student that the brakes stop the bicycle. It is very important for them to be in good working condition. [It would be helpful to demonstrate on a bicycle.] Also, explain the use of reflectors and that they reflect the light and make it easier for a motorist to see the bicycle. [If you have a bicycle, show the student the reflector.])

- **Ride as close to the side of the street as you can.** If you ride in the street, stay as close to the side as you can. This gives cars and other vehicles enough room to pass you.

- **When you ride on the sidewalk, let people know you are coming.** It is very important for people to know you are coming. That way they won't step in front of your bicycle.

- **Wear light- or bright-colored clothing so motorists can see you.** Very often people in cars cannot see or do not notice a person on a bicycle. Light-colored clothing is more noticeable and catches their eye.

- **Don't do unsafe tricks or ride a friend on your bicycle.** Tricks can be dangerous and can hurt you and others. Don't ride a friend on the handlebars or the back of your bike. You can easily lose your balance. It is also difficult to see with someone on your handlebars.

2. Have the student complete Activity Sheet 5–4. The student will look at an illustration and decide if the person is practicing good bicycle safety. If not, he/she should draw an X on what is wrong. Ask the student to describe each picture and what rule it shows. **Answer Key:** (*Part One*) 1. X—Riding without a helmet. (2.) Good—Walking bike across the street. (3.) X—Doing unsafe tricks and no helmet. (4.) Good—Wearing a helmet. (5.) Good—Riding single file, with traffic at the side of the street. (6.) X—Riding on a crowded sidewalk. (*Part Two*) Right, Stop, Left.

Extension Activity: Ask your local law enforcement agency for information about programs that would supply bike helmets to the students, either free or at a nominal cost.

Name_____ Date_____

Be Safe on Your Bike!

Part One: Look at each picture. Decide if the bicycle riders are showing good or poor bicycle safety. Put an X on those who are not. Discuss.

Part Two: Practice each arm signal and tell what it means. Then match it to the correct word.

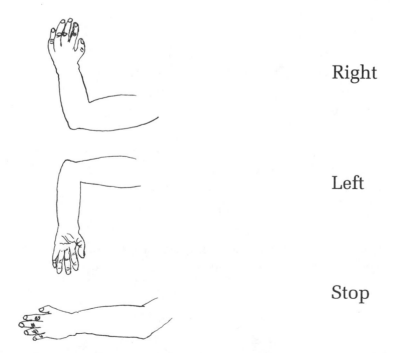

Right

Left

Stop

Lesson 5-5: Bus Safety

• • • • • • • • • • • • • • • • • • •

Objective: The student will understand the safety rules for boarding and riding a bus.

Vocabulary: bus; ten feet; Danger Zone; five steps; curb; seatbelt

Materials: Activity Sheet 5–5; Large piece of chart paper (yellow, if possible) with a bus drawn on it; Masking tape; Pencil

Teaching Notes: It would be helpful for the students to practice in and around a real school bus. Also, invite a bus driver to class to discuss safety rules on the bus.

Directions:

1. Say, "Today we are going to talk about being safe when you ride the bus." Show the student the chart paper with the outline of the bus drawn on it. Ask, "Why do people ride the bus?" (go to school, work, shopping)

2. Discuss the following rules for bus safety. You may want to write them on the chalkboard or chart paper. Draw pictures or gesture as needed.

   • **Get out of the "Danger Zone" quickly.** The Danger Zone for a bus is ten feet in the front and back of the bus and on each side. Put the chart paper (bus) on the floor. Explain to the student that there is a Danger Zone around every bus. Discuss the meaning of the Danger Zone and explain that it is hard for the bus driver to see people in the Danger Zone. It is also difficult for passing cars to see. Tell the student that the Danger Zone is ten feet in the front (point), in the back (point), and on each side (point) of the bus. Put the chart paper (bus) on the floor. Stand at the edge of the chart paper (bus) and pace off ten feet. Then say, "This is ten feet. From the bus to here is the Danger Zone." Ask the student to stand at the side of the bus (chart paper) and pace off ten feet. Now walk around the front, sides, and back of the bus at a ten-foot distance. Say, "This is the Danger Zone. Get out of it as fast as you can." Remind the student that if he/she drops anything in the street or parking lot while walking in front or back of the bus, **don't stop and pick it up**. Instead, tell the bus driver, then go, and pick it up.

   • **If you can't see the bus driver's eyes, then he/she can't see you.** Tell the student to remember this rule when getting on or off the bus. (**Gesture:** Pretend you are driving the bus. Point to your eyes and then the student's eyes. Ask the student to stand in various spots and to tell you if the bus driver can see him/her.)

   • **Stand five steps away from the curb.** Explain to the student that when he/she waits for the bus, it is important to stand five steps away from the

184

curb or stopping point. Put a piece of masking tape on the floor and pretend this is the curb. Pace off five steps. Ask the student to follow.

- **Wear seatbelts.** If the bus is equipped with seatbelts, the student must wear one. Discuss the safety advantages of seatbelts. (keeps you from being thrown around or out of the bus)

- **Always sit down in the bus.** Never stand in the bus. It makes sharp turns and quick stops, so you could lose your balance and fall.

- **Talk quietly. Don't scream or yell.** Explain that noisy voices and yelling can make the bus driver nervous and upset. (Pretend to shake and be upset, then slam on the brakes.)

- **Tie loose shoelaces and drawstrings for clothes.** These can get caught in the doors. (Pretend to tie shoes.)

3. Give the student a copy of Activity Sheet 5–5 to complete. The student will match the correct rule to the picture. If necessary, help with reading. **Answer Key:** (1.) C; (2.) E; (3.) D; (4.) F; (5.) A; (6.) B.

Name_____ Date_____

Be Safe on the Bus!

Directions: Match the pictures to the rules below. Put the correct letter next to the rule.

A.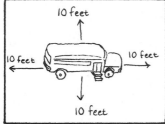

B.

C.

D.

E.

F.

© 2001 by The Center for Applied Research in Education

_____ 1. Sit down. Don't stand up or walk around the bus.

_____ 2. Always wear a seatbelt.

_____ 3. Stand 5 steps back from the curb or stopping point.

_____ 4. Talk quietly. Don't scream or yell.

_____ 5. Get out of the Danger Zone (10 feet) quickly.

_____ 6. If you can't see the bus driver's eyes, then he/she can't see you.

Lesson 5-6: Emergency Help–9-1-1

Objective: The student will understand how to use the emergency number 9-1-1 and the appropriate reasons for using it.

Vocabulary: emergency; 9-1-1; "I need help!"; name; address; sick; hurt; prank; break-in; directions; police; fire; doctor; cross street

Materials: Activity Sheet 5–6; Practice telephone; Pictures of police officer/police car, firefighter/firetruck, doctor/ambulance

Teaching Notes: It is very important for the ESL student to understand the use of 9-1-1. Learning and practicing this procedure can greatly aid the student if a real emergency situation occurs. Also, it is essential that the student understand what constitutes a 'real' emergency and one that can be handled without calling 9-1-1. (NOTE: Most communities have 9-1-1; however, some areas do not, so be sure to check your particular area first before beginning this lesson.)

Directions:

1. Say, "Today you are going to learn what to do in an 'emergency.' An emergency means that you need help 'right now'!" (Show the pictures of each as you say the name Police, Fire Department, Doctor.) "If you need the police, fire department, or a doctor, you can dial a special number, 9-1-1." Ask the student to repeat the number.

2. Discuss what a "real" emergency is. Draw pictures and gesture as needed. Brainstorm with the student: Your father can't breathe and has chest pain; someone is bleeding very badly and it won't stop; someone is breaking into your house; there is a fire in the garage; there has been a very bad accident in front of your home; an adult is hurting you and won't stop. Next, discuss the situations where it would *not* be appropriate to call 9-1-1. Examples: your cat is in a tree; your neighbors are too noisy; you cut your finger and can't find a bandage; etc. Explain to the student that it is against the law to call 9-1-1 for non-emergency reasons, to give false information, or to play a prank or joke. Explain that this can keep help from getting to someone who really needs it.

3. Discuss what to do when 9-1-1 is called.

   (1.) **Stay calm.** Give your name, address, and description of the emergency. Explain that the operator may ask for the name of a cross street. Explain the meaning of the cross street by drawing this diagram:

187

(2.) **Listen.** The operator will ask you questions. Answer them clearly and slowly. If you don't understand a question say, "Repeat, please." Or say, "No English."

(3.) **Do what the operator tells you.**

(4.) **NEVER hang up on the operator until he/she tells you to.**

4. Have the student practice dialing 9-1-1 on a practice telephone. Give him/her a situation, e.g., your grandmother fell and is not moving. Practice the following role play:

STUDENT: "I need help! Grandmother has fallen."
TEACHER (OPERATOR):   "What is your name and location?" (address)
STUDENT: (Gives his/her name and address.)
TEACHER (OPERATOR)   "Is your grandmother moving?"
STUDENT: "No."
TEACHER (OPERATOR):   "Help will be there soon. Don't move your grandmother. You can hang up now."
STUDENT: (Gets off the phone.)

5. Tell the student that it is very important to keep a card with important information next to the telephone. Explain that sometimes people get upset and forget their address and other information. It is also important for the student to be able to give cross streets or directions to his/her home.

6. Give the student a copy of Activity Sheet 5–6. Ask the student to complete the emergency card. Explain that this should be kept by the telephone at home. Then the student is asked to write 9-1-1 under the pictures that show a valid emergency. **Answer Key:** (1.) 9-1-1; (2.) No; (3.) 9-1-1; (4.) No; (5.) 9-1-1; (6.) 9-1-1; (7.) No; (8.) No; (9.) No.

Name_____ Date_____

Emergency Help—9-1-1

Part One: Write the information on this emergency card. Cut it out and put it by your phone.

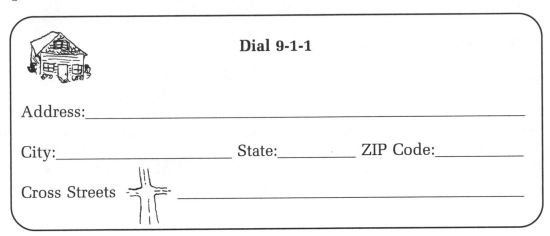

Dial 9-1-1

Address:_____

City:_____ State:_____ ZIP Code:_____

Cross Streets _____

Part Two: Write 9-1-1 next to each picture that shows a real emergency where 9-1-1 is needed.

1.
The house is on fire!

2.
Sally skinned her knee.

3.
Father can't breathe.

4.
You and your brother are fighting.

5.
Someone is breaking into your house.

6.
You see a very bad accident.

7.
You didn't clean your room and Mom yelled at you.

8.
Your cat is in a tree.

9.
You are home alone and the lights go out.

Lesson 5-7: Lost! What Do You Do?

Objective: The student will learn strategies to help him/her handle dangerous situations.

Vocabulary: lost; found; find; security guard; ID card; "Lost. Help, please."

Materials: Activity Sheets 5–7A and 5–7B; Sample of a "Safe House" sign for your area; Copy of ID card; Pen; Set of keys; 1 die; Game markers.

Teaching Notes: It is very important for the newcomer to know what to do if he/she should get lost. It is also essential that the student make an ID card to carry with him/her. (See Lesson 1–7. If you have not done this activity, include it as part of this lesson.)

Directions:

1. Say, "Today we are going to talk about what to do if you get lost. What does it mean to be lost?" *Demonstrate*: Take your keys in your hand and pretend to walk and drop them. Then begin looking for them. Say, "My keys are 'lost.' I do not know where they are." (**Gesture:** Shake your head, shrug your shoulders, and raise your palms up.) Ask the student, "Can you 'find' them?" When the student finds your keys, say, "Thank you, you 'found' them!" Tell the student that sometimes people get lost. Ask, "What happens when people get lost?" (go the wrong way, can't find parents, do not know where they are) Discuss where and how children can get lost, e.g., in a theater, walking home from a friend's house, at the mall, don't stay with parents, get separated in a crowd, not knowing the way home.

2. Discuss the following guidelines with the student. *If you get lost:*

   - **Know how to say, "Lost. Help, please."** (Have the student point to him-/ herself when saying 'lost.'

   - **(In the mall) Go to a store clerk or security guard** and tell him/her that you are lost.

   - **(Outside) Look for a 'safe house' sign or go to a store, gasoline station, or busy place and ask for help. A police station or fire station is a good place to get help.** (*Teacher*: Make sure the student knows what the 'Safe House' sign for your area looks like.)

   - **Always carry an ID card.** This will give people the correct information so they can help you.

   - **Know your Mom and Dad's name, where they work, and their phone number at their job.** Review this information with the student.

- **These people can help you: Police Officer, Security Guard, Firefighter, Mail Carrier.** (If the student cannot find an official person to help, security experts suggest it is safer to ask a female for help rather than a male.)

- **Dial 'O' for Operator on a pay phone.** Tell the student that he/she does not need money to dial 'O' and that the operator is trained to help in these situations.

3. Give the student a copy of Activity Sheet 5–7A. Have the student complete #1 on the activity sheet, where the student is asked to make an ID card. This is an excellent time to review the student's Emergency Information. In #2, the student is asked to find two ways home through a maze.

4. Give the student a copy of Activity Sheet 5–7B. In "Lost and Found!" the student rolls the die and, on an exact roll, stops at each Safe Place and names it. A player must visit each Safe Place. The first player to reach "Found" wins the game.

Extension Activities:

1. Enact the following role-plays with the student. Brainstorm ideas and discuss.

   - The student is lost in the mall.

   - The student gets lost walking to a friend's house.

   - The student gets on the wrong bus.

   - The student is lost at the airport.

   - The student is lost at a sports stadium.

2. Hide an object in the room and ask the student to find it. Give clues as the student is looking for it. Then ask the student to hide an object and give you clues as to where it is hidden.

Name_____ Date_____

Lost and Found!

1. **Complete the information on the ID card. Cut out the card and carry it with you.**

> ### Identification Card
>
> Name: _____
>
> Address: _____
>
> Home Telephone #: _____
>
> Parent work telephone #: _____

2. **Find two ways home through this maze.**

Lost and Found!

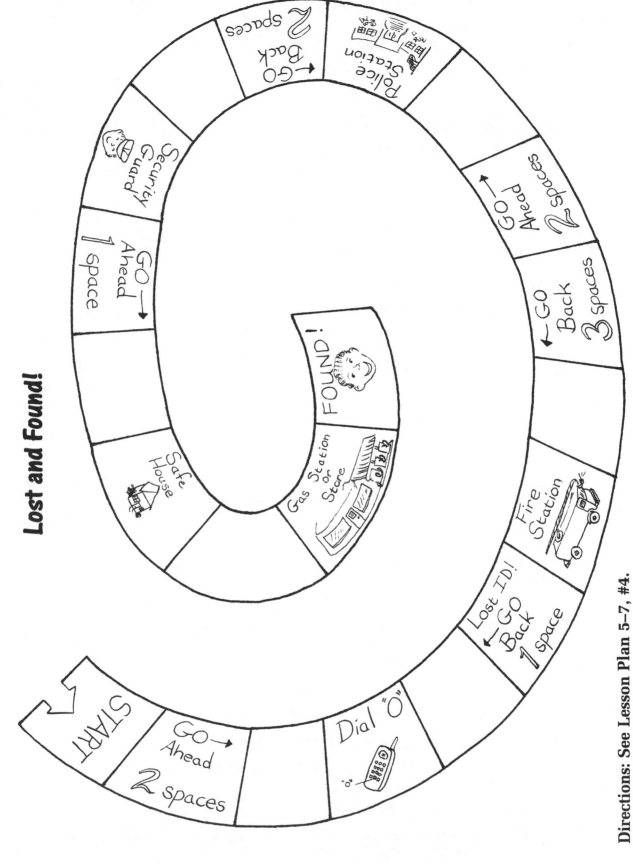

START

GO → Ahead
2 spaces

Dial "O"

Lost I.D.!
← GO Back
1 space

Fire Station

← GO Back
3 spaces

GO → Ahead
2 spaces

Police Station

← GO Back
2 spaces

Security Guard

GO → Ahead
1 space

Safe House

Gas Station or Store

FOUND!

Directions: See Lesson Plan 5–7, #4.

Lesson 5-8: Stranger Danger

• •

Objectives: The student will understand the safety guidelines in regard to strangers. The student will learn what to do in a "Stranger Danger" situation.

Vocabulary: stranger; scream

Materials: Activity Sheet 5–8; Pen; Photographs of people the students know (teachers, classmates); Photographs of people the students don't know (bring in photos of your adult family members, neighbors, etc.)

Directions:

1. Say, "Today you are going to learn about 'Strangers.' Who is a stranger?" (Someone you have never seen before.) Show the student a picture of a person they "know" or have seen before. Say, "Who is this?" (Student gives name.) "Have you seen this person many times?" (Yes) "Have you spoken to this person?" (Yes) "This person is not a stranger. You 'know' them." Now show the student a picture of a person he or she has not seen before. Ask, "Who is this?" (Student doesn't know.) "Have you seen this person many times?" (No) "Have you spoken to this person?" (No) "This person is a stranger. You do not 'know' them."

2. Explain to the student that most strangers are nice people, but that there are some strangers who are not nice to children. Discuss the fact that we cannot tell who are the nice strangers and who are not nice. That is why children need to be careful around strangers.

3. Give the student a copy of Activity Sheet 5–8. Discuss the safety rules. Use the illustrations for clarification.

   • **Never stop and talk to strangers.** Remind the children that for no reason at all should he/she talk to a stranger. If a stranger approaches and asks a child for help or directions, tell the student to not respond and leave. An adult should ask another adult for help.

   • **Never take gifts or rides from strangers.**

   • **Always walk and play with friends.**

   • **Stay in well-lighted areas where someone can see you.**

   • **Learn to write down and report the license numbers of people who offer you rides or follow you.**

   • **Never play in the street or close to the curbs.**

   • **Learn the safe places to run to in an emergency (safe houses, stores, gas stations, police and fire stations).**

- If someone grabs you, SCREAM as loud as you can.

- Always tell your parents or caretaker where you are going, how you will get there, who you will be with, and what time you will be home.

- Look out for other kids' safety. Report anything that doesn't seem right.

Name_____ Date_____

Stranger Danger

Look at the pictures. Match each one to a "Stranger Danger" safety rule.

"Mom, I'm going to the mall with Juanita. We'll be home at six o'clock."

Always walk and play with friends.

Never take rides from strangers.

"Do you want a ride?"

Stay in well-lighted areas where someone can see you.

Always tell your parents or caregiver who you will be with, where you will be going, and what time you will be home.

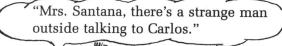

Look out for other kids' safety. Report anything that doesn't seem right.

"Mrs. Santana, there's a strange man outside talking to Carlos."

Learn the safe places to run to in an emergency.

Lesson 5-9: Latchkey Safety

• •

Objective: The student will learn safety guidelines for staying at home alone.

Vocabulary: latchkey; plan

Materials: Activity Sheets 5–9A and 5–9B; Pen or pencil

Teaching Notes: In many ESL families, both parents work. Most states have laws regulating the age at which a child can be left alone. This may be a new concept, especially to the newcomer. If you suspect that young children are being left alone, or with an unreliable sibling, inform the parents of the regulations and help them divise a plan for a safe latchkey situation.

Directions:

1. Ask, "Do you ever stay at home alone?" (Yes or no) "When do you stay alone?" (parents working, mom or dad is shopping, etc.) "Some children stay at home alone everyday, especially if both mother and father work. This is called 'latchkey.' It means the key that will open the door to the house. Latchkey children carry a key with them to open the door."

2. Explain that there are some important rules to obey to stay safe when home alone. Brainstorm some rules with the student. Then discuss the following rules.

    (1.) **Keep your key in a safe place.** Discuss some safe places to keep a key: wallet or purse, zippered space in a backpack, key ring, string around your neck.

    (2.) **Go straight home.** If your parents expect you home after school, go home. If you want to go somewhere, call and ask permission.

    (3.) **Check in with an adult when you get home.**

    (4.) **Know how to call 9-1-1 in an emergency.**

    (5.) **Know how to give directions to your home.** (In an emergency, you may need to give directions to your home.)

    (6.) **Never open the door to a stranger.**

    (7.) **Never let a caller at the door or on the phone know that you are home alone. Say, "Mom (Dad) can't come to the phone right now."**

    (8.) **Do not go into an empty house if things don't look right:** a door is open, a screen is ripped, a window is broken, a pet who usually greets you doesn't come to the door.

(9.) **Use your time wisely.** Have a routine. This is a good time to do homework, read a book, or clean up the house.

(10.) **Know at least two escape routes out of the house.** These may be needed in case of a fire or other emergency.

(11.) **Know how to lock the windows, doors, and use the alarm system** (if you have one).

(12.) **Keep a flashlight handy in case the power goes out.**

3. Give the student a copy of Activity Sheet 5–9A. The student will be asked to brainstorm ideas about different activities that he/she can do at home, e.g., *Helpful Activities*—do dishes, clean room, pick up toys, etc; *good books to read*—give the student suggestions or ask the librarian to assist; *fun activities*—play board games, sports, play toys, sew, crafts, draw/color, video games; *school activities*—homework, read, projects, review math facts, etc.

4. Give the student a copy of Activity Sheet 5–9B. The student will be asked to find ten hidden keys in a picture.

Extension Activities:

1. Play *Hide the Key*. Cut several keys out of paper and put the student's name on them. Hide the keys. The first student to find his/her key wins.

2. *Latchkey Plan*. Help the student make a weekly plan for his/her time that is spent alone. Check off each activity as it is done.

Name_____ Date_____

My Latchkey Plan

Write down ideas on how to spend your latchkey time.

Helpful Activities

_____

_____

_____

_____

_____

Good Books to Read

_____

_____

_____

_____

_____

Fun Activities

_____

_____

_____

_____

School Activities

_____

_____

_____

_____

Name_____ Date_____

Hidden Key Picture

Circle the ten hidden keys. Then color the picture.

Lesson 5-10: Playing It Safe Around Electricity

• •

Objective: The student will understand the safety rules and vocabulary associated with safety around electricity.

Vocabulary: electricity; HIGH VOLTAGE; DANGER; wire; cord; plug; outlet; switch; ON; OFF; safety plug

Materials: Activity Sheet 5–10; Pen or pencil; Small lamp or appliance (radio, TV, tape recorder) that works with electricity; Safety plug for an outlet

Directions:

1. Say, "Today you are going to learn about being safe around electricity. What is electricity?" (Discuss answers.) Tell the student that electricity is a force that goes through wires and makes many things work. Now, brainstorm with the student all the things that work with electricity (appliances, TV, computers, etc.).

2. Show the student the lamp or other appliance. Point to the cord and say, "This is called the electrical cord or wire." (Student repeats.) Point to the plug and say, "This is called the plug." (Student repeats.) "We put the plug into an outlet." (Student repeats.) Point to an outlet and put the plug into it. Ask, "What do we have to do to make the lamp (appliance) work?" (Turn it on.) Say, "Most lamps and appliances that work with electricity have a 'switch.'" Show the student the switch on the lamp and other electrical items in the room. Say, "Many switches have the words 'ON' and 'OFF' printed on them." (Find a switch in the room that has this feature and show the student, then ask the student to read the words as he/she flips the switch on and off.) Inform the student that the phrase "Flip the switch" can mean to turn the electrical item on or off. Next say, "When we turn on the lamp, the electricity moves from the outlet, through the wire, to the lamp." (Follow the route with your finger as you say the sequence.) Ask the student to repeat.

3. Say, "Electricity helps us in many ways but it is dangerous." Explain to the student that electricity can go through our bodies. Every year people are killed because they have not been careful using electricity.

4. Tell the student that electricity gets into our homes from the tall poles or underground wires that are outside. Write the words DANGER and HIGH VOLTAGE on the chalkboard. Inform the student that these words mean that dangerous electricity is in that spot. It may be a tall pole or a square green box. DO NOT TOUCH!

5. Write the following safety rules on the chalkboard and discuss:

- **Check for a wire before climbing a tree.** If you see electrical wires near a tree, don't climb it. The wind or your own weight could make the branch touch a wire and bring electricity to you. Just a small touch can hurt or kill you.

- **Check out the sky before flying a kite.** If you see electrical lines in the sky over you, don't fly your kite or model airplane there. If you fly a kite, use only nonmetal, dry string. If your kite or plane gets tangled in a wire or tree, never use a pole or rake to get it down. Ask an adult to help.

- **Don't go near a wire that is on the ground.** You could be hurt or killed. Tell an adult and ask them to call the electric company or 9-1-1.

- **Don't play around utility equipment.** Stay away from those green boxes and tall electric poles.

- **Never stick anything but a plug into an outlet.** Electricity moves through objects and can move through you!

- **"Call before you dig!"** Most electrical companies have a similar slogan. Tell the student that some electrical wires are underground, so it is very important for a person who is digging deep holes in the ground to call the electrical company and find out if it is safe to dig.

- **If you have a young child in your home, ask your parents to put child-safe plugs into the outlets.** Show the student an example of one and how it works.

6. Ask the student to complete Activity Sheet 5–10. In #1, the student will find and circle dangerous situations in regard to electricity. Ask the student to describe and discuss what he/she has found. In #2, the student will be asked to match a picture to a vocabulary word.

Extension Activities:

1. Ask the student to walk around his/her neighborhood and map out any dangerous electrical hazards. Do the same for the area around the school.

2. Invite a speaker from your local electric company to talk about electrical safety.

Name_____ Date_____

Play It Safe Around Electricity!

1. **Put an X on the danger spots. Tell what is wrong.**

2. **Look at each picture. Choose the correct word from the word box and write it in the spaces below each item.**

electricity	HIGH VOLTAGE	DANGER	wire	cord
OFF	safety plug	plug	switch	ON

_ _

_ _

_ _

Lesson 5-11: Stay Away from Guns and Fireworks

Objective: The student will understand the safety rules involving guns and fireworks.

Vocabulary: guns; BB gun; laser gun; air rifle; fireworks; firecrackers

Materials: Activity Sheets 5–11A and 5–11B; Pen or pencil; Crayons or colored pencils; Pictures of guns and fireworks (*optional*)

Directions:

1. Draw or find illustrations of guns and fireworks. Then say, "Today we are going to talk about two very dangerous things, guns and fireworks." (point) "They both can hurt and even kill you."

2. Ask the student to brainstorm some safety rules regarding guns:

   - **Never touch or handle a gun.** Many accidents happen because a gun goes off accidentally. If you are with friends and someone shows you a gun, leave. Never be around someone who is playing with a gun.

   - **If you find a gun or see one lying around, tell an adult as quickly as possible.**

   - **If there is a gun in your home, tell your parents to lock it away in a safe place.**

   - **Don't play with BB guns, laser guns, or air rifles. These are not toys and can be very dangerous.** (If hit in the eye, blindness can occur.)

3. Explain to the student that fireworks are also dangerous for children to play with. Discuss the fact that although fireworks can be fun and very beautiful, we must be very careful when around them. Give examples of different kinds of fireworks, firecrackers, sparklers, large displays, etc. Discuss when people use fireworks (on holidays: 4th of July, Chinese New Year; at theme parks; special celebrations, etc.). Explain that some fireworks can be dangerous and are against the law. Others that you can buy in the retail stores are allowed. Remind the student that children should always have an adult present when using fireworks. Discuss these rules for fireworks:

   - **Always use fireworks with adult supervision.** Fireworks can explode and cause severe injuries to eyes and hands. They can burn you.

   - **Never play jokes or pranks with fireworks.** Fireworks are not a joke, but a serious matter. Be responsible if you use them.

4. Ask the student to complete Activity Sheet 5–11A. The student will be asked to match an unsafe situation to a safe solution. If needed, help with the reading. **Answer Key:** (1.) C; (2.) A; (3.) B; (4.) E; (5.) D.

5. Ask the student to complete Activity Sheet 5–11B. The student will draw a picture of a fireworks display. Discuss it when completed.

Extension Activity: Draw a picture of colorful fireworks. Using crayons, have the student color a white sheet of paper with bright, vivid colors. Then color completely over in black crayon. Use the end of a scissors to scratch out the patterns and forms of the colorful fireworks.

Name_____ Date_____

Stay Away from Guns and Fireworks

Look at the "unsafe" pictures. Then match each one to a "safe" solution.

1. "Let's go outside and shoot this BB gun."

   A. "That's not a funny joke. We could hurt ourselves and Maria!"

2. "Hey, let's put this firecracker under this can and light it. That will really scare Maria!"

   B. "Dad, it would be a good idea to lock up your hunting rifles."

3.

   C. "No! BB guns can kill small animals and hurt children."

4. "Let's get some fireworks from Freddie. He sells stuff you can't buy in the stores."

   D. "Mom, Aunt Carmen has a gun hidden under her pillow."

5.

   E. "Those fireworks are illegal. Let's go to the big show at the park tonight."

Name_____ Date_____

Stay Safe Around Guns and Fireworks

Draw a picture of a colorful fireworks show.

Lesson 5-12: Fire Safety

• •

Objectives: The student will learn the rules for fire safety. The student will learn important vocabulary associated with fire safety.

Vocabulary: matches; lighters; escape plan; smoke detector; battery; Fall and Crawl; Stop–Drop–and Roll; 9-1-1; meeting place

Materials: Activity Sheets 5–12A and 5–12B; Smoke detector with a battery in it; Pencil; Container to hold safety cards

Directions:

1. Say, "Today you are going to learn some important rules for staying safe around fire. You will also learn what to do if you are in a fire."

2. Give the student a copy of Activity Sheet 5–12A. Discuss the following safety rules. Help with reading and use the illustrations as needed.

   • **Never play with matches or lighters. If you find them, give them to an adult.**

   • **Ask your parents to put in smoke detectors. Remind them to: "Change the clock, change the batteries."** Show the student what a smoke detector looks like. Let the student hear the alarm by pressing the tester button. Take out the batteries and show that the smoke detector will not work if it doesn't have batteries or if the batteries don't work.

   • **If you are on fire, "STOP–DROP–and ROLL."** Don't run; it makes the fire worse.

   • **If your house is on fire, "Don't hide, go outside."** When there is smoke or a fire, go outside. If you can't get outside, stay low to the floor. Stay some-place where firefighters can see you. Look for their masks and clothes.

   • **Have a family meeting place.** A tree or a neighbor's house is a good spot.

   • **Plan an escape route.** Know at least two ways to get out of the house.

   • **"Fall and crawl."** When there is smoke and you need to get out, stay low; it is easier to breathe.

   • **Never go back into a burning house.**

   • **Know the emergency number to call. Call from a neighbor's house.**

   • **Tell an adult when you see a fire or smell smoke. Never keep it a secret, even if you started the fire.**

3. Cut out the cards on Activity Sheet 5–12A and put them in a container. The student will take the cards from the container, one by one, and describe/read the rule that goes with the picture.

4. Ask the student to complete Activity Sheet 5–12B. The student will be asked to fireproof his/her home. When each item on the list is checked out, the student will put a check mark in the box next to it. In addition, the student will be asked to draw an escape plan with two exits from his/her home. The location of smoke detectors should be included.

Extension Activity: Ask the student to describe the escape routes that he/she has planned.

Rules for Fire Safety

1. Never play with matches or lighters. If you find them, give them to an adult.

2. Ask your parents to put in smoke detectors. Remind them, "Change the clock, change the batteries."

3. If you are on fire, "STOP–DROP–and ROLL."

4. If your house is on fire, "Don't hide, go outside."

5. Have a family meeting place.

6. Plan an escape route from your home.

7. "FALL and CRAWL."

8. Never go back into a burning house.

9. Know the emergency number to call. Call from a neighbor's house.

10. Tell an adult when you smell or see fire or smoke.

Name_____ Date_____

Fire Safety—Home Checklist

Part One: Take this fire safety checklist home. Read each item and check YES or NO. If you check NO, ask your parents to fix the problem.

	YES	NO
1. Are matches or lighters lying around the house?	1.	
2. Is the space heater far away from drapes and furniture?	2.	
3. Are emergency numbers close to the telephone?	3.	
4. Is there a smoke detector on every floor?	4.	
5. Do the smoke detectors work? Check the batteries.	5.	
6. Do you have an emergency escape route?	6.	

Home Escape Route

Part Two: Draw a plan of your home and show at least two escape routes (exits). Show the location of smoke detectors.

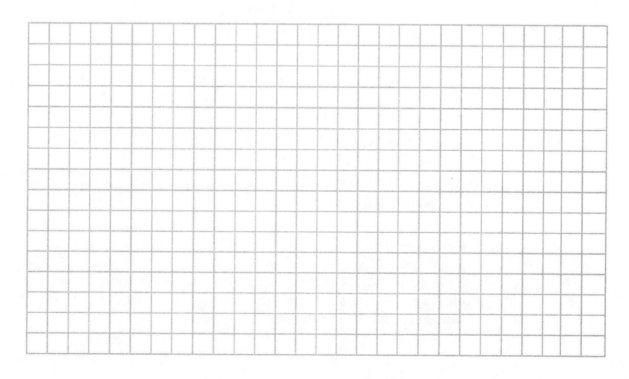

Lesson 5-13: Railroad Safety

Objectives: The student will learn the safety rules when near a train or railroad track. The student will learn and understand the necessary vocabulary.

Vocabulary: train; warning signs; Railroad Crossing; flashing red light; tracks; gates; STOP! LOOK! LISTEN!

Materials: Activity Sheet 5–13; Pen or pencil

Directions:

1. Say, "Today you are going to learn some safety rules and signs to help you stay safe when you are near a train or railroad track."

2. Give the student a copy of Activity Sheet 5–13. Point to the illustrations in #1. Explain to the student that these are the warning signs that are by a railroad track: (**A.**) This sign tells you that a railroad crossing is near. It gives you time to Stop, Look, and Listen for a train. Inform the student that the engineer will blow a whistle at the railroad crossing to warn people that the train is coming. (**B.**) This mark is on the street and has a Stop Line before the tracks. Stop behind the Stop Line when you are waiting for the train to pass. (**C.**) This sign says RAILROAD CROSSING. (Ask student to repeat.) It has flashing red lights and bells. If the lights are flashing and you hear the bells, STOP! A train is coming. (**D.**) These are the gates at a railroad track. When these gates move down, STOP! A train is coming.

3. Read the rules for train safety in #2 on the activity sheet. Discuss.

   - **Never play on the train tracks.** You can trip and fall or get caught in the tracks.

   - **If you come to a train track, STOP! LOOK! and LISTEN!** Listening is very important. You may not be able to see the train, but you will be able to hear the whistle. It is always blown at a crossing.

   - **If the train passes by, LOOK and LISTEN before you cross. Another train may be coming on the next track.**

   - **NEVER try to race a train to cross the tracks. Trains cannot stop quickly and many people have lost this race.**

4. Ask the student to complete #2 on Activity Sheet 5–13. The student will identify railroad signals that he/she has seen and will be asked to put an RR by people who are practicing safe behavior by the train tracks. Ask the student to discuss the answers. **Answer Key**: A. Child waiting for train to pass—RR; B. Children playing on tracks—No RR; C. Child riding around the gate—No RR; D. Child saying STOP, LOOK, LISTEN—RR.

Extension Activities:

1. Read *The Little Engine That Could,* a wonderful motivational story. Ask the student to draw a picture of something that he/she thought was too difficult, but after trying, he/she was successful.

2. Older children will enjoy reading the series about *The Boxcar Children* by Gertrude C. Warner.

Name_____ Date_____

Here Comes the Train!

Part One: Discuss the following RR safety signs. Put an RR next to each sign you have seen before.

A.

This sign tells you railroad tracks are nearby.

B.

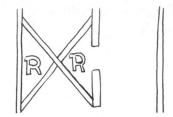

This sign is on the street. Stop and look!

C.

This sign has flashing red lights and bells. Stop!

D.

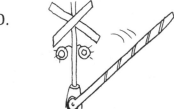

These gates go down. Stop! Don't go around them!

Part Two: Put an RR by the people who will be safe when the train passes.

A.

Ding! Ding!

B. "Playing on the tracks is fun!"

C. "I'm faster than the train!"

Ding! Ding!

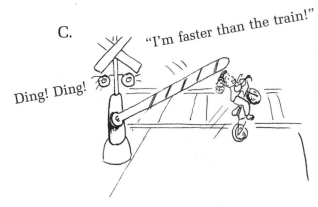

D.

Toot! Toot!

STOP! LOOK! LISTEN!

Lesson 5-14: Water Safety

• •

Objective: The student will learn safety rules associated with swimming and boating.

Vocabulary: dive; wave; current; shallow; deep; pool; float; dunk; beach; swim; drown; sink; life preserver; seat cushion; lifeguard; "NO DIVING"; "NO SWIMMING"

Materials: Activity Sheet 5–14; Life preserver or seat cushion; 1 or 2 small stones; Container for water

Directions:

1. Say, "Today you are going to learn important rules that will keep you safe when you are by water." Ask, "How do people have fun in the water?" (swim, ride in boats, dive, play, etc.) "Water can be a lot of fun and it can also be dangerous." Ask, "How is water dangerous?" Take a small stone and drop it in a glass of water. Ask, "What happens to the stone when I drop it in the water?" (It sinks.) Then say, "This small stone is like a person in the water. If a person cannot swim or has problems in the water, he/she will sink." Explain to the student that people cannot breathe under the water. If a person is under the water too long, his/her lungs fill with water and the person dies. This is called "drowning."

2. Brainstorm with the student some safety rules for swimming and boating. You may want to write these on the chalkboard, e.g.:

   • **Never swim alone.** If you swim alone and start to have problems, no one can hear you. Always swim with at least one other person.

   • **If you start to have trouble and go under, yell "Help!"** Never yell "help" unless you really need it. The water is not a place to play jokes.

   • **Swim where there is a lifeguard.** *Always* listen to the lifeguards. They are trained to save lives in the water. They will tell you if something is dangerous.

   • **Don't swim at night.** Nighttime is a dangerous time to swim. If you go under or get into trouble, no one can see you. It is hard to see where you are going or what is in the water.

   • **Wear a life preserver or sit on a floating cushion in a boat.** It is the law and it can save your life if your boat sinks or tips over. (If one is available, show the student a life preserver, how to wear it, and how it floats.)

   • **Always obey the safety signs: NO SWIMMING, NO DIVING**, etc.

   • **Never swim or dive in unknown water.** You don't know how deep or shallow the water might be. If you dive, you could hit your head on a rock or break your back. Also, some water has a current. That means it is moving underneath and can pull you under or out to deeper water.

- **Don't run on the pool deck.** Water makes things slippery. You could fall and hurt yourself or someone else.

- **Don't "dunk" people or horseplay in the water.** Holding people under the water (dunking) or roughhousing is dangerous. A person can drown this way.

- **If you see someone in trouble, get help.** Don't try to save the person unless you are a lifeguard. Throw a life preserver or something that floats to the person in the water.

3. Ask the student to complete Activity Sheet 5–14. In #1, the student is asked to write the correct word in the blank. Discuss. **Answer Key:** (1.) Alone; (2.) Run; (3.) Help; (4.) Night; (5.) Lifeguard; (6.) Dive; (7.) Horseplay; (8.) Life preserver. In #2 the student circles those who are not practicing water safety. Discuss. **Answer Key:** Person in boat without a life preserver; person diving by a NO DIVING sign; person swimming alone; two people fooling around on the dock, one yelling "Help."

Extension Activities:

1. Do a floating and sinking experiment. Get small articles that float and sink. Ask the student to predict what will happen to each item.

2. Read the Big Book *Who Sank the Boat?* by Pamela Allen.

Name_____ Date_____

Be Safe by the Water!

Part One: Write the correct word in the blank.

1. Never swim _____.   "Help!"

2. Don't _____ on the pool deck.   night

3. If you are in trouble, yell _____.   lifeguard

4. Don't swim at _____.   dive

5. Always listen to the _____.   alone

6. Don't _____ in shallow water.   run

7. No _____ in the water!   horseplay

8. Wear a _____ when you ride in a boat.   life preserver

Part Two: Circle the people who are not being safe in the water. Discuss how they can improve their behavior.

Lesson 5-15: Caring for Younger Children

• •

Objectives: The student will understand how to care for younger children. The student will learn safety procedures associated with caring for younger children.

Vocabulary: childproof; routine hazard; baby-sitting

Materials: Activity Sheet 5–15; Pencil

Teaching Note: Many ESL students are responsible for caring for younger siblings while both parents work. This lesson is designed for the older student. However, often young children are asked to supervise younger siblings. Because many countries do not have laws regulating the age of the caretaker, be aware and report any inappropriate situations. The suggestions given in this lesson can help the student become more responsible when caring for younger children.

Directions:

1. Ask, "Have you ever taken care of a younger child?" (Student answers.) Inform the student that in America this is called baby-sitting.

2. Explain that there are certain things a baby-sitter can do to help make the job easier and also keep the younger child safe. Brainstorm some ideas with the student. Then write these ideas on the chalkboard or chart paper. Discuss each one as you write it.

   • **Keep emergency telephone numbers near the phone** (9-1-1, parents' work, parents' location, emergency contact person).

   • **Always know where parents can be reached** (name of workplace, people they are visiting, a place they will spend the evening, etc.).

   • **If the child is a baby, make sure you can always see him/her. If the child is older, know where (what room) he/she is playing in, what he/she is playing, and who is with the child.**

   • **Keep small objects off the floor or in a place where a small child (baby or toddler) cannot reach them.** Small children like to put things in their mouths and may swallow a small object.

   • **Block off dangerous areas, such as stairs.**

   • **Keep the doors and windows locked.**

   • **Put away all sharp objects** (knives, forks, scissors, pins, needles, thumbtacks, nails).

   • **Cover electrical outlets with safety plugs. Never allow a small child to play with electrical cords or by outlets.** (If possible, show the student a sample of a safety plug and how to use it.)

- **Keep poisons in a childproof cabinet or locked away** (cleaners, bleach, insect repellent, paint, nail polish remover, gasoline, medicine, etc.).

- **If a pot or pan is on the stove, turn the handle to the inside.** (Small children are very curious and may grab the handle.)

- **Keep cords and pulls from blinds and drapes tied and out of reach.** (Children can get tangled in long cords or put them around their necks.)

- **Have an escape plan in case of fire.** Know at least two ways out of the house.

- **Never leave the child alone** (e.g., if the child is napping, don't walk over to a friend's house or go outside).

- **Don't get distracted from your job by phone calls, TV shows, video games, etc.**

- **Establish a routine for the child** (e.g., snack, nap, play, dinner, storytime, bed). The routine depends upon the age of the child. If an older child, don't forget homework time.

3. Ask the student to complete Activity Sheet 5–15. The student will be asked to make a judgment concerning a statement and then place a + or a – next to that statement. Help with reading, if necessary. **Answer Key:** 1. +; 2. –; 3. +; 4. +; 5. –; 6. +; 7. –; 8. +; 9. –; 10. +; 11. +; 12. +; 13. –; 14. +; 15. +; 16. +; 17. –; 18. +; 19. +; 20. –; 21. +.

Extension Activities:

1. Have the student make a list of games, art activities, songs, and books that a young child would enjoy.

2. Using the guidelines above, ask the student to make a tour of his/her home. Then the student should list ideas as to how to childproof the home.

3. Many hospitals have programs teaching childcare. Ask a speaker to come and address the special needs of your students who are responsible for childcare.

Name_____ Date_____

Taking Care of Younger Children

Pretend you are caring for a younger child named Carmen, who is two years old. Read the following statements. If the statement describes a responsible action, mark it with a +. If the statement is irresponsible, mark it with a −.

_____ 1. Carmen has been crying for a long time. When you touch her, she's very warm. You call her mother at work.

_____ 2. Your friend Marco calls. You talk on the phone for 30 minutes.

_____ 3. You see scissors on the table and put them in a drawer.

_____ 4. When you want to go into another room, you take Carmen with you.

_____ 5. You spray an insect with repellent and leave the open can on the table.

_____ 6. You plan games, books, and activities that Carmen will enjoy.

_____ 7. You are giving Carmen a bath. The doorbell rings and you leave to answer it.

_____ 8. A large, shiny button is lying on the floor. You pick it up and put it on a high shelf.

_____ 9. It is warm outside so you keep the front door open.

_____ 10. Carmen is playing with an electrical wire. You take her away even though she cries.

_____ 11. You are making dinner on the stove and turn the pot handles to the inside.

_____ 12. You check for two escape routes out of the house.

_____ 13. Carmen is playing in the kitchen. You are in the living room watching TV.

_____ 14. You notice the blinds in Carmen's bedroom have a long cord. You tie it and put it out of reach.

_____ 15. Carmen falls and hits her head. She is not moving. You call 9-1-1.

_____ 16. You take Carmen to play outside. A man approaches and says he is her uncle and wants to take her to the park. You take her inside and call her mother at work.

_____ 17. There is a bowl of hard candy on the coffee table. You give Carmen a piece.

_____ 18. Carmen wants to walk up the stairs. You hold her hand and help her.

_____ 19. You notice that there are no safety plugs on the electrical outlets. You suggest to the parents that safety plugs are a good idea.

_____ 20. Three of your friends come to the door while you are babysitting. You invite them in.

_____ 21. You write down emergency numbers and put them by the telephone.

Part 2

SCHOOL AND ACADEMIC SKILLS

New ESL students enter school with many and varied educational experiences. Some students may have had access to an outstanding and consistent education, while others may have encountered great hardships and long interruptions in their exposure to formal education. It is the latter student who presents the greater challenge to the ESL professional and classroom teacher. Interrupted and sporadic access to the educational environment can leave the student with little knowledge of academic and behavioral expectations within the school community. It is the responsibility of the entire school staff, with assistance from the ESL professional, to help the new student to adjust, conform, and succeed in his/her new school life.

Part 2 attempts to help the ESL student understand not only basic academic content, but also the behavior that is expected in American schools. Often, if a student has come from a strict disciplinary environment, American teachers and schools seem "easy" and relaxed. Kindness is often mistaken for weakness. In most instances, a stern verbal reminder will be sufficient to curtail negative actions. If not, loss of a privilege or removing the student from the situation usually gets the message across.

Curriculum requirements differ from state to state and certainly from country to country. It is often difficult to ascertain what academic skills the new ESL student has mastered. Each academic section begins with a pre-/posttest to help identify strengths and weaknesses in the student's knowledge of basic skills. Some students may have mastery in one academic area and exhibit large gaps in another. Very often, the process or concept is mastered in the student's first language, but the English terms are unknown. The lessons in Part 2 are designed to teach the most commonly used English terms (academic and social) that are used in a school setting.

One danger for the older ESL student is that in our need to present grade-level curriculum, the basic skills that serve as the foundation of higher level learning are often overlooked. Part 2 presents many of these basic skills and draws them to the attention of the teacher.

Many of the life skills introduced in Part 2 will be useful not only in an academic setting, but also as a part of everyday life. These are life skills the new ESL student will use for a lifetime.

Section 6

School Information

The new ESL student is not only adjusting to a new social culture but also a new school culture. The school experience the new ESL student had in his/her native country was most likely very different from American schools. Demands of the curriculum, expected behavioral patterns, classroom management, and social interaction are all aspects of school life to which the newcomer must become accustomed. The simple act of finding your room in a large school can be a challenge for the new student.

The older ESL student may not be used to following a schedule where each period brings a change of location and a new teacher. The act of learning a locker combination and actually opening a locker can be a huge hurdle to overcome. Homework assignments, grade reports, recess, lunch routines, etc., are all part of the student's new school culture. Learning how to cope and survive in the school environment can be very stressful. In order for successful academic progress to occur, the new student must be comfortable with his/her new environment and feel in control of it.

The lessons in Section 6 expose the new ESL student to important information about his/her new school life and environment in an attempt to help him/her gain confidence in managing another part of this new world.

Lesson 6-1: My School

• • • • • • • • • • • • • • • • • • •

Objective: The student will become familiar with his/her new school, its name, and the rooms (places) in it.

Vocabulary: (*outside*) name of the student's school, entrance, flagpole, playground, parking lot, bike rack, sidewalk, windows, school sign, school bus; (*inside*) restroom, gym, cafeteria (lunchroom), office, nurse's office, classroom, hallway, library, lockers, drinking fountain, showcase

Materials: Activity Sheets 6–1A and 6–1B; Pencil; Crayons or colored pencils; Picture or photograph of your school (if possible)

Teaching Notes:

1. A student guide will be needed for this lesson. The job of the student guide will be to show the newcomer the various rooms/places in the school. It is always helpful to take pictures of the actual rooms/places in your specific school.

2. The lesson divides the items into two categories, those found on the inside and those found on the outside of the school. Thus, you might want to teach this lesson in two sessions.

Directions:

1. Give the student a copy of Activity Sheet 6–1A. Point to the picture of the school and say, "This is a school." Ask the student to repeat. If possible, show the student a picture of your school and say, "The name of our school is (name of school)." Ask the student to repeat the name of your school. Now write the name of your school on the chalkboard or a piece of paper. Read the sentence in #1 on the activity sheet and include the name of your school. Ask the student to write the name of his/her school on the line and repeat the sentence: "My school is (name of school)."

2. Point to the other items on the picture: flagpole, playground, parking lot, bike rack, sidewalk, entrance, windows, school bus, school sign. For each item, say the sentence, "This is the/a (name of item)." Ask the student to repeat.

3. Ask the student to complete Activity Sheet 6–1A. The student will find the item by number and then write the name on the correct line. Help with reading may be needed, which could be done with a student helper.

4. Give the student a copy of Activity Sheet 6–1B. Read the names of the various rooms in the school and ask the student to repeat. Then say, "This is the _____." Ask the student to supply the name of the room as you point to it. If possible, ask the student to repeat the entire sentence.

5. Ask a student guide to take the newcomer to each room. The student should take Activity Sheet 6–1B with him/her. When the student visits each room, he/she should put a check mark by the name of that room. Tell the student guide to say, "This is the (name of room)." Then the newcomer should repeat the sentence and make the check mark.

6. After the student returns to the classroom, he/she can complete Activity Sheet 6–1B. The student will be asked to locate a room/place by number and write the name on the corresponding line. This can be done with the student guide. Then the student can color the picture of the school and the rooms on the two activity sheets.

7. **Answer Key:** (*Activity Sheet 6–1A*) (1.) Entrance, (2.) Flagpole, (3.) Playground, (4.) Parking lot, (5.) Bike rack, (6.) Sidewalk, (7.) Windows, (8.) School sign, (9.) School bus.

   (*Activity Sheet 6–1B*) (1.) Classroom, (2.) Hallway, (3.) Restroom, (4.) Gym, (5.) Cafeteria (Lunchroom), (6.) Library (Media Center), (7.) Nurse's office, (8.) Office, (9.) Lockers, (10.) Drinking fountain, (11.) Showcase.

Extension Activities:

1. Play "Can You Take Me?" In this game, a classmate of the newcomer will choose a room/place in the school and ask, "Can you take me to the (gym)?" The ESL student must then take the student to that location. After they arrive, another location is requested. The students can use Activity Sheet 6–1B for reference.

2. Ask the newcomer to accompany student messengers around the school as they deliver messages to various locations.

3. Make a copy of Activity Sheet 6–2, "People Who Work in My School," from Lesson 6–2. Ask the student to tell you at what location each person can be found.

4. Give the student a piece of graph paper and, with a partner, make a map of the school. (This activity is appropriate for older students.)

Name_____ Date_____

My School—Outside

1. **Write the name of your school on the line.**

   The name of my school is _____.

2. **Find each number on the picture. Match it to the number below and write the name.**

entrance	flagpole	playground	parking lot	bike rack
sidewalk	windows	school sign	school bus	

1. _____   6. _____

2. _____   7. _____

3. _____   8. _____

4. _____   9. _____

5. _____

Name_____ Date_____

My School—Inside

Find each number on the picture. Match it to the number below and write the name.

classroom	hallway	restroom	gym	cafeteria	library
nurse's office	office	showcase	lockers	drinking fountain	

1. _____   7. _____

2. _____   8. _____

3. _____   9. _____

4. _____   10. _____

5. _____   11. _____

6. _____

Lesson 6-2: The People Who Work in Your School

Objective: The student will become familiar with the names and the jobs of the staff members in his/her school building.

Vocabulary: Principal; Teacher; Bus Driver; Gym Teacher; Librarian; Nurse; Secretary; Custodian

Materials: Activity Sheet 6–2; Pencil; Snapshots of the various staff members in your building (This is optional but is a very helpful tool in teaching the student the identities of these staff members. An instant camera or recent yearbook are good sources for obtaining snapshots.)

Directions:

1. Give the student a copy of Activity Sheet 6–2. Point to the various pictures of people who work in a school. Say, "These people work in a school." Point to each illustration and follow this procedure for each job title:

   - **Say the name of the job.** "This is the principal."

   - **Tell what that job means.** "He/She is the head of the school."

   - **Ask the student to identify the name of the person who holds that job at your school.** "Who is the principal at (name of your school)?" If needed, supply the name for the student.

   - **Write the name of the person on the line under the illustration.**

   - **Repeat the name and the title.** "(Principal's name) is the principal." Ask the student to repeat.

2. Ask the student to complete #2 on the activity sheet. The student will be asked to complete each sentence by writing the correct name on the line. (The name will have already been written in #1, so the student can use this for reference.)

3. After the student has completed Activity Sheet 6–2, say the name of the job and ask the student to tell you the name of the person who has that job at your school. This is to be done from memory. Then say the name of the person and ask the student to tell you the name of his/her job, also from memory.

Extension Activities:

1. Ask a student guide to introduce the newcomer to each of the people listed on the activity sheet. After the student has met each one, ask that person to sign the sheet.

2. Give the more advanced student a situation and ask who at the school would be able to help. *Examples:* "You don't feel well." (the nurse) "Your locker doesn't open." (the custodian) "You need to call home." (the secretary) "You don't know where your bus stops." (the bus driver)

Name_____ Date_____

People Who Work in My School

Part One: Say the name of the job and the name of the person. Then write the name of that person at your school under the picture.

Principal

_____

Teacher

_____

Bus Driver

_____

Gym Teacher

_____

Librarian

_____

Nurse

_____

Secretary

_____

Custodian

_____

Part Two: On the blank, write the name of the person who has that job at your school. Then read each sentence.

(1.) The principal is_____.

(2.) My teacher is _____.

(3.) My bus driver is _____.

(4.) My gym teacher is _____.

(5.) The librarian is _____.

(6.) The nurse is _____.

(7.) The secretary is _____.

(8.) The custodian is _____.

Lesson 6-3: Classroom Facts

• •

Objective: The student will learn pertinent, informational facts about his/her classroom.

Vocabulary: grade; students; teacher; girls; boys; pet; fish; grade; room number; recess; Gym class

Materials: Activity Sheet 6–3; Pencil or pen; Crayons

Teaching Note: Ask a classmate to assist the ESL student with this activity. This is a wonderful opportunity for the ESL student to interact with a classmate.

Directions:

1. Choose a student to help the ESL student obtain the information for Activity Sheet 6–3. Explain to the ESL student that he/she will do this activity with another student. (**Gesture:** Point to the student helper, the ESL student, and then Activity Sheet 6–3.)

2. Familiarize the student helper with the activity sheet before he/she begins the activity.

3. After the ESL student has completed Activity Sheet 6–3, ask him/her to repeat the information to you.

Extension Activity: Ask another classmate to help the ESL student learn the names of the other children in the classroom. Ask the students to write their name on small pieces of paper. The student helper can choose name cards and ask the ESL student to indicate where that student is sitting.

Name_____ Date_____

Classroom Facts

Work with a partner and write the correct information in the blanks.

1. I am in the _____ grade. Kdg. 1st 2nd 3rd 4th 5th 6th 7th 8th

2. My teacher's name is _____.

3. There are _____ students in my classroom.

4. There are _____ girls in the classroom.

5. There are _____ boys in the classroom.

6. My room number is _____.

7. My classroom has a pet _____.

8. My classroom has _____ fish.

9. _____ sits next to me.

10. I have recess in the (circle): **morning**   **at lunch time**   **afternoon**

11. I have gym class _____ times a week.
     (number)

Lesson 6-4: Classroom Objects

Objective: The student will become familiar with the vocabulary of objects found in his/her classroom.

Vocabulary: desk; pencil; chair; table; crayons; notebook; stapler; book; bookshelf; notebook paper; eraser; ruler; computer; chalk; board; glue; scissors; calendar; globe; flag; clock; map; pencil sharpener; tape; pencil case; binder; paper clip; pen; loudspeaker

Materials: Activity Sheets 6–4A (2 pages), 6–4B, 6–4C; Pen or pencil

Teaching Note:

1. Activity Sheet 6–4A contains the names and illustrations of various classroom objects. A few blank squares have been provided for you to add any items that may be specific to your classroom, e.g., fish tank, microscope, etc.). Activity Sheet 6–4B is a word search of these items designed for the older student. Activity Sheet 6–4C, "What's in Your Desk?" is designed for the younger student.

2. Because of the large number of objects presented in this lesson, you may want to teach this vocabulary over several sessions.

Directions:

1. Give the student a copy of the 2-page Activity Sheet 6–4A, "Classroom Objects." Point to each illustration and say its name. Ask the student to repeat.

2. Ask the student to find each object in the classroom. This is a nice activity to do with a partner. When the student finds each object, he/she should say, "This is a (name of object)."

3. (According to the level of the student) choose either Activity Sheet 6–4B or 6–4C. Ask the student to complete the activity sheet. Make sure the student understands how to do a word search activity. For Activity Sheet 6–4C, the student should use the illustrations of the objects as a reference guide.

4. After the student has completed the activity sheet, ask him/her to describe what is on it.

5. **Answer Key** for Activity Sheet 6–4B:

```
p  x  o  q  s  c  i  s  s  o  r  s  z  n
a  e  b  n  m  t  a  p  e  d  e  k  g  o
h  i  n  l  u  e  a  z  m  x  c  n  f  t
f  r  l  s  q  t  a  p  y  o  b  a  g  e
m  a  p  i  j  n  r  u  l  e  r  k  m  b
p  r  a  d  l  z  b  c  y  e  u  i  c  o
a  z  b  c  p  u  i  r  y  r  r  m  p  o
u  d  y  r  f  g  n  l  o  a  d  g  a  k
h  c  j  a  k  p  d  m  q  s  r  v  p  w
t  o  b  y  l  k  e  z  d  e  s  k  e  x
k  m  s  o  w  b  r  a  e  r  f  g  r  h
t  p  e  n  c  i  l  l  o  v  m  x  c  y
a  u  k  b  e  d  p  c  f  g  j  n  l  q
k  t  x  w  n  e  u  h  t  y  l  r  i  h
l  e  r  f  z  f  l  a  g  s  v  o  p  t
o  r  q  m  v  a  y  i  k  r  z  u  b  s
c  a  l  e  n  d  a  r  n  r  e  a  b  e
z  l  o  u  d  s  p  e  a  k  e  r  d  l
```

Extension Activities:

1. *Classroom Object Memory.* Make a duplicate copy of the 2-page Activity Sheet 6–4A. Cut out the cards and turn them face down. The first player turns over two cards and tries to make a matching pair of objects. The student should say the name of the object as he/she turns over the card. If a pair is made, the player puts it in his/her pile and takes another turn. If not, the player turns the cards over and the next player goes. The player with the most pairs is the winner. This game can also be played individually.

2. Say the name of an object and ask the student to draw that object.

3. Cut out the object cards and put them in a container. The student chooses one and must say, "This is a (name of object)." If correct, the student keeps the card. If not, the card goes back into the container for another try.

4. Play *What am I?* Cut out the object cards and put them in a container. Describe what the object is used for, e.g., "I cut paper." The student must guess the name of the object.

Name_____ Date_____

Classroom Objects

desk	pencil	chair	table
crayon	notebook	stapler	book
bookshelf	notebook paper	eraser	ruler
computer	scissors	glue	board

Name_____ Date_____

Classroom Objects

chalk	pencil sharpener	tape	calendar
pencil case	paper clip	binder	globe
flag	clock	map	pen
loudspeaker	wastebasket		

Name_____ Date_____

Classroom Objects

Look at the word list. Find each word in the puzzle, circle it, then cross it off the list.

p	x	o	q	s	c	i	s	s	o	r	s	z	n
a	e	b	n	m	t	a	p	e	d	e	k	g	o
h	i	n	l	u	e	a	z	m	x	c	n	f	t
f	r	l	s	q	t	a	p	y	o	b	a	g	e
m	a	p	i	j	n	r	u	l	e	r	k	m	b
p	r	a	d	l	z	b	c	y	e	u	i	c	o
a	z	b	c	p	u	i	r	y	r	r	m	p	o
u	d	y	r	f	g	n	l	o	a	d	g	a	k
h	c	j	a	k	p	d	m	q	s	r	v	p	w
t	o	b	y	l	k	e	z	d	e	s	k	e	x
k	m	s	o	w	b	r	a	e	r	f	g	r	h
t	p	e	n	c	i	l	l	o	v	m	x	c	y
a	u	k	b	e	d	p	c	f	g	j	n	l	q
k	t	x	w	n	e	u	h	t	y	l	r	i	h
l	e	r	f	z	f	l	a	g	s	v	o	p	t
o	r	q	m	v	a	y	i	k	r	z	u	b	s
c	a	l	e	n	d	a	r	n	r	e	a	b	e
z	l	o	u	d	s	p	e	a	k	e	r	d	l

scissors

crayon

chair

stapler

binder

computer

pencil

eraser

notebook

flag

clock

calendar

desk

ruler

map

globe

paper clip

pen

loudspeaker

tape

Name_____ Date_____

What's in Your Desk?

Look in your desk. Draw a picture of everything that is in it. Then write the word and say what it is.

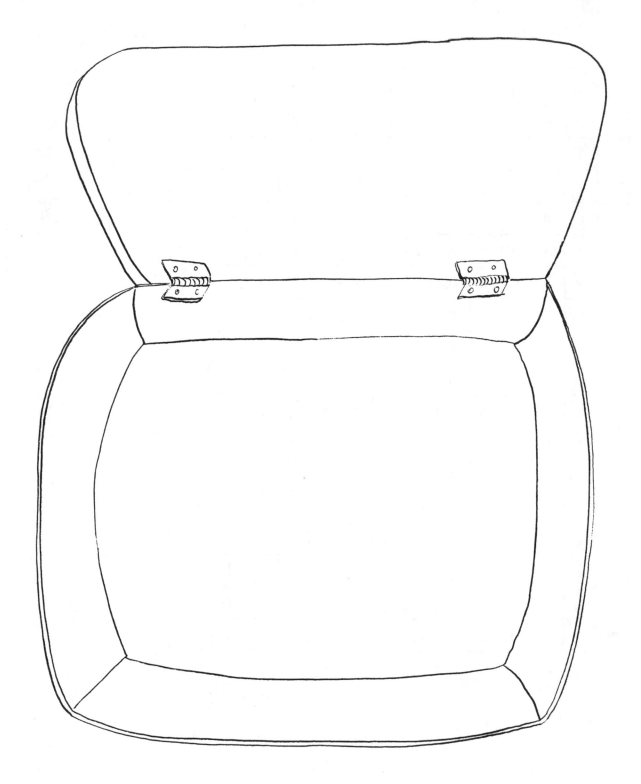

Lesson 6-5: Classroom Directions and Commands

Objective: The student will become familiar with the conduct and vocabulary associated with common classroom commands.

Vocabulary: Listen; Look; Pay attention; Think; Raise your hand; Don't be late; Open; Close; Turn the page; Turn to page; Stand up; Sit down; Walk; Come back; Take out; Put away; Take one and pass it back; Collect; Line up; Homework; Continue; Ask a question; Answer the question; Come here; Begin; Stop/Don't; Say the Pledge of Allegiance; Erase; Point to; Pick up; Sharpen your pencil; Bring; Get; Write the words; Copy; Times; Read the words; Color; Draw; Cut; Glue; Work with a partner; Spell

Materials: Activity sheet 6–5 (two pages); Pencils; Common classroom materials

Teaching Note: Many of the common commands and directions used in the classroom every day are not part of the newcomer's vocabulary. Although the behavior or concept is understood, the language associated with it may not be. This lesson provides a list of common classroom commands and directions. Gestures and activities are suggested for each one.

Directions:

1. The classroom directions are listed below (and on Activity Sheet 6–5). A description of the command and an action are given. Some commands are grouped according to their relationship to each other. Model and ask the student to perform the command. Introduce a few new commands every day. Review the commands that have already been introduced. For action commands, play "The Commander" game. The Commander begins by saying, "Listen to me!" Point to your ears and then yourself. Give the student several commands to perform, such as Stand up, Sit down, Open your desk, Take out a book, Walk to the door, etc. Begin with a few commands and add more. Mix and alternate the commands. Say them slowly at first, then gradually more quickly. The students can then take turns being the Commander and giving the directions. This game is a lot of fun as the pace quickens! (This is also an excellent way to practice "classroom objects" and "locations" vocabulary.)

2. The best way for a student to learn the vocabulary is to practice it in authentic classroom situations. *Classroom Directions*: Say and model the command. Ask the student to repeat the words and to perform the action.

   - **Listen:** Point to your ears.

   - **Look:** Point to your eyes. Say "Look at the board." Point to your eyes and then the board. Choose other objects and ask the student to look at them.

- **Raise your hand:** Raise your hand.

- **Stand up:** Stand up. Move your arm in an upward motion.

- **Sit down:** Sit down. Move your arm in a downward motion.

- **Walk to:** Walk to the door, walk to the flag, walk to the board.

- **Come here:** Come here. Motion with your hand toward yourself.

- **Take out:** Sit at a desk and say "Take out your book." "Take out a pencil." etc.

- **Put away:** Sit at a desk and place a number of items that you have taken out in front of you. Say "Put away the book." "Put away the pencil." etc.

- **Open:** "Open the door." "Open your book." "Open the window." Open the drawer." etc.

- **Close:** "Close the door." "Close your book." "Close the window." "Close the drawer." etc.

- **Turn the page:** "Open your book." "Turn the page." "Turn the page." "Turn the page." "Close the book."

- **Turn to page:** "Open your book." "Turn to page 5." "Turn to page 8." "Turn to page 20." etc.

- **Hand out:** Hand out papers to each student.

- **Collect:** Collect papers that have been handed out.

- **Take one and pass it back:** Have the students sit in rows and pass a stack of papers. For fun, use candy.

- **Begin:** Put your finger to your mouth indicating the "quiet sign." Say "Begin" and begin singing "Happy Birthday." Have the students follow the same procedure.

- **Stop:** Start jumping (or some other action). Say "Stop!" and stop the action. Do this several times with different actions. Hold up your palm facing the student and make a stopping gesture similar to a traffic police officer.

- **Point to:** "Point to the flag." "Point to the board." "Point to the door." etc.

- **Pick up:** Drop a pencil on the floor. Say "Pick up the pencil, please." Do this with other items.

- **Bring/Go get:** Choose classroom objects and say "Bring me the globe, please." Or, "Go get the markers, please." If clarification is needed, ask the student to stand and walk with you to the item, place the item in the student's hands, walk back to your original location, and motion for the student to give the object to you.

- **Write:** "Write your name." "Write your telephone number."

- **Erase:** Ask the student to write his/her name. Then say "Erase your name." Write a word on the board. Ask the student to erase it.

- **Copy/Times:** Write familiar words on the board. Give the student a sheet of paper and say "Copy the words." Then write a word on the board and say "Copy the word two times." "Write the word twice." Choose other words and other amounts to copy, e.g., "Copy the word three times."

- **Read:** Write familiar words on the board. Say "Read the words." Point to your mouth. Ask the student to read the words. Model silent reading by holding a book and reading silently.

- **Draw, Color, Cut, Glue:** Give the student a piece of blank paper and say "Draw a picture of yourself." Then "Color the picture." "Cut out the picture." "Glue your picture." Provide a large piece of chart paper and make a classroom collage of the students' pictures.

- **Think:** Point to your head.

- **Pay attention:** Point to your head, then your eyes, then your ears.

- **Ask a question/Answer the question:** Write this question on the board, point to yourself, and say "Ask a question. What is your name?" Point to the student and say "Answer a question." (Student says his/her name.) Model other questions/answers.

- **Come here:** Gesture with your index finger in a "come here" motion.

- **Spell:** Say "Spell your name." Write the student's name on the board with dashes between each letter and spell it out loud, e.g., J-o-s-e.

- **Work with a partner:** Point to the student and then to another student. Then clasp your hands together.

- **Homework:** Draw a picture of a house on the board, point to the student and the homework, then back to the house again. You may want to point to a clock and indicate after-school hours.

3. For an appropriate school behavior guide, see the Visual Behavior Chart on page 242.

Name_____ Date_____

Classroom Direction and Command Chart

Pay attention.

Line up.

Raise your hand.

Look at the board.

Sit down.

Stand up.

Open your book.

Close your book.

Take one and pass one back.

Don't be late.

Do your homework.

Continue.

Name_____ Date_____

Classroom Direction and Command Chart

Ask a question.

Answer the question.

Come here.

Begin.

Stop.

Turn the page.

Listen to the announcements.

Say the Pledge of Allegiance.

Read the words.

Write the words.

Work with a partner.

Spell the word.

Visual Behavior Chart

 happy

 sad

walk

run

sit down

stand up

shout/yell

quiet

raise your hand

line up

keep hands to yourself

nice/friend

listen

don't chew gum

Lesson 6-6: What's in Your Backpack?

Objective: The student will understand the use of a backpack and the vocabulary associated with it.

Vocabulary: backpack; sack lunch; comb; ID card; keys; book; notebook

Materials: Activity Sheet 6–6; Pencil; Crayons or colored pencils; Backpack; Paper lunch bag; Plastic food (sandwich, apple, chips, drink container) to represent a lunch (or draw pictures and cut them out); Comb; ID card; Set of keys; Book; Notebook; Any other items student may keep in his/her backpack

Teaching Notes:

1. Place all of the items on the Materials list (except Activity Sheet 6–6) in the backpack.

2. This is an excellent opportunity to teach the spatial concepts of "in" and "out."

Directions:

1. Show the backpack to the student and say, "This is a backpack." Ask the student to repeat. Ask the student to describe the backpack (color, zippers, straps, size, decorations). (Give help as needed.) Then give the backpack to the student and ask him/her to show you how to wear it. Most of the students will know how to wear it on their back, but if there is any question, model for the student. Now ask, "Why do we call it a backpack?" ("It is worn on the *back*.") (Point to your back.) "We *pack* things in it." (Pretend to be putting things in it.)

2. Ask the student, "What do students put in their backpacks?" (**Gesture for "in"**: Put your hand down into the backpack.) Let the student brainstorm ideas.

3. Ask the student to take the items out of the backpack. (**Gesture "out"**: Pull your hand out of the backpack.) The student should say the name of the item as it is taken out of the backpack. If necessary, help with vocabulary.

4. If the student has his/her own backpack, ask him/her to get it, and describe the backpack and what he/she keeps in it.

5. Give the student a copy of Activity Sheet 6–6. The student is asked to draw a picture of items that are put in a backpack. If needed, help with the spelling of the names.

Extension Activities:

1. Ask for student volunteers who would be agreeable to show the ESL student what they keep in their backpacks. The ESL student then names the items along with the student volunteer. This is a good opportunity for the ESL student to participate in a group or partner activity.

2. Give the name and description of a person, e.g., a teacher, a football player, a doctor, a mother, a father, etc., and ask what he/she might put in his/her backpack.

Name_____ Date_____

What's in Your Backpack?

Think of some things a student would put in this backpack. Draw a picture of each and write the word underneath.

Lesson 6-7: The Playground

Objectives: The student will learn the names of items found on a playground, and the vocabulary associated with them. The student will discuss the concept of recess.

Vocabulary: recess; playground; play structure; blacktop; slide; swings; basketball hoop; jungle gym; bars; bench; hopscotch; four-square

Materials: Activity Sheets 6–7A and 6–7B; Pencil; Crayons or colored pencils

Teaching Notes: The ESL student may not understand the concept of "recess." It has happened that ESL students have gone home thinking that school was over. You can use the following illustrations and gestures to explain this concept. Draw the "start" and "end" times of recess on the clocks below.

1. Say, "At (time) our class goes to the playground. This is called recess." Point to the time on the clock, the classroom, and then the children walking to the playground.

2. "At (time) we come back to the room." Point to the time on the clock and the children coming back into the school.

3. Explain to the ESL student what signal is used when recess has ended and the children line up.

4. It is always helpful to assign a student helper to the newcomer at recess. The responsibility of the student helper is to line up with the ESL student, teach him/her games, and include the newcomer in play groups.

Directions:

1. Give the student a copy of Activity Sheet 6–7A. Point to the illustration of the playground and say, "This is the playground." Ask the student to repeat.

2. Then point to each item on the playground and ask the student to repeat the name in a short sentence: "This is the slide," etc. The student will circle each item as he/she says the name. (Supply help when needed.) The student can then draw him-/herself playing on the playground and color the picture.

3. Give the student a copy of Activity Sheet 6–7B. The student will complete the sentences by writing the correct word on the line. If needed, help with reading the sentences. **Answer Key:** (1.) swing; (2.) jungle gym; (3.) bench; (4.) blacktop; (5.) basketball hoop; (6.) hopscotch; (7.) four-square; (8.) slide; (9.) play structure; (10.) bars.

Extension Activities:

1. Ask the student to draw a picture of recess in his/her native country and then describe it.

2. Ask the student to teach his/her classmates a favorite game from his/her native country.

Name_____ Date_____

The Playground

Look at the picture of the playground. Find and circle each item listed in the word box. Say each word. Now draw yourself and your friends playing on the playground. Describe what everyone is doing.

swings	blacktop	slide	climbing bars	hopscotch
basketball hoop	bench	bars	play structure	four-square

Name_____ Date_____

The Playground

Look at the word list below. Write the correct word on the line. The pictures will help you. Then read each sentence.

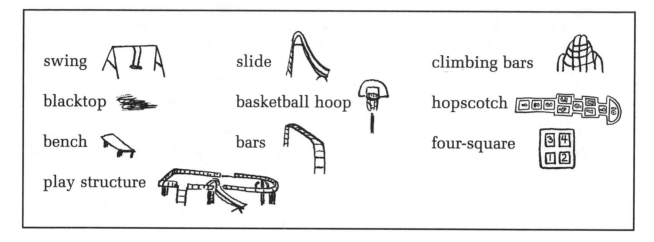

swing   slide   climbing bars

blacktop   basketball hoop   hopscotch

bench   bars   four-square

play structure

1. She is on the_____.

2. They are on the _____.

3. He is sitting on the _____.

4. They are jumping on the _____.

5. The ball is in the _____.

6. The girls are playing _____.

7. The boys are playing _____.

8. They are going down the_____.

9. They are on the _____.

10. He is hanging on the _____.

Lesson 6-8: How Do You Get to School?
When Do You Go to School?

• •

Objectives: The student will learn the various means of transportation for getting to (and from) school and the vocabulary associated with it. The student will learn the starting and end times for the school day, and the days of the week that school is in session.

Vocabulary: bus; bus stop; car; carpool; bicycle; walk; passenger; begin; end; time

Materials: Activity Sheet 6–8; Pencil; Picture of a school bus, a car, a bicycle, a person walking (if none are available, draw the pictures on the board); Teaching clock

Directions:

1. Say to the student, "There are many ways a student can get to school." Draw a picture of a student with the following modes of transportation. Read the following sentences and ask the student to say the missing word as you point to each picture.

   "This student takes a _____." (bus)
   "This student comes in a _____." (car)
   "This student rides a _____." (bicycle)
   "This student _____." (walks)

2. Ask the student to repeat each sentence. Help, when needed.

3. Explain to the student that the place where the bus stops to "pick up" (get on) and "drop off" (get off) the students is called the *bus stop*. Draw a simple illustration of students waiting at a bus stop.

4. Tell the student that sometimes people take turns driving a group of students in a car, and that is called a *car pool*. Explain that children who ride in a bus or a car are called *passengers*.

5. Ask the student how he/she gets to school. Ask that the response be in a complete sentence, e.g., "I walk to school."

6. Now ask the student if he/she rides/walks to school with other students. Ask the student to identify the students, if possible.

7. Say to the student, "What time does school begin?" (If necessary, supply the answer.) "School begins at (time)." Ask the student to repeat. Write the time on the board. Now ask the student to show the time on the teaching clock. (Help as needed.) Ask the student what time school ends. "School ends at (time)." Write the time on the board. Ask him/her to show that time on the teaching clock.

8. Ask the student, "On what days do you come to school?" If help is needed, point to a calendar and recite the days of the week, shaking your head "yes" or "no" in response to the question. Ask the student to repeat.

9. Give the student a copy of Activity Sheet 6–8. The student will be asked to answer various questions covered in the lesson. If needed, help with reading.

Extension Activities:

1. Ask the student to pretend he/she lives on another planet. "How do those children get to school? Draw a picture and tell about it."

2. Pretend you live in the desert or the jungle. How would you get to school? Draw a picture and write about it.

Name_____ Date_____

How Do You Get to School?
When Do You Go to School?

Part One: Read the sentences and circle the one that tells how you get to school. The pictures will help you.

I ride my bicycle to school.

I walk to school.

I take a bus to school.

I ride in a car to school.

Other: I _____ to school.

Part Two: Answer the questions. Write YES or NO on the line.

Are you a **passenger** in a car? _____

Are you in a **car pool**? _____

Do you wait at the **bus stop**? _____

Do you **walk** with your friends to school? _____

Part Three: Draw the correct time on each clock. Then write the time on the line.

School **begins** at: _____

School **ends** at: _____

Part Four: Circle the days of the week that you come to school.

Sunday   Monday   Tuesday   Wednesday   Thursday   Friday   Saturday

Lesson 6-9: The Lunchroom

• •

Objectives: The student will learn the routine for lunch time. The student will learn appropriate lunchroom behavior.

Vocabulary: lunchroom; cafeteria; tray; lunch line; trash; food choices; sack lunch

Materials: Activity Sheet 6–9; Pencil; Items from your school cafeteria (tray, cup, plate, knife, fork, spoon, napkin); Brown paper lunch bag (*optional*: plastic food to represent a lunch); Teaching clock

Teaching Notes: One of the most important—and worrisome—times in a student's day is lunch time. Will they have anyone to sit with? How do they get lunch? It is very beneficial to introduce this lesson as soon as possible to help alleviate any anxiety/ worry on the part of the newcomer.

1. Be sure to ask the office or the child's caretaker for the correct information regarding the student's lunch: Do they receive free or reduced lunch tickets? Do they stay at school or go home for lunch? Does the lunch monitor know there is a new student and his/her name? Ask the lunch monitor to help the newcomer.

2. Before he/she has lunch, it is a good idea to show the student the cafeteria; where it is located; where to get trays, utensils, and food; where to sit. This is especially helpful for the older student.

3. Ask a student helper to assist and sit with the newcomer for the first few days. This is especially helpful in aiding the ESL student to feel welcome in his/her new surroundings.

Directions: This lesson is designed for the student who eats lunch at school.

1. Say, "When we eat at school, we eat in a room called the *cafeteria/lunch-room*." Use the illustration on Activity Sheet 6–9 as a reference. Then tell the student what time lunch begins and ends. Use the teaching clock to model. Ask the student to repeat.

2. Show the student the tray with the items placed on it and the sack lunch. Say, "Some students have the school lunch" (point to the tray) "and some students bring a sack lunch from home" (show the student the paper sack). Name the items on the tray and ask the student to repeat.

3. Explain the procedure your school uses for lunch, i.e., a ticket, a card, etc. Also explain how the food *choices* in your school are announced (PA system, school bulletin, etc.). Inform the student that *choices* mean what food will be given on that day. Inform the student of some choices that your school offers. Draw pictures, if needed.

4. Tell the student that he/she is expected to use good manners in the school cafeteria. Review your school's cafeteria/lunchroom rules. If none are available, brainstorm with the student what good manners (behavior) would mean. (Demonstrate or use Activity Sheet 6–9 for reference.)

   - Use "just right" (indoor) voices.

   - Stand in line politely. Give enough personal space. *Don't* cut in front of people in line.

   - Don't throw food.

   - If you drop something, pick it up. If someone else drops something and doesn't notice, pick that up also.

   - If you spill something, clean it up.

   - Talk about nice things (not, "My dog threw up last night.").

   - Clean up your spot for the next person who sits there.

   - Throw your trash away.

   - Put your tray back in the proper place.

5. Give the student a copy of Activity Sheet 6–9. The student will be asked to find and circle six pictures of good behavior and put an X on six pictures of poor behavior. **Answer Key:** (*good*) two girls talking in quiet voices, a boy wiping his mouth with a napkin, a girl putting her tray away, a boy throwing his trash away, a boy picking up some trash on the floor, students standing politely in the lunch line; (*poor*) a boy pulling a girl's hair, a girl shouting, a student putting gum under the table, a boy throwing food, a girl throwing trash on the floor, a girl cutting in front of someone in line.

Name_____ Date_____

Lunchroom Lookout!

Look at this lunchroom! Circle 6 students with good manners. Put an X on 6 students with bad manners.

Lesson 6-10: Using the School Library

Objectives: The student will understand the procedure used in the school library and how the library is organized. The student will learn how to handle a book and use appropriate behavior for the library.

Vocabulary: library; book; pages; quiet; fiction; nonfiction; periodicals; videos; music; borrow; due date; fine; overdue; renew; check out; reference; call numbers; librarian; title

Materials: Activity Sheets 6–10A and 6–10B; Backpack or bag; Calendar; Crayons or colored pencils

Directions: This lesson should be done in the school library.

1. Take the student to the school library. Ask, "What is a *library*?" (A place with many books) Then say, "At the library, you can *borrow* a book. That means you can take it out of the library and keep it for a certain amount of time and then bring it back again."

2. Inform the student that there are rules for good behavior in the library. Discuss the following rules. (Add any rules that are specific to your library.)

   • **Use a quiet voice.** (Model this.)

   • **After looking at a book, put it back where you found it.** (Model.)

   • **Review the rules developed for your school's library.**

3. Explain that the person who works in the library is called the *librarian*. Introduce the student to your school's librarian.

4. Explain to the student how the library is organized. Show the student the section for *Fiction*. Explain that fiction means books that tell make-believe stories. Show the student various examples.

5. Now show the student the *Nonfiction* section. Explain that nonfiction books tell real stories or give information about a subject. Show the student various examples.

6. Visit the area for *Reference* material and explain that reference books are books of facts and information. Show the students the various types of reference books found in your library.

7. Now visit the *Periodical* section. Explain that this is the area where magazines and newspapers are found. Show the student examples of the periodicals found in your library.

8. Show the student any other sections that your library may contain, e.g., video, music, etc.

9. Use a library book to explain each term. Explain that the *title* is the name of the book and is found on the cover. Explain that the name of the *author* is the person who wrote the book and it is also found on the cover. Explain that the numbers or letters on the spine of the book are called the *call numbers*, which help us locate the book.

10. Show the student how to use the library computer to select a book. Ask the student to write down the title and call numbers of the books he/she would like to find.

11. Help the student locate the area where his/her selections would be found. Help the student locate his/her books by using the call numbers.

12. Show the student the proper procedure for *checking out* a book from your library. Explain that the term "checking out" means to let the library know you are borrowing the book. Help the student check out a book.

13. Explain to the student that he/she will be given a day when the book is to be returned to the library. This is called the *due date*. Tell the student the amount of time he/she will be allowed to keep the book. Use a calendar to clarify. Show the student the due date for the book he/she has checked out.

14. Explain that if the book is not brought back by the due date, it is late and that is called *overdue*. (Use a calendar to illustrate.) Inform the student that if the book is overdue, he/she may have to pay a *fine*. Explain that a fine is money that has to be paid.

15. Inform the student that it is very important to take good care of the book he/she has borrowed. Discuss the following guidelines:

    - **Turn the pages from the top.** (Model this.)

    - **Have clean hands when you handle a book.** (Pretend to wash your hands.)

    - **Put your book in your backpack or bag.** (Demonstrate.)

    - **Keep the book in a safe place at home.**

16. For reinforcement, ask the student to complete Activity Sheets 6–10A and 6–10B. **Answer Key:** (*Activity Sheet 6–10A*) borrow, due date, overdue, fine; (*Activity Sheet 6–10B*) Nonfiction, Periodical, Fiction, Reference.

17. Take the student to the library regularly so he/she becomes familiar with the procedures.

Name_____ Date_____

Be Kind to Your Books

1. **Complete these sentences. Choose a word from the word box and write it on the line.**

due date	borrow	fine	overdue

"You can _____ a book from the library. Don't forget to look

for the _____. If your book is _____,

you might get a _____."

2. **Match the picture to the rule.**

Use a quiet voice.

Turn the pages from the top.

Have clean hands.

Keep your book in a safe place at home.

Carry your book in a backpack or bag.

Name_____ Date_____

Understanding the Library

Part One: Look at the pictures. Circle the correct area where each can be found.

Fiction	Fiction	Fiction	Fiction
Nonfiction	Nonfiction	Nonfiction	Nonfiction
Reference	Reference	Reference	Reference
Periodical	Periodical	Periodical	Periodical

Part Two: Find an example for each: Fiction and Nonfiction. On the lines below, write the title, the author, and the call number for the book you found.

Fiction

Title: _____

Author: _____

Call Number: _____

Nonfiction

Title: _____

Author: _____

Call Number: _____

Part Three: Find an example of a Reference book. Write the information on the lines below.

Title: _____

Call Number: _____

Part Four: Find an example of a Periodical. Write the information on the line below.

Title: _____

Lesson 6-11: Using an Assignment Book

Objective: The student will understand the format and the importance of writing down homework assignments.

Vocabulary: assignment; Assignment Book; subjects; Reading; English; Spelling; Math; Science; Social Studies; Other

Materials: Activity Sheets 6–11A and 6–11B; Examples of books or materials from the following subject areas: Reading, Math, Science, Social Studies, English, Other (Art or other electives that might be offered)

Teaching Notes:

1. The activity sheet that you choose for your student will depend upon his/her age and language level. Activity Sheet 6–11A is formatted with the older student in mind (grades 3–8). Activity Sheet 6–11B is more suited to the younger student (grades 1–3).

2. The concept of keeping an Assignment Book/Log may be a new concept for the ESL student. In many countries, this is not part of the daily school routine.

Directions:

Activity Sheet 6–11A

1. Explain to the student that the word "assignment" means school "work" that is to be done by the student. When that work is done at home, it is called "homework." If clarification is needed, point to the illustration of a student doing homework at the top of Activity Sheet 6–11B.

2. Give the student a copy of Activity Sheet 6–11A. Say, "Today I am going to show you a way to help you remember your homework assignments. This will also help you know what assignments you have completed." (**Gesture:** Point to your head and then the words Homework Assignments on Activity Sheet 6–11A.)

3. Ask the student to recite the days of the week that are listed on the assignment sheet. (Monday–Friday). Ask, "Why are these days listed?" (Those are school days.) Explain that an assignment given on Friday would be done over the weekend—Saturday or Sunday.

4. Now point to the words "Week of _____." Explain that Sunday's date would go on the line because it is the first day of the week. It is also a good idea to write the numerical date (month and day) next to each word, e.g, Monday 3/17.

5. Read the word "Subjects" and ask the student to repeat. Explain the meaning of the word "Subjects": different things students study in school. Read the subjects with the student. Show examples of books and specific subject material.

6. Say the name of a subject and then show the student the row of empty squares next to it. (Trace your finger along the row, from Monday to Friday.) Explain that this is where the assignments for that day are written. (**Model:** Choose a subject, a day, and a homework assignment. Write it in the correct square.) Give the student practice assignments to write on the assignment sheet. Check for accuracy.

7. Now point to the little empty box in the corner of each large assignment square. Explain to the student that when an assignment is completed, he/she should put a check mark in the little box.

8. If you want to require a parent signature, point to the words at the bottom of each row. Say, "Mother or Father must write his/her name here." (Model.)

9. Give the student an Assignment Sheet/Log to use routinely. Monitor for consistency.

Directions:

Activity Sheet 6–11B

1. Give the student a copy of Activity Sheet 6–11B. Define "homework" as school work that a student does at home. To clarify, point to the illustration at the top of the sheet. Next, explain to the student that you can show them a way to help them remember what homework needs to be done. (**Gesture:** Point to your head.) Explain that the word *Log* means to write down and know (keep track of) what was done. Say, "Students write down what they need to do for homework in a *Homework Log*." Point to the heading at the top of Activity Sheet 6–11B.

2. Now ask the student to recite the days of the week that are printed on the assignment sheet (Monday–Friday). Help, if necessary.

3. Point to each day and trace your finger along the empty space next to it.

4. Model writing an assignment in one of the spaces, e.g., say, "Monday. Your homework is to write your spelling words." Write that assignment in the correct space. Give the student practice assignments to write. Give the name of the day and the assignment. Help with spelling, if necessary.

5. Now show the student the small box under the name of the day. Explain that when all the homework for that day is done, a check mark goes in the box.

6. Give the student a homework sheet to use regularly each week. Monitor for consistency.

Name _____

Date _____

Homework Assignments

Week of _____

Subjects	Monday	Tuesday	Wednesday	Thursday	Friday
Reading					
English					
Spelling c-a-n s-i-t					
Math 5×5=25 30÷6=36					
Science					
Social Studies					
Other					

Parent's Signature: Parent's Signature: Parent's Signature: Parent's Signature: Parent's Signature:

Name_____ Date_____

My Homework Log

Monday

☐

Tuesday

☐

Wednesday

☐

Thursday

☐

Friday

☐

Lesson 6-12: School in Your Native Land

Objectives: The student will have an opportunity to share information about school in his/her native country. The student will learn to compare similarities and differences. The student will learn to use a graphic organizer.

Materials: Activity Sheets 6–12A and 6–12B; Pencil; Crayons or colored pencils; World map; Illustration of a school; Realia from student's native country

Teaching Note: This lesson is a wonderful opportunity for the student to share information about school in his/her native country. Most children are very interested in learning what school is like in other places. The activity sheets are formatted according to age and language level. Activity Sheet 6–12A is designed for the younger student. Activity Sheet 6–12B is suited for the older, more advanced student.

Directions:

Activity Sheet 6–12A

1. Give the student a copy of Activity Sheet 6–12A. Show the student an illustration of a school, then say the name of his/her country, and point to it on the map. Indicate that the student is to draw a picture of school in his/her native land. (Point to crayons/colored pencils.)

2. Ask the student to write the name of his/her native country on the line at the top of the activity sheet. The student can use the map as a spelling aid.

3. After the picture has been drawn, ask the student to describe it. Help with vocabulary, as needed.

4. Encourage the student to bring realia (report card, school yearbook, etc.) from his/her native country. Make a classroom display.

Directions:

Activity Sheet 6–12B

1. Give the student a copy of Activity Sheet 6–12B. Show the student the graphic organizer. Point to the illustration of the school and explain that one side is used to describe his/her American school; the other side, the native school. Ask the student to write the name of his/her country on the line provided: "School in _____."

2. Brainstorm some categories, e.g., transportation (is already included on the activity sheet as an example), clothing, time (days, start time and end time), subjects, teachers, etc. Ask the student to write the categories in the spaces provided on the graphic organizer.

3. Now ask the student to write the information on the graphic organizer. The student should then compare and describe which things are the same (alike) and which are different.

Extension Activity: Assign a research assignment to the entire class called "Schools in Other Countries." Each student is to choose a country and research its schools. Each student then shares that information with the class.

Name_____ Date_____

School in _____

Draw a picture of school in your native land.

Name _____

Date _____

School in . . . .

America

(Native Country)

Transportation

Transportation

SCHOOL

Section 7

The Alphabet and Handwriting

This section provides lessons and teaching suggestions pertaining to the alphabet. Alphabet flash cards are provided along with small letter cards that can be used for games and with decoding strategies.

A lesson on directionality has been included for those students whose alphabet in their first language is not read or written from left to right.

An initial sheet teaching the basic strokes for letter formation begins the handwriting sequence.

Alphabet practice sheets in both manuscript and cursive letters are provided. For your convenience a blank, generic practice sheet that can be copied has been included. Remember, when teaching cursive writing, it is important to show the student how to connect the letters. This often presents a challenge for new language learners.

Alphabet and Handwriting Pretest–Posttest

Student:_____   Grade:_____

Date: _____

1. Ask the student to recite the alphabet.

2. Give the student the Alphabet Assessment (visual recognition), Activity Sheet 7–2G. Circle the correct responses.

3. Show the student these two letters and say, "There are two kinds of letters. This is the letter *B* and this is the letter *b*. What kind of a *B* is this?" (capital) "What kind of a *b* is this?" (lower case)

B   b

4. On a separate sheet of paper, ask the student to **print** the alphabet in both capital and lower-case letters.

5. On a separate sheet of paper, ask the student to **write** the alphabet in both capital and lower-case letters.

6. On a separate sheet of paper, ask the student to write the numbers from 1 through 10.

7. Ask the student to put these words in alphabetical order:

    drop   cry   apple   eat   book

8. Ask the student to rewrite the following sentence, putting capital letters where they should be used:

    may i go to denver, colorado on friday, november sixth?

Lesson 7-1: Directionality–Left to Right

• •

Objective: The student will understand that the correct direction when reading or writing English is from left to right.

Vocabulary: go; stop; "turn and go back"

Materials: Activity Sheet 7–1; Paint/paintbrushes, fingerpaints, markers, or prepared pudding on fingerpaint paper; Green marker or crayon; Red marker or crayon; Small toy (Matchbox™) cars (*optional*); Red circle made from construction paper with the word "Stop" printed on it; Green circle made from construction paper with the word "Go" printed on it

Teaching Note: This lesson will be necessary if the ESL student comes from a culture whose language does not observe left-to-right directionality. Many Arabic and Asian languages are indicative of this. Also, it is not necessary for the student to know the terms "left" and "right." It is sufficient that he/she understands the concept of "left-to-right directionality." It is always helpful for any student to understand this concept before teaching the alphabet.

Directions:

1. Hold up the red and green circles and say, "Let's play a game. Green means 'go'" (point to the word) "and red means 'stop'" (point to the word). "I will tell you to do something. When I hold up the green circle, it means 'go'" (point to the word) "and when I hold up the red circle, you must 'stop.'" (point to the word) Model: Say, "Jump!" Hold up the green circle and say, "Go!" Begin jumping and have the student jump also. Now hold up the red circle and say "Stop!" Everyone stops jumping. Repeat until the student understands that green means Go and red means Stop. Choose other actions such as running in place, jumping jacks, twirling arms, etc. Then let the student think of an action, hold up the cards, and say "Go" or "Stop."

2. Give the student a copy of Activity Sheet 7–1. Point to the circles at the top of the page and, with the student, read "Go" and "Stop." Now ask the student to color the GO circle green, and the STOP circle red.

3. Point to the illustration of the bee at the beginning of the first line. Say "Go" and trace with your finger on the dotted line until you reach the beehive at the end of the line. Now say "Stop." Ask the student to repeat.

4. Show the student how to follow the arrows and go back to the beginning of the next line. Say, "Turn and go back." Trace with your finger; ask the student to do so and repeat.

5. Ask the student to follow the same procedure for the rest of the lines. (Tracing with his/her finger and then moving down to the next line.)

6. Ask the student to go back to the first line and draw on the dotted line in a left-to-right direction. (Use colored pencils, markers, paint, pudding, etc.) Ask the student to continue until all the lines are drawn.

7. *Optional:* Younger students enjoy rolling small toy cars from left to right along the lines.

Extension Activities:

1. Give the student manipulatives and ask him/her to put them in a line from left to right.

2. Copy a page from a textbook, magazine, or newspaper and ask the student to highlight or underline the lines going in a left-to-right direction.

Name_____ Date_____

Left to Right!

Directions: Color the Go circle green and the Stop circle red. Next, trace each line with your finger. Then go back and draw on the dotted lines, left to right!

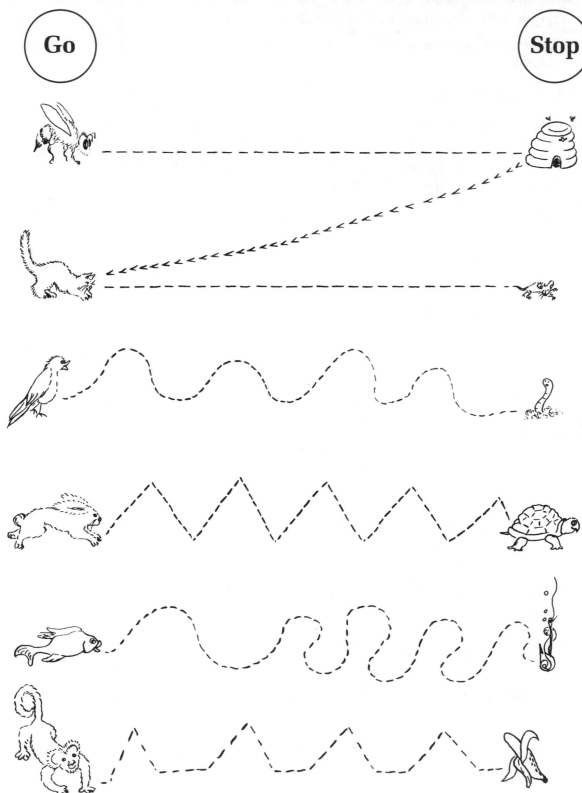

Lesson 7-2: Tips for Teaching the Alphabet

Objective: The student will learn to visually recognize and say the letters of the alphabet.

Vocabulary: alphabet; letters; *specific names of the alphabet letters*

Materials: Activity Sheets 7–2A, 7–2B, 7–2C, 7–2D, 7–2E, 7–2F, 7–2G; Pencil; Specific items mentioned in suggestions below

Teaching Note: This lesson consists of suggestions for teaching the alphabet, which is an ongoing process. Use as many methods as possible to help make the lesson interesting for the student. Once the alphabet has been mastered, it is very important to review frequently. It is also very important for the older student to recognize the alphabet in cursive writing, which is the style that most teachers use when writing information.

Teaching Suggestions:

1. **Use the word "Alphabet."** This is the correct name and is what the student will hear in the academic world of school. *Teaching idea:* Draw a circle around the entire alphabet and say, "This is called the alphabet." Then give the student a copy of the alphabet and ask him/her to draw a circle around it and repeat, "This is the alphabet."

2. **Define the term "letter."** Say, "The alphabet has twenty-six letters." Point to each letter and identify it as belonging to the category of "letter." Ask the student to count the letters with you and repeat, "The alphabet has twenty-six letters." *Teaching idea:* Place plastic letters on the floor or table with other plastic objects. Ask the student to put all the letters in one group and all the objects that are *not* letters in another. (If the student knows "numbers," use letters and numbers and ask the student to put each in a group.) The student may use an alphabet chart for reference. *Variations*: (1.) Have the student put all the capital letters in one group and all the lower-case letters in another. (2.) Have the student put all the "tall" letters in one group and all the "short" letters in another.

3. **Teach the alphabet in a rhythm or song.** It is much easier for the student to remember the letters if presented in a rhythm, chant, or the traditional "Alphabet Song."

4. **Teach the letters in chunks.** First, say the entire alphabet. Then, if necessary, divide the letters into chunks of no more than 6–8 letters.

5. **Define Capital and Lower Case.** Use the terms "capital" and "lower case," which are what the student will hear in his/her classroom. Stress the fact that

this is the same letter, written in a different way. *Teaching idea*: (1.) Make copies of Activity Sheet 7–2D, "Alphabet Game Cards." Cut out the capital and lower-case cards. Mix them up and ask the student to put them into pairs. (2.) Ask the student to put all the capital letters in a group and the lower-case letters in another group. (3.) Play "Memory." Cut out the capital and lower-case game cards. Mix them up and turn them face down. Each player takes a turn to turn over two cards, trying to make a matching pair. The player with the most pairs at the end of the game is the winner.

6. **Identify book type/print.** This is an important feature to teach. Some book-type letters are very different from the manuscript form and will be encountered in reading, so the student must know the identity of these letters. See the alphabet chart on Activity Sheet 7–2A. Find examples of these letters in books and magazines and show them to the student. *Teaching idea:* Copy a page from a newspaper or magazine. Ask the student to find and highlight an example of book type for each letter.

7. **Alphabet Desk Chart.** Cut out Activity Sheet 7–2F and tape this chart to the student's desk in a location where it is easily visible. This can be a convenient aid to which the student can refer.

8. **Alphabet assessment sheet.** Use Activity Sheet 7–2G as a pretest and a posttest. Ask the student to identify each letter by name. Circle the correct answers.

9. **Alphabet plastic letters.** A very effective way to teach the alphabet is to use this type of manipulative. When purchasing the letters, choose manuscript form, both capital and lower case. Some letters that have nubby surfaces can be traced with the finger, which provides for tactile reinforcement. Whichever style you choose, use these letters for games, categorization activities, and for future reading/spelling activities.

Alphabet Games and Activities:

1. **Alphabet Bingo.** Use Activity Sheet 7–2E. Copy several sheets and make different Bingo cards by putting different letters on the squares. Use the letters from Activity Sheet 7–2D as the letters to be called. Cut them out, place them in a container, and ask a student to be the Caller. Give the players markers for the Bingo cards. When a called letter is on the card, the player puts a marker on the square. The first player to make a line vertically, horizontally, or diagonally across the card is the winner. This can be played with only capital letters, only lower-case letters, or a mixture of both.

2. **Alphabet Memory.** Use Activity Sheet 7–2D. Cut out the letters and use as game cards. The letters are turned face down and mixed up. The players then take turns trying to remember and choose the correct letter in order of the alphabet. For example, the first player must try to find an A. If he/she fails,

the card is turned over and the next player tries. If that player is successful, he/she then tries to find the B, etc. The player with the most cards at the end of the game wins. *Variation*: Use pairs of capital and lower-case letters. (See #5 under Teaching Suggestions.)

3. **Mixed-up Alphabet Cards:** Give each student several alphabet game cards (Activity Sheet 7–2D). The students must put the cards in correct order. This is an excellent activity for group work and to stimulate conversation. *Variation*: Give each student both capital and lower-case letters, but *not* of the same kind. He/She must then try to make pairs by finding the person with the letters he/she needs. The players should ask each other, "Do you have a capital __?" or "Do you have a lower-case __?" That person must then give the player the card. The person who finishes first wins.

4. **Alphabet Go Fish.** Make a copy of the alphabet game cards on Activity Sheet 7–2D. Each player is dealt five cards. Put the remainder of the cards into the "Go Fish" pool in the middle, face down. The first player begins and asks another player for a card, e.g., "Do you have a capital __ or lower-case __?"— trying to make a pair of a capital and lower-case letter. If the other player has the card, he/she must give it to the player. If not, the player who is asked says, "Go Fish" and the other player must choose from the pool. If a pair is made, the player gets another turn. The player who makes all of his/her pairs wins.

5. **Alphabet Spin the Bottle.** Use the flash cards from Activity Sheet 7–2C. Cut out the cards and place them face up in a circle. Put a glass soda bottle on its side in the middle of the circle. The student goes to the middle of the circle, spins the bottle, and names the letter the bottle points to when it stops. If correct, the student gets one point and another turn. The player with the most points wins.

6. **Alphabet Hide and Seek.** Hide alphabet letters (either plastic or flash cards) around the classroom. The student must find them and put them in correct order. *Variations:* (1.) The student must find them in order. (2.) Hide lower-case letters. Place capital letters in order on the floor or table. The student must then find and match the lower case to the capital letter.

7. **Alphabet Basketball.** This game is particularly fun for a group. An empty wastebasket is the basket and a soft foam ball is the basketball. Divide the students into teams. One team member from each team competes to identify a letter you show them. (Each team member must have a turn.) The first one to identify the letter gets to shoot a basket. Each basket is worth one point. The team with the most points at the end of the game wins. *Variation*: This can also be played with an individual student. Give the student a goal to achieve, e.g., 15 points. Then continue as above. If he/she achieves the goal, offer a treat or reward.

8. **Alphabet Collage.** Ask the student to find large letters of the alphabet in magazines, catalogs, etc. Then the student cuts them out and pastes them in order. *Variation:* Create a "Hidden Alphabet Collage." The student uses magazine letters of the alphabet, but places them in random order on a collage. Another student must find and identify all the letters.

9. **Alphabet Search.** Give the student a copy of a newspaper or magazine page. He/She must then circle or highlight the letters of the alphabet in order. This can be done choosing capital or lower-case letters.

10. **Alphabet Roll.** This game is fun for a group. The first player rolls the die and says the number rolled. (Help, if needed.) Then show him/her a letter to identify. If correct, he/she gets the number on the die as points. The player with the most points wins. (This game is also helpful in practicing numbers and addition.)

Bibliography of Alphabet Books:

All About Arthur by Eric Carle
Alligator All Around by Maurice Sendak
The Alphabet Tree by Leo Lionni
Animalia by Graham Base
Anno's Alphabet by Mitsumasa Anno
A to Z Picture Book by Gyo Fujikawa
Brian Wildsmith's ABC by Brian Wildsmith
Chicka Chicka Boom Boom by Bill Martin
Dr. Seuss' ABC by Dr. Seuss
Norman Rockwell's Americana ABC by Norman Rockwell
Pooh's Alphabet Book by A. A. Milne
Richard Scarry's ABC Word Book by Richard Scarry

Alphabet Chart—Manuscript

Alphabet Chart—Cursive

A a   B b   C c   D d

E e   F f   G g   H h

I i   J j   K k   L l

M m   N n   O o   P p

Q q   R r   S s   T t

U u   V v   W w

X x   Y y   Z z

Alphabet Flash Cards

A a   B b

C c   D d

Alphabet Flash Cards

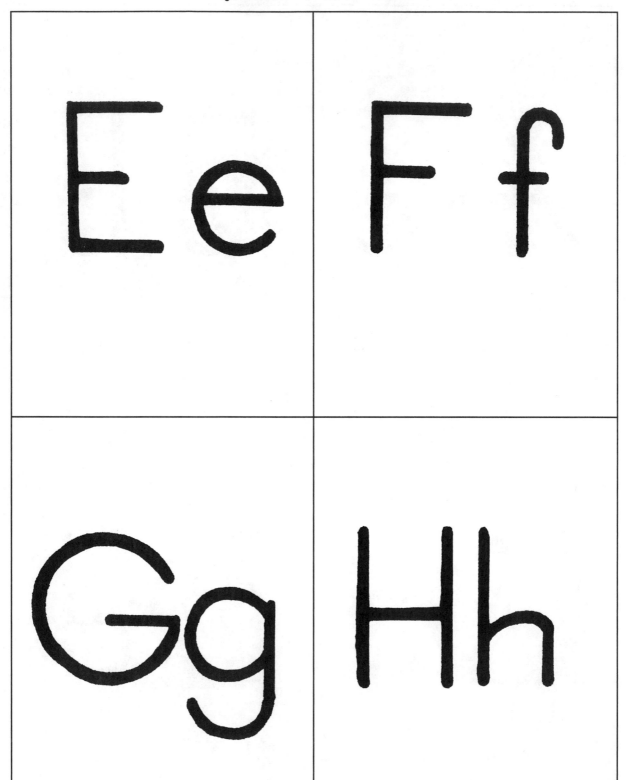

Alphabet Flash Cards

I i

J j

K k

L l

Alphabet Flash Cards

Mm	Nn
Oo	Pp

Alphabet Flash Cards

Qq

Rr

Ss

Tt

Alphabet Flash Cards

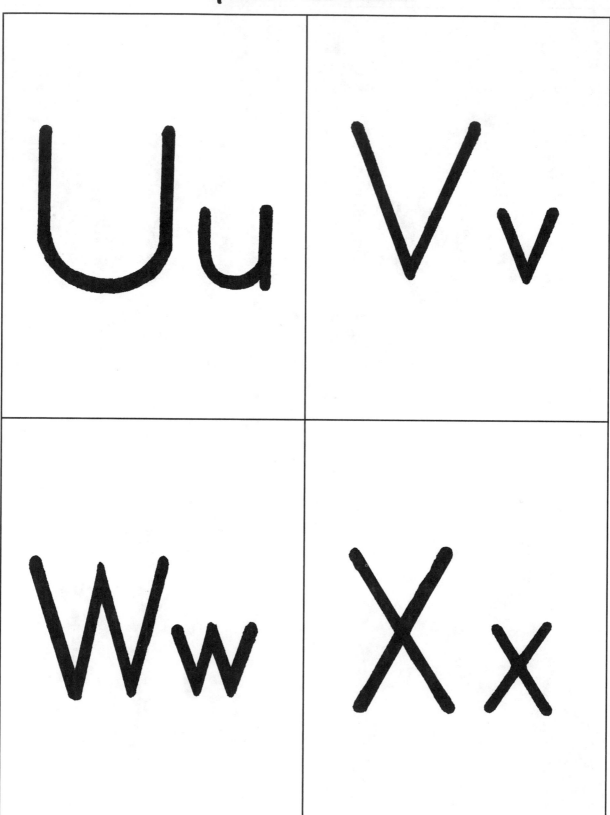

Alphabet Flash Cards

Y y | Z z

Alphabet Game Cards

A	a	B	b
C	c	D	d
E	e	F	f
G	g	H	h

Alphabet Game Cards

I	i	J	j
K	k	L	l
M	m	N	n
O	o	P	p

Alphabet Game Cards

Q	q	R	r
S	s	T	t
U	u	V	v
W	w	X	x

Alphabet Game Cards

Y	y	Z	z

Alphabet Bingo

		FREE		

Alphabet Desk Chart

Aa Bb Cc Dd Ee Ff Gg Hh Ii
Jj Kk Ll Mm Nn Oo Pp Qq Rr
Ss Tt Uu Vv Ww Xx Yy Zz

Name_____ Date_____

Alphabet Assessment

L	P	Y	A	K	N	X
H	S	Z	F	D	E	O
W	R	B	V	U	J	C
Q	I	M	T	G		

g	t	m	l	q	c	j
u	v	b	r	w	o	e
d	f	z	s	h	x	n
k	a	y	p	i		

Lesson 7-3: Alphabetical Order

Objectives: The student will understand the concept of alphabetical order. The student will learn to put words in alphabetical order.

Vocabulary: alphabetical order

Materials: Activity Sheet 7–3; Pencil; Alphabet chart; Alphabet letter cards; Index cards or pieces of paper (make word cards for the following words: apple, boy, cat, dog, Aaron, about, act, add, each, eagle, ear, eat); Tape

Teaching Note: It is important to use the term "alphabetical order" as opposed to "ABC order." This is the correct academic term and is the language that will be used in the student's classroom.

Directions:

1. Place the letter cards in alphabetical order on the board. Point and say, "These letters are in alphabetical order. They are just the way you see them in the alphabet." Ask one student to read the alphabet from the chart and another to read the letter cards. Ask, "Are the letters in the same place (order)?" (**Response:** Yes.)

2. Next, take a sequential series of letters from the board and give one to each student (e.g., a, b, c, d, e). Tell the students to stand in alphabetical order. Continue this procedure with another series of letters. Then take letters that are not in a sequential series and ask the student to stand in alphabetical order (e.g., b, g, k, o, t).

3. Secure the word cards *apple*, *boy*, *cat*, and *dog* to the board. Read the words with the student. Explain that words can be put in alphabetical order by looking at the order of their letters. Say, "We look at the first letter of the word." Point to the first letter on the word cards and ask the student to read the first letter with you, "a, b, c, d." Now say, "These words are in alphabetical order." Now, take the words, give each one to a different student, and ask the students to stand in alphabetical order according to the word he/she is holding.

4. Next, secure these word cards to the board: *Aaron*, *about*, *act*, *add*. Read the words with the student. Point to the first letter of each word and say, "A, A, A, A. The first letter is the same." Explain that when that happens we look at the second letter and use that to put the words in alphabetical order. Point to the second letter of each word and ask the student to say them with you ("a, b,c,d"). Take the words from the board, give them to different students, and ask the students to put the words back on the board in alphabetical order.

293

5. Next, secure these word cards to the board: *each*, *eagle*, *ear*, *eat*. Read the words with the student. Ask the student, "What letter do we look at to put these words in alphabetical order?" (**Response:** The third letter.) Take the word cards from the board and give them to different students. Ask the student to put the words in alphabetical order.

6. Write the students' first names on the board (not in alphabetical order). Ask the students to stand in alphabetical order. Continue this with the last names, and ask them to stand in alphabetical order.

7. Give the student Activity Sheet 7–3. **Answer Key:** 1. abc, jkl, pqr, mno; 2. aunt, ball, cry, dear, east; 3. about across, add, after, again; 4. baby, back, bad, ball, band; 5. Answers will vary.

Extension Activities:

1. *For a group:* Put letters of the alphabet in a container. Each student closes his/her eyes and takes several letters. The first one to put his/her letters in alphabetical order wins. *Variation:* Use words.

2. Give the student a list of words. Ask him/her to highlight the letter that will determine alphabetical order (e.g., dinner, dime, diet—the student will highlight third letter). Then the student should put the words in alphabetical order.

Name_____ Date_____

Alphabetical Order

1. **Play alphabet tic-tac-toe. Look at each tic-tac-toe game. Find three letters in each game that are in alphabetical order. Draw a line through them. You can go down, across, or corner to corner.**

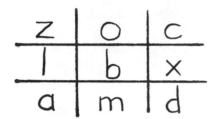

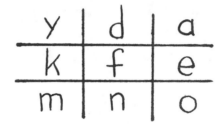

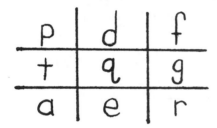

2. **Put these words in alphabetical order. (Circle) the letter that you will use.**

   cry, aunt, dear, east, ball

   _____ _____ _____ _____ _____

3. add, about, after, across, again

   _____ _____ _____ _____ _____

4. band, ball, back, baby, bad

   _____ _____ _____ _____ _____

5. **Put the first names of your classmates in alphabetical order. Use the back of this paper.**

Lesson 7-4: Rules for Capital Letters

Objective: The student will learn basic rules for using capital letters.

Vocabulary: capital letter; letter; initials; greetings; closings

Materials: Activity Sheet 7–4; Pencil; Copy of a newspaper article

Teaching Note: These are basic rules. More detailed capitalization rules can be presented as the student progresses. You may want to make a copy of the rules to give to the student.

Directions:

1. Say to the student, "There are certain times when you will need to use capital letters. Sometimes a capital letter is the first letter or sometimes it stands alone."

2. Write the following rules on the board. Give examples to support each rule.

Use capital letters for:

1. **The word I.**   Do I have to go?

2. **Initials.**   Mary Smith's initials are M.S.   Directions: North—N   South—S

   East—E   West—W

3. **The first letter of a person's name.**   Rutila Sanchez

4. **The first letter in the name of streets, cities, states, countries.** Maple Street, Chicago, Texas, Mexico

5. **The first letter in the name of days, months, and holidays.**   Monday, November, Halloween

6. **The beginning word of each sentence.**   The dog is barking.   Five cats are howling.

7. **Greetings and closings of letters.**   Dear, Sincerely

---

3. Give the student a copy of a newspaper article. Ask him/her to circle the capital letters and explain what rule applies.

4. Give the student a copy of Activity Sheet 7–4. The student is asked to rewrite sentences using capital letters appropriately in situations pertaining to the above rules. **Answer Key:** (1.) Do I have to go to Dallas, Texas? (2.) Robert Brown's initials are R.B. (3.) My new friend is Hung Tu. (4.) Her address is 122 Avon Street, Detroit, Michigan. (5.) My favorite holiday is Halloween. (6.) My birthday is Thursday, May 19. (7.) Dear Sandy, I would love to come to your party. Sincerely, Maria

Name_____ Date_____

Capitals, Please!

Rewrite the following sentences using capital letters where they belong.

1. do i have to go to dallas, texas?

   _____

   _____

2. robert brown's initials are r.b.

   _____

   _____

3. my new friend is hung tu.

   _____

   _____

4. her address is 122 avon street, detroit, michigan.

   _____

   _____

5. my favorite holiday is halloween.

   _____

   _____

6. my birthday is thursday, may 19.

   _____

   _____

7. dear sandy, i would love to come to your party. sincerely, maria

   _____,

   _____

   _____

   _____,

   _____

Lesson 7-5: Tips for Teaching Handwriting

Objectives: The student will learn the correct posture, pencil grip, and position of the paper when printing or writing. The student will learn how to correctly form the letters of the alphabet, both in manuscript and cursive writing. The student will understand the difference between the terms *print* and *write*. The student will be able to recognize letters formed in *book* print. The student will learn correct spacing between words.

Vocabulary: print; write; cursive writing; book print; grip; slant; circle; forward; backward; straight; tail; line; legibly

Materials: Activity Sheets 7–5A through 7–5E; Pencil; Paper

Teaching Note: Introduce the letters one at a time; include both the capital and the lower-case form. A practice paper has been included as Activity Sheet 7–5E. Make additional copies and use as practice paper for handwriting. Be sure to model how to "connect" the cursive letters.

Directions:

Model the following processes for the student and ask him/her to repeat the action.

1. *Pencil grip and paper position.* Use a pencil and piece of paper to model the correct pencil grip and paper position for the student. Ask the student to repeat the actions. Emphasize the idea that the hand not holding the pencil holds the paper in place.

2. *Good posture for writing.* Model good posture for writing: back straight, feet flat on the floor.

3. *Basic strokes for printing.* Before the student begins printing letters, ask him/her to complete Activity Sheet 7–5A. Model the correct method of formation.

4. *Manuscript alphabet practice sheet.* Model the formation of each letter and ask the student to complete Activity Sheet 7–5B.

5. *Cursive alphabet practice sheet.* Model the formation of each letter and ask the student to complete Activity Sheet 7–5C.

6. *Numbers.* Model the formation of the numerals 1–10. Ask the student to complete Activity Sheet 7–5D.

7. *Spacing.* Model the correct amount of space that should be left between words. For younger students, use the example of one finger space.

Extension Activity: Have the student form letters and numbers in clay, sand, with fingerpaint, pudding, etc.

Name_____ Date_____

Basic Strokes for Printing

Name_____ Date_____

Manuscript Alphabet

Trace. Then print.

Name_____ Date_____

Manuscript Alphabet

Trace. Then print.

N n n	o o o
O O O	o o o
P P P	p p p
Q O O	q q q
R R R	r r r
S S S	s s s
T T T	t t t
U U U	u u u
V V V	v v v
W W W	w w w
X X X	x x x
Y Y Y	y y y
Z Z Z	z z z

3

Name_____ Date_____

Cursive Alphabet

Trace. Then write.

Name_____ Date_____

Cursive Alphabet

Trace. Then write.

Name____________________________ Date____________________________

Numbers

Trace. Then practice.

1 1 1

2 2 2

3 3 3

4 4 4

5 5 5

6 6 6

7 7 7

8 8 8

9 9 9

10 10 10

1 2 3 4 5 6 7 8 9 10

Name_____ Date_____

Practice Paper

Section 8

Introduction to Literacy

This section provides you with the basic concepts necessary to introduce the literacy process in English. One very important factor to the success of the student is his/her literacy level in the first language. It is the foundation upon which literacy in the second language is built. It would be very advantageous to obtain this information not only for ESL class but for other teachers as well. In some cases, this can be a challenge particularly if former school records are not available. The following suggestions may help you get this information: obtain former school records; speak with parents or relatives about the student's progress and curriculum in school; ask a native speaker to interview the student and determine the type and content of curriculum that was required in the student's native country; conduct an evaluation (writing sample, oral reading passage, comprehension questions, and story retell) by an interpreter or native speaker (preferably a professional person who can gauge the student's level of competency in academic first language).

It would also be helpful to know the literacy level of the student's parents or primary caregiver. The literacy level in the home can indicate the student's exposure to and experience with early literacy in his/her native language. A solid literacy foundation in the home can be an indication of future success in the second language.

Section 8, Introduction to Literacy, gives you basic guidelines, tools, and information to begin the English literacy process for levels Zero through High Beginner. Some ESL students may have had some exposure to English in their native countries, but most have some "gaps" in the skill areas that need to be addressed. The lessons included in this section can help you accomplish this.

It is very important to involve the ESL student in all the processes of literacy: reading, writing, speaking, listening, and thinking. You are encouraged to accommodate lessons and assignments in the content areas to meet the needs and language level of the ESL student. Participating and practicing literacy skills in authentic learning situations is key to the student's success. Literacy terms and processes used frequently in the classroom should be understood by the ESL student.

Note: If your school participates in a sustained silent reading (SSR) time, encourage the ESL student to bring literature from his/her native country. It is an excellent opportunity for the ESL student to participate in a literacy activity and remind others that he/she is a literate student, who happens to be in the process of learning a new language. It also serves as a stress reliever and enhances the self-esteem of the ESL student.

Incorporating the use of a *Daily Writing Journal* in your classroom is an invaluable writing tool and also serves as an excellent vehicle for assessment. Even at the beginning stages of literacy, journal writing enables a student to communicate thoughts and ideas. The following are some suggestions for implementing the use of journal writing into your classroom:

- Have the student use a simple spiral notebook as a daily journal. It keeps papers secure and in sequence.

- Ask the student to date each entry.

- Encourage the beginning literacy student to draw pictures and write beginning sounds or simple decoding underneath the picture. Ask the student to tell about the picture. You, or a journal partner, can then write the correct spelling or dictated sentences on the journal page. The ESL student then reads the words/sentences on the journal page.

- Set aside time every day for journal writing. The beginning of class works well; it provides a time for the student to become focused and settled.

- Have a specific topic or idea (reaction to events, opinions, challenges, problem solving) for the student to write about. For the beginning student topics such as family, native country, friends, and school work well. Write the topic on the board each morning or draw a picture. If the student requests to write about an alternative topic, allow him/her to do so.

- Ask students to share their journal writing with the class or a journal partner. Don't force a student to share, however, particularly if he/she is shy or not yet ready to do so.

- Use the journal as an assessment tool. Collect the student journals periodically and assess the progress of the student's literacy skills. Compare early and recent entries. Look for strengths and challenges the student may be experiencing regarding the language process.

Literacy Pretest-Posttest

Student:_____   Grade:_____

Date: _____

1. Ask the student to identify the letters that are vowels and consonants.

2. Administer the Alphabet Assessment, Activity Sheet 7–2G. Ask the student to produce the sound of each letter. Circle the correct responses.

3. Administer a sight-word evaluation. Use Activity Sheet 8–13B, "First Hundred Instant Words." Circle the correct responses.

4. Say these words: **run, sit, man.** Ask the student to respond with a rhyming word for each one. Write responses under the word.

5. Ask the student to compare these circles using the word **big.** (big, bigger, biggest).

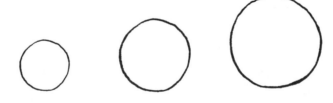

6. Point to the pictures and say, "One pencil. Two _____."
   Response: **pencils.** "One child. Three _____." Response: **children.**

7. Ask the student to put the proper punctuation in this sentence:

   did carlos daniel and jose make the basketball team

8. Ask the student to write the verb **play** in the present, past, and future tenses.

Lesson 8-1: Position–Beginning, First, Middle, End, Last

Objective: The student will learn the vocabulary and position of the terms: Beginning, First, Middle, End, Last.

Vocabulary: beginning, first, middle, end, last

Materials: Activity Sheet 8–1; 4 squares of colored paper (1 red, 1 green, 1 blue, 1 yellow); Clear plastic bingo chips, one for each child; Paper with the letters **c a t** on it, one sheet for each student (the letters should be large and spaced so that a bingo chip can cover one letter); Black marker; Tape to secure paper to the chalkboard; Index cards; Pencil

Teaching Note: This is an important concept for beginning literacy. The terms "beginning"—"first" and "last"—"end" are used interchangeably in many books and by many teachers.

Directions:

1. Ask three students to stand in line. Then say, "(Student's name) is **first**. (Student's name) is in the **middle**. (Student's name) is **last**." Ask the students to repeat. Ask other students to do the same until everyone has had a turn. Others identify who is first, middle, and last in line.

2. Put three colored pieces of paper in a row on the board. (Secure with tape.) Place them in this order: red, green, blue. Say, "Red is first, green is in the middle, blue is last." Ask the students to repeat.

3. Take the colors down and ask different students to put them back in a specific order, e.g., "Put blue first, red in the middle, green last." Change the order.

4. Next, place four colors on the board: red, green, blue, yellow. This time explain that two colors are in the middle. Identify the colors. Change the order of the colors and ask the students to identify the first, middle, and last colors.

5. Use the terms *beginning* and *end*. Put three colors in a row and say, "Red is at the **beginning**, green is in the **middle**, blue is at the **end**." Ask the student to repeat. Now, change the order and ask the student to put the colors in the correct location. Use *beginning*, *middle*, and *end* as location words.

6. Explain that we can do the same thing with letters. Secure the letters **d o g** (written on index cards) to the board. Say, "This is the word *dog*." Point to the first letter and say, "**D** is the **first** letter. It is at the **beginning** of the word." Point to the *o* and say, "**O** is the **middle** letter. It is in the **middle** of the word." Point to the *g* and say, "**G** is the **last** letter. It is at the **end** of the word." Ask the student to repeat.

7. Now, ask the student the following questions:

What is the first letter?   What is the beginning letter?
What is the middle letter?   What letter is in the middle?
What is the last letter?   What letter ends the word?

8. On a sheet of white paper write (with marker) the word **c a t**. Write the letters large enough and leave enough space so that a bingo chip can cover one letter. Give each student a copy. Then ask the student to cover the *beginning* letter with the bingo chip, then the *middle* letter, then the letter at the *end* of the word. Say the positions in random order and ask the student to cover the appropriate letter. Also use the alternate vocabulary words of *first* and *last*. Write other words and continue with this procedure.

9. Give the student a copy of Activity Sheet 8–1. He/she will be asked to identify letters according to their position in a word.

Extension Activity: Give the student plastic letters. Write three columns on a sheet of paper: **begins/first**, **middle**, **last/end**. Give the student a list of words and ask him/her to put the letters in the correct position.

Name_____ Date_____

Where Am I?

1. **Circle the beginning letter of each word.**

   look   see   house   little   book   desk

2. **Circle the middle letter of each word.**

   cat   box   cry   day   boy   the

3. **Circle the last letter of each word.**

   pan   cup   big   stay   fire   word

4. **Circle the first letter of each word.**

   pink   blue   green   red   black   gray

5. **Circle the middle letters of each word.**

   dress   card   find   bird   rock   stop

6. **Circle the letter that is at the end of each word.**

   sock   tree   walk   bug   jump   feel

7. **Circle the letters.**

Beginning or First	**Middle**	**End or Last**
paper	run	cook
happy	play	game

Lesson 8-2: Letter Name–Letter Sound

Objectives: The student will understand the meaning of the terms "letter name" and "letter sound." The student will learn the difference between letter name and letter sound.

Vocabulary: letter name, letter sound

Materials: Activity Sheet 8–2; Pencil; Small drum or musical instrument (triangle); Small bell; Picture of lion or other wild animal; Picture of dog or cat, or stuffed animal of each

Teaching Note: The concepts of letter name and letter sound can be very confusing for an ESL student, especially if the native language is not phonetic. This is a very important concept for the student to master.

Directions:

1. Hold up the drum and ask, "What is the name of this instrument?" (a drum) Now say, "This drum makes a sound." (**Gesture:** Point to your ear.) Ask the student to beat on the drum to make a sound. Then review, "The name is drum. The sound is (beat the drum)." Ask the student to repeat.

2. Follow the same procedure with the bell and the pictures of the animals. Ask the student to repeat the sentences: "The name is _____. The sound is _____."

3. Now give the student a copy of Activity Sheet 8–2. The student will be asked to match the name and sound to a picture. It may be necessary to help with reading the name and making the sound. This can be done as a directed group activity or individually.

Extension Activities:

1. Play "What am I?" Ask the student to think of other things that have a name and make a sound. The student then makes the sound and the others must guess the name.

2. Read *Polar Bear, Polar Bear, What Do You Hear?* by Bill Martin, Jr., with illustrations by Eric Carle (Holt, 1991).

Name_____ Date_____

Name—Sound

Look at the picture. Draw a line to the name of the picture and then to the sound it makes.

Name		Sound

| Bird | | Oom-pa-pa |

| Lion | | Tweet |

| Tuba | | S-S-S-S-S |

| Cow | | Gr-r-r-r-r |

| Telephone | | Moo |

| Snake | | Vroooooom |

| Race car | | Ring, Ring |

Lesson 8-3: "Pardon Me, Are You a Vowel or a Consonant?"

● ●

Objective: The student will learn the terms *vowel* and *consonant*. The student will recognize the difference between a vowel and a consonant.

Materials: Activity Sheet 8–3; Blue and red colored pencils/markers; Alphabet flash cards from Lesson 7–2 (one for each letter of the alphabet, except Y—make two Y cards); Tape

Teaching note: This lesson should be presented before the consonant and vowel lessons are introduced. Knowing the terms *vowel* and *consonant* are important in the early literacy process. These are the terms used in reading programs and by classroom teachers. It is an excellent opportunity for categorization activities.

Directions:

1. Secure the 26 letters of the alphabet on the board or place them on the floor or table. Point to the letters and ask, "What are these called?" (**Response:** Letters)

2. Ask different students to get the letters A, E, I, O, U, Y. Ask the students to stand in a line holding the letters. Then explain that these letters are a special group of letters called *vowels*. Write the word "vowels" on the board. Point to and read the word *vowels*. Ask, "What are these letters called?" (**Response:** Vowels) Ask, "What letters are vowels?" (**Response:** A, E, I, O, U, Y) Ask the students to secure the letters A, E, I, O, U, Y on the board under the word *vowels*.

3. (Place the second Y card on the board with the remaining consonant letters.) Point to the letters and say, "These letters are called *consonants*. Any letter that is not a vowel is a *consonant*." Write the word "consonants" over the remaining letters. Ask, "What are these letters called?" (**Response:** Consonants) "What letters are consonants?" (**Response:** [Students name the consonant letters])

4. Next, point to the two Y cards and explain that Y can be a vowel or a consonant. Point back and forth. Tell the student that when we say the vowels, we say "A-E-I-O-U and sometimes Y." (**Gesture:** When you say the word "sometimes," hold your hand flat and shake it back and forth.) Ask the student, "What are the vowels?" (**Response:** A, E, I, O, U and sometimes Y)

5. Next, give the students various letters of the alphabet and give these commands: "Vowels—jump. Consonants—sit." Change alphabet letters and continue with this type of action command for each group.

6. Remove all the letters from the board and give a few to each student. Then ask the students to put the letters in two groups: vowels and consonants.

7. Give the student a copy of Activity Sheet 8–3. The student will be asked to identify vowels and consonants. The student will need a blue and a red crayon or colored pencils.

Answer Key: 2. | cfgkmt | | aei y | | wpsr y | | ou |

Extension Activities:

1. Give the student a copy of a magazine and ask him/her to highlight the vowels one color and the consonants another color.

2. *Find the Vowels.* Take 26 alphabet cards, turn them face down, and mix them up. Each student takes a turn turning over a card and naming it. If it is a vowel, he/she keeps it. If it is a consonant, it goes back into the pile. The student with the most vowels at the end wins.

Name_____ Date_____

VOWELS and CONSONANTS

Vowels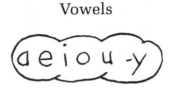

Consonants

1. **Look at the alphabet letters. Circle the vowels red and the consonants blue. Put two circles around Y.**

a	b	c	d	e	f	g
h	i	j	k	l	m	n
o	p	q	r	s	t	u
v	w	x	y	z		

2. **Look at the letters on the balls. Each juggler has vowels and consonants. Write the letters in the correct box. The Y's are done for you. Color the vowels red and the consonants blue.**

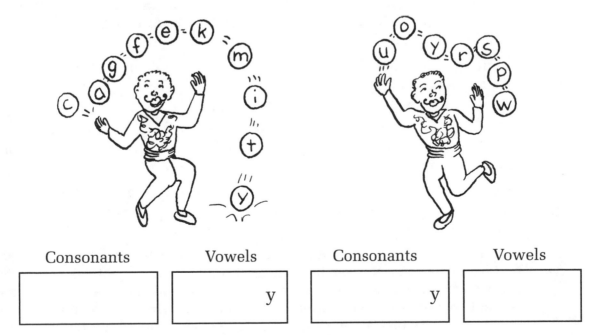

Consonants	Vowels	Consonants	Vowels
	y	y	

3. **Write your first and last name on the line. Circle the vowels red and the consonants blue.**

_____

Lesson 8-4: Teaching Consonants

Objective: The student will learn the identification of letters that are consonants and each individual sound.

Vocabulary: consonants

Materials: Activity Sheets 8–4A and 8–4B; Magazines; Glue; Scissors; Pencil

Teaching Note: The sound of each individual consonant should be taught in isolation and then as a beginning sound. ESL students can become confused when the sound is not isolated and can confuse it with the word. Lessons 8–1 and 8–2 should be taught before letter sounds are attempted. The teaching of consonants will cover a number of weeks.

Directions:

Give the student a copy of Activity Sheet 8–4A, the Consonant Chart.

1. Say, "I am going to show you a special group of letters called *consonants.* Each letter has a name and makes a sound." (Point to your ear.) "Some consonants have two sounds." Explain that the capital letter and the lower-case letter share the same sound.

2. Tell the student that all of the letters on the chart are called *consonants.* Ask the student to "name" all of the letters that are consonants. Explain that the number 2 on some of the cards means that letter has two sounds.

The following part of the lesson is an example of a lesson plan to teach one consonant sound.

3. Go to the letter B, point to it, and say, "B makes the sound ____." (Say the sound for b.) Ask the student to repeat the sound of B. Next say, "It is the sound you hear at the beginning of the word *book.*" (Point to the picture on the consonant card.) Ask the student to repeat the word *book.*

4. Together with the student brainstorm words that begin with B. Ask the student to find objects in the classroom that begin with B. Write a list on the chalkboard. Share.

5. Give the student a copy of Activity Sheet 8–4B. Write the letter Bb in the middle of the page, and ask the student to find magazine pictures of objects or items that begin with b, cut them out, and glue them in the boxes. The student should write the word under the picture. Help with spelling, if necessary. (If magazines are not available, the student may draw the pictures.) The student then shares his/her words and pictures with the class.

6. Continue with this procedure for the other consonants.

Extension Activities:

1. Play "Going to Grandma's House." Students sit in a circle. One student begins by saying, "I'm going to Grandma's house and I'm taking a _____." The item must begin with a B sound. Each student must think of something that begins with a B sound and cannot say an item that has already been chosen.

2. Play "I've Got a Secret." Students sit in a circle. You whisper a word that begins with a B sound in one student's ear. That student whispers it to the person sitting next to him/her. The last person in the circle announces the word. (This game can have some very funny results!)

3. Play this alphabet rhyme. Use the sound that is being taught in the lesson for that day. The student must complete the rhyme by supplying names and words that begin with that sound, e.g., "B my name is *Betty* and my husband's (or wife's) name is *Bob*. We come from *Boston* with a carload full of *baskets*." Each student takes a turn and cannot use words that have already been chosen.

4. Play "Thumbs Up, Thumbs Down." Say a word. If it begins with a consonant sound that was taught, the student points his/her thumb up. If the word does not begin with the sound that was taught, the student points his/her thumb down.

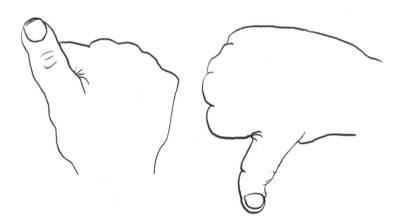

Name_____ Date_____

Consonant Chart

B b	² **C c** hard	² **C c** soft	**D d**
book	cat	cent	dog
F f	² **G g** hard	² **G g** soft	**H h**
fish	goat	giraffe	hat
J j	**K k**	**L l**	**M m**
jacket	key	lion	moon
N n	**P p**	**Q q**	**R r**
net	pig	queen	ring

Name_____ Date_____

Consonant Chart

S s	**T t**	**V v**	**W w**
<u>s</u>un	<u>t</u>urtle	<u>v</u>ase	<u>w</u>indow
X x	**Y y**	**Z z**	
bo<u>x</u>	<u>y</u>awn	<u>z</u>ebra	

Name_____ Date_____

Consonant Boxes

Write the consonant in the circle. Look in magazines and find pictures of objects that begin with that sound. Cut out the pictures and glue them in the boxes. Write the word under the picture.

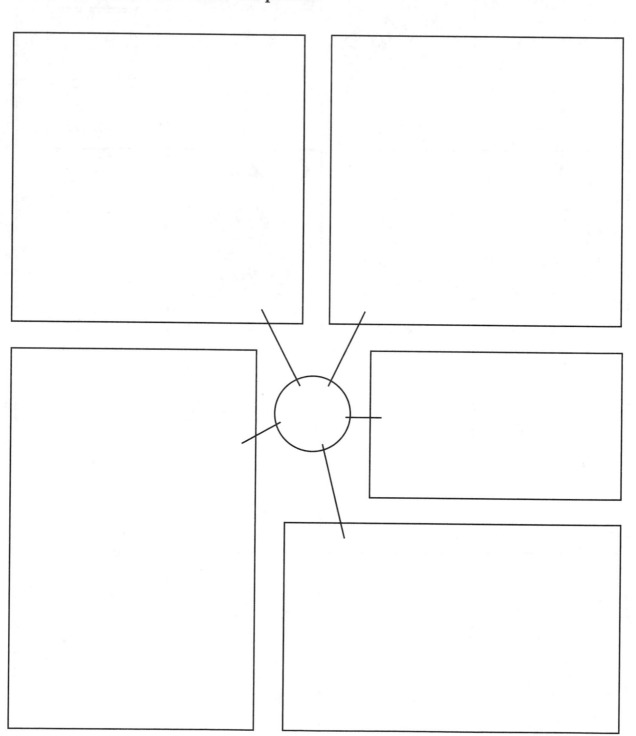

Lesson 8-5: Teaching Vowels

• •

Objectives: The student will learn that **a,e,i,o,u and sometimes y** are called vowels. The student will know that all words contain vowels. The student will learn the difference between the long and short sounds of vowels.

Vocabulary: vowel, long, short

Materials: Activity Sheet 8–5; Activity Sheet 8–6 (from Lesson 8–6); Pencil; Magazines and newspapers

Teaching Note: One of the most difficult decoding skills for the ESL student to learn is the short vowel sound. Depending upon the student's native language, some sounds are very difficult to reproduce or even "hear." This process takes time and a great deal of practice and review. When teaching the vowel sounds, say them in isolation first, then as part of a word.

Directions:

Short Vowel Sounds

Here is a sample lesson for teaching short vowel sounds.

1. Give the student a copy of Activity Sheet 8–5. Explain that there is a special group of letters called *vowels*. The vowel letters are: *a,e,i,o,u, and sometimes y*. Ask the student to repeat. Explain that all words have at least one vowel in them.

2. Tell the student that he/she will learn the *short sound of a*. Explain that vowels have two sounds: a short sound and a long sound. Point to the vowel card that shows the short sound of *a*. Say, "Short *a* sounds like ă." (Make the sound in isolation.) Ask the student to repeat. Now tell the student that short *a* is the sound that is heard at the beginning of the word *apple*.

3. Brainstorm other words that begin with the short *a* sound: ant, ask, alligator, ax, astronaut, add.

4. Ask the student to listen and raise his/her hand when you say a word that begins with the short *a* sound. Randomly, mix in words that begin with other sounds.

5. Next, use Activity Sheet 8–6 (from Lesson 8–6). Write *a* on the blending sheet. Continue with the blending procedure and ask the student to blend *a* as the middle sound in words.

6. After the blending procedure is done, write a list of *a* words, e.g., cat, tab, add, am, and. Help the student decode them.

7. Ask the student to *listen and write*. (Say words that were used for blending and decoding and with the short *a* sound.) Say the word and ask the student to write it. Check for accuracy. Follow the same procedure for the rest of the vowels.

8. NOTE: When teaching the short vowel sounds in depth, *e* and *i* should not be taught in sequence. The two sounds are very similar and can be confusing if taught together.

Long Vowel Sounds

Here is a sample lesson for teaching long vowel sounds.

9. Ask the student, "What is your name?" (Student says name.) Now ask, "What is the name of this letter?" (Point to *A*, student says the letter name *A*.) Now say, "When a vowel is long, it says its name: A,E,I,O,U." You can clap and say this in rhythm. Ask the student to repeat. Now model the long vowel sounds. Ask the student to repeat.

10. Point to the vowel card *A* and say, "The long sound of *a* is *ā*." Ask the student to repeat. Now say, "It is the sound you hear at the beginning of the word *ape*." Ask the student to repeat, "*a—ape*." Follow the same procedure for each long vowel sound.

11. Practice the two most consistent long vowel phonics rules: (1.) When two vowels go walking, the first one does the talking. (seat, rain, road, soap, tree) (2.) Silent *e* rule: When a word has two vowels and one is a silent *e* at the end of the word, the other vowel is usually long. (made, cute, time) Brainstorm examples of these rules and ask the student to decode the words. A third rule is: When a vowel is the last letter in a one-syllable word, it is usually long. (go, no, so, me, he, hi)

12. Explain that *Y* is sometimes a vowel. Tell the student to use these guidelines: (1.) When *Y* comes at the end of a one-syllable word, it usually sounds like long *i*. (cry, shy, fly, fry, my) (2.) When *Y* comes at the end of a word with more than one syllable, it usually sounds like long *e*. (puppy, funny, jelly, baby)

Extension Activities:

1. Give the student a page from a magazine or newspaper. Give specific vowel sounds for the student to highlight.

2. Make a word wall of silent *e* words. As the student comes across silent *e* words, he/she can write them on cards and add them to the word wall. Do the same for the rule, "When two vowels go walking, the first one does the talking" or the vowel *Y* words. This can also be done for the short vowel sounds.

Name_____ Date_____

Vowel Chart—Long and Short

A a	A a	E e	E e
ăpple	āpe	ĕlephant	ēagle

I i	I i	O o	O o
ĭnch	īce	ŏctopus	ōpen

U u	U u	Y y (i)	Y y (e)
ŭmbrella	ūniform	cr<u>y</u>	sunn<u>y</u>

Lesson 8-6: Blending Sounds

Objective: The student will understand how to blend the sounds of letters to form a word.

Vocabulary: blending

Materials: Activity Sheet 8–6; Pencil; Transparency of Activity Sheet 8–6; Overhead projector (or write the letters and the format of the blending sheet on the board)

Teaching Notes:

1. Blending sounds can be difficult for some ESL students, especially those whose first language is not phonetic or exhibits extensive linguistic distance from English. A list of English sounds not in other languages is included at the end of this lesson. It is an excellent reference when teaching phonics.

2. The exercise in this lesson can be adapted for a combination of blending situations. The blending sheet is designed to be used with all the short vowel sounds (also "ee"). For variety, you may want to format your own blending sheet and change the beginning and final consonant sounds.

Directions:

1. Show a transparency of Activity Sheet 8–6. In the center print a vowel of your choice. This will represent the short sound of the vowel. Give the student a copy of Activity Sheet 8–6 and ask him/her to print the vowel sound on the line in the middle of the page.

2. Explain to the student that words can be made by blending sounds. Point to the consonant letters printed down the left side of the activity sheet and explain that these are the beginning sounds. Model each sound. Ask the student to point and repeat each sound.

3. Next, point to the vowel in the middle of the page and say, "This is the middle sound. It is the short sound of the vowel _____." Model the sound. Ask the student to point and repeat the sound. Explain that this will be the same middle sound for each word.

4. Go back to the beginning column of consonants, point to, and blend each initial consonant sound with the short vowel sound (point); e.g., ba, ha. Ask the student to point and repeat the sounds.

5. Next, go to the right-hand column of consonants, point to, and model each sound. Ask the student to repeat the sounds.

6. (This last step should be done more quickly, in a smooth blending pace and moving your finger in a smooth connected line to each sound.) Ask the stu-

dent to blend the sounds with you. Go back to the first column, point to a consonant, and say the sound; point to the vowel, and say the sound; point to the ending consonant, and say the sound. Say the word. (**NOTE:** Be careful not to ask the student to "spell" the words that have been blended. Spelling is a sound-segmenting activity and the opposite process of blending. It can cause confusion. Also explain that actual words will not always be made, e.g., mep, sen, hig, bot.) Continue this procedure using various combinations. Ask the student to practice blending sounds into words using his/her blending sheet.

7. **Reading:** Write a list of words on the board that the student has previously blended. Ask the student to read the words. Then ask the student to copy the words on the back of the blending sheet. The student can then practice reading the words.

ENGLISH SOUNDS NOT IN OTHER LANGUAGES

Language	Sounds Not Part of the Language
Chinese	b cd d dg g oa sh *s* th *th* v z
French	ch ee j ng oo th *th*
Greek	aw ee I oo schwa
Italian	a ar dg h I ng th *th* schwa
Japanese	dg f I th *th* oo v schwa
Spanish	dg j sh th z

Extension Activity: Give the student plastic letters or letter cards (see Lesson 7–2). Ask him/her to make as many words as possible using a specific combination of letters. The team or student with the most words wins a treat or privilege.

Name_____ Date_____

Let's Get Together!

b   t

m   p

h   _____   g
              (Vowel)

f   d

s   n

Lesson 8-7: Seven Important Phonics Rules

Objective: The student will be introduced to seven basic phonics rules.

Vocabulary: hard, soft, VC pattern, VV pattern, VCE pattern, CV pattern, R rule

Materials: Activity Sheet 8–7; Pen/pencil

Teaching Note: English is a very inconsistent language. Many phonics rules do not apply a large percentage of the time. The seven rules presented in this lesson are considered by experts as the most consistent phonics rules. It is helpful for the ESL student to be aware of these rules and know how to apply them; this will require practice and reinforcement on a regular basis during authentic reading situations.

Directions:

1. Give the student a copy of Activity Sheet 8–7. Explain the following phonics rules:

   - The soft *c* sound: cent, city. The hard *c* sound: car, cat.

   - The soft *g* sound: gem, giraffe. The hard *g* sound: game, go.

   - A single vowel letter followed by a consonant letter, digraph, or blend usually has a short sound: hat, bath, fast.

   - When two vowels go walking, the first one does the talking: seat, boat.

   - The silent *e* pattern. When a one-syllable word has two vowels, one of which is a silent *e*, the vowel is usually long: sale, nice.

   - A single vowel at the end of a one-syllable word is usually long: go, my.

   - The letter *r* modifies the long or short sound of a preceding vowel: car, short, first.

2. Ask the student to decode the words in #1 on Activity Sheet 8–7. The student works with classmates for #2.

Name_____ Date_____

Seven Basic Phonics Rules

- The soft *c* sound: cent, city. The hard *c* sound: car, cat.

- The soft *g* sound: gem, giraffe. The hard *g* sound: game, go.

- A single vowel letter followed by a consonant letter, digraph, or blend usually has a short sound: hat, bath, fast.

- When two vowels go walking, the first one does the talking: seat, boat.

- The silent *e* pattern. When a one-syllable word has two vowels, one of which is a silent *e*, the vowel is usually long: sale, nice.

- A single vowel at the end of a one-syllable word is usually long: go, my.

- The letter 'r' modifies the long or short sound of a preceding vowel: car, short, first.

Part One: Read the following words. Use the rules to help you.

carpet	gift	cup	coat	vote	cry
far	circle	germ	kite	so	barn
cent	gave	meat	yard	why	jump

Part Two: Work with a partner. Find three words that show each phonic rule. Use books from your classroom and make a list.

_____

_____

_____

_____

_____

_____

_____

Lesson 8-8: Silent e

. . . .

Objective: The student will understand that when a *silent e* is added to the end of a word, the preceding vowel becomes long.

Vocabulary: silent e

Materials: Activity Sheet 8–8; Pencil; 8½ × 11 word cards for each word: mad, cub, cap, kit, can, mop, rob; 8½ × 11 word card with an *e* printed on it and a picture of the "quiet" sign

Directions:

1. Ask a student to come to the front of the room and hold the word card **mad**. Now ask, "What is this word?" (**Response:** mad)

2. Say, "I'm going to add a special letter to the end of the word *mad*. It is called a *silent e*. Silent e is very shy and doesn't say anything." (**Gesture:** Put your finger to your mouth in the "quiet" gesture.)

3. Hold the *silent e* card and stand next to the student who is holding the word card *mad*. Then say, "*Silent e* doesn't say anything but it is very strong." (**Gesture:** Flex a muscle.) "It makes the vowel closest to it say its name." Ask, "What is the vowel closest to *silent e*?" (**Response:** *a*) Ask, "How does *a* say its name?" (**Response:** $\bar{a}$) "What word is this now?" (**Response:** made) Say, "*Silent e* changed the word *mad* to *made*."

4. Continue with this process: One student holds the word card, the others identify it. Another student then holds the *silent e* card and the others identify the new word.

5. Give the student a copy of Activity Sheet 8–8. He/she will be asked to write words with the *silent e* and circle the vowel that is long. **Answer Key:** home, snake, time, cape, plane, game, bike, cane, smile, kite, rake, cake, rope, flake, same, pine.

Extension Activity: Write various letter combinations on index cards. Make a *silent e* card. The student places the *silent e* next to the combinations and decodes the word.

Name_____ Date_____

Silent e

Read the *silent e* words in the word box. Then look at the pictures and write the correct words. Circle the vowel that says its name.

cane	time	kite	smile	cape	pine	plane	home
snake	bike	rake	same	cake	rope	flake	game

Lesson 8-9: Digraphs: th, wh, sh, ch

● ●

Objective: The student will learn the sound of the digraphs: th, wh, sh, ch.

Materials: Activity Sheets 8–9A through 8–9D; Pencil; 1 plastic letter or paper letter of each: c, t, s, w, h; 3 index cards cut in half (write each blend on a separate card: ch, sh, wh, th); 1 jar or container with a lid

Teaching Note: This lesson combines the digraph sounds of *th, wh, sh,* and *ch.* Teaching suggestions for each digraph are included in the lesson. A separate activity sheet has been designed for each digraph sound.

Directions:

1. Follow these steps for teaching each digraph. ***Ch* will be used as a model.**

   • Ask a student to identify the individual letters of the digraph. (c,h)

   • Then ask a student to place the letters in a container.

   • Put on the lid and ask a student to shake the container. Then ask the student to open the container.

   • You put in the digraph card *ch.*

   • Ask a student to pull out the digraph card. Explain that when the letters *c* and *h* are mixed together, they make the new sound "ch" (digraph sound).

2. **Suggestions for teaching each digraph:**

   • *Ch*—It is fun to call this the cha-cha-cha sound. Model the phrase (with rhythm) "1-2 cha-cha-cha!" Then dance with it. Ask the students to repeat and dance. It's fun to do this with maracas. (The students shake the maracas as they say the phrase.) **Answer Key:** 1. (*Row 1*) —ch, —ch, ch—, ch/ch; (*Row 2*) ch—, —ch, ch—, —ch; (*Row 3*) ch—, —ch, ch—, ch—. 2. chimpanzee, chipmunk, chow, chinchilla.

   • *Sh*—Call this the quiet sound. Place your index finger in front of your mouth and say, "Shhhhhh." Give situations [draw illustrations, if necessary] and have the student say, "Shhhhhh." ("The baby is sleeping." Or "We are in the library.") **Answer Key:** (*Row 1*) crash, shoe, dish; (*Row 2*) brush, shop, cash; (*Row 3*) shell, fish, shine; (*Row 4*) trash, ship, shark.

   • *Wh*—Call this the windy sound. Ask the student to hold his/her finger in front of his/her mouth and feel the wind as the "wh" sound is said. For fun, have the student hold a piece of tissue in front of his/her mouth and watch the tissue move as he/she says "wh." In season, take the students outside and blow on dandelion seeds using the "wh" sound. **Answer Key:** (*Part One*) 1. whale, 2. wheel, 3. whines, 4. white, 5. whistle; (*Part Two*) Answers will vary.

333

- *Th*—This digraph is undoubtedly the most difficult because of its two sounds. It is helpful to ask the student to place his/her hand on the throat when saying the "th" sound. The "th" sound (made in the word *them*) will produce a vibration in the throat. The "th" sound (made in the word *thumb*) will produce no vibration. Also, calendar time is a good time to emphasize the "th" sound when used in ordinal numbers: fourth, fifth, sixth, etc. **Answer Key:** (*Th*—*them*) that, this, these, mother, there, the, weather; (*Th*—*think*) third, thin, thing, bath, thumb, fifth, thank.

Name_____ Date_____

"One, Two Cha, Cha, Cha!" (The Ch Sound)

1. **Look in the word box and read the words. Then write *ch* in the correct place under the picture. In one word you hear *ch* in two places.**

chick	chair	church	catch	lunch	chin
inch	chain	watch	witch	chess	cherry

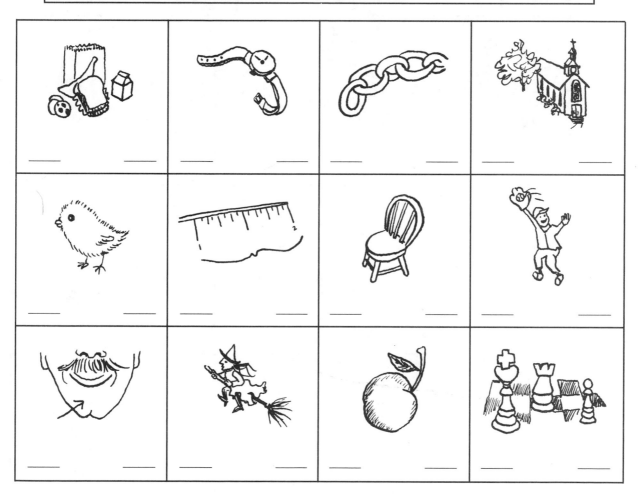

2. **Write *ch* on the lines and find out the names of these mystery animals.**

____ ____impanzee   ____ ____ipmunk   ____ ____ow   ____ ____in____ ____illa

Name_____ Date_____

"Shhhh"—The Quiet Sound

Look in the word box and read the words. Then write the correct word under each picture.

shell	dish	ship	fish	crash	shark
brush	shop	shoe	cash	trash	shine

Name_____ Date_____

Is That the Wind? (The Wh Sound)

Part One: Read each sentence. Then write *wh* on the line to complete the word. The pictures will help you.

1. The ___ ___ale swam in the ocean.

2. The ___ ___heel fell off the wagon.

3. The puppy ___ ___ines for his ball.

4. The puffy clouds are ___ ___ite.

5. The police officer blew his ___ ___istle.

Part Two: Read the question words. Then answer the questions. Write the answer on the line.

Who?   What?   When?   Where?   Why?

1. Who is your teacher? _____

2. What is your favorite food?_____

3. When is your birthday? _____

4. Where are you from? _____

5. Why did you come to America?_____

Part Three: Ask a classmate the five "Wh" questions from Part Two.

Name_____ Date_____

The Trickers ("Th and Th")

The "Th" twins lost their balloons! Help each one get the words back. Read the word on each balloon. Then write it on the line under the correct "th" sound. (If you need help, put your hand on your throat as you say the sound.)

Th—them

Th—think

_____   _____

_____   _____

_____   _____

_____   _____

_____   _____

_____   _____

Lesson 8-10: Beginning Blends

Objective: The student will learn that two to three sounds can blend together to form a blended sound. (These basic blends will be introduced: bl, sl, cr, dr, sp, st, str, spl, tw.)

Vocabulary: blend

Materials: Activity Sheet 8–10; Pencil; 2 pitchers (one should be clear); Water; Mixing spoon; 1 pkg. powdered drink mix; 1 paper cup for each student; Index cards cut in half (print each of these blends on a separate card: bl, sl, cr, dr, sp, st, str, spl, tw); Paper or plastic alphabet letters (b, l, c, r, d, s, p, t, w)

Teaching Note: This lesson presents *some* basic blends. You can add others as an extension to this lesson.

Directions:

1. Ask a student to put the powdered drink mix into the clear pitcher. Ask another student to add the water. Then say, "Let's *blend* the drink mix and the water together." Ask a student to stir the drink mix. Ask, "What happened to the drink mix and the water?" (**Response:** They blended together.)

2. Next, tell the students that letter sounds do the same thing. Show the student letter *b* and ask him/her to say the sound. Ask a student to put the letter *b* in the empty pitcher.

3. Then take the letter *r* and ask the student to say the sound. Then ask a student to put the letter *r* in the pitcher. Ask another student to stir the letters.

4. Take the *br* blend card and place it in the pitcher while the student is stirring. Then ask the student to stop stirring and take out the *br* card. Say, "(b-sound) and (r-sound) mixed together to make the blend (br-sound)." Then write the word *bread* on the board and say, "(br-sound) is the sound you hear at the beginning of the word *bread*." Brainstorm other words that begin with *br* (break, bring, bright, brick, brown).

5. Continue this process with the other two-letter blends. Then do the three-letter blends of *str* and *spl*.

6. Ask a few students to pour and pass out the drink.

7. Give the student a copy of Activity Sheet 8–10. The student will be asked to write various beginning blends. **Answer Key:** 1. skirt; 2. drink; 3. smile; 4. bread; 5. trunk; 6. grape; 7. cloud; 8. swim; 9. trash; 10. spoon; 11. frog; 12. splash; 13. street; 14. twin.

Extension Activity: Write various blends on cards. Then write the ending of the words. For example: eak, ash, y. Turn the ending cards face down. Each player gets a blend card and tries to make words by turning over an ending card. If a word is made, the student keeps it and chooses another blend. If not, play moves on to the next player. The player with the most words wins.

Name_____ Date_____

Let's Get Together!

Read the sentence. Look in the blend box and write the correct blend on the line. The pictures will help you.

1. Rosa wore a ___ ___irt to school.

2. May I have a ___ ___ink of water?

3. Lee has a nice ___ ___ile.

4. Sammy likes to eat ___ ___ead.

5. The elephant has a long ___ ___ unk.

6. I like ___ ___ape juice.

7. The sun is behind a ___ ___oud.

8. Danny likes to ___ ___im.

9. Throw your gum in the ___ ___ash can.

10. I eat ice cream with a ___ ___oon.

11. The ___ ___og sat on a log.

12. Jason made a ___ ___ ___ash!

13. The car is on the ___ ___ ___eet.

14. Ling is my ___ ___in.

br	**sm**
bl	**st**
cl	**tw**
sl	**tr**
gr	**str**
cr	**fr**
dr	**spl**
sw	**sk**
sp	

Lesson 8-11: Ending Blends

Objectives: The student will learn that some blends occur at the end of a word. The student will learn several of the basic ending blends.

Vocabulary: blend, end

Materials: Activity Sheet 8–11; Pencil; Index cards cut in half (on separate cards write the blends: nd, nk, nt, st, lt, mp, ft, ck); Index cards or pieces of plain paper (write each word on a separate card: send, bank, tent, first, jump, neck, belt, lift—underline the ending blend); Tape

Teaching Note: This lesson should be done after the student understands beginning blends. (See Lesson 8–10.)

Directions:

1. Secure the word cards to the board and place the blend cards in a row next to them. Point to the row of blends and say, "Some blends come at the end of a word. I'm going to say a word. Listen to the sound at the end." Point to and say the word "send." Point to the blend at the end of the word. Ask the student to repeat the word. Then ask, "What blend did you hear at the end of the word *send*?" (**Response:** "nd"). Ask a student to secure the *nd* blend card underneath the word card *send*. Brainstorm other words that end with the *nd* blend (bend, round, found). Write them on the board by the *nd* blends.

2. Continue with this process for the other blends. Use the following words/blends as examples: nk—bank, nt—tent, st—first , mp—jump, ck—neck, lt—belt, ft—lift.

3. Next, clear the chalkboard except for the blend cards and *say* a word containing one of the blends. Ask the student to repeat the word. Then *write* the letters that come before the blend on the board. For example, say,"felt"; write: fe ____. Ask a student to come to the board and write the correct blend on the line. Student reads the word.

4. Give the student a copy of Activity Sheet 8–11. The student will be asked to write the ending blend of words. **Answer Key:** nd—bend, ground; nk—sank, thank; nt—went, tent; ft—left, gift; st—test, fist; mp—stamp, bump; lt—felt, melt; ck—luck, clock.

Extension Activity: Write several ending blends on cards. Then write beginning parts of words on cards. Pass out to the students in random order. The students then try to find a "partner" that will make a word. The students then write their word on the board. When all the words are made, the class reads the words that have been written on the board.

Name_____ Date_____

Ending Blends

The bees are looking for flowers! Help them get there. Look at the ending blends on the flowers. Read the word on each bee and circle the ending blend. Then write the word under the correct flower.

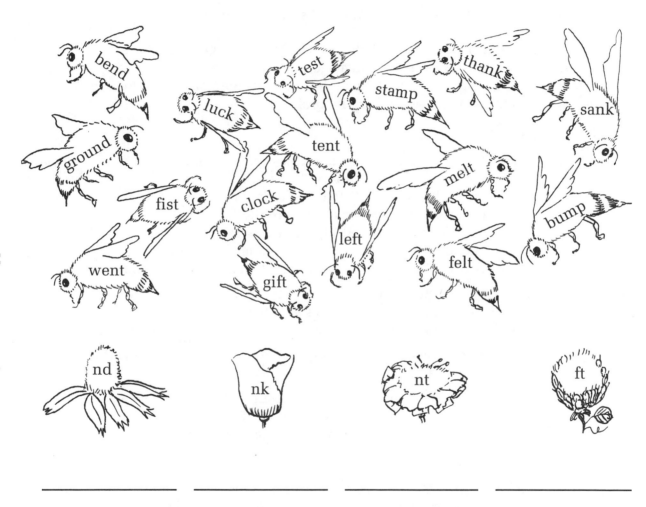

nd   nk   nt   ft

_____ _____ _____ _____

st   mp   lt   ck

_____ _____ _____ _____

Lesson 8-12: Rhyming Words

• •

Objective: The student will understand the concept of rhyme and learn to produce rhyming pairs.

Vocabulary: rhyme

Materials: Activity Sheet 8–12; Pencil; Assorted poetry books

Teaching Note: The concept of rhyme can be challenging for some ESL students, particularly those whose native language does not have this structure. Listening to poetry regularly can greatly aid the student in developing an "ear" for rhyme. Songs and jump-rope rhymes are also very helpful.

Directions:

1. Explain to the student that sometimes words sound the same. This usually happens when the ends of the words have the same letters. On the board print a row of the pattern *et*. Tell the student that *et* sounds like "et." Ask the student to repeat. Next, write a *p* before the first pattern. Ask the student to try to identify the word *pet*. Help, if necessary. Next, write the letters *s, w, g* before the rest of the patterns. Ask the student to identify these words. Now, reread the row of words in a rhythmic manner. Ask the student to repeat.

2. Point out to the student that the end of these words is the same and that makes them sound the same. When words sound the same, they rhyme. Ask the student to think of other words that can be made from the *et* pattern and that rhyme.

3. Put other patterns on the board and generate rhyming patterns (in, it, an, en, ack, up, ot, un, ake).

4. Give the student a copy of Activity Sheet 8–12. The student will be asked to identify rhyming words and generate rhyming words to complete simple rhyming sentences. **Answer Key:** hot, cake, fun, bike.

Extension Activities:

1. Play "I Rhyme, You Rhyme." One player says a word chosen from rhyming patterns. The other players must respond with a rhyming word. If correct, that player gets one point and then he/she gives a rhyming word to which the others must respond. The player with the most points wins.

2. Teach the student jump-rope rhymes to be played at recess. This can also be coordinated with the physical education teacher.

3. Read poems to the student and stop before the ending word. Have the student predict what that word will be.

4. Big Books are excellent resources for poetry in a story. Locate several in the school library to use with your students.

Name_____ Date_____

You're a Poet

Part One: Look at the rhyming patterns. Make words and then read them.

en	**in**	**up**	**op**
_____en	_____in	_____up	_____op
_____en	_____in	_____up	_____op
_____en	_____in	_____up	_____op
_____en	_____in	_____up	_____op

ack	**ake**	**ike**	**eat**
_____ack	_____ake	_____ike	_____eat
_____ack	_____ake	_____ike	_____eat
_____ack	_____ake	_____ike	_____eat

Part Two: Choose a rhyming word to complete each sentence.

Don't touch the pot!

I fear that it's_____.

"Mother, what did you make?"

"A birthday_____."

Look at the sun!

Let's go have some_____.

What would you like?

A shiny, new_____.

Lesson 8-13: Sight Vocabulary

Objective: The student will learn to recognize by sight the most commonly used sight words in the English language.

Vocabulary: sight words

Materials: Activity Sheets 8–13A, 8–13B, 8–13C; Pencil

Teaching Note: The method for teaching sight vocabulary presented in this lesson is very effective. It utilizes the auditory, visual, and tactile modalities. Review is a key part of the process in mastering sight vocabulary.

Directions:

Do not present more than 6–8 new sight words in one session. You can determine the number of words from the success of the student.

1. Begin by making a copy of the blank word cards on Activity Sheet 8–13A. On each card, write the sight word to be learned. (See Activity Sheet 8–13B.) Then follow these steps.

   - Point to each word in order and say it. The student listens.

   - Say each word in order and have the student point to it. Say each word in random order and have the student point to it.

   - Point to each word in order and have the student say it.

   - Point to each word in random order and have the student say it.

   - Cut the squares into individual cards. Mix them up and flash them at the student, who says each word. The student puts the correct responses in his/her pile. Keep the incorrect responses and review these with the student.

   - The student keeps the word cards (an envelope works well). At the next session, review the previous words and then add new ones.

2. This method is also helpful when presenting phonetically irregular words. (See Activity Sheet 8–13C.)

Sight Word Cards (Blank)

First Hundred Instant Words

These are the most common words in English, ranked in frequency order. The first 25 make up about a third of all printed material. The first 100 make up about half of all written material.

Words 1–25	*Words 26–50*	*Words 51–75*	*Words 76–100*
the	or	will	number
of	one	up	no
and	had	other	way
a	by	about	could
to	word	out	people
in	but	many	my
is	not	then	than
you	what	them	first
that	all	these	water
it	were	so	been
he	we	some	call
was	when	her	who
for	your	would	oil
on	can	make	now
are	said	like	find
as	there	him	long
with	use	into	down
his	an	time	day
they	each	has	did
I	which	look	get
at	she	two	come
be	do	more	made
this	how	write	may
have	their	go	part
from	if	see	over

Common suffixes: *-s, -ing, -ed*

From *The Reading Teacher's Book of Lists,* Fourth Edition, by Edward Fry, Dona Fountoukidis, and Jacqueline Kress. © 2000 by Prentice Hall.

Reading Rascals

about	edge	none	thought
address	eight	of	through
again	enough	off	tried
along	every	often	together
although	February	once	tomorrow
any	few	only	too
balloon	fierce	other	trouble
because	find	people	Tuesday
been	friend	piece	two
both	from	please	use
bought	goes	practice	usually
brought	great	quarter	very
built	group	quite	walk
busy	guard	receive	wear
buy	guess	right	weather
caught	half	rough	weigh
close	heard	said	were
color	height	Saturday	we're
come	here	says	where
cough	hour	science	which
could	house	shoes	who
couldn't	instead	some	whole
county	kind	straight	women
country	knew	sure	world
dies	know	surprise	would
does	love	talk	write
door	laugh	tear	you
early	many	the	young
easy	minute	their	your
	mouth	there	
	neither	they	
	night	though	

Lesson 8-14: Plurals and Irregular Plurals

• •

Objectives: The student will learn how to form plurals by adding *s* and *es*. The student will learn the irregular form of common verbs.

Vocabulary: plural, irregular plural

Materials: Activity Sheet 8–14; 2 pencils; 2 crayons or markers; 2 books; 2 small boxes

Directions:

1. Hold up one pencil. Ask the student, "What is this?" (a pencil) Write the word *pencil* on the board. Now hold up two pencils. Ask the student, "What are these?" (pencils) Help, if necessary. Ask, "Do you hear the *s* sound at the end of the word *pencils*?" Write the word *pencils* on the board. Explain that when there is more than one of something, we usually add an *s*. Explain that the word "plural" means *more than one*. Follow the same procedure for *book*, *crayon*, *marker*.

2. Next, show the student the box. Ask, "What is this?" (a box) Write *box* on the board. Now, show the student two boxes. Ask, "What are these?" (boxes) Write *boxes* on the board. Ask, "How did I write boxes?" (b-o-x-e-s) Ask, "How is that different from what I did before?" (*es* instead of *s*) Explain that when words end with *ch*, *sh*, *ss*, *z*, and *x*, we add *es* to form the plural.

3. Explain that in order to make a word plural that ends in *y*, the *y* is changed to *i* and *es* is added. Write *baby* and *babies* on the board. Ask the student to change *lady* to a plural. Other examples: bunny, candy, pony, twenty, thirty.

4. Ask one child to stand at the front of the room. Say, "This is one child." Write the word *child* on the board. Ask another child to stand next to the first child. Say, "Now we have two _____." (Ask the student to predict what word is the correct plural. Help, if necessary.) Write the word *children* on the board. Explain that sometimes a word is changed to make the plural. Give other examples: foot—feet, mouse—mice, goose—geese.

5. Give the student a copy of Activity Sheet 8–14. The student will be asked to form the plural of words by adding *s*, *es*, or the irregular form. **Answer Key:** (2.) books, benches, eggs, cups, bushes, friends, foxes, glasses; (3.) children, women, feet, mice, ladies, geese, oxen, babies, men, teeth.

Extension Activity: Ask the student to find groups of objects around the classroom and write a list of the plural forms of the words.

Name_____ Date_____

Plurals

Part One:

s	es	change
1 bird	1 box	1 child

2 bird<u>s</u>   3 box<u>es</u>   4 child<u>ren</u>

Part Two: Make these words plural. Add *s* or *es*. Remember, words that end in *ch*, *sh*, *ss*, *z*, or *x* need *es*.

book _____   bench _____

egg _____   cup _____

bush _____   friend _____

fox _____   glass _____

Part Three: Find the plurals of these words. Be careful! The words will change.

child _____   woman _____

foot _____   mouse _____

lady _____   goose _____

ox _____   baby _____

man _____   tooth _____

Lesson 8-15: Categorization

Objective: The student will learn to identify the concept of *category* and its relationship to the items that belong in it.

Vocabulary: category

Materials: Activity Sheet 8–15; Pencil; 8–10-foot long piece of yarn or string (big enough to make a circle in which several children can stand); Letter cards and number cards; Random items from the classroom (book, eraser, paper, crayon); Pictures from your picture file representing different categories: people/animals/food/furniture/clothing, etc.

Teaching Note: Your picture file will come in handy for this lesson. If you haven't had time to update it, this is a wonderful opportunity for the students to help you locate pictures of items in various categories. Categorization is a beneficial vehicle for providing opportunities rich in language.

Directions:

1. Ask the students to sit on the floor or around a table. Make a circle on the floor with the string. Next, point to each boy in the class and say, "Boy, boy, boy, etc." Now, ask the boys to stand in the circle. With your hand make a big circle and say, "Boy." Ask the students to repeat. Now, point to each boy in the circle and say, "(name) is a boy." Next, point to a girl and then to the circle and ask, "Does (girl's name) go in the circle?" (**Response:** No) Then say, "(girl's name) is not a boy. She does not go in the circle." Next, follow the same procedure for the girls.

2. Point to the circle, trace around it in the air, and say, "Students." Point to several students (boys and girls) and ask them to stand in the circle. Point to yourself and ask, "Do I go in the circle?" (**Response:** No) Then say, "I am not a student, I am a teacher. I do not go in the circle." Give each student a chance to stand in the circle.

3. Put several letters in the circle. Put other items, including more letters, in a group outside the circle. Point to the circle and ask, "What are these?" (**Response:** Letters) Ask a student to look at the other items and choose the ones that belong in the *category* letters. The student places the letters in the circle and names them. Do the same procedure for numbers.

4. Continue this process with other items/pictures such as animals, people, food, clothing, books, etc. Provide help with naming the categories and items.

5. Next, put several items of the same category in a group. Put one item that does not belong. Ask the student to name the category and remove the item that does not belong.

6. Give the student a copy of Activity Sheet 8–15. He/she will be asked to find three category items in a row (Category tic-tac-toe). Then he/she will be asked to find pictures of items in two different categories: Food and Clothes. **Answer Key:** 1. mouse, lion, giraffe; boy, baby, man.

Extension Activities:

1. Choose a number of pictures from your picture file, mix them up, and ask the student to put them in categories. The student then says the category and the items that belong in it.

2. Have each student make a book of categories. Write the name of the category on the top of the page. The student finds pictures in magazines/catalogs of items in that category. The pictures are glued on the page and the name of the item written next to it. This can be used during reading time or shared with a friend.

Name_____ Date_____

Categorization

1. Play category tic-tac-toe. Look for three items in a row that belong in the same category. Draw a circle around the items in the category. You can go down, across, or corner to corner. Name the category and the items.

2. Look in magazines. Find pictures of items in each category. Cut them out and glue them in the box. Name the item.

Food	Clothing

Lesson 8-16: Same and Different

• •

Objective: The student will learn the meaning of the concepts *same* and *different*.

Vocabulary: same, different, alike

Materials: Activity Sheet 8–16; Pencil; Bag of M&M™ candy; 3 identical pencils (new, unsharpened); 1 large pencil eraser; 3 identical pieces of colored construction paper; 1 piece of lined paper; 3 identical plastic/paper letters; 1 plastic/paper number

Teaching Note: Any kind of identical items can be used for this lesson. Use what is convenient and available to you in your classroom. The lesson moves the student from identifying obvious differences to differences within a category.

Directions:

1. Put the three identical pencils next to each other. Point to each pencil and say, "The pencils are the **same**." Model and describe the features that are the same (same color, same length, not sharpened). Now place three identical pieces of colored construction paper next to each other. Point to each paper and say, "The papers are the **same**." Ask the student to describe what features are the same (size, color). Provide help, if necessary. Then follow the same procedure for the plastic/paper letters.

2. Place a large pencil eraser next to the three identical pencils. Point to each pencil and then the eraser and say, "Same, same, same, different." Ask the student to repeat. Now say the sentence and point to the items, "The pencils are the *same*, the eraser is *different*." Ask the student to repeat. Place a piece of lined paper next to the construction paper and ask the student to point and say, "Same, same, same, different." Now ask the student to say, "These papers are the *same*, this paper is *different*." Follow the same procedure for the letters and the number.

3. Finally, place three identical M&M™ candies next to each other, followed by one that is a different color. Ask the student to follow the same procedure as described above. When done correctly, the student can eat the candy.

4. After the student has mastered the concepts of *same* and *different*, explain that *alike* is another way to say *same*. Place several items that are identical next to each other, followed by one that is different. Ask the student, "What items are alike?" The student should then indicate which items are alike and say the sentence, "The _____ are *alike*, the _____ is *different*." Ask the student to draw three things that are *alike*.

5. Give the student a copy of Activity Sheet 8–16. The student will be asked to identify items that are the same/alike and different.

Extension Activity: Ask the student to find items in the classroom that are the *same* and place them in a group. If possible, ask the student to describe what is the same. The student should also use the sentence, "The _____ are the same." Then ask the student to find an item that is *different* and place it in the group. The student then says the sentence, "The _____ are the same, the _____ is different."

Name_____ Date_____

Same and Different

1. Circle the ones that are the *same* in each row.

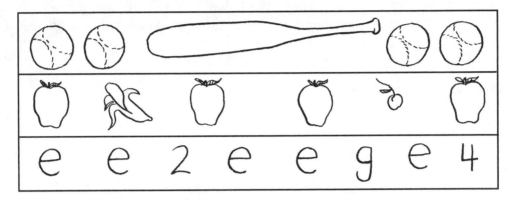

2. Put an X on the one that is *different* in each box.

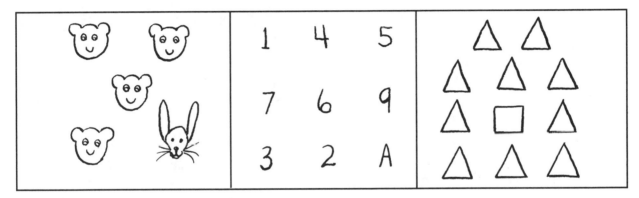

3. Circle the ones that are *alike* in each row.

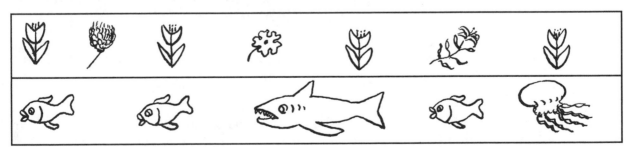

4. Draw a picture of three things that are the *same* and one thing that is *different*.

Lesson 8-17: Story Sequence

Objectives: The student will understand that story events are placed in sequence. The student will place story events in order and write a story to describe those events.

Vocabulary: event, beginning, next, end

Materials: Activity Sheet 8–17; Pencil

Directions:

1. Give the student a copy of Activity Sheet 8–17. Say, "Today we are going to make some stories. When something happens in a story, it is called an *event*. Let's look at events in this story." Point to #1 on the activity sheet. Explain that events happen "in order" so that the story makes "sense." (In this way, you know what's happening.)

2. Point to the four events in #1 and say, "This story has four events. The pictures tell what is happening in the story."

3. Point to event A and say, "This is the *beginning* of the story. How does the story *begin*?" The student should describe; help, if necessary: The boy is taking his dog for a walk. Ask the student to write a sentence that tells about the event. Provide help, if necessary.

4. Point to event B and ask, "What happens *next*?" The student should describe: A cat runs in front of the dog. Ask the student to write a sentence describing the event. Provide help, if necessary.

5. Point to event C and ask, "Then what happens?" The student should describe: The dog runs away from the boy and chases the cat. Ask the student to write a sentence describing the event. Help, if necessary.

6. Now point to event D and say, "This is the *end* of the story. How does the story *end*?" (The cat runs up a tree and the boy gets his dog back.) Ask the student to write a sentence describing the end of the story. Discuss if this is a happy ending or a sad ending.

7. Now, go back and ask the student to read the sentences or tell the story from the beginning to the end.

8. Next, point to #2 on Activity Sheet 8–17. Ask the student to make up a story and draw the events in the boxes. Upon completion, ask the student the following questions: "How does your story begin? What happens next? Then what happens? How does your story end?" Now ask the student to write a sentence to describe each event.

9. The story boxes can be cut out, mixed up, and placed back in order again. If you have several students, have them exchange story boxes and try to put each other's stories in order.

Extension Activities:

1. Read stories aloud to the student and ask him/her to draw story boxes showing the sequence of events in the story. Then write sentences to describe what happened.

2. Ask the student to work with a partner and develop a story to share with the class. This is a good activity in which to pair a native speaker with an ESL student. The native speaker can write the sentences, and the ESL student can draw the pictures.

Name_____ Date_____

Story Sequence

Part One: Describe what is happening in each event box. Write a sentence for each one.

Part Two: Make up your own story. Draw the events in the boxes. Describe the event and write a sentence for each one. Share your story with a classmate.

A	B
C	D

Lesson 8-18: Nouns

• • • • • • • • • • • • • • • • •

Objectives: The student will learn that nouns are words that name people, places, and things. The student will learn to identify a proper noun and know that it is capitalized.

Vocabulary: noun, proper noun, name, people, places, things

Materials: Activity Sheet 8–18; Pencil; Pictures of people, places, and things (*National Geographic* magazine is a good source)

Directions:

1. Ask the student, "What is your name?" (Student answers.) Now ask, "What is my name?" (Student answers.) Now ask, "What is the name of your school?" (Student answers.) Then hold up a pencil and ask, "What is the name of this?" (Student answers.)

2. Explain that a word that names a person, place, or thing is called a *noun*.

3. Next, tell the student that you will be showing him/her pictures of people, places, and things. Say, "I will ask you the name. All the names you say will be *nouns*." Provide help, if necessary.

4. Explain to the student that when a noun names a specific person, place, or thing, it is called a *proper noun* and is capitalized. Write these examples on the board: boy, girl—(the specific name of a boy or girl in the class), school—(your school's name), soda—Coca-Cola, movie—(name a current movie).

5. Give the student a copy of Activity Sheet 8–18. He/She will be asked to identify words that are nouns in isolation and in sentences. **Answer Key:** (1.) book, computer, teacher, store, doctor, yard, ball, school; (2.) Field Museum, Chicago, Illinois, Lake Shore Drive, Lake Michigan, Tyrannosaurus Rex, Jose, M&M's.

Extension Activities:

1. Ask the student to make a list of nouns he/she finds in the classroom. For homework, he/she can make a list of nouns found in the home.

2. Make three columns and label them PEOPLE, PLACES, THINGS. Ask the student to find ten proper nouns for each category.

Name_____ Date_____

Nouns

A noun is the name of a:

| **Person** | **Place** | **Thing** |
| teacher | school | pencil |

Part One: Read these words. Circle the nouns.

book	hot	computer	teacher
store	look	doctor	messy
yard	ball	pretty	school

Part Two: Read this story. Circle the proper nouns.

Our class took a trip to the Field Museum in Chicago, Illinois. The bus drove on Lake Shore Drive and we saw Lake Michigan. The museum had a large skeleton of a Tyrannosaurus Rex. On the ride back, I sat next to Jose. He shared his M&M's with me. It was a wonderful trip.

Part Three: Complete these sentences. Write a noun on the line. Remember to capitalize proper nouns.

My name is _____.

My native country is _____.

I am a _____.

My favorite subject is _____.

My favorite sport is _____.

My favorite food is _____.

Lesson 8-19: Pronouns

• • • • • • • • • • • • • • • • • • • •

Objective: The student will learn pronouns that are subject pronouns. The student will discuss object pronouns and possessive pronouns.

Vocabulary: I, you, he, she, it, we, they

Materials: Activity Sheet 8–19; Pencil

Teaching Note: This lesson will present the subject pronouns in depth. Once these have been learned, present the object pronouns and possessive pronouns that are listed at the end of this lesson plan.

Directions:

1. Say, "A *pronoun* is a word that takes the place of a noun." (name)

2. Give the student a copy of Activity Sheet 8–19. Point to the pronoun chart and explain each one:

   • **I**—means yourself. Point to yourself and say "I am a teacher." Ask the student to point to him-/herself and either say, "I am a boy/girl."

   • **You**—can be singular or plural. Hold up one finger, count "one," point to the student, and say, "You are a student." Ask the student to point to you and say, "You are a teacher." Next, point to a group of students, count the number of students, and say, "You are students." Point to the illustration on Activity Sheet 8–19 for clarification.

   • **He**—Point to the boys in the classroom and say, "He, he, he." If there is a girl in the classroom, shake your head indicating "no." Explain that *he* is used for a man or boy. Model sentences such as, "He is a boy." Ask the student to repeat. Use the illustrations on the activity sheet for clarification.

   • **She**—Point to the girls in the classroom and say, "She, she, she." Point to a boy and say "He." Model sentences such as, "She is sitting." Ask the student to repeat.

   • **They**—Point to a group of students and say, "They." Use the illustration for clarification. Explain that *they* is used for more than one person. Ask several students to stand, point to them, count them, and say, "They are standing." Have one of the students sit down and repeat, "They are standing." Each student should take a turn. Now ask one student to stand, count "one," and shake your head indicating "no." Use the illustration on the activity sheet for clarification.

   • **We**—Sit with a group of students, point to yourself and the others in the group, and say, "We." Say the sentence, "We are sitting." Ask the student to repeat.

- **It**—Explain that *it* is used for things. Point to objects in the room and say, "It, it, it, etc." Now point to a person and shake your head to indicate "no." Use the illustrations for clarification. Ask the student to point to objects and say "It." If possible, ask the student to use sentences such as, "It is on the floor." "It is on the shelf." "It is big."

3. Ask the student to complete Activity Sheet 8–19. The student will be asked to use the correct pronoun in a sentence. **Answer Key:** (1.) I, He, She, We (or They), They (or We), It, You; (2.) 1. I, 2. She, 3. He, 4. They (or We), 5. you, 6. It, 7. We (or They).

Extension Activity: After the student understands the subject pronouns, introduce the following pronouns:

Object Pronouns		**Possessive Pronouns**	
me	it	my, mine	its
you	us	your, yours	our
him	them	his	their, theirs
her		hers	

Name_____ Date_____

Pronouns

Part One: Complete the following story frame. Use the correct pronoun and write it on the line. You will write each pronoun once. Cross it off once you have used it.

I	**you**	**He**	**She**	**They**	**We**	**It**

My name is Miguel. _____ am from Mexico. Josh is my cousin. _____ is from

Panama. Carla is my friend. _____ sits next to me in English class. There

are ten other students in our class. _____ are from different countries. _____

like our teacher. All of us go to George Washington School. _____ is a good

school. We would like _____ to visit us soon.

Part Two: Use the pronouns *I, you, he, she, it, we*, and *they* for the following sentences. Use each pronoun only once. Write it on the line.

1. _____ like to read books.   2. _____ is going to Girl Scout Camp.

3. _____ is on the football team.   4. _____ are in the band.

5. I can show _____ how to play.   6. _____ is under the table.

7. _____ walk to school together.

Lesson 8-20: Verbs

• • • • • • • • • • • • • • • •

Objective: The student will learn that a verb is a word that shows action.

Vocabulary: verb, action

Materials: Activity Sheet 8–20; Pencil

Teaching Note: The basic action verb will be taught in this lesson. As the student progresses, introduce more complicated forms of verbs.

Directions:

1. Ask the student to stand, then say, "I'm going to tell you to do some things." Then say, "Jump!" (Model, if necessary.) Next say, "Spin!" Then, "Run!" (in place) Ask the student to be seated.

2. Explain that the words *jump*, *spin*, and *run* are called verbs. Say, "Verbs tell what a person or thing does. *Action* means to do something." Ask the student to brainstorm action verbs and do the action, e.g., read, write, hop, sing, look, talk, etc.

3. Play the game "Simon Says." One student is Simon who thinks of an action verb. The others do it only if the student says "Simon says" before the verb. Example: "Simon says, jump!" (Others jump.) If the student says, "Jump" and someone does the action, he/she must sit down.

4. Give the student a copy of Activity Sheet 8–20. The student will be asked to identify verbs, and generate words that are verbs. **Answer Key:** (1.) walk, read, catch, write, talk, jump, draw, hop, run, climb; (2.) bake, hide, yell, sing; (3.) Answers will vary.

Extension Activities:

1. Ask the physical education teacher to provide a list of verbs that the student will need to know for gym class. The students can then write the words, do the action, and make an Action Verb Word Wall in the gym.

2. Play "Verb Jeopardy." Make several categories of action verbs—At Home, At School, In Gym Class, In Art Class, At the Park, On the Playground, etc. Write the categories in rows. Then write five verbs for each category on index cards and write a money amount on the back of each card. Put the cards in the correct column with the money-side up. The teams then choose a category and money amount. Turn the card over. If the teams say the word correctly and use it in a sentence, they earn that money amount and another turn. If incorrect, the other team gets a chance. The team with the most money wins. *Variation:* Draw a picture of the verb and write the word on the card. The student must do the action and say the word.

Name_____ Date_____

Verbs

Part One: Circle all the words that are verbs.

walk	book	read	catch	ball	write
talk	pencil	jump	art	draw	lamp
juice	green	hop	run	gym	climb

Part Two: Choose a word from the box and write it under the correct picture.

bake	hide	yell	sing

1. _____   2. _____

3. _____   4. _____

Part Three: Complete each sentence with a verb.

1. I _____very fast.   2. My dog_____.

3. The fish _____.   4. The lion _____.

5. The frog _____.   6. The cat_____.

7. The flower _____.   8. My friend _____.

9. My teacher_____.   10. My mother _____.

Lesson 8-21: Verbs–Present Tense

●●●●●●●●●●●●●●●●●●●●●●●●●●●●●

Objective: The student will learn the meaning of present tense in relationship to verbs.

Vocabulary: tense, present

Materials: Activity Sheet 8–21; Pencil; Magazines

Directions:

1. Explain to the student that there is a way verbs tell when the action happened. This is called *tense*. Ask the student to repeat.

2. Tell the student that if action is happening right now, it is called the *present tense*. Ask the student to repeat. Ask a student to walk toward the door. As he/she is walking, say, "(Student's name) walks." Ask the student to repeat. Say, "*Walks* means the action is happening right now." (If further clarification of *now* is needed, point to today's date on the calendar, point to the clock and say the current time, then say *now*.) Choose other verbs, such as jumps, hops, walks. Ask one student to do the action and the others say, "(Student's name) jumps." Follow the same procedure for the other verbs (runs, writes, hops, spins).

3. Write the sentence on the board: **(Student's name) walks.** Underline the "s" at the end of the word *walks*. Explain that when it is just one person or thing doing the action, an *s* is added to the verb. Write sentences for the other actions that a student performed. Write: **(Student's name)** and ask a student to write (on the board) the verb, e.g., jumps, hops, walks. (Student underlines the *s* at the end of each verb.) Students repeat the sentence.

4. Now, ask two or three boys or girls to jump. Change the sentence and write: **The (boys/girls) jump**. Explain that when there is more than one person doing the action, an *s* is not added to the verb. Give the student other plural subjects and a verb and ask him/her to write the correct verb form on the board (e.g., teachers talk, students read, birds fly). Students repeat the sentence.

5. Next, mix singular and plural nouns and give the student a specific verb. Ask him/her to write the correct verb form for both singular and plural (e.g., dog barks, dogs bark, horse runs, horses run). Students repeat the sentences.

6. Ask the student to find pictures of people or things showing action. Ask the student to say, e.g., "He _____." "She _____." "The children _____." "The dogs _____." (This is a good time to ask the student to cut out the pictures, glue them to index cards, and place them in your picture file as examples of present tense verbs.)

368

7. Give the student a copy of Activity Sheet 8–21. He/she will be asked to choose the correct present tense verbs in a story frame and in sentences. **Answer Key:** (1.) rings, get, stands, walks, slides, climbs, jump, play, hears, runs, run, stand, talks, walk; (2.) 1. plays, 2. chase, 3. sing, 4. drives.

Extension Activity: Give the student a piece of large art paper. Ask him/her to find pictures of people or things showing action, cut them out, glue them to the paper, and write the noun and verb under the picture. Examples: He reads. The lady shops. The dog runs.

Name_____ Date_____

Verbs—Present Tense

Part One: Read this story. Choose the correct present tense verb and write it on the line.

On the Playground

The bell _____. The children _____ in line.
 ring, rings   get, gets

Greta _____ in the front. Then she _____ to
          stand, stands   walks, walk

the playground. First, she _____ down the slide. Next, she
                                      slide, slides

_____ on the jungle gym. Greta and her friends
    climb, climbs

_____ rope. Then they _____ basketball.
    jump, jumps   plays, play

Greta _____ the bell. She _____ to the door.
          hears, hear   run, runs

The other children also _____. They _____ in line. Greta
                              run, runs   stand, stands

_____ to her friend. Then they _____ back
    talk, talks   walk, walks

to their classroom. Recess is over.

Part Two: Circle the correct present tense verb in each sentence.

1. Sasha (play, plays) cards with her sister.

2. The cats (chase, chases) the ball.

3. The students (sing, sings) in the choir.

4. Mother (drive, drives) Sergei to school.

Lesson 8-22: Verbs–Past Tense

●●●●●●●●●●●●●●●●●●●●●●●●●●●●

Objective: The student will learn the meaning of past tense as it relates to verbs.

Vocabulary: past, tense

Materials: Activity Sheets 8–22A and 8–22B; Pencil; History book or historical pictures; Calendar

Teaching Notes:

1. Past tense can be a very difficult concept for the ESL student, especially when his/her native language does not have this form. Review and use it in authentic writing situations to foster better understanding of this concept.

2. Irregular verbs are addressed in this lesson, but they should only be done after the regular past tense has been presented. These should be two separate lessons.

Directions:

Regular Verbs

1. Show the student the calendar and today's date. Make a backward line with your finger and point to yesterday. Say, "Yesterday is past. It already happened." Now, turn back the calendar and point to a few months that have passed. Include some holidays or important events. Say, "_____ is past." Ask the student to repeat. (**Gesture:** Motion your hand toward your back.)

2. Now, explain that verbs can also tell about action that already happened in the past. Tell the student that this is called the *past tense*. Ask the student to repeat. Model the following action: Begin walking, stop, turn to the student, and say, "I walked." Give the student an action to perform, e.g., say, "Jump!" (Student jumps. Ask him/her to stop.) Now, direct the student to say, "I jumped." (Or "We jumped.") Ask certain students to do actions and the others to say the sentence, "(Student's name) walked." Or "(Student's name) opened the door."

3. Open the history book and locate pictures that are obviously in the past. Model a sentence with a past tense verb. Look for verbs with *ed* endings as opposed to irregular verbs, e.g., "The wagons rolled." "The boy walked." "The farmer planted." Ask the student to repeat.

4. Explain that verbs that tell about past actions usually end in *ed*. NOTE: For the advanced student, you may want to present the following rules for adding *ed*: (1.) If the verb ends in *e*, drop the *e* and add *ed* (bake, baked). (2.) If a one-

371

syllable verb ends with a consonant preceded by a vowel, double the final consonant and add *ed* (hop, hopped). (3.) If a verb ends in *y* preceded by a consonant, change the *y* to *i* and add *ed* (carry, carried).

5. Point to yesterday's date on the calendar. Write yesterday's date on the board. Write the sentence: "Yesterday I _____." Ask the student to brain-storm verbs about things they did yesterday, e.g., "Yesterday I watched TV." "Yesterday I brushed my teeth." Ask the student to say and then copy the sentences from the board.

6. Give the student a copy of Activity Sheet 8–22A. The student will be asked to choose the correct past tense of a verb to complete a story frame. The student will then choose the correct past tense for sentences. **Answer Key:** (1.) baked, mailed, guarded, knocked, looked, walked, yelled, screamed, laughed, played, opened, huffed, puffed, clapped, smiled. (2.) cried, planned, hopped, carried.

Irregular Verbs

7. After the student has completed Activity Sheet 8–22A, introduce the concept of *irregular verbs*. Explain that some verbs form the past tense by forming another word. Write the following example on the board: "I wrote on the board." Explain that the past tense of write is *wrote*.

8. Give the student a copy of Activity Sheet 8–22B. The student will be asked to write the irregular past tense of some common verbs. This activity sheet should be saved and used by the student as a reference tool. Most likely, the student will require help completing this activity sheet. This would be an excellent activity in which to work with a partner. **Answer Key:** began, bit, blew, broke, brought, caught, chose, dug, drank, ate, fell, fed, felt, flew, forgot, froze, fought, gave, hid, held, kept, knew, laid, left, lit, lost, made, read, rode, said, saw, sold, sang, sat, spoke, stood, took, taught, told, thought, wore, won, wrote.

Extension Activities:

1. Ask the student to look at pictures in various history books and make a list of past tense verbs.

2. Ask the student to keep a diary for a week. The student should describe what he/she did: e.g., I woke up. I ate breakfast. I dressed for school.

Name_____ Date_____

Past Tense—Regular Verbs

Part One: Read the story. Make the past tense of the verbs by adding *ed* and write them on the line.

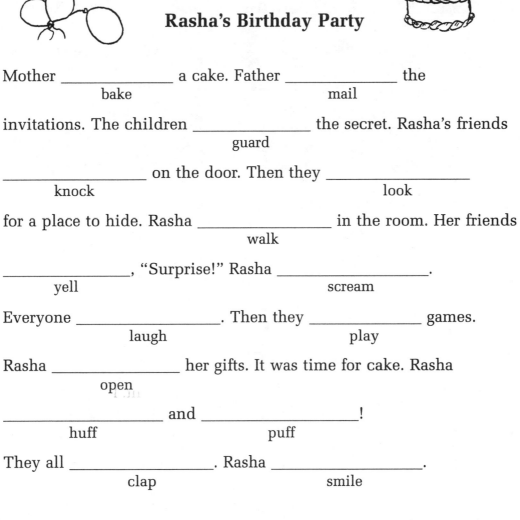

Rasha's Birthday Party

Mother _____ a cake. Father _____ the
             bake   mail

invitations. The children _____ the secret. Rasha's friends
                              guard

_____ on the door. Then they _____
      knock   look

for a place to hide. Rasha _____ in the room. Her friends
                           walk

_____, "Surprise!" Rasha _____.
    yell   scream

Everyone _____. Then they _____ games.
           laugh   play

Rasha _____ her gifts. It was time for cake. Rasha
         open

_____ and _____!
    huff   puff

They all _____. Rasha _____.
       clap   smile

Part Two: Write the past tense of these verbs. Review the spelling rules for adding *ed*.

1. cry _____ 2. plan _____

3. hop_____ 4. carry _____

Name_____ Date_____

Past Tense—Irregular Verbs

Find the past tense of these verbs and write them on the line. Keep this sheet to help you remember.

Past Tense	Past Tense	Past Tense
begin_____	hide_____	take _____
bite _____	hold_____	teach _____
blow _____	keep _____	tell _____
break _____	know _____	think _____
bring_____	lay _____	wear_____
catch _____	leave_____	win_____
choose_____	light _____	write_____
dig_____	lose _____	
drink_____	make _____	Others:
eat _____	read _____	_____
fall _____	ride _____	_____
feed_____	say _____	_____
feel _____	see _____	_____
fly_____	sell _____	_____
forget_____	sing _____	_____
freeze _____	sit_____	_____
fight_____	speak _____	_____
give_____	stand _____	_____

Lesson 8-23: Verbs–Future Tense

• •

Objective: The student will learn the meaning of future tense as it relates to verbs.

Vocabulary: future, tense, verb, helping verb, will

Materials: Activity Sheet 8–23; Pencil; Lined paper; Calendar

Directions:

1. Show the student the calendar and ask him/her to say today's date. Then draw a line with your finger to tomorrow and say, "Tomorrow is the future. It hasn't happened yet." Then turn the calendar to future months and important holidays that are in the future. Model this sentence: "(Halloween) is in the future." Ask the student to repeat. Choose other holidays/events and ask the student to say the sentence for them: "_____ is in the future."

2. Explain that verbs can also tell about action that will be done in the future. Tell the student that this is called the *future tense*. Explain that to make the future tense of a verb, the helping verb *will* goes before the main verb. Say, "I will walk." (You walk.) Next, say a student's name and an action, e.g., "Rosa will spin." Then ask, "What will Rosa do?" (**Response:** "Rosa will spin." Then Rosa spins.) Choose other actions and other students to perform them. Follow the same directive, question, response procedure as described above. Next, make a sequence of actions, e.g., "I will spin. Then I will walk." (Spin and walk.) Ask the student to generate a sequence of actions and say what they will be, e.g., "I will jump. Then I will walk." (Student jumps and walks.) For a group, one student can decide what the group will do. "We will _____." Everyone does the actions.

3. Again, show the student the calendar and point to tomorrow. Then write the date and the following sentence on the board: "Tomorrow, I will _____." The student supplies the last part of the sentence, e.g., go to ESL, learn English, say words, write words. Ask the student to generate other ideas. This is a good activity for group/partner work. The student should repeat the sentences and copy them from the board.

4. Give the student a copy of Activity Sheet 8–23. The student will be asked to write the future tense of verbs. **Answer Key:** (1.) will blast, will land, will get, will walk, will be, will gather, will drive, will look, will find, will come, will greet; (2.) will wear, will look, will stop/look/listen, will keep.

5. For reinforcement, assign this as homework. Ask the student to write about his/her routine for tomorrow, e.g., First, I will wake up. Then I will eat breakfast. I will take a shower. I will brush my teeth. etc. Ask the student to share with a partner.

Extension Activities:

1. Ask the students to bring their baby pictures to school. Display them and ask others to guess the identity of the baby. The student can use these pictures to generate sentences about the future, e.g., This baby will be president. This baby will play basketball.

2. Ask the student to write about what the world will be like in the future. They can draw pictures to illustrate their ideas.

Name_____ Date_____

Verbs—Future Tense

Part One: Read the story. Make the verbs future tense by adding the helping verb *will* to the main verb. Write them on the line.

A Trip in Space

The spacecraft _____ off! It _____
                 blast   land

on Mars. The astronauts _____ out of the ship. They
                                 get

_____ in space. They _____
    walk   be

weightless. One astronaut _____ information.
                                 gather

One astronaut _____ the rover. Another
                      drive

_____ for Martians! Do you think the astronaut
    look

_____ them? Then the astronauts _____
    find   come

back to Earth. Their families _____ them.
                           greet

Part Two: Add the helping verb *will* to the main verb and make the verb future tense. Write them on the line.

1. I _____ a seatbelt.
        wear

2. I _____ both ways before I cross the street.
        look

3. I _____ by the railroad tracks.
      stop/look/listen

4. I _____ myself healthy and safe.
      keep

Lesson 8-24: Verbs–"To Be"

· ·

Objective: The student will learn to use the correct form of the verb "to be."

Vocabulary: am, is, are, was, were

Materials: Activity Sheets 8–24A and 8–24B; Pencil

Teaching Note: The forms of the verb "to be" can be difficult for the ESL student to understand. Practice and review will foster automaticity and reinforce the patterns of the verb "to be."

Directions:

Am, Is, Are

1. Give the student a copy of Activity Sheet 8–24A. Point to the verb chart. Explain that these verbs are present tense and tell about now. Explain that they are usually used with another verb. Point to and read **I am—I'm** on the chart. Ask the student to repeat. Explain that the verb *am* is used with the word *I*. Practice the following speaking exercises with the student.

   TEACHER: (Point to yourself) "I am from America. Where are you from?"
   STUDENT: (Point to him-/herself) "I am from _____."

   TEACHER: (Walk) "I am walking." (Ask the student to walk) "What are you doing?"
   STUDENT: "I am walking."

   Choose other actions to reinforce the dialogue.

2. Tell the student that when one person or thing (hold up one finger) is doing the action, we use the verb *is*. Point to and read **he is—he's, she is—she's, it is—it's** on the activity sheet. Ask the student to repeat. Explain that for the pronouns *he*, *she*, and *it*, we use the verb *is*. Tell the student that **he's, she's,** and **it's** are short ways to say *he is*, *she is*, and *it is*. Practice the following speaking exercise with the student.

   TEACHER: (Point to a boy) He is (<u>Student's name</u>)." (Pause) "Who is he?"
   STUDENT/S: "He is (<u>Student's name</u>)."

   TEACHER: (Point to a girl and ask her to jump) "She is jumping." (Pause) "What is she doing?"
   STUDENT/S: "She is jumping.

   TEACHER: (Point to the calendar) "It is (<u>Name of the day</u>)." (Pause) "What is today?"
   STUDENT/S: "It is (<u>Name of the day</u>)."

You may want to ask different students to do different actions (spin, run, etc). Then ask the others to respond by first saying the student's name and then the action, e.g., "Ruben is running." You can also ask different students to hold up different pieces of colored paper and have the others respond to the question, "What color is it?" "It is blue."

3. Tell the student that the verb *are* is used when more than one person or thing (hold up 2, 3, 4, 5 fingers) is doing the action. Point to and read from Activity Sheet 8–24A **we are**, **they are**, **you are**. Ask the student to repeat. Explain that *are* is always used with *you*, both for singular and plural. Practice the following speaking exercise with the student.

TEACHER: (Point to yourself and the class) "We are in English (ESL) class." (Pause) "Where are we?"

STUDENT/s: "We are in English (ESL) class."

TEACHER: (Ask several students to stand and point to them) "They are standing." (Pause) "What are they doing?"

STUDENT/s: "They are standing."

TEACHER: (Point to the students who are sitting, and ask the students who are standing) "What are they doing?"

STUDENT/s: "They are sitting."

Choose other actions and ask the students to practice the dialogue.

4. Give the student a copy of Activity Sheet 8–24A. The student will be asked to write the correct form of the verb "to be" in a sentence and answer questions using the verb "to be." **Answer Key:** (1.) am, is, is, is, are, am, is, are, is, is, are, are, is, is, is, are, is, is, am, are, am. (2.) am, am, rattlesnake; are, are, monkeys; is, is, lion.

Directions:

Was, Were

1. Give the student a copy of Activity Sheet 8–24B. Point to the chart and explain that the verbs *was* and *were* are used to tell what happened in the past. (It already happened. It's over.) Explain that was and were are usually used with another verb.

2. Point to and read from the chart **I was**, **she was**, **he was**, **it was**. Ask the student to repeat. Explain that the verb *was* is used when one person or thing has done the action. Practice the following speaking exercise.

TEACHER: (Point to yesterday on the calendar) "I was tired yesterday." (Yawn) "Please repeat."

STUDENT/s: " I was tired yesterday."

Brainstorm other sentences using "I was _____ yesterday."

TEACHER: (Point to a girl and ask her to spin.) "Stop!" (Pause) "She was spinning." (Pause) "What was she doing?"
STUDENT/S: "She was spinning."

Brainstorm other actions for "She was _____."

TEACHER: (Point to a boy and ask him to run in place.) "Stop!" (Pause) "He was running." (Pause) "What was he doing?"
STUDENT/S: "He was running."

Brainstorm other actions for "He was _____."

TEACHER: (Ask a student to bounce a ball one time, and let it stop by itself.) "It was bouncing." (Pause) "What was it doing?"
STUDENT/S: "It was bouncing."

Brainstorm other actions for "It was _____." (roll, spin)

3. Explain that the verb *were* is used to show action that happened in the past. *Were* is used when more than one person or thing does the action. Explain that it is usually used with another verb. Point to and read **we were, they were, you were**. Ask the student to repeat. Explain that *were* is used with *you,* singular or plural. Practice the following speaking exercise.

TEACHER: (Have everyone in the class sitting, including yourself. Now ask everyone to stand, including yourself.) "We were sitting." (Pause) "What were we doing?"
STUDENT/S: "We were sitting."

TEACHER: (Ask several students to walk.) "Stop!" (Pause) "They were walking." (Pause) "What were they doing?"
STUDENT/S: "They were walking."

Switch groups so everyone has a turn walking and responding.

TEACHER: (Ask one student to march around the room.) "Stop!" (Point to him/her) "You were marching." (Ask all the students to march around the room) "Stop!" (Point to all of the students) "You were marching."
TEACHER: (March and stop) "What was I doing?"
STUDENT/S: "You were marching."
TEACHER: (When the lesson is done) "You were wonderful students today."

4. Ask the student to complete Activity Sheet 8–24B. The student will be asked to write the correct form of the verbs *was* and *were*. **Answer Key:** (1.) was, were, were, was, were, were, was, were, was, was, were; (2.) The tyrannosaurus was the most fierce. The velociraptor was a fast runner. The mammoths were like elephants. The pterodactyls were like birds.

Extension Activities:

1. Play "Who/What am I?" The student chooses a person or an animal and gives clues that begin with the words "I am . . ." *Examples:* I am big. I am gray. I am an animal. "What am I?" (an elephant) This can be played with partners or in groups. *Variation:* Clues begin with "It is . . ." or clues begin with "She is . . ." or "He is . . ."

2. Play "Where am I?" The student gives clues with the words *was* and *were*. The others guess the location. *Example:* "The weather was warm. The sand was hot. The lake was cool. Where am I?" (at the beach) This can be played with partners or in groups.

Name_____ Date_____

Am, Is, Are

I am—I'm	he is—he's	they are—they're
	she is—she's	we are—we're
	it is—it's	you are—you're

Part One: Read the story. Use *am*, *is*, or *are* to complete the sentences. Write the word on the line.

 A Trip to the Zoo

I _____ happy. Today _____ Friday. The weather _____

beautiful. My ESL class _____ going to the zoo. We _____

taking a bus. I _____ sitting next to Sara. She _____ my best

friend. The bus stops. We _____ finally here. The lion _____

roaring. He _____ very hungry. The monkeys _____ doing

tricks. Chico says, "You _____ silly." The snake _____ sunning

itself on a rock. The alligator _____ floating in the pond. Leo _____

throwing peanuts to the elephant. We _____ having a wonderful time. It

_____ getting late. The bus driver _____ waiting for us. I _____

tired. My eyes _____ closing. Soon I _____ dreaming of the jungle!

Part Two: Choose *am*, *is*, or *are* and write the word on the line. Then solve the riddle. Work with a partner and make up your own riddles to share.

- I _____ long and sleek. I _____ sunning myself. I rattle.

  What am I?_____

- We _____ funny and playful. We _____ eating bananas.

  What are we? _____

- He _____ big and powerful. His mane _____ furry and thick. ROAR!

  What is he? _____

Name_____ Date_____

Was, Were

I was	we were
she was	they were
he was	you were
it was	

Part One: Read the story. Write *was* or *were* on the line.

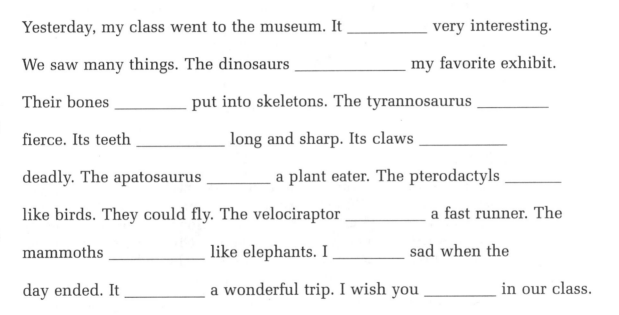

The Museum

Yesterday, my class went to the museum. It _____ very interesting.

We saw many things. The dinosaurs _____ my favorite exhibit.

Their bones _____ put into skeletons. The tyrannosaurus _____

fierce. Its teeth _____ long and sharp. Its claws _____

deadly. The apatosaurus _____ a plant eater. The pterodactyls _____

like birds. They could fly. The velociraptor _____ a fast runner. The

mammoths _____ like elephants. I _____ sad when the

day ended. It _____ a wonderful trip. I wish you _____ in our class.

Part Two: Use another sheet of paper to answer the questions with complete sentences. Use *was* or *were* in your answer.

- What dinosaur was the most fierce?

- What dinosaur was a fast runner?

- What dinosaurs were like elephants?

- What dinosaurs were like birds?

Lesson 8-25: Adding "ing"

Objectives: The student will learn that *ing* is an ending that can be added to words. The student will learn the spelling rules for adding *ing* to a word. The student will learn that when *ing* is added to a verb, it usually has a helping verb.

Vocabulary: ing, ending

Materials: Activity Sheets 8–25A and 8–25B; Pencil

Directions:

1. Ask the student to walk to the door. While he/she is walking, ask, "What are you doing?" (**Response:** I am walking.)

2. Write the sentence on the board, and ask the student to read it with you. Then point to the word "walking" and say, "The word *walking* has an ending on it. We add *ing* to the end of the word *walk*." Underline the *ing* ending. Ask the student, "What word is this?" (**Response:** Walking)

3. Explain that *ing* is called an ending because it is added to the end of a word. (Point to the end of the word.) Give the student other actions to perform, e.g., jump, stand, laugh, read, whisper. Write the word on the board. After the student has done the action, ask him/her to add the *ing* ending to the verb on the board. Student reads the word.

4. Next, tell the student to run to the door. Ask, "What are you doing?" (**Response:** I am running.) Write the word *running* on the board. Explain that when a one-syllable word ends with a CVC (consonant–vowel–consonant) pattern, the last letter is *doubled* and *ing* is added. Give other examples and ask the student to do the action and again add *ing* to the end of the word, but this time doubling the final consonant (e.g., skip, hop, spin).

5. Explain that words that end with *l*, *w*, and *x* are exceptions to the rule. Write the word *wax* on the board and add *ing*. Write other examples on the board and ask the student to add *ing* (e.g., grow, know, blow).

6. Ask a student to hold a pencil. Then take the pencil from him/her and say, "I am taking the pencil." Ask, "Did you hear a word with the *ing* ending?" (**Response:** taking) Write the word *take* on the board and explain that when there is a *silent e* (doesn't make a sound) at the end of a one-syllable word, the *e* is dropped and *ing* is added. Cross out the final *e* and add *ing* to the word *take*. Ask the student, "What word is this?" (**Response:** taking) Write other examples on the board and ask the student to cross out the final *e* and add *ing* to the word (e.g., bake, bike, skate). Student reads the words.

7. Explain that when *ing* is added to the end of a verb, usually a helping verb is added: am, is, are, was, were. Give the student commands with actions that generate these patterns: She is (jumping). He is . . . , They are . . . , We are . . . , It is . . . , I am . . . , They were . . . , He was . . . , I was . . . .

8. Give the student a copy of Activity Sheet 8–25A. The student will be asked to add *ing* to words using the spelling rules taught in this lesson. **Answer Key:** Answers will vary. Activity Sheet 8–25B provides further practice writing the *ing* ending. **Answer Key:** (1.) playing, climbing, looking, drawing, jumping, crying, seeing, reading, holding; (2.) running, sitting, planning, begging, zipping, getting, humming, kidding, swimming; (3.) riding, skating, taking, giving, biting, raking, smiling, sliding, driving.

Name_____ Date_____

Adding "ing"

Look at each piture below. Use the patterns to help you make sentences to go with the pictures. Add *ing* to the verb.

| I am | He is | She is | It is | You are | They are | We are |

1. _____ (run)

2. _____ (climb)

3. _____ (skate)

4. _____ (eat)

5. _____ (hop)

6. _____ (dance)

7. _____ (sleep)

8. _____ (play)

9. _____ (blow)

10. _____ (smile)

Name_____ Date_____

Adding "ing"

1. Write the verb on the line and add the ending *ing*.

play _____   climb_____   look _____

draw_____   jump _____   cry_____

see _____   read_____   hold _____

2. Add *ing* to the verbs. Don't forget to double the last consonant.

run _____   sit_____   plan _____

beg _____   zip _____   get_____

hum _____   kid_____   swim_____

3. Add *ing* to the verbs. Don't forget to drop the silent *e*.

ride_____   skate _____   take_____

give_____   bite _____   rake_____

smile _____   slide _____   drive_____

4. Write a sentence for each *ing* word above. Use another sheet of paper.

Lesson 8-26: Compound Words

Objectives: The student will understand that two words can be put together to make one larger word. The student will learn that these are called compound words.

Vocabulary: compound word, pound

Materials: Activity Sheet 8–26; Pencil; Word cards with the following words written on them: in, side, out, sun, set, pan, cake, bed, time, him, self, her, side, walk, to, basket, ball, foot, base, rise, tan; 1 pad of small self-stick notes; Tape; (*optional*) Modeling clay

Directions:

1. Tape the word cards *in* and *to* on the chalkboard. Ask, "What are these words?" (**Response:** in, to) Now tell the students that *in* and *to* can be put together to make a bigger word. Write *in* on one self-stick note and *to* on another. Make two fists and stick the words on the front of each hand below the knuckles.

2. Now say, "I'm going to *pound* 'in' and 'to' together and make a new word." Then pound your fists together and ask, "What is the new word?" (**Response:** into) Explain that when two words are put together to make a new word, it is called a *compound word*. (Pound your fists together when you say "pound.") Ask the student to repeat and do the action.

3. Next, give each student two self-stick notes and ask him/her to write different combinations of words that will make a compound word (for example, outside). The student sticks the words on his/her fist and pounds them together to make a compound word. Ask the student to read the compound word.

4. *Variation*: Give the student two pieces of modeling clay or play dough. The student scratches two words in each piece, then pounds them together to make a compound word.

5. Secure the word cards to the board. Say a new compound word and ask the student to choose the two words that are in the compound word. The student sticks the words together on the board to make the compound word. Student reads the compound word. Next, say two separate words and ask the student to make a new compound word from them. Student reads the compound word.

6. Give the student a copy of Activity Sheet 8–26. The student will be asked to put two words together to make a compound word. **Answer Key:** (*Part One*) 1. ladybug, 2. cupcake, 3. bathtub, 4. outside, 5, grasshopper, 6. sunshine, 7. snowflake, 8. jellyfish, 9. popcorn, 10. bedtime; (*Part Two*) 1. back/pack, 2. snow/flake, 3. sail/boat, 4. base/ball, 5. flash/light.

Extension Activity: *Compound Match.* Write small words on index cards. Turn them face down. The players take turns turning over two cards, trying to make a compound word. If successful, he/she keeps the word. If not, the cards are turned face down and play continues with another player. The player with the most compound words wins.

Name_____ Date_____

Compound Words

Part One: Read the two small words. Pound them together and make one big word.

1. lady + bug = _____

2. cup + cake = _____

3. bath + tub = _____

4. out + side = _____

5. grass + hopper = _____

6. sun + shine = _____

7. snow + flake = _____

8. jelly + fish = _____

9. pop + corn = _____

10. bed + time = _____

Part Two: Read each compound word. Then write the words that made it.

 1. backpack = _____ + _____

 2. snowflake = _____ + _____

 3. sailboat = _____ + _____

 4. baseball = _____ + _____

 5. flashlight = _____ + _____

Lesson 8-27: Syllables

Objectives: The student will learn the basic rules for dividing words into syllables. The student will learn to "hear" syllables in words.

Vocabulary: syllables, part

Materials: Activity Sheet 8–27; Colored pencil or pen

Teaching Note: The first part of the lesson develops the student's awareness to "hearing" the parts of words. The second part deals with separating the words according to phonetic rules.

Directions:

1. Say to the student in a loud voice and *clap* the syllables, "Qui-et!" Ask the student to repeat and clap the syllables of "qui-et." Ask, "How many *parts* did you hear when you said 'quiet'?" (**Gesture for "parts"**: Hold your hands apart, palms facing each other, first on one side, then move them to the other side.) (**Response:** Two parts) Explain that parts of words are called *syllables*. Ask the student to repeat.

2. Continue to say words, and ask the student to repeat and clap the syllables. For variety, ask the student to stomp out the syllables (or use percussion instruments or sticks). Suggestions for *one-syllable words*: gum, pen, read, book, sit, boy, girl, desk, draw; *two-syllable words*: teacher, pencil, student, backpack, jacket, paper, staple, window, standing; *three-syllable words*: eraser, attention, repeating, wonderful, beautiful, triangle. Ask the student to generate words, too.

3. Ask each student to clap out the syllables of his/her first and last name.

4. Give the student a copy of Activity Sheet 8–27. Explain these basic rules for dividing words into syllables. Ask the student to complete the examples on the page. **Answer Key:** cup/cake, jump/ing, rab/bit, nap/kin, bath/tub, thank/ful, sum/mer, thun/der, base/ball, fish/ing, mit/ten, win/ter, sun/shine, cry/ing, zip/per, bas/ket.

Extension Activity: We're going on a vacation! The student must prepare a list of things to take on vacation; a one-syllable list, two syllables, three syllables, etc.

Name_____ Date_____

Syllables

Words can be divided into syllables between:
- 2 little words (back / pack)
- 2 consonants that are the same (lit / tle)
- a word and its ending (jump / ing)
- 2 consonants that come between 2 vowels (vc/cv—sis / ter)

Read the words and draw a line between the syllables.

cupcake

jumping

rabbit

napkin

bathtub

thankful

summer

thunder

baseball

fishing

mitten

winter

sunshine

crying

zipper

basket

Lesson 8-28: A, An, The

• • • • • • • • • • • • • • • • • • •

Objective: The student will learn that *a* is used before a word that begins with a consonant, and *an* is used before a word that begins with a vowel.

Vocabulary: a, an, vowel, consonant, the

Materials: Activity Sheet 8–28; Pencil

Teaching Note: Before presenting this lesson, review the letters that are vowels and the letters that are consonants. *A* should be pronounced ə, not long *a*.

Directions:

1. Write the words *a* and *an* on the board. Tell the student that sometimes we use *a* or *an* before nouns that are singular (one). Read the words and ask the student to repeat.

2. Explain that *a* is used before singular nouns that begin with a consonant or a consonant sound. Write these examples on the board: a car, a house, a teacher. Explain that "a car" means one car. Ask the student to supply other words that begin with a consonant and write *a* before them. Ask the student to read the examples.

3. Next, explain that *an* is used before singular nouns that begin with a vowel or a vowel sound, or a silent *h*. Write these examples on the board: an apple, an orange, an hour. Ask the student to supply other words that begin with a vowel and write *an* before them. Ask the student to read the examples.

4. Explain that the word *the* is used before singular and plural nouns. Write *the car* and *the cars* on the board. Ask the student to supply other singular and plural pairs and write *the* before them. The student then reads the words.

5. Give the student a copy of Activity Sheet 8–28. The student will be asked to write *a*, *an*, or *the* before words in a sentence. **Answer Key:** (1.) a, an, a, an, an, a, a, a, an, a, an, a; (2.) the, the, the, The.

Extension Activity: Ask the student to look at magazines, newspapers, and books. Have him/her find examples of *a* and *an* used before a word, and examples of *the* before singular and plural words. Write the examples on a sheet of paper, and then read.

Name_____ Date_____

A, An, The

Part One: Read the sentence. Choose *a* or *an* and write the word on the line.

a   an

1. I wanted _____ dog for my birthday.

2. My brother ate _____ ice cream cone.

3. My sister rode _____ pony.

4. My father fried _____ egg.

5. My cousin peeled _____ orange.

6. Our cat chased _____ mouse.

7. Grandmother baked _____ cake.

8. The ball broke _____ window.

9. It took me _____ hour to do my homework.

10. The baby wanted _____ bottle.

11. My father is _____ honest man.

12. My grandfather bought _____ new car.

Part Two: Write *the* on the line. Then read the sentence.

1. He saw _____ two cats fighting.

2. He saw _____ cat.

3. We saw _____ dolphins jump.

4. _____ dolphin swam away from the boat.

Lesson 8-29: Possessive Pronouns and Nouns

Objective: The student will learn to recognize possessive pronouns and to make the possessive form of a noun.

Vocabulary: mine, yours, his, hers, ours, theirs, my, your, its, her, our, their, apostrophe

Materials: Activity Sheet 8–29; Pencils

Directions:

1. Hold a pencil in your hand and say, "This is *my* pencil. I own it. I have it." Explain that the word *my* means that "I own it" or "I possess it" (or "have it"). Explain that there are certain pronouns that tell that someone owns or possesses (has) something.

2. Give a pencil to each student. Point to a boy and then his pencil and say, "This is *his* pencil." Explain that the word *his* is used for a man or a boy and means "he owns it" or "possesses (has) it." Now ask the question, "Whose pencil is this?" **Response:** "It is his."

3. Now, point to a girl and then her pencil and say, "This is *her* pencil." Explain that the word *her* is used for a girl or a woman and means "she owns or possesses (has) it." Point to a girl and ask the question, "Whose pencil is this?" **Response:** "It is hers."

4. Give the student a copy of Activity Sheet 8–29. Read the possessive pronouns on the chart. Give examples using each in a sentence. Use objects in the classroom that belong to the students, such as: "Open your desks." "Take their papers." "Get his jacket." "Show me which backpack is yours."

5. Tell the student that we can show that an object belongs to a specific person or thing by adding an "apostrophe s" to the end of the word. Write this sentence on the board: **This is the teacher's desk**. Read the sentence with the student. Show the student how to write an *apostrophe s*. Ask the student to choose one thing that belongs to him/her. Write the sentence on the board: **That is** _____. Choose students to show the others their object and the others respond; e.g., "That is Rosa's jacket." Ask a student to write the words **Rosa's jacket** on the line to complete the sentence. Check for accuracy. Continue until each student has had a turn.

6. Tell the student that if an object belongs to *more* than one person or thing, we add an "s apostrophe" at the end of the word. Ask girls in the class to form a line. Write "This is the girls' line" on the board. Ask the student to brainstorm and write other examples on the board (boys' football, girls' shower, boys' locker room).

7. Ask the student to complete the activity sheet. The student will be asked to identify possessive pronouns in a sentence and write possessive nouns in sentences. **Answer Key:** (1.) hers, theirs, my, his, mine, its, hers, yours, our, their, theirs, yours, ours, yours. (2.) farmers' crops, Juan's backpack, girls' club, Nicole's dress, boys' gym, dog's bone.

8. Ask the student to write sentences using the possessive pronouns listed on the chart.

Extension Activity: Ask the student to make a list of one thing that belongs to each student in the room, e.g., Juan's desk, Lainie's jacket, etc.

Name_____ Date_____

Possessive Pronouns and Nouns

┌───┐
│   **Possessive Pronouns**   │
│   my, its, her, his, your, our, their, │
│   mine, yours, hers, ours, theirs   │
└───┘

1. Read the sentences. Then circle the possessive pronoun in each one.

This new jacket is hers.

This basketball is theirs.

Do you like my new dress?

Those gym shoes are his.

I think that suitcase is mine.

The puppy chased its tail.

The keys I found are hers.

This book is yours.

We like our ESL teacher very much.

This is their new house.

The lost kitten is theirs.

These papers are yours.

The jump ropes are ours.

The classroom books are yours.

2. Make the nouns possessive. Add an 's or s'.

farmer_____ crops *(plural)*   Juan_____ backpack   girl_____ club *(plural)*

Nicole_____ dress   boy_____ gym *(plural)*   dog_____ bone

Lesson 8-30: Adjectives

• • • • • • • • • • • • • • • • • • • •

Objectives: The student will understand that adjectives are words that describe nouns and pronouns. The student will learn to identify and supply adjectives for nouns and pronouns.

Vocabulary: adjective, describing

Materials: Activity Sheet 8–30; Pencil; Stuffed teddy bear; Objects or vivid pictures that the student can describe; Brown grocery bag

Directions:

1. Hold up the teddy bear and ask the student to think of some words that tell about the teddy bear. Supply help, if necessary. Write the words on the board, e.g., soft, cute, cuddly, small, furry, lovable, etc. Explain that words that tell about a noun or pronoun are called *adjectives*. Tell the student that adjectives answer these questions: (1.) Which one? (2.) What kind? (3.) How many? Write these questions on the board.

2. Put various objects (pictures) in a brown grocery bag. Ask each student to close his/her eyes and choose an object (picture). Then give the student a few minutes to generate words that describe the object and answer the question **What kind?** Supply help as needed. Then each student shows his/her object (picture) and shares the adjectives. Other students can then suggest more adjectives. Write the words on the board.

3. Next, tell the student that if a number word or a word that describes an amount is used before the noun, it is usually an adjective. Write on the board: ten students, five dogs, a few pennies, several children. Ask the student to identify which words answer the question **How many?**

4. Explain that the words *this*, *that*, and *those* can be adjectives because they answer the question **Which one?** Give the following examples and ask the student to do the action: "Bring me *that* book, please." "Is *this* your jacket" (hold up a jacket) "Give me *those* papers, please."

5. Give the student a copy of Activity Sheet 8–30. The student will be asked to identify words that are adjectives and supply adjectives for specific nouns. **Answer Key:** (*Part One*) (1.) Three, How many? (2.) scary, What kind? (3.) That, Which one? (4.) Sixteen, How many? (5.) This, Which one? (6.) green, What kind? (7.) new, What kind? (8.) Those, Which one? (9.) Several, How many? (10.) apples, What kind?; (*Part Two*) Answers will vary.

Extension Activities:

1. Give each student a brown paper lunch bag. Ask him/her to bring a "mystery object" from home and place it in the bag. The student shares adjectives describing his/her mystery object and the class tries to guess the identity of it.

2. Play "Password." The students form teams. Give one person a password (a noun). That person must give adjectives describing the noun. The first team to guess the noun gets a point. The team with the most points at the end of the game wins.

Name_____ Date_____

Adjectives

Adjectives describe nouns or pronouns and answer these questions:

Which one? **What kind?** **How many?**

Part One: Circle the adjective that describes the underlined noun. Then write the question it answers at the end of the sentence.

Example: The (little) dog barked at the cat. What kind?

1. Three <u>monkeys</u> jumped through the trees. _____

2. The scary <u>monster</u> hid in the forest. _____

3. That <u>backpack</u> is not mine. _____

4. Sixteen <u>students</u> went to the zoo. _____

5. This <u>jacket</u> belongs to my teacher. _____

6. The green <u>pen</u> is Juan's. _____

7. I want a new <u>computer</u> for my birthday. _____

8. Those <u>books</u> belong in the ESL classroom. _____

9. Several <u>children</u> came to my birthday party. _____

10. Mother made an apple <u>pie</u> for dinner. _____

Part Two: Think of two adjectives to describe the following nouns. Write them on the lines.

 Lion

 Parrot

 Race Car

_____   _____   _____

_____   _____   _____

 Mountain

 Clown

Pizza

_____   _____   _____

_____   _____   _____

Lesson 8-31: Adverbs

• • • • • • • • • • • • • • • • • • •

Objectives: The student will understand that an adverb is a word that describes verbs. The student will learn to identify adverbs.

Vocabulary: adverb

Materials: Activity Sheet 8–31; Pencil

Directions:

1. Say in a very *loud* voice, "Hello, boys and girls!" Now, ask the students, "How was I speaking?" **Response:** loud, loudly. Write this sentence on the board: **She spoke loudly.** Explain that there are words that describe the verb (action word). These words are called *adverbs*. The verb in the sentence is *talk* and the word that describes it is *loudly.*

2. Tell the student that adverbs tell these three things about the verb: (1.) **When**, (2.) **Where**, (3.) **How** the action takes place. Write these on the board.

3. Now, point to the sentence **She spoke loudly.** Ask the student what the adverb *loudly* tells about the verb *talk.* **Response:** How.

4. Ask a student to walk quickly toward the door. Write this sentence on the board: **He/She walked quickly.** Ask the other students to identify the adverb and what it tells about the verb. Use other actions and adverbs, e.g., jumped high, ran fast, walked slowly, whispered softly, etc.

5. Now, point to the calendar and to yesterday's date. Say, "I walked to school yesterday." Write the sentence on the board. Ask the student to find an adverb that tells *when* the action took place. **Response:** yesterday. Write other examples on the board and ask the student to find the adverb that tells when, e.g., "He played basketball today." "She will play tomorrow." "We will go soon." "We will read later." Choose adverbs that tell *when* and ask the student to generate sentences.

6. Write this sentence on the board: **We played outside.** Ask the student to find an adverb that tells *where.* **Response:** outside. Generate a list of words that tell where, e.g., inside, everywhere, around, outdoors, indoors. Ask the students to work in partners and create sentences using the adverbs that tell *where.*

7. Give the student a copy of Activity Sheet 8–31. The student will be asked to find adverbs and write them on a chart under the categories: *When, Where,* and *How.* The student will also be asked to add an adverb to a sentence. **Answer Key:** *When*—yesterday, finally, later, soon, someday; *Where*—outside, inside, everywhere, nearby, around; *How*—slowly, patiently, quickly, happily, wildly, loudly, thankfully, sadly.

Name_____ Date_____

Adverbs

Adverbs tell this about a verb:

1. When	2. Where	3. How

Read the story and circle the adverbs. Then write the adverbs under the correct heading on the chart.

A Trip to Walt Disney World

Our ESL class went to Walt Disney World yesterday. We stood outside to buy tickets. The line moved slowly. Finally, we walked inside. People were rushing everywhere. We saw the roller coaster nearby. We patiently stood in line again. This line moved quickly. We happily boarded the roller coaster. It moved wildly. We were shoved around. Sasha screamed loudly. The roller coaster stopped. We thankfully climbed out of the car. Later, we saw our teacher. Sasha told her about the wild ride. Soon, it was time to go home. We sadly boarded the bus. Someday, I will bring my whole family to Walt Disney World.

Adverb Chart

WHEN	WHERE	HOW

Lesson 8-32: Comparisons: "er" and "est"

Objective: The student will understand that the ending *er* is added to adjectives to compare two nouns and the ending *est* is added to compare three or more nouns.

Vocabulary: compare, *er*, *est*

Materials: Activity Sheet 8–32; Pencil; Crayons or colored pencils; 3 pieces of yarn cut in 3 varying lengths (about 6 in., 3 in., and 1 in.), enough for each student to have one piece of each length

Teaching Note: When lining up the students to do *tall, taller, tallest*, be careful not to put your hand on the top of the students' heads. In some cultures, this is an insulting gesture.

Directions:

1. Choose three students of varying height. Arrange them in a line from tall to taller to tallest. Say to the class (move your hand up to indicate the increasing height), "(Student's name) is *tall*." "(Student's name) is *taller*." "(Student's name) is the *tallest*." Ask the students to repeat the sentences in sequence. Then say, "We are *comparing* these students to each other."

2. Give the student the piece of yarn that is the longest of the three. Have the student lay the string on the desk or table. Then say, "This piece of yarn is *short*." Ask the student to repeat. Then give the student the next shortest piece of yarn and lay it next to the other piece. Say, "This piece is *shorter*." Ask the student to repeat. Explain that when we compare two items (nouns), the ending *er* is used. Then give the student the shortest piece of yarn to lay next to the other pieces and say, "This piece is the *shortest*." Ask the student to repeat. Explain that when more than two items (nouns) are compared, the ending *est* is used. Then point to each piece of yarn and say, "Short, shorter, shortest." Student repeats. Ask the students to find other objects in the classroom to compare, e.g., long, big, small, large, soft, etc.

3. Give the student a copy of Activity Sheet 8–32. The student will be asked to make comparisons and draw comparisons of his/her own. **Answer Key:** (*Part One*) a. fast, c. faster, b. fastest; 2. a. high, b. higher, c. highest; 3. c. strong, b. stronger, a. strongest; 4. b. long, c. longer, a. longest; (*Part Two*) Answers will vary.

Name_____ Date_____

Using "er" and "est"

Part One: Look at the pictures in the boxes. Match each picture to the correct word. Write the letter on the line.

1

a. _____ fast

b. _____ faster

c. _____ fastest

2

a. _____ high

b. _____ higher

c. _____ highest

3

a. _____ strong

b. _____ stronger

c. _____ strongest

4

a. _____ long

b. _____ longer

c. _____ longest

Part Two: Draw your own pictures like the ones above. Write the correct word by the picture. Use *er* and *est* endings.

Lesson 8-33: Can–Can't and Do–Don't

Objectives: The student will understand the meaning of the terms *can* and *can't* and *do* and *don't* and their relationship to each other. The student will understand that *can* and *do* are positive in nature; *can't* and *don't* are negative.

Vocabulary: can, can't, do, don't

Materials: Activity Sheet 8–33; Pencil; Book; Pictures of various kinds of food; 1 piece of hard candy for each student

Directions:

1. Put a light chair by your desk. Say to the student, "I *can* (**shake you head "yes"**) lift the chair." (Lift the chair.) Then say, "I can't (**shake your head "no"**) lift the desk." (Try to lift the desk.) Ask each student to do the action and repeat the sentences.

2. Next, give the student other examples of *can* and *can't*. Draw illustrations or do the actions. ("I can touch the wall. I can't touch the ceiling.—I can sing a song. I can't play the trumpet.—I can ride a bike. I can't skate on roller blades.) Shake your head "yes" for can; "no" for can't. Ask the student to generate sentences of I can.—I can't.

3. Show the student the candy and say, "I *do* (**shake your head "yes"**) like candy. I *don't* like _____ ." (Hold up a picture of food that you don't like and shake your head "no.") Give the student a piece of candy and let him/her choose a food he/she doesn't like and repeat the sentences, using *do* and *don't*.

4. Generate *do* and *don't* sentences. (Draw illustrations, if necessary.) For example, "I do my homework. I don't watch TV.—I do the dishes. I don't leave a mess.—I do play games. I don't play with matches." Ask the student to generate do—don't sentences.

5. Give the student a copy of Activity Sheet 8–33. The student will be asked to draw pictures of *can* and *can't* and write the words *do* and *don't* under illustrations. **Answer Key:** (*Part One*) 1. can, 2. can't, 3. can, 4. can't, 5. can, 6. can't; (*Part Two*) 1. do, 2. don't; (*Part Three*) Answers will vary.

Extension Activities:

1. Give the student another "I do like . . . I don't like" paper. Decide on a category (clothes, food, cars). Then give the student magazines and catalogs and ask him/her to cut out pictures of items for each list. Then ask the students to share.

2. Make a class behavior chart of *Do's* and *Don'ts*. The students can generate types of behavior for each chart.

3. Ask the student to make an "I Can" book. The student draws pictures of him-/herself doing things he/she can do. This is a wonderful self-esteem booster.

Name_____ Date_____

Can—Can't and Do—Don't

Part One: Look at the pictures. Read the sentence and write *can* or *can't* on the line.

1. He _____ open the jar.

2. He _____ open the safe.

3. She _____ eat the corn.

4. She _____ eat the corn.

5. He _____ kick the ball.

6. She _____ kick the ball.

Part Two: Look at the pictures. Write *do* or *don't* on the line.

1. I _____ wear a seat belt.

2. I _____ talk to strangers.

Part Three: Look at the lists below. Write or draw pictures of things you do like and things you don't like. If you need more room, use the back of the paper.

I do like . . .   I don't like . . .

Lesson 8-34: Kinds of Sentences and Basic Punctuation

Objectives: The student will learn that there are different kinds of sentences: statement, question, command, and exclamatory. The student will learn the correct punctuation to put at the end of each kind of sentence: period, question mark, exclamation point.

Vocabulary: sentence, statement, question, command, exclamatory, period, question mark, exclamation point

Materials: Activity Sheet 8–34; Pencil; *Optional*: M&M™s (several for each student), licorice sticks (cut in 1-inch pieces, 2 for each student), jelly candy rings that can be cut into half circles (1 for each student)

Teaching Note: The candy is optional and can be used to do an activity called "Punctuation is sweet," which is described at the end of the lesson.

Directions:

1. Write the following words on the board: **are**, **different**, **from**, **we**, **countries**. Read the words with the student. Explain that these words can be put in a certain order so that they tell you something, an idea, or a complete thought. Next, write this sentence on the board: **We are from different countries.** Read the sentence and ask the student to repeat. Tell the student that this is called a *sentence*.

2. Write the following words on the board: **are**, **English**, **learning**, **we**. Ask the student to read them. Now ask the student to put the words in order to make a sentence that tells a complete idea. **Response:** "We are learning English."

3. Have the students work with partners and think of word groups that can be made into sentences. Write the words on the board and share with the class. Other groups try to put the words into sentences.

4. Tell the student that there are four kinds of sentences. Write **statement** on the board. Explain that a statement is a sentence that tells something. It begins with a *capital letter* and ends with a *period*. Write this sentence on the board: **We are in ESL class.** Read the sentence with the student. Explain that a statement begins with a capital letter and ends with a period. Show the student that a *period* is a small dot at the end of the sentence. It is placed on the line. Now, ask the student to generate sentences that are statements and write them on the board. Check for accuracy with capital letters and periods.

5. Write the word **question** on the board. Read it with the student. Explain that a question is a sentence that asks something. Write this question on the board: **Where are you from?** Explain that a question begins with a capital letter and

ends with a *question mark*. Demonstrate how to write a question mark. Ask the student to practice. Now, ask the student to think of a question, write it down, and ask a partner. Check for capital letters and question marks.

6. Tell the student that an *exclamation* is a sentence that shows strong feeling or surprise. Write this sentence on the board and read it with a lot of expression: **I lost my money!** Ask the student to repeat. Explain that a sentence that is an exclamation begins with a period and ends with an *exclamation point*. Demonstrate how to make an exclamation point. Give the student situations where he/she might use an exclamatory sentence and write a sentence, e.g., "Your dog is lost!" "There is an accident outside your house!" Ask the student to think of a sentence that is an exclamation and write it on the board. Share with the class. Check for capital letters and exclamation points.

7. Tell the student that a *command* is a sentence that tells someone to do something. Write this sentence on the board: **Pick up the paper.** Next, ask the student to work with a partner. Give each pair a sheet of paper. One student drops the paper on the floor and says, "Pick up the paper." The other student does the command. Then switch so that each has a turn. Explain that a command begins with a capital letter and ends with a period. Ask the student to think of a sentence that can be a command for the entire class, e.g., "Take out a book." "Raise your hand." Write it on a piece of paper. Each student reads his/her command and the class does the command. Check for capital letters and periods.

8. Give the student a copy of Activity Sheet 8–34. The student will be asked to identify sentences and supply the proper punctuation. **Answer Key:** (*Part One*) 1. E, 2. Q, 3. S, 4. C, 5. Q, 6. S, 7. E, 8. S; (*Part Two*) 1. Call 9-1-1! 2. I like vanilla ice cream. 3. Where do you live? 4. Put the dishes away.

Optional: Play "Punctuation is sweet!" Give the student a large piece of blank white paper (11 × 14 works well). Ask the student to copy sentences from the board and put the correct punctuation at the end. Use the following candy to make punctuation marks: *Period*—1 M&M™; *Exclamation point*—cut a short piece of licorice and an M&M™; *Question mark*—cut half of a candy jelly ring, a short piece of licorice, and an M&M™. At the end of the activity, announce, "Now you may eat your question mark," etc.

Name_____ Date_____

Sentences and Punctuation

A statement tells something. It begins with a capital letter and ends with a period.   **.**

A question asks something. It begins with a capital letter and ends with a question mark.   **?**

A command tells someone to do something. It begins with a capital letter and ends with a period.   **.**

An exclamation shows strong feeling or surprise. It begins with a capital letter and ends with an exclamation point.   **!**

Part One: Read the sentence. Write S for statement, Q for question, C for command, or E for exclamation.

1. Don't stop now! _____

2. What country are you from? _____

3. The name of our school is John Page Public School. _____

4. Pick up the papers now. _____

5. Is Jatin your neighbor? _____

6. This is not his jacket. _____

7. I lost my wallet! _____

8. Close the door after you leave. _____

Part Two: Rewrite the following sentences. Use the correct punctuation.

Capital letters   **.**   **?**   **!**

1. call 9-1-1   _____

2. i like vanilla ice   _____

_____

3. where do you live   _____

_____

4. put the dishes away _____

_____

Lesson 8-35: Question Words: Who? What? When? Where? Why?

● ●

Objectives: The student will understand the meaning of the questions words *who*, *what*, *when*, *where*, and *why*. The student will learn to ask and answer questions using these question words.

Vocabulary: question, answer, who, what, when, where, why, because

Materials: Activity Sheet 8–36; Pencil; Picture of your school; World map/globe; Wristwatch; From your picture files, pictures to go with the categories Who—people, What—objects, When—calendar/watch, Where—places.

Directions:

1. Ask a student to come to the front of the class. Write the question "**Who is this?**" on the board. Ask "Who is this?" (**Response:** [Student's name].) Continue and point to other students, asking the question, "Who is this?" Draw a picture of a person above the word *Who* and tell the students that *who* goes with a person. Then ask the students to point to another student and ask the question, "Who is this?"

2. Hold up a pencil and ask, "What is this?" (**Response:** A pencil) Show a picture of an animal and ask, "What is this?" (**Response:** [Name of the animal]) Continue to show various objects using the question "What is this?" Let the students point to objects and ask the question.

3. Show the student a picture of your school and ask, "Where are you?" (**Response:** at school, [your school's name]) Point to a map and ask, "Where are you from?" (**Response:** [Student's native country]) Give the student an opportunity to ask other students the question, "Where are you from?"

4. Show the student the calendar and ask, "When is your birthday?" (**Response:** [The date of the student's birthday]) Ask, "When is ESL class?" Point to the clock. (**Response:** [The time]) Ask, "When do you go to school?" (**Response:** Monday, Tuesday, Wednesday, Thursday, Friday) Ask the student to generate *when* questions.

5. Next, begin to shake and shiver. Say "Brrrrrr." Ask, "Why am I shaking?" (**Response:** Because you are cold) Explain to the student that after a *why* question, the word *because* is usually used in the answer. Pretend to cry. Ask, "Why am I crying?" (**Gesture:** Make a sad face.) (**Response:** Because you are sad) Next, ask a student to pretend to eat. Ask, "Why are you eating?" (**Response:** Because I am hungry) Have the student act out other Why–Because situations (running–late, angry–hold breath, laughing–funny, etc.).

6. Next, give the student a copy of Activity Sheet 8–35. He/she will be asked to identify *Who*, *What*, *When*, and *Where* questions. He/she will practice questions and answers with a partner. **Answer Key:** (*Part One*) who—the people; what—dog, plane; when—clock, calendar; where—USA, house; why—because; (*Part Two*) Students will practice the conversation.

Extension Activities:

1. Place a variety of pictures in a group: people, places, objects, animals, a calendar, a watch. Ask the student to categorize them according to the question words *Who*, *What*, *When*, *Where*. The student then uses the pictures to generate questions.

2. Show pictures of action. The student can generate questions asking *Why*? Examples: Why is he running? Why is she laughing? etc. The student then gives an answer to the Why question.

Name_____ Date_____

Who? What? When? Where? Why?

Part One: Draw a line to the picture that matches the question word.

Who?

What?

When?

Where?

Why?

Part Two: Practice this conversation with a friend. Then switch parts.

PERSON 1—Questions?

PERSON 2—Answers.

Who is that? ⟶ That's Jose.

Where is he going? ⟶ He's going to Mexico.

What will he take? ⟶ He'll take a gift.

When does he leave? ⟶ He leaves at 4 o'clock.

Why is he going? ⟶ Because it's his grandmother's birthday.

Lesson 8-36: Dictation–A Sentence a Day!

Objective: The student will learn to listen to a sentence, repeat it, write it, and then correct it.

Vocabulary: sentence, word

Materials: Activity Sheet 8–36; 1 pocket folder for each student; Pencil

Teaching Note: Dictation is a very supportive tool to use in the development of literacy. The strategy described in this lesson includes the literacy elements of listening, speaking, and writing. It would be beneficial to make this a daily activity.

Directions:

1. Say, "It's time for a sentence a day." Students take out dictation folder, the current dictation sheet (Activity Sheet 8–36), and a pencil. Student writes the date above the new dictation line.

2. *First*—Say a simple sentence. Student listens. ("It is Monday.") *Second*—Student repeats the sentence with you. You repeat the sentence and hold up a finger for each word. Student does the same. You ask, "How many words in the sentence?" (**Response:** [The number of words]) *Third*—Student repeats the sentence without you. *Fourth*—Student writes the sentence on the dictation sheet. *Fifth*—You call students to the board to write a word from the sentence. ("Carlos, write the first word in the sentence.") At this point corrections are made (capital letter, spelling, punctuation, etc.). Other students are asked to help with corrections. Continue and ask, "What word comes next?" Ask a student to write the next word on the board, and continue with the process. *Sixth*—After the sentence is complete, the student writes the correct sentence from the board under his/her sentence on the dictation sheet. Student compares sentences.

Tips for Using This Strategy:

- It is important to keep the dictation papers dated and together in a folder. In that way, you and the student can see his/her progress. It is also a good evaluation tool to determine any challenges the student may be having regarding decoding or grammar skills. This is also a nice piece of information to share at conference time.

- As the student progresses, add more words and more difficult sentence structures.

Name _____

Date _____

A Sentence a Day—Dictation Sheet

Date:

Date:

Lesson 8-37: Contractions

• •

Objectives: The student will understand that a contraction is a word that is made when two words are joined together and one (or more letters) is omitted. The student will learn that an apostrophe is used in place of the missing letters.

Vocabulary: apostrophe, contraction, shortcut

Materials: Activity Sheet 8–37; Pencil; Chairs (classroom or folding)

Directions:

1. Place the chairs in a line at the front of the room. Say, "Oh no! I don't want to walk all the way around these chairs." (Point down the line of chairs.) "I'll take a shortcut." (Walk halfway down the line and cut through the middle.) Explain to the student that a *shortcut* means a shorter way; it's faster. Brainstorm situations when people take shortcuts, e.g., walking to and from school, riding your bike to your friend's house, etc.

2. Tell the student that words can do the same thing. Write the sentence **I am from America** on the board. Underneath that sentence, write the sentence **I'm from America**. Read the two sentences with the student. Ask, "Do the sentences tell you the same thing?" (**Response:** Yes.) Now, ask the student if he/she notices anything different about the two sentences. (**Response:** The words "I am" and "I'm.") Ask the student to identify the difference between *I am* and *I'm*. (**Response:** The missing *a*.) Explain that some words can be put together to make a shorter word and that one or more letters is left out. These words are called *contractions*. Have the student repeat.

3. Next, point to the apostrophe and explain that when a letter is missing, an apostrophe is added. Show the student how to make an apostrophe. Ask the student to write the word *I'm* using the apostrophe. Check for accuracy.

4. Write other word pairs and contractions on the board. Model by crossing out the missing letters and writing the contraction underneath. Ask the student to copy. Examples:

    can n͞o͞t   will n͞o͞t
    can't   won't

5. Give the student a copy of Activity Sheet 8–37. He/she will be asked to write the correct contraction in a sentence. **Answer Key:** 1. I'm; 2. We'll; 3. Don't; 4. They're; 5. can't; 6. We've; 7. Where's; 8. What's; 9. Here's; 10. How's.

Extension Activities:

1. Write various contractions in large letters on plain white paper. Use uncooked elbow macaroni for the apostrophe. The student then glues the apostrophe in the correct position for the contraction.

2. Ask the student to write a sentence for each contraction listed on Activity Sheet 8–37.

Name_____ Date_____

Let's Take a Shortcut—Contractions

is	*are*	*will*	*not*	*have*
I am—I'm	they are—they're	I will—I'll	can not—can't	I have—I've
he is—he's	you are—you're	he will—he'll	will not—won't	we have—we've
she is—she's	we are—we're	she will—she'll	are not—aren't	you have—you've
it is—it's		we will—we'll	do not—don't	they have—they've
what is—what's			have not—haven't	
here is—here's			did not—didn't	
where is—where's			was not—wasn't	
how is—how's				

Write the correct contraction on the line. Don't forget the apostrophe!

1. _____ a student.
   <u>I am</u>

2. _____ help you.
   <u>We will</u>

3. _____ chew gum in school.
   <u>Do not</u>

4. _____ going on a field trip.
   <u>They are</u>

5. I_____ lift this box.
   <u>can not</u>

6. _____ a wonderful ESL teacher.
   <u>We have</u>

7. _____ your new house?
   <u>Where is</u>

8. _____ your name?
   <u>What is</u>

9. _____ your new book.
   <u>Here is</u>

10. _____ your stomachache?
    <u>How is</u>

Lesson 8-38: Commas

• • • • • • • • • • • • • • • • • •

Objective: The student will learn the basic rules for using commas.

Materials: Activity Sheet 8–38; Pencil; Uncooked elbow macaroni (enough for each student to have several); Glue; White paper

Vocabulary: comma

Teaching Note: One of the most important punctuation marks for the student to learn is the comma. It is often forgotten, so it should be reviewed and practiced frequently.

Directions:

1. Write a comma on the board. Tell the student that this is a special mark used in writing. It is called a *comma*. Demonstrate how to write a comma.

2. Give the student a copy of Activity Sheet 8–38. Read and explain the following rules for using commas:

   (1.) **Commas are used between words in a series. A series contains three or more items.** *Example:* I brought my pencil, paper, scissors, and glue to art class.

   (2.) **Commas are used between digits in numbers.** *Examples:* 1,000 2,000,000

   (3.) **Commas are used in dates between the number of the day and the year.** *Example:* Today is March 15, 2001.

   (4.) **Commas are used between items in an address: between street name and city or town and between city or town and state. Do not put a comma between the state and the ZIP Code.** *Example:* 2020 Yale Avenue, Arlington Heights, Illinois 78906

   (5.) **Commas are used to set off dialogue (exact words of the speaker).** *Example:* Jose said, "Let's go to the baseball game."

   (6.) **Use commas after the greeting and closing in a letter.** *Example:* Dear John,   Sincerely yours,

3. Ask the student to walk around the classroom and write a list of classroom objects. Use the list to write a sentence similar to this one on the board (use the items that your student found): **I found paper, pencils, crayons, pens, and books in my classroom.**

4. Give the student some elbow macaroni, glue, and blank white paper. Ask the student to write the sentence and glue the macaroni where the commas

419

belong. (You may also wish to practice other uses for commas using other sentences or numbers.)

5. Refer to Activity Sheet 8–38. The student will be asked to write commas in the correct locations. **Answer Key:** (*Part One*) (1.) 1,000,000; (2.) 2,000; (3.) 109,999; (4.) 4,005,450; (5.) 60,050: (*Part Two*)

Dear Grandmother,

   Thank you for the beautiful birthday presents. I received many gifts. Mother and Father bought me a soccer ball, pajamas, a radio, and candy. We are moving on April 10, 2001. Our new address is 5118 Park Street, Detroit, MI 48009. Mother said, "The house is perfect!" I hope you can come to visit us soon.

                          Love,

                          Carlos

Name_____ Date_____

Please, Don't Forget the Comma!

Basic Rules for Using Commas

1. **Commas are used between words in a series. A series contains three or more items.** *Example:* I brought my pencil, paper, scissors, and glue to art class.

2. **Commas are used between digits in numbers.** *Examples:* 1,000   2,000,000

3. **Commas are used in dates between the number of the day and the year.** *Example:* Today is March 15, 2001.

4. **Commas are used between items in an address: between street name and city or town and between city or town and state. Do not put a comma between the state and the ZIP Code.** *Example:* 2020 Yale Avenue, Arlington Heights, Illinois 78906

5. **Commas are used to set off dialogue (exact words of the speaker).** *Example:* Jose said, "Let's go to the baseball game."

6. **Use commas after the greeting and closing in a letter.** *Example:* Dear John, Sincerely yours,

---

Part One: Put commas in the numbers. Don't forget part of the comma goes below the line.

(1.) 1000000   (2.) 2000   (3.) 109999   (4.) 4005450   (5.) 60050

Part Two: Read the letter and put commas in the correct places.

Dear Grandmother

    Thank you for the beautiful birthday presents. I received many gifts. Mother and father bought me a soccer ball   pajamas   a radio   and candy. We are moving on April 10   2001. Our new address is: 5118 Park Street Detroit   Michigan 48009. Mother said   "The house is perfect!" I hope you can come to visit us soon.

                Love

Lesson 8-39: Quotations

Objectives: The student will learn that quotations are the words that are the exact words of the speaker. The student will learn the correct placement of quotation marks.

Vocabulary: quotation marks

Materials: Activity Sheet 8–39; Pencil; Uncooked elbow macaroni (enough for each student to have at least 5 pieces); Glue; White paper

Directions:

1. Say to the students, "You are very good students." Now write this sentence on the board, **(Your name)** said, "You are very good students." Read the sentence with the students.

2. Ask the students, "What were the exact words that I spoke?" (Or, "What were the exact words that came out of my mouth?") (**Response:** "You are very good students.")

3. Ask the student if he/she notices anything different around these words. (**Response:** little marks) Explain to the student that special marks called *quotation marks* are put before the first word spoken and after the last word spoken. (**Gesture** for quotation: Hold up both hands and move your index and middle fingers up and down.) Also show the student how to write quotation marks and in what direction they face. Model by moving your fingers in the correct direction, and then ask the student to do so.

4. Point to the part of the sentence that says, **(Your name)** said,. Tell the student that you did not speak these words so they do not have quotation marks around them. Tell the student that a *comma* is placed after the word *said* and before the quotation begins. Tell the student that ending punctuation is written inside the last quotation mark. Point to the sentence that was written on the board and the period that is placed inside the quotation marks.

5. Give the student a plain sheet of white paper, five pieces of macaroni (enough for one set of quotation marks and a comma), and glue.

6. Write a short sentence using quotation marks on the board, e.g., **Rosa said, "I like candy."** Ask the student to glue the macaroni in the correct places for the comma and the quotation marks. (Check to be sure the macaroni is facing the correct direction.)

7. Give the student a copy of Activity Sheet 8–39. The student will be asked to supply the correct punctuation in sentences that contain quotations. **Answer Key:** (1.) Mother said, "Wake up." (2.) Father said, "It's time to go to the beach." (3.) "Hooray!" yelled the children. (4.) Juan said, "Let's pack our

things in the beach bag." (5.) Maria said, "I'm getting in the car." (6.) "We're coming," said Juan and Mother. (7.) "Here we go!" laughed Father. (8.) "When will we be there?" asked Maria. (9.) "Soon, dear," said Mother. (10.) "We're here!" called Father. (11.) Maria said, "Juan, let's go swimming." (12.) "Time for lunch," called Mother. (13.) "Okay, we're coming," Maria and I answered. (14.) "Where's Father?" asked Mother. (15.) "He's asleep on the blanket," said Maria. (16.) "You need to rest, too," said Mother. (17.) "Then we'll go swimming again," said Juan. (18.) "I love the beach," said Maria.

Extension Activity: Give the student a newspaper. Ask him/her to find and highlight quotation marks. *Variation*: Highlight the quotation marks and the speaker.

Name_____ Date_____

Who Said That?—Quotations

Read the sentences. Put quotation marks in the correct places. Don't forget the comma!

1. Mother said   Wake up!

2. Father said   It's time to go to the beach.

3. Hurray!   yelled the children.

4. Juan said   Let's pack our things in the beach bag.

5. Maria said   I'm getting in the car.

6. We're coming   said Juan and Mother.

7. Here we go!   laughed Father.

8. When will we be there?   asked Maria.

9. Soon dear   said Mother.

10. We're here!   called Father.

11. Maria said   Juan let's go swimming.

12. Time for lunch   called Mother.

13. Okay, we're coming   Maria and I answered.

14. Where's Father?   asked Mother.

15. He's asleep on the blanket   said Maria.

16. You need to rest too   said Mother.

17. Then we'll go swimming again   said Juan.

18. I love the beach   said Maria.

Lesson 8-40: Writing a Friendly Letter

• •

Objectives: The student will learn the correct form and punctuation to use when writing a letter. The student will learn how to address an envelope.

Vocabulary: heading, greeting (salutation), body, closing, signature, letter, note, address the envelope, return address, stamp

Materials: Activity Sheet 8–40; Transparency of Activity Sheet 8–40; Pencil; Sheet of blank paper on which to write a letter; Plain envelope; Stamp; Overhead projector

Teaching Note: This is an activity in which the student can write a letter to a family member or friend in his/her native country. Before presenting the lesson, ask the student to bring the address of a person to whom he/she would like to write. Explain that the letter will be written in English.

Directions:

1. Give the student a copy of Activity Sheet 8–40. Tell the student that today he/she is going to learn how to write and send a friendly letter. Brainstorm different situations for which the student would write a friendly letter and to whom that letter might be written.

2. Place a transparency of Activity Sheet 8–40 on the overhead and explain that a friendly letter has five parts. Explain that in a friendly letter to a close friend or relative, the letter may not need all of the parts. If you don't know someone very well, it is best to include all five parts.

3. Discuss the name and meaning of each part and ask the student to fill in his/her information as that part is discussed.

   • **Heading:** Your address and the date.

   • **Greeting (Salutation):** Begins with *Dear* and then the name of the person who will receive the letter. It begins with a capital letter and ends with a comma after the name. **Dear Flora,**

   • **Body:** The main part of the letter and where you write your thoughts. Indent the paragraphs.

   • **Closing:** Tells the reader the letter is ending. The closing begins with a capital letter and is followed by a comma. Some common closings for a friendly letter are: **Love,   Sincerely,   Your friend,**

   • **Signature:** In a friendly letter you usually write your first name only.

425

4. Point to the front of the envelope on the activity sheet. (This lesson shows the student the traditional method of addressing an envelope. Some new methods do not include punctuation and use all capital letters.)

- **Address of the person to whom the letter is being sent:** Write this a little to the left of the middle of the envelope.

- **Return address:** Write your name and address in the upper left-hand corner.

- **Stamp:** Place in the upper right-hand corner.

5. Using a piece of lined paper or blank white paper, model how to fold the letter. Begin from the bottom and fold one third of the way to the top edge. Now fold the top part down over the bottom part. Show the student how to fold the paper if it is too large for the envelope: First fold in half and then into thirds.

6. Using a real envelope, show the student how to seal the envelope.

7. Supply the student with writing paper, an envelope, and a stamp. Ask him/her to write a letter that will be sent, using the practice letter as a model. Hopefully, he/she will receive a letter in return!

Extension Activity: As a class project, have the students write letters to their favorite authors in care of the books' publishers.

Name_____ Date_____

Writing a Friendly Letter

Use this page for practice. Write the information on the lines.

(Heading: address, and the date) _____

_____

_____

_____

Dear _____, (Greeting)

(Body: Your thoughts)

_____

_____

_____

_____

_____

_____

(Closing) Love, Sincerely, _____

(Signature: Write your first name) _____

(Return Address: Your name and address)

_____

Stamp

_____

_____

(Name and address of the person receiving the letter)

_____

_____

_____

Lesson 8-41: Story Elements

Objective: The student will learn to identify the important elements of a story including title, characters, setting, problem, resolution, and ending.

Vocabulary: title, characters, setting, problem, resolution, ending, elements

Materials: Activity Sheet 8–41; Pencil

Teaching Note: This is an important concept for the student to understand. These terms will be used throughout his/her school experience.

Directions:

1. Ask, "What is your favorite story?" (Answers will vary.) Explain there are certain parts a piece of writing must have in order to be a story. These parts are called story *elements*. When the story elements are put together, they make a story.

2. Give the student a copy of Activity Sheet 8–41. Say, "Today we are going to read a short story and learn about important story elements." Read aloud the story 'The Picnic.'

3. Discuss the story elements. Begin with the *title*. (Use an overhead projector or write the word on the board.) Explain that the title of the story is the name of the story. Ask, "What was the title of this story?" (**Response:** The Picnic.) Ask the student to write his/her answer on the activity sheet.

4. Discuss *setting*. Define *setting* as where the story takes place. Ask the student, "What is the setting of this story?" Ask the student to write the answer on the activity sheet.

5. Next, define *characters* as who (people) or what (animals, things) is doing the action in the story. Ask the student to identify the characters in the story and to write the answer on the activity sheet.

6. Define *problem* as something that is wrong and needs to be fixed. Ask the student to identify the problem in the story and write the answer on the activity sheet.

7. Discuss *resolution*. Define *resolution* as how the problem is fixed or solved. Ask the student to describe the resolution to the problem and write it on the activity sheet.

8. Define *ending* as the conclusion or result. Explain that an ending is usually one of two things: happy or sad. Discuss the ending to the story and ask the student to write if it was happy or sad.

Extension Activity: Ask the student to choose one of his/her favorite stories and identify each of the story elements.

Name_____ Date_____

Story Elements

Title: The *name* of the story

Setting: *Where* the story takes place

Characters: *Who* or *What* is doing the action

Problem: What's *wrong*

Resolution: How the problem is *fixed*

Ending: Happy or Sad

Read this story. Then write the story elements on the lines below.

The Picnic

It was a beautiful day. Mother, Gina, and Tony went to the park for a picnic. They brought food to eat and games to play. They chose a picnic table near the flowers. Tony and Gina went to play and Mother read a book. Later, Mother put out the food. "Come and eat!" she called. Tony and Gina sat down. Soon, they had many visitors. Bees! The bees landed on the food, they sat on Gina's head, and buzzed in Tony's ear. Mother swatted at them but they wouldn't go away. "I think I have an idea," said Mother. She put jelly and fruit on a plate. Then she put the plate on the ground away from the table. The bees followed her! Now the bees had their own picnic. Mother, Tony, and Gina ate their food. Mother read a story and then it was time to go home. It was a fun-filled afternoon.

Title: _____

Setting:_____

Characters: _____

Problem: _____

Resolution: _____

Ending:_____

Lesson 8-42: Written Directions

Objective: The student will learn to read and execute the vocabulary of common written directions.

Vocabulary: circle, cross out, underline, trace, fill in the blank, erase, match, connect the dots, write the answer on the line, fill in (mark) the bubble, draw a line from

Materials: Activity Sheet 8–42; Pencil; Colored chalk (*optional*)

Teaching Note: The directions presented in this lesson are the ones most commonly found on worksheets and on tests. Depending upon the level of the students, you may want to divide this lesson into two sessions.

Directions:

1. Write this pattern on the board. **A B C D** _____ **F.** Tell the student that he/she is going to practice following directions. First, give the direction and model how to do the action. Ask the student to do the movement with his/her finger on the desktop or table (for tactile reinforcement). Say and model: "Circle the A. Cross out the B. Underline the C. Trace the D. Fill in the the blank. (Print an E.) Erase the F."

2. Write the same pattern for each student: **A B C D** ____ **F.** Ask the students to come to the board. Give the same directions as before and each student performs the action on the board. Check for accuracy.

3. Put these patterns on the board:

   A   B   . . . . . .   ◯ ◯   **A   Z**
   B   A   _____

   First, give the direction and then model the action. Each student should do the movements on his/her desk or table. Say, "Match the letters. Connect the dots. Write your name on the line. Fill in the bubble. Cross out the bubble. Draw a line from A to Z."

4. Write the same patterns on the board, give the directions, and ask the student to execute the actions.

5. Give the student a copy of Activity Sheet 8–42. The student will be asked to follow written directions. Help with reading, if necessary.

Name_____ Date_____

Following Written Directions

1. **Circle these letters   B b   when you find them.**

   A   C   a   B   d   N   r   b   H   B   o   b   M   D   B   b

2. **Cross out these numbers: 3   5   7.**

   3   6   9   5   4   7   2   3   9   5   0   1   7   5   3

3. **Underline the number words.**

   one   look   five   three   read   two   run   six   ten

4. **Trace these shapes.**

5. **Fill in the blanks.**

   My name is _____.

   I am _____ years old.

6. **Match the numbers.**

   1   5   6   3   4   8

   5   1   3   6   8   4

7. **Connect the dots.**

8. **Write the answer on the line.**

   What country are you from?_____

9. **Fill in the bubble.**   ◯   **Cross out the bubble.**   ◯

10. **Draw a line from A to Z.**

   A   Z

Lesson 8-43: Understanding Test Questions

• •

Objectives: The student will understand the different types of questions used on tests. The student will practice the various formats.

Vocabulary: True–False, Multiple Choice, Matching, Fill in the Blank, Short (essay) Answer

Materials: Activity Sheet 8–43; #2 pencil

Teaching Note: The activity sheet in this lesson provides examples of, and practice for, the different types of questions. It is part of the presentation of the lesson itself. Remember to incorporate a number of different styles of questions when writing a test. This gives the student an opportunity to practice the various kinds of questions.

Directions:

1. Give the student a copy of the two-page Activity Sheet 8–43. Explain that there are different ways to answer a question. Tell the student that on tests he/she may see different kinds of questions.

2. Point to Example 1 on Activity Sheet 8–43. Explain that this kind of question is called *True–False*. Tell the student that *True* means "yes" and *False* means "no." Explain that many times a capital *T* means *True* and a capital *F* means *False*. Ask the student to read question 1 and to answer it with a T or F. Next, explain that true–false questions can also be answered with a O for false or a + for true. Student reads question 2 and answers it with a O for false or a + for true. Check for accuracy.

3. Explain that another kind of question is called *Multiple Choice*. Explain that in this type of question, different answers are given and the student must choose the correct answer. Show the student the example of the Scantron® answer form. Explain that many times multiple-choice questions are answered on a special answer sheet with a special pencil. Read and explain the directions. Model. Explain that some answers will be one right answer (question 1) and others will give a choice. Explain the two-choice option (question 2) and "All of the above" and "None of the above" (question 3). Ask the student to answer the multiple-choice questions using the Scantron® sample. Check for accuracy.

4. Point to Example 3, *Fill in the Blank*, and explain that for some questions, the answer is to be written on a line usually as part of a sentence. The line is the "blank." Ask the student to answer the questions and check for accuracy.

5. Point to the *Matching* questions. Explain that in matching questions a line is drawn from one answer to another. Ask the student to answer the questions. Check for accuracy.

6. Next, point to *Short Answer*. Explain that short answer means that you need to write the information in a few sentences. Ask the student to answer the short-answer question. Check for accuracy.

Extension Activity: Ask the student to write different kinds of test questions for a unit you are currently studying. The students exchange questions and answer them.

Name_____ Date_____

Different Types of Test Questions

Example 1: True or False.

    Mark T for True, F for False.

      1. _____ I am a boy.

      _____ I am a girl.

    Mark + for True, O for False.

      2. _____ I am a student.

      _____ I am not a student.

Example 2: Multiple Choice. Write the information on the Scantron® sheet. Then read the questions and mark the correct answer on the sheet.

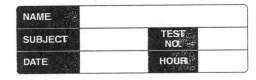

```
1  cA⊐  cB⊐  cC⊐  cD⊐  cE⊐
2  cA⊐  cB⊐  cC⊐  cD⊐  cE⊐
3  cA⊐  cB⊐  cC⊐  cD⊐  cE⊐
4  cA⊐  cB⊐  cC⊐  cD⊐  cE⊐
5  cA⊐  cB⊐  cC⊐  cD⊐  cE⊐
6  cA⊐  cB⊐  cC⊐  cD⊐  cE⊐
7  cA⊐  cB⊐  cC⊐  cD⊐  cE⊐
8  cA⊐  cB⊐  cC⊐  cD⊐  cE⊐
9  cA⊐  cB⊐  cC⊐  cD⊐  cE⊐
10 cA⊐  cB⊐  cC⊐  cD⊐  cE⊐
```

1. I came to America by:
   a. train
   b. plane
   c. bus
   d. bicycle

2. The American flag has:
   a. stripes
   b. stars
   c. circles
   d. a and b

3. My body has:
   a. one head
   b. two eyes
   c. one nose
   d. all of the above
   e. none of the above

Example 3: Fill in the blank. Read each sentence. Write the correct answer on the line.

  1. My native country is _____.

  2. _____ is the capital of the United States.

Example 4: Matching. Draw a line from the item to its matching category.

      jacket   food

      zebra   clothing

      hamburger   animal

Example 5. Short Answer. Write a description of school in your native country.

_____

_____

_____

_____

Lesson 8-44: Reading a Schedule

• •

Objectives: The student will learn how to read a school class schedule and a bus schedule. The student will understand the basic items included in that schedule.

Vocabulary: schedule, Monday through Friday

Materials: Activity Sheet 8–44; Pencil

Teaching Note: A school class schedule and a bus schedule will be presented in this lesson.

Directions:

1. Give the student a copy of Activity Sheet 8–44. Explain that this is a school class schedule. Discuss the various elements and the abbreviations for each:

   Hour: Hr Time
   Days: MTWTF Explain that the days of the week are usually abbreviated in this manner. Also explain that "Monday through Friday" means Monday, Tuesday, Wednesday, Thursday, Friday.
   Subject: Sub The name of what is being taught. Abbreviations: **soc. st. = social studies**, **PE = physical education (gym)**
   Room: Rm The classroom number. **cafe = cafeteria**
   Teacher: Teacher's name
   Lunch: Lunch

   If your school has different terms, explain these to the student.

2. Next, look at the bus schedule. Explain the following items:

   Departure The time the bus leaves. Sometimes it is abbreviated **LV** for leaves.
   Arrival The time the bus gets there. Sometimes it is abbreviated **AV** for arrival.
   One-way A ticket to ride on the bus (one time) to the place you want to go.
   Round Trip Takes you to the place you want to go and back where you came from.
   Cost How much money you need to buy a ticket.
   a.m./p.m. Is sometimes abbreviated with just an **a** or a **p**.
   Information The telephone number to call if you have a question.

3. Ask the student to answer the questions for each schedule on Activity Sheet 8–44.

Answer Key: (*Part One*) 1. Mon., Tues., Wed., Thurs., Fri., 2. Sill, 3. Tues. and Thurs., 4. Room 6, 5. 4th hour, 6. Mon., Wed., Fri., 7. 2nd hour, 8. Jarbo; (*Part Two*) 1. $45.00/$25.00, 2. 8:30 a.m./12:40 p.m., 3. 7:00 p.m., 4. 12:00 a.m., 5. 802-555-6213.

Extension Activity: Get samples of other schedules (train, airline, etc.). Ask the student various questions regarding these schedules. Discuss the differences in schedules.

Name_____ Date_____

Reading a Schedule

Part One: This is Maria's class schedule. Read it to answer the questions below.

Hr.	Sub.	Days	Teacher	Rm#
1	math	MTWThF	Stevens	6
2	ESL	MTWThF	Jarbo	112
3	soc. stud.	MTWThF	Sill	232
4	lunch	MTWThF	Staff	cafe
5	PE	T-Th	Kenyon	gym
6	art	M-W-F	Henshaw	101

1. On what days does Maria have ESL?

   _____

2. Who is her Social Studies teacher?

   _____

3. On what days does Maria have gym?

   _____

4. Where is her math class?

   _____

5. When is lunch?

   _____

6. On what days does she have art?

   _____

7. What hour is ESL?

   _____

8. Who is the ESL teacher?

   _____

Part Two: Read the bus schedule and answer the questions.

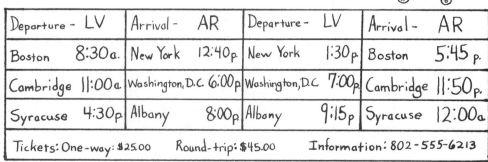

Departure - LV	Arrival - AR	Departure - LV	Arrival - AR
Boston 8:30a.	New York 12:40p.	New York 1:30p.	Boston 5:45p.
Cambridge 11:00a.	Washington, D.C. 6:00p.	Washington, D.C. 7:00p.	Cambridge 11:50p.
Syracuse 4:30p.	Albany 8:00p.	Albany 9:15p.	Syracuse 12:00a.
Tickets: One-way: $25.00	Round-trip: $45.00	Information: 802-555-6213	

1. How much does a one-way ticket cost? _____ A round-trip ticket? _____

2. What time does the bus leave Boston for New York? _____

   Arrival time? _____

3. What time does the bus leave Washington, D.C. for Cambridge? _____

4. What time does the bus arrive in Syracuse from Albany? _____

5. What telephone number do you call for information? _____

Lesson 8-45: Idioms

• • • • • • • • • • • • • • • • •

Objectives: The student will learn that an idiom is a phrase or expression in which the meaning is different from the actual words. The student will learn the meaning of some common idioms.

Vocabulary: idiom

Materials: Activity Sheet 8–45; Pencil

Teaching Note: Americans frequently use idioms in daily conversation. It is very helpful for the ESL student to learn the meaning of some common idioms. It is also helpful for the ESL student to understand that idioms exist and to ask a teacher for the meaning if he/she hears an idiom and does not understand its meaning.

Directions:

1. Say to the student, "Heads up!" Now ask the student what you meant by saying the words, "Heads up!" (**Response:** varies) If a student offers a correct response, reply with the idiom, "You've hit it on the head!" Explain that when you said "Heads up!" you wanted the student to pay attention (listen and look) at you. Explain that "You've hit it on the head!" means you're right.

2. Tell the student that sometimes we use phrases and expressions that mean something different from what the words are saying. Say, "I got it straight from the horse's mouth." Ask the students to guess what that idiom means. (**Response:** Got information from a reliable/good source) Discuss other idioms that the student might have heard.

3. Give the student a copy of Activity Sheet 8–45. He/she will be asked to match an idiom to a meaning. The student will also be required to find out the meaning of selected idioms by asking other people for the meaning. They may not ask you, so this is a good activity in which the student can also develop speaking/social skills. Practice the polite way to approach a person and ask for help. After the activity sheet is completed, discuss the idioms with the class.

Extension Activity: Ask each student to listen to conversations on the bus or in the cafeteria or on TV and find three idioms and their meanings. Share the idiom and the others in class guess its meaning.

Name_____ Date_____

Idioms

Idioms are sayings in which the words have little to do with the actual meaning of the saying.

Part One: Match the idiom to its meaning. Ask a teacher or adult for help, if needed.

1. I have a sweet tooth.

2. Keep a stiff upper lip.

3. You're in hot water.

4. Time flies.

5. Stop bugging me.

6. It's time to hit the hay.

7. Drop me a line.

8. She let the cat out of the bag.

9. Get off my back!

10. It's raining cats and dogs.

_____ in trouble

_____ bothering me

_____ likes candy/dessert

_____ write

_____ told a secret

_____ goes quickly

_____ be brave

_____ work hard

_____ go to bed

_____ stop pressuring me

Part Two: Be a detective. Find out the meaning of these idioms. You can't ask your ESL teacher—you must ask another person at school.

1. Cat got your tongue? _____

    _____

2. You've hit it on the button. _____

    _____

3. Don't be nosey. _____

    _____

4. She's over the hill. _____

    _____

5. Straight from the horse's mouth. _____

    _____

6. Go jump in the lake. _____

    _____

7. We don't see eye to eye._____

    _____

Section 9

Numbers, Math, and Money

Math is truly the universal language. Many ESL students arrive in America very adept at math calculations and processes. Math is the content area in which most ESL students have some background with which to relate. In many cases, the ESL student will excel in mathematics over and above his/her American counterpart.

The issue for the ESL student is the language of math. Most math symbols are universal. However, slight differences can occur from culture to culture. Section 9 provides a lesson introducing the ESL student to the math symbols most generally used in America. Also, the processes may have been taught differently, although each arrives at the same answer. Generally, once the language is taught and the connection is made with the first language, the ESL student will find success in the field of mathematics.

One very obvious challenge to the ESL student is the story problem. A strategy called RADS is taught in this section to help the ESL student solve various types of story problems. It involves drawing the equation before solving it.

Section 9 teaches the Standard System of Measurement that is used in the United States. In many life situations and in many content areas, the student will be given information defined by the Standard System. It is an important concept to master.

Math provides a comfort level for most ESL students because it is an area to which they can more easily draw comparisons to their native language and school curriculum. Once again, it is the English language of math that is the challenge, not the processes themselves.

Numbers, Math, and Money Pretest–Posttest

Student:_____   Grade:_____

Date: _____

1. Ask the student to recite the numerals 1 through 100.

2. Ask the student to write the numerals 1 through 100.

3. Ask the student to solve the following problems:

   2 + 4   8 − 3   10 ÷ 5 ⌐ 6 12   7 × 3

   5 · 5   (4) (3)

4. Ask the student to write the multiplication tables to 12. (Use the chart on Activity Sheet 9–7B.)

5. Ask the student to identify the name and amount of each coin and bill:

6. Ask the student to measure this line in inches; then centimeters.

   _____

   _____ inches   _____ centimeters

7. Ask the student to solve this problem: Jon has three dogs. Jose gives him six more. How many dogs does Jon have in all? Write an equation.

8. Using an ordinal number, ask the student to point to and identify each person standing in line.

Lesson 9-1: The Hundred Chart

Objective: The student will learn to count verbally and visually recognize numerals from 1–100.

Vocabulary: names of the numerals—one to one hundred

Materials: Activity Sheets 9–1A and 9–1B; Pencils

Teaching Note: The Hundred Chart can be used to teach and provide practice for many skills. This lesson will explain many of these uses and suggest activities to complement them.

Skills that Can Be Taught Using the Hundred Chart:

1. *Rote counting of numerals from 1–100.* Break the numbers into manageable numbers depending upon the level and ability of the student. In some cases, the word "teen" (thirteen) is difficult to distinguish from the numerals that end in "ty" (thirty).

2. *Writing the numerals from 1–100.* The student can use the blank Hundred Chart (Activity Sheet 9–1B) to practice writing the numerals.

3. *Skip counting.* The student can use the chart to help learn the concept of skip counting. Begin teaching this concept counting by tens. Be sure to use the term "Counting by . . ." (10's, 5's, 2's, etc.) This is the term most commonly used. (Skip counting is an important concept for the student to master, particularly before learning to tell time.) It is helpful for the student to circle the numerals on the chart with a colored marker when learning a specific pattern. For example: Circle ⑤ ⑩ ⑮. This provides visual organization and helps the student focus on the pattern.

4. *Number patterns.* Write various number patterns on a sheet of paper or on the board. The student must supply the missing number, e.g., 2, __, 6, __, 8, etc. Eventually make the patterns more difficult, e.g., 1, 3, __, 7, 9, __, etc. This is an important cognitive skill to develop. (See Lesson 9–17, Patterns.)

5. *Odd and even numbers.* If the student understands the concept of division, introduce odd and even numbers. Explain that odd numbers *cannot* be divided by two; even numbers *can* be divided by two. Ask the student to circle all the even numbers on the chart and him/her to read the numbers. Give the student another chart and ask him/her to circle all the odd numbers. Play "Odd or Even": Give the students two dice. Each player rolls the dice; if the number is even, a point is scored. The player with the most points wins. *Variation:* The odd numbers score a point.

6. *Backward counting.* The student can use the Hundred Chart to help him/her understand the concept of counting backwards. Begin with 10, 9, 8, 7, 6, 5, 4, 3, 2, 1. Then move on to higher numbers.

Name_____ Date_____

The Hundred Chart

1	2	3	4	5	6	7	8	9	10
11	12	13	14	15	16	17	18	19	20
21	22	23	24	25	26	27	28	29	30
31	32	33	34	35	36	37	38	39	40
41	42	43	44	45	46	47	48	49	50
51	52	53	54	55	56	57	58	59	60
61	62	63	64	65	66	67	68	69	70
71	72	73	74	75	76	77	78	79	80
81	82	83	84	85	86	87	88	89	90
91	92	93	94	95	96	97	98	99	100

Name_____ Date_____

The Hundred Chart

Lesson 9-2: Number Words

• •

Objective: The student will learn the relative amount associated with number words.

Vocabulary: many, a few, some, several, all, none, both, couple

Materials: Activity Sheet 9–2; Pencil; Colored pencils or crayons; 1 bag of Styrofoam packaging filler (popcorn or peanut style)

Teaching Note: Styrofoam can be purchased very cheaply at a packaging store or an office supply store. If that is not possible, any item—such as a bag of dried beans, etc., that comes in a large quantity and can be used as a manipulative—will do.

Directions:

1. Hold up one piece of Styrofoam packaging filler and tell the student that this is called "filler" and is used to put in packages. Ask, "How many pieces do I have?" (**Response:** One) Next, say, "I have *a* piece of Styrofoam." Explain that the word *a* means "one." Ask each student to take *a* piece of Styrofoam from the bag. Ask the student to repeat, "I have a piece of Styrofoam."

2. Next, point to the bag of Styrofoam packaging pieces and say, "How many pieces are in the bag?" (**Response:** Guesses or I don't know) Explain that we can use a number word *many* to explain that there is a large number in the bag. Say, "There are *many* pieces in the bag." Ask the student to repeat.

3. Ask the student to take a *dozen* pieces of popcorn from the bag. Ask, "How many pieces are in a dozen?" (**Response:** Twelve) Ask each student to take a dozen pieces from the bag.

4. Next, tell the student that he/she is going to use these pieces to learn other number words. Explain that some number words aren't an exact amount: several, few, most, some, a lot. Tell the student the number word and ask him/her to repeat it and count out the number you say. Then ask the student to repeat, "I have (several) pieces." The following guidelines are relative to twelve pieces of popcorn:

   Several—six or seven   **Both**—two
   Few—three or four   **All**—the entire amount
   Couple—two   **None**—zero
   Most—ten pieces   **A lot**—nine or ten
   A/an—one

5. Ask the student to put *all* of his/her Styrofoam pieces back in the bag. Now ask, "How many pieces do you have?" (**Response:** I have none.)

6. Give the student a copy of Activity Sheet 9–2. The student will be asked to draw a relative number of items relating to a number word. **Answer Key:**

445

Check pictures for accuracy.

Extension Activities:

1. Give a student the bag of Styrofoam filler and ask him/her to give each class-mate a few pieces. Then change the amount and ask another student to give each classmate a dozen pieces. Vary the number words.

2. Find pictures of various amounts in your picture file, e.g., *many*—a crowd of people. Ask the student to name the correct amount using one of the number words.

Name_____ Date_____

How Many?

1. **Read the number word and draw the amount in each place.**

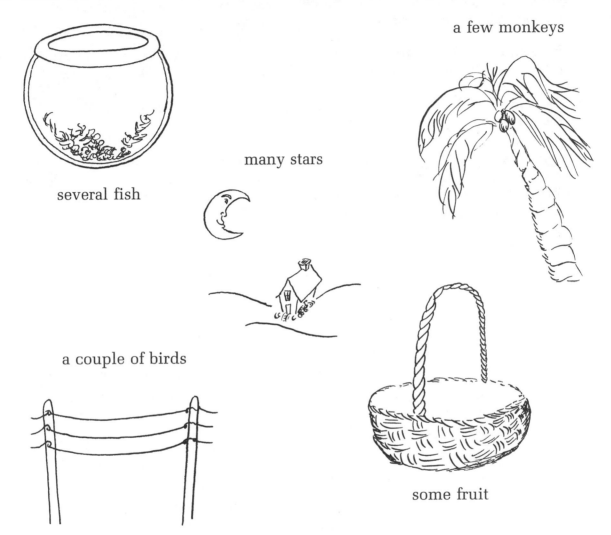

a few monkeys

several fish

many stars

a couple of birds

some fruit

a cat

a lot of circles

2. **Read the directions and do what they tell you.**
    *   Circle *all* of the monkeys.
    *   Circle *none* of the birds.
    *   Cross out *most* of the fish.

Lesson 9-3: Basic Math Symbols and Vocabulary

Objective: The student will learn the symbols used in basic math operations and the vocabulary associated with them.

Vocabulary: sign; addition; add; plus; subtraction; minus; take away; multiplication; times; division; divide; divided by; equals; is; greater than; less than; answer

Materials: Activity Sheet 9–3; Transparency of Activity Sheet 9–3; Overhead projector; Pencil

Teaching Note: This lesson is not intended to teach the operations of the math concepts; rather, it teaches the basic English vocabulary associated with math operation. This lesson is for the student who knows the operation, but does not know the English vocabulary used to define it.

Directions:

1. Give the student a copy of Activity Sheet 9–3. Place the transparency on the overhead (or write the information on the board).

2. Begin with *equation/problem*. Tell the student that a math *problem* is also called an *equation*. It includes everything in the problem, from the first number to the last number. Read the equation, then draw a circle around each equation. (Student circles the equations on his/her activity sheet.)

3. Explain the symbol and vocabulary for *addition*. Tell the student that this is called a *plus* sign. It tells us to *add* the numbers together. Read the equations and ask student to repeat.

4. Explain the symbols and vocabulary for *subtraction*. It can also be called *minus* or *take away*. Read the equations using both terms. Then have student repeat.

5. Explain the symbols and vocabulary for *multiplication*. It can also be called *times*. Read the equations, and have the student repeat.

6. Explain the symbols and vocabulary for *division*. Explain the term *divided by*. Read the equations and have the student repeat.

7. Explain the symbols and vocabulary for *equals*. Read the equations, and have the student repeat.

8. Explain the symbol for *greater than*. Read the math sentence, and have the student repeat. A simple way to remember this concept is that the large part of the arrow opens to the larger number.

9. Explain *less than*. Read the math sentence, and have the student repeat. A simple way to remember this concept is that the narrow (small) part of the arrow points to the smaller number.

10. Explain that *answer* is a word that can be used to define the final result of the problem. (It is used here in the general sense and not specific to the operation.)

11. Ask the student to complete Activity Sheet 9–3. The student will be asked to identify and write math signs and to identify vocabulary. **Answer Key:** (*Part One*) 1. +, 2. −, 3. <, 4. ×, 5. −, 6. =, 7. >, 8. =, 9. ÷, 10. ×; (*Part Two*) $4 + 7 = 11$ $15 \div 5 = 3$ $10 - 6 = 4$ $7 \times 2 = 14$; (*Part Three*) 12>6 5<10; (*Part Four*) Multiply—Times, Plus—Add, Equals—"is"

Extension Activities:

1. Write different kinds of problems on the board, but leave out the sign of operation. Ask the student to come to the board, supply the sign, and "read" the equation using the correct vocabulary. Examples: 4 4 = 8; 5 5 = 20. For operations that can be represented by more than one sign (multiplication, division), ask one student to supply the sign and another to rewrite the problem using an alternate sign.

2. Say the problem using the words of operation, e.g., "Six minus three equals three." The student then writes the equation.

Name_____ Date_____

Basic Math Symbols and Vocabulary

	Equation or Problem $5 + 6 = 11$ $10 - 5 = 5$
+	**Addition, Add, Plus** $12 + 10 = 22$
–	**Subtraction, Minus, Take away** $6 - 4 = 2$
× or · or ( )	**Multiplication, Multiply, Times** $4 \times 5 = 20$ $4 \cdot 5 = 20$ $(4)(5) = 20$
÷ or ⌐	**Division, Divide, Divided by** $20 \div 5 = 4$ $5\overline{)20}\,^{4}$
= or ___	**Equals, "is"** $4 + 6 = 10$ $\begin{array}{r}2\\+2\\\hline\end{array}$ ✐
>	**Greater than** $15 > 6$
<	**Less than** $4 < 8$
	Answer (General Term) $4 + 4 = 8$ $6 \times 6 = 36$ $20 \div 5 = 4$

© 2001 by The Center for Applied Research in Education

Part One: Write the correct math sign next to the word.

1. Plus ____   2. Minus ____   3. Less than ____   4. Times ____

5. Take away ____   6. Equals ____   7. Greater than ____   8. "is" ____

9. Divide ____   10. Multiply ____

Part Two: Circle the equations.

$4 + 7 = 11$ $15 \div 5 = 3$ $10 - 6 = 4$ $7 \times 2 = 14$

Part Three: Write these math sentences.

Twelve is greater than six.   Five is less than ten.

_____   _____

Part Four: Match the words that mean the same thing.

Multiply   Times

Plus   "is"

Equals   Add

Lesson 9-4: Ordinal Numbers

● ●

Objective: The student will learn the correct position of and the correct word for ordinal numbers to ten.

Vocabulary: first; second; third; fourth; fifth; sixth; seventh; eighth; ninth; tenth

Materials: Activity Sheet 9–4; Pencil; $8\frac{1}{2} \times 11$ plain paper (write each word on a separate piece of paper: first, second, third, fourth, fifth, sixth, seventh, eighth, ninth, tenth; underline the *th* ending); Tape to secure the words to the board

Teaching Note: This is a helpful concept for the ESL student to learn, especially when learning to say the date. The ending "th" sound is difficult for some ESL learners to "hear." Emphasize it when teaching the words *fourth, fifth, sixth, seventh, eighth, ninth, tenth.*

Directions:

1. Tape the ordinal number words to the board. Directly over them write the number that coincides with the ordinal number. Explain that the words mean order (or place). Read the ordinal number words and ask the student to repeat.

2. Take the words off the board and give them to the student(s). Ask the students to put the words back in the correct order. Ask, "What word means number one?" (**Response:** "First.") Continue this procedure with the rest of the numbers.

3. Ask the students to form a line. Ask, "Who is first?" Student responds, "I am first." Then continue through the rest of the ordinal numbers with the same question–response method. Continue until all the students have had an opportunity to stand in line and respond.

4. Ask the students to mix up again and stand in another position. This time the students identify their position in line by counting off "First, Second, Third, etc." Continue until all students have had a turn.

5. Give the student a copy of Activity Sheet 9–4. The student will be asked to identify and write the ordinal number words from first to tenth. The student will also be asked to identify the name of a student standing in a specific position. **Answer Key**: (*Part Two*) Rosa, Kara, Kirsten, Mike, Sonja, Maria, Jabar, Ling, Taro, Helene.

Name_____ Date_____

Ordinal Numbers

Part One: Write the ordinal number words on the lines.

first

second

third

fourth

fifth

sixth

seventh

eighth

ninth

tenth

Helene

Taro

Ling

Jabar

Maria

Sonja

Mike

Kirsten

Kara

Rosa

Part Two: Answer the questions.

Who is first?_____

Who is second?_____

Who is third?_____

Who is fourth?_____

Who is fifth? _____

Who is sixth?_____

Who is seventh?_____

Who is eighth?_____

Who is ninth?_____

Who is tenth?_____

Lesson 9-5: Addition

Objectives: The student will learn the operation of addition and the vocabulary associated with it. The student will learn to use a number line in relation to addition.

Vocabulary: add; plus sign; equals; addends; sum; how many in all

Materials: Activity Sheets 9–5A and 9–5B; Pencil; Enough manipulatives for each student to have 20 (dried beans or macaroni work well); Plastic sandwich bags in which to store sets of manipulatives; 1 sheet of lined paper for each student

Directions:

1. Ask two students to stand at the front of the room. Ask, "How many students are standing?" (**Response:** "Two.") Write **2** on the board. Now say, "I want to *add* two *more* students to this group." Write **+ 2** next to the 2 that is already on the board. Ask two students to join the group. Ask, "How many students are there *in all*?" (**Gesture:** Move your arms out to indicate "all.") (**Response:** "There are 4 students in all.") Write **= 4** on the board so that the equation reads **2 + 2 = 4.**

2. Now tell the students that the *equation* (number sentence) is read, "Two plus two equals four." Run your finger under the equation as you read it. Have the student repeat.

3. Point to the numerals 2 and 2 and tell the students that these numbers are called *addends*. The student repeats. These are the numbers that are being added together. Then point to the + sign and explain that this is called the *plus sign* and tells what to do in the equation. The student repeats. Inform the student the plus sign means *add*.

4. Point to the *equal* sign and explain that it comes before the answer. Tell the student that it is read "equals" with an "s" at the end of the word. Have the student repeat.

5. Point to the numeral 4 and say, "This is called the *sum*." Explain that the answer to an addition equation is called the *sum*. Student repeats. Explain that the sum answers the question, "How many in all?"

6. Give the student 20 manipulatives and write various equations on the board. The student should read the equation aloud and copy it on a sheet of paper. Then he/she solves the equation using manipulatives. (Demonstrate how to use the manipulatives.) *Example*: 3 + 2 = 5. The student puts 3 manipulatives in one set, 2 manipulatives in another set, and then counts them together to tell how many in all.

7. Show the student that equations can be written with the addends (numerals) underneath each other with the + sign to the left side of the bottom addend

453

(numeral). The equal sign is a line under the bottom addend. Write an equation on the board using this method, read it aloud, and ask the student to repeat. Then the student copies the equation on a sheet of paper and solves it using his/her manipulatives. Write various examples on the board, e.g.,

$$
\begin{array}{ccc}
2 & \quad 3 & \quad 4 \\
+4 & +3 & +1 \\
\hline
6 & \quad 6 & \quad 5
\end{array}
$$

Student reads, copies, and solves the equations.

8. Give the student a copy of Activity Sheet 9–5A. Point to the number line at the top of the page. Explain that this is another way to help solve an addition problem. Use the first equation in Part One: Show the student how to begin at the first *addend* and move forward the number of spaces indicated by the second *addend.* Then explain that the number you land on is the *sum.* Practice using other equations.

9. Ask the student to complete the activity sheet. Students should use the number line for help. The student will be asked to solve addition equations, solve number puzzles (explain), and write an equation (number sentence) using two different styles. **Answer Key:** (*Part One*) 5, 6, 7, 8, 12, 13, 10, 17, 9; (*Part Two*) 5, 10, 12, 17; 5, 11, 8, 14; 4, 8, 10, 14; 10, 12, 9, 5, 7; 6, 8, 10, 11, 5, 12; (*Part Three*) 4 + 2 = 6

$$
\begin{array}{c}
4 \\
+2 \\
\hline
6
\end{array}
$$

Extension Activities:

1. *Solving addition equations with three addends.* Give the student a copy of Activity Sheet 9–5B. It explains the process of solving adding equations with three addends. **Answer Key:** (*row one*) 12, 16, 13, 16; (*row two*) 11, 13, 14, 17; (*row three*) 11, 13, 16, 12.

2. *Domino addition.* Give the student several dominoes and ask him/her to write an addition equation using the dots and the position of the domino. Examples:

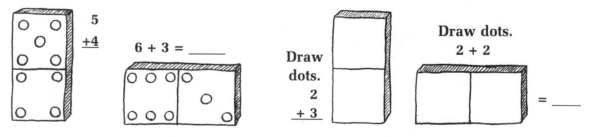

3. *Number line addition.* Write addition problems using the words *more than.* The student then supplies the correct number. *Example:*

3 more than 7

_____

Name_____ Date_____

Addition

0 1 2 3 4 5 6 7 8 9 10 11 12 13 14 15 16 17 18 19 20

Part One: Use the number line to help you find the sum of these addition equations.

1 + 4 = _____   3 + 3 = _____   2 + 5 = _____   6 + 2 = _____

$$\begin{array}{c} 6 \\ +6 \\ \hline \end{array}\qquad \begin{array}{c} 5 \\ +8 \\ \hline \end{array}\qquad \begin{array}{c} 5 \\ +5 \\ \hline \end{array}\qquad \begin{array}{c} 8 \\ +9 \\ \hline \end{array}\qquad \begin{array}{c} 4 \\ +5 \\ \hline \end{array}$$

Part Two: Solve the number puzzles.

+	1	8
4		
9		

+	4	7
1		
7		

+	0	6
4		
8		

+	5	7	4	0	2
5					

+	3	5	7	8	2	9
3						

Part Three: Look at the picture. Write this equation two different ways.

   +   **=**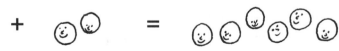

_____

Name_____ Date_____

Addition—3 Addends

To add three addends (numbers) together, you:

1. Add the first two addends together.

2. Then add that sum to the last addend.

3. In this example, the sum is 8.

$$
\begin{array}{r}
5 \\
2
\end{array} \Bigg] = 7
$$
$$
\begin{array}{r}
+1 \\
\hline
8
\end{array}
$$

Directions: Solve the equations. Find the sums.

$$
\begin{array}{r} 4 \\ 1 \\ +7 \\ \hline \end{array}
\qquad
\begin{array}{r} 8 \\ 6 \\ +2 \\ \hline \end{array}
\qquad
\begin{array}{r} 5 \\ 5 \\ +3 \\ \hline \end{array}
\qquad
\begin{array}{r} 7 \\ 6 \\ +3 \\ \hline \end{array}
$$

$$
\begin{array}{r} 2 \\ 0 \\ +9 \\ \hline \end{array}
\qquad
\begin{array}{r} 6 \\ 3 \\ +4 \\ \hline \end{array}
\qquad
\begin{array}{r} 5 \\ 8 \\ +1 \\ \hline \end{array}
\qquad
\begin{array}{r} 8 \\ 6 \\ +3 \\ \hline \end{array}
$$

$$
\begin{array}{r} 6 \\ 3 \\ +2 \\ \hline \end{array}
\qquad
\begin{array}{r} 5 \\ 8 \\ +0 \\ \hline \end{array}
\qquad
\begin{array}{r} 7 \\ 6 \\ +3 \\ \hline \end{array}
\qquad
\begin{array}{r} 3 \\ 2 \\ +7 \\ \hline \end{array}
$$

Lesson 9-6: Subtraction

• •

Objectives: The student will learn the operation of subtraction and the vocabulary associated with it. The student will learn to use a number line in relation to subtraction.

Vocabulary: equation; subtract; minus; take away; difference; How many are left?

Materials: Activity Sheet 9–6; Pencil; Enough manipulatives for each student to have 20 (dried beans or macaroni work well); Plastic sandwich bags in which to store the manipulatives; 1 sheet of lined paper for each student

Directions:

1. Ask five students to stand at the front of the room. Ask, "How many students are standing?" (**Response:** "Five students.") Write **5** on the board. Now say, "I am going to take two students from this group." Write **– 2** on the board. Ask two of the students to return to their seats. Now ask, "How many are left?" (**Response:** "Three students are left.") Write **= 3** on the board so that the equation reads **5 – 2 = 3.**

2. Tell the student that the *equation* (number sentence) is read "Five minus two equals three." Run your finger under the entire equation and read it. Have the student repeat.

3. Point to the – (minus sign) and explain that this is called the *minus sign* and tells us what to do in the equation. Inform the student the minus sign means *take away.* Ask five students to stand at the front of the room again. Then ask two of them to return to their seats. As they are moving, say "minus."

4. Now point to the *equal sign* and explain that it comes before the answer. Tell the student that this sign is read "equals" with an "s" at the end. The student repeats.

5. Point to the numeral 3 and tell the student that this is called the *difference.* Explain that the answer in a subtraction equation is called the difference. Have the student repeat. Explain that it answers the question *How many are left?*

6. Give the student 20 manipulatives. Write various equations on the board. Ask the student to read the equation aloud and copy it on a sheet of paper. Then he/she should solve the equation using manipulatives. (Demonstrate how to use the manipulatives.) *Example:* 6 – 3 = 3. The student should put six manipulatives in one set; then remove three and count the difference.

7. Show the student that subtraction equations can be written with the numbers in a vertical pattern with the minus sign to the left of the bottom number. Write an equation on the board using this form, read it, and ask the student to repeat. Then the student copies the equation on a sheet of paper and solves it

457

using his/her manipulatives. Write other examples on the board. The student then reads, copies, and solves the equation. *Examples:*

$$
\begin{array}{r} 7 \\ -\ 4 \\ \hline 3 \end{array}
\qquad
\begin{array}{r} 6 \\ -\ 2 \\ \hline 4 \end{array}
$$

8. Give the student a copy of Activity Sheet 9–6. Point to the number line at the top of the page and explain that this is another way to help solve an equation. Tell the student that in subtraction, we begin at the first number and move backward the number of spaces that is after the minus sign. The number we land on is the difference.

9. Ask the student to complete the activity sheet. The student will be asked to solve subtraction equations and number puzzles, and write a subtraction equation using two different forms. **Answer Key**: (*Part One*) 2, 5, 3, 4, 1, 8, 4, 7; (*Part Two*) 4, 6, 2, 4; 3, 1, 4, 2; 3, 6, 1, 4; 6, 3, 5, 4, 7; 3, 1, 2, 4, 2, 6; (*Part Three*) $5 - 3 = 2$

$$
\begin{array}{r} 5 \\ -\ 3 \\ \hline 2 \end{array}
$$

Extension Activities:

1. *Domino subtraction.* Give the student several dominoes and ask him/her to write a subtraction equation. First, the student adds the total number of dots on the domino and then writes a subtraction equation subtracting the number of dots in the first or second square or both. Or the student can draw dots to represent the equation. *Examples*:

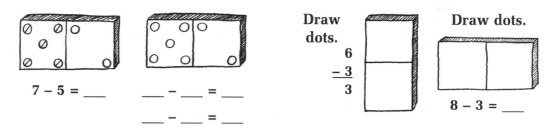

$7 - 5 = \underline{}$ $\underline{} - \underline{} = \underline{}$

Draw dots.
$$
\begin{array}{r} 6 \\ -\ 3 \\ \hline 3 \end{array}
$$

Draw dots.
$8 - 3 = \underline{}$

$\underline{} - \underline{} = \underline{}$

2. *Number line subtraction.* Write subtraction problems using the words *less than*. The student uses the number line to supply the correct number.

3 less than 8

_____

Name_____ Date_____

Subtraction

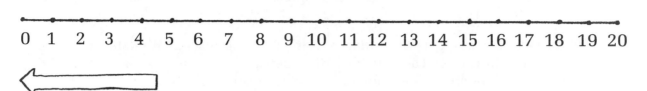

0 1 2 3 4 5 6 7 8 9 10 11 12 13 14 15 16 17 18 19 20

⟵_____

Part One: Use the number line to help you find the difference in these subtraction equations.

6 − 4 =	9 − 4 =	8 − 5 =	4 − 0 =

$$\begin{array}{r} 5 \\ -4 \\ \hline \end{array} \qquad \begin{array}{r} 8 \\ -0 \\ \hline \end{array} \qquad \begin{array}{r} 7 \\ -3 \\ \hline \end{array} \qquad \begin{array}{r} 9 \\ -2 \\ \hline \end{array}$$

Part Two: Solve the number puzzles.

−	8	6
4		
2		

−	6	7
3		
5		

−	10	8
7		
4		

−	9	6	8	7	10
3					

−	7	5	6	8	6	10
4						

Part Three: Look at the picture. Write the equation two different ways.

 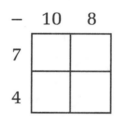

_____

Lesson 9-7: Multiplication

Objectives: The student will understand the concept of *set* as it relates to the operation of multiplication. The student will understand that multiplication is addition repeated. The student will memorize the multiplication tables to 12.

Vocabulary: set; multiply; product

Materials: Activity Sheets 9–7A and 9–7B: Pencil; Heavy yarn or string cut in two pieces long enough to make two large circles on the floor in which three students can stand; 1 sheet of lined paper for each student

Teaching Note: Although the older ESL student may know the multiplication tables in his/her native language, it would be beneficial to present this lesson to him/her so that the English terms for multiplication can be learned.

Directions:

The Operation of Multiplication

1. Make one large circle on the floor with string or heavy yarn. Tell the students that you are going to make one *set*. Now ask three students to stand inside the circle. Say, "This is *one set of three students*." (**Gesture:** Hold up one finger, then make a circle motion. Next, point to the students and hold up three fingers.) You may want to explain that a set is similar to a group.

2. Say, "I want *two sets of three* students." Make another circle and ask three more students to stand inside that set. Say, "There are *two sets of three*." (**Gesture**.) Ask, "How many students *in all*?" (**Gesture:** Open your arms wide.) (**Response:** "Six.") Draw and write this pattern on the board, then explain each item as you read it:

Two sets of three

2 sets of 3 = 6

3 + 3 = 6

2 × 3 = 6

Write the words that name the set: Two sets of three

Write the equation: 2 sets of 3 = 6

Multiplication is repeated addition: 3 + 3 = 6

Multiply: 2 × 3 = 6 (Explain that the × is the sign for multiplication and is read, "Two times three equals (is) six." Also explain that the answer in multiplication is called the product.) Ask the student to copy and repeat.

3. Draw and write other examples on the board. The student is to draw the set and then copy the pattern as was used in step 2. *Variation*: Ask several students to draw sets on the board and have other students "name" them. Then everyone writes the pattern.

4. Explain that multiplication problems can be written with the numbers underneath each other with the × sign to the left of the bottom number.

$$\begin{array}{r} 2 \\ \times\,3 \\ \hline 6 \end{array}$$

Write various problems on the board (3 × 4 =) and ask the student to rewrite them in the other formation.

$$\begin{array}{r} 3 \\ \times\,4 \\ \hline 12 \end{array}$$

5. Give the student a copy of Activity Sheet 9–7A. The student will be asked to draw a set, name a set, and write a multiplication equation for a set.
   Answer Key: (*Part One*) , ;
   (*Part Two*) 3 sets of 3, 4 sets of 4; (*Part Three*) 3 × 2 = 6, 2 × 4 = 8, 2 × 2 = 4, 4 × 3 = 12

Directions:

Memorizing the Multiplication Tables

1. Give the student a copy of Activity Sheet 9–7B. Explain that these are called the *Multiplication Tables* and that each problem is called a *Multiplication Fact*. Explain that the facts represent the sets learned earlier. Then discuss the importance of memorizing the tables to make solving math equations much quicker. Inform the student that knowing the multiplication tables also helps with division.

2. Show the student how to use the Multiplication Table: Look at the number on the top line and move down to the number along the left side. The answer is located in the answer square at which they meet. Give examples for practice.

3. The student can use the blank chart on the activity sheet to write and practice each table.

Extension Activity: Use the charts on Activity Sheet 9–7B. Play "Five in a Row." Each student gets a different color marker or colored pencil. A caller gives a multiplication fact to each player. The player responds and, if correct, writes the answer in the correct square. The player tries to get five answers written in a row. The other players try to block their opponents. The first player with five in a row wins. *Variation*: Players try to get three in a row or four in a row.

Name_____ Date_____

Multiplication

Part One: Draw the sets.

4 sets of 2   3 sets of 5

Part Two: Write the words to name each set.

  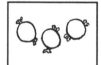 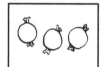    

_____   _____

Part Three: Write a multiplication problem for each set.

_____ × _____ = _____   _____ × _____ = _____

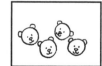    

_____ × _____ = _____   _____ × _____ = _____

Name_____ Date_____

	0	1	2	3	4	5	6	7	8	9	10	11	12
0	0	0	0	0	0	0	0	0	0	0	0	0	0
1	0	1	2	3	4	5	6	7	8	9	10	11	12
2	0	2	4	6	8	10	12	14	16	18	20	22	24
3	0	3	6	9	12	15	18	21	24	27	30	33	36
4	0	4	8	12	16	20	24	28	32	36	40	44	48
5	0	5	10	15	20	25	30	35	40	45	50	55	60
6	0	6	12	18	24	30	36	42	48	54	60	66	72
7	0	7	14	21	28	35	42	49	56	63	70	77	84
8	0	8	16	24	32	40	48	56	64	72	80	88	96
9	0	9	18	27	36	45	54	63	72	81	90	99	108
10	0	10	20	30	40	50	60	70	80	90	100	110	120
11	0	11	22	33	44	55	66	77	88	99	110	121	132
12	0	12	24	36	48	60	72	84	96	108	120	132	144

	0	1	2	3	4	5	6	7	8	9	10	11	12
0													
1													
2													
3													
4													
5													
6													
7													
8													
9													
10													
11													
12													

MULTIPLICATION

Lesson 9-8: Division

• • • • • • • • • • • • • • • • •

Objectives: The student will learn the vocabulary and the process of basic division. The student will be aware of the relationship between multiplication and division.

Vocabulary: set; divide; divided by; quotient; dividend; divisor

Materials: Activity Sheet 9–8; 12 manipulatives for each student (dried beans or macaroni work well); Pencil; Yarn or string cut in two large pieces long enough to make two large circles on the floor in which two students will stand

Teaching Note: The student must know multiplication facts before starting division.

Directions:

1. Ask four students to stand in the front of the room. Say, "There are four students in all." (Ask the students to count with you.)

2. Next say, "There are four in all. From these four, I want to make *sets* with two students in each *set*." (You might want to explain that a set is similar to a group.) Make two circles on the floor with yarn/string and tell the students that these are the sets. Ask the four students who are standing, "Can you make two sets of two?" Give the students an opportunity to perform the task themselves. Provide help, if necessary, by asking two of the students to stand in one circle and the other two in the other circle. Ask, "How many sets of two are there?" (**Response:** "There are two sets of two.") Continue with other examples.

3. Write the following words on the board, read, and ask the student to repeat: "**Four in all**, **divided by two in each set, equals two sets**."

4. Explain to the student that this can be written as a division problem: 4 ÷ 2 = 2. Inform the student that this is read, "Four *divided by* two equals two." Ask the student to repeat and then write the problem. Practice with other problems.

5. Tell the student that there is another way to write this division problem. It is called *long division*. Write this problem on the board. Ask the student to copy.

$$2\overline{)4}$$ with quotient 2

6. Tell the student that there are important parts to a division problem. The number that is being divided is called the *dividend*, the number that it is divided by is called the *divisor*, the answer is called the *quotient*. Write these words on the board by the correct number in the problem. Show the student how to line up the answer with the ones or tens in the dividend. Practice with other problems.

$$\text{divisor} \rightarrow 2 \overline{\smash{\big)}\, 4} \leftarrow \text{dividend} \qquad \overset{2 \; \leftarrow \text{quotient}}{}$$

7. Remind the student that when finding the quotient of a division problem, he/she should think of the multiplication fact that goes with it, e.g., $5 \times 4 = 20$, $20 \div 5 = 4$, $20 \div 4 = 5$.

8. Give the student a copy of Activity Sheet 9–8. The student will be asked to identify sets, write, and solve division problems. **Answer Key:** (*Part One*)
00000 00000; (*Part Two*) $8 \div 4 = 2$, $6 \div 2 = 3$; (*Part Three*) 4, 4, 6, 10, 8, 12, 8, 5, 3, 8, 7, 10; (*Part Four*) $\overset{7}{5\overline{\smash{\big)}35}}$ $\overset{4}{6\overline{\smash{\big)}24}}$ $\overset{10}{9\overline{\smash{\big)}90}}$ $\overset{7}{7\overline{\smash{\big)}49}}$;

(*Part Five*) 27 is the dividend, 3 is the divisor, and 9 is the quotient.

Extension Activities:

1. Ask a group of students to stand at the front of the room. Ask them to form different sets; e.g., two sets of three, four sets of two, etc.

2. Ask the students to work in pairs and create various division problems by drawing sets. Another pair of students writes and solves the equation.

3. Give the student a number of manipulatives. Ask him/her to follow these directions, for example, using the manipulatives. Say, "Six in all" (student counts out six manipulatives) "divided by two sets" (student makes two sets of three using manipulatives) "equals?" (student responds "Three") Then write the equation $6 \div 2 = 3$. Student also writes the equation. Continue with other examples.

Name_____ Date_____

Division

Part One: Draw the set.

10 in all, divided by 2 sets = 5 in each set. $10 \div 2 = 5$

Part Two: Write each division problem.

_____ ÷ _____ = _____   _____ ÷ _____ = _____

Part Three: Find the quotient. Line it up in the correct place with the dividend (tens or ones).

7⟌28   3⟌12   6⟌36   4⟌40   8⟌64   12⟌144

7⟌56   5⟌25   8⟌24   9⟌72   6⟌42   10⟌100

Part Four: Rewrite the division problems using long division. Then find the quotient.

35 ÷ 5 =   24 ÷ 6 =   90 ÷ 9 =   49 ÷ 7 =

Part Five: Label each part of the division problem. Write the word by the correct number.

| Divisor, Quotient, Dividend |

9 ←——— _____

————→ 3⟌27 ←——— _____

_____

Lesson 9-9: Fractions

• • • • • • • • • • • • • • • • • • • •

Objectives: The student will learn that a fraction is a part of a whole. The student will learn to read and write the fractions.

Vocabulary: part; whole; half; names of fractions

Materials: Activity Sheet 9–9; Colored pencils; 1 white paper circle about 12–18 inches in diameter (write the words "Happy Birthday" on the circle and color to look like the top of a birthday cake); Tape to secure the paper to the board; 2 sheets of plain white paper for each student

Directions:

1. Tape the circle to the board and tell this story: "Joseph had a birthday party. He invited his four friends. His mother made a birthday cake." (Point to the circle.) "After they sang 'Happy Birthday,' Joseph cut the cake into six pieces. Joseph, his four friends, and his mother had a part of the cake."

2. Draw lines to show the six pieces of cake. Explain to the student that each of these pieces is a *part* (point to the pieces) of the *whole*. (Run your hand over the whole circle.) Explain that we call each part a *fraction*.

3. Write the fraction $\frac{1}{6}$ on each piece of the circle. Explain that this is the way to write a *fraction*. Then explain that the bottom number, 6, is called the *denominator* (student repeats) and shows the whole or the total number of parts (point to the whole cake). The top number, 1, is called the *numerator* (student repeats) and shows a part of the whole. (Point to the pieces.) Tell the student that we read the fraction as *one-sixth*.

4. Say, "Everyone at the birthday party got one-sixth of the birthday cake." Point to the pieces. Ask a student to come to the board and cut out one-sixth of the birthday cake. Ask the student to say the sentence, "I cut one-sixth of the birthday cake." Continue this procedure with other students until all of the pieces are cut.

5. Give the student a piece of plain white paper. Ask him/her to fold it in half from top to bottom. Ask, "How many parts do you see?" (**Response:** "Two.") Explain that each part is called *one-half*. (Student repeats.) Write $\frac{1}{2}$ on the board. Ask the student to write $\frac{1}{2}$ on each part of the paper.

6. Show the student how to fold a paper into thirds. Then ask the student, "How many parts do you see?" (**Response:** "Three.") Ask the student to color one part of the paper red. Explain that this can be shown by the fraction $\frac{1}{3}$. Explain that we call this fraction *one-third*. Ask the student to repeat and write $\frac{1}{3}$ on the red section of the paper.

7. Ask the student, "How many parts are left?" (two). Ask the student to color the remaining two parts blue. Write $\frac{2}{3}$ on the board. Ask, "What do you think this fraction is called?" (**Response:** "Two-thirds.") Ask the student to repeat and write $\frac{2}{3}$. Review and ask, "How many parts are red?" (**Response:** "One-third.") Ask, "How many parts are blue?" (**Response:** "Two-thirds.")

8. Write the fraction $\frac{3}{3}$ on the board. Ask the student, "How many parts are in this whole paper?" (**Response:** "Three.") Then ask, "If the paper is divided into three parts" (point to the denominator) "and you have all three parts," (point to the numerator) "then you have one whole paper. This is written 1." Explain that the fraction three-thirds equals one whole. Write $\frac{3}{3} = 1$ on the board. Explain that if the numerator and the denominator are the same number, the fraction equals 1. Write $\frac{4}{4} = 1$. Give other examples and ask the student to write $= 1$ on the board.

9. Give the student a copy of Activity Sheet 9–9. The student will be asked to identify fractions and write fractions. **Answer Key:**

(*Part One*)   (*Part Two*)   (*Part Three*)

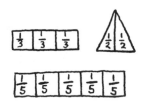

$\frac{3}{3} = 1, \frac{2}{2} = 1$

Name_____ Date_____

Fractions

Part One: Color the parts that show the fraction.

$\dfrac{5}{8}$
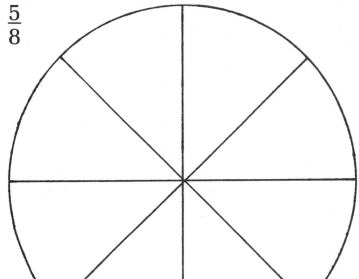

$\dfrac{3}{4}$
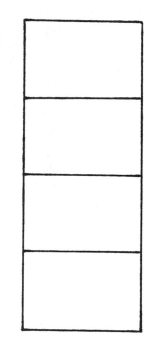

Part Two: Write the fractions inside each part.

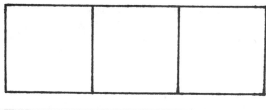

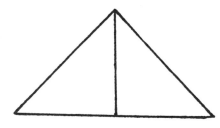

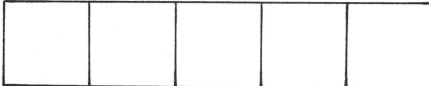

Part Three: Write the correct answer.

$\dfrac{3}{3} = $ _____ $\dfrac{2}{2} = $ _____

Lesson 9-10: Place Value and Reading Numbers

● ●

Objectives: The student will learn the place value of numbers from ones to millions. The student will learn to read, write, and say numbers.

Vocabulary: ones; tens; hundreds; thousands; ten thousands; hundred thousands; millions

Materials: Activity Sheet 9–10; Transparency of Activity Sheet 9–10; Overhead projector; Pencil

Teaching Note: This is an important skill for the ESL student to master because he/she will encounter these terms in many areas of the curriculum. The student will also need to read, write, and say these numbers in many academic and life situations.

Directions:

1. Give the student a copy of Activity Sheet 9–10. Explain that we know the value of numbers (how much) by their position (where they are) in the number. Explain that this is called *place value*.

2. Begin with the ones and tens place values. While the student uses the activity sheet and you use the transparency, say and write the number 25 on the place value chart and ask the student to say the number, write it in the correct position on the place value chart, and then read it. Explain that the 2 in the tens column means 2 sets of 10, and the 5 in the ones column means 5 ones. Give other examples and follow the same procedure.

3. As each place value is mastered, move on to the next one, including the previous ones learned. The student should be able to read, say, and write the numbers with multiple place values.

Extension Activities:

1. Play "Who Wants to Be a Millionaire?" On one side of an index card, write a number with multiple place values. On the other side, write a question that deals with a subject the students are studying. The student reads the money amount on the card and then answers the question. If the question is answered correctly, the student keeps the card. At the end of the game, the values of the cards are added and the student with the most money is the winner.

2. Play "Number Memory." Write various numbers with multiple place values on pairs of cards. Turn them face down and mix them up. Each student must turn over one card and read the number. He/She then tries to find a matching number by turning over another card and reading it. If a pair is made, the student keeps the cards. The player with the most pairs wins.

Name_____ Date_____

Place Value Chart

millions	hundred thousands	ten thousands	thousands	hundreds	tens	ones

Lesson 9-11: Money! Money! Money!

Objectives: The student will learn the names and the value of U.S. currency. The student will learn to write the cent sign and the dollar sign with a decimal.

Vocabulary: coin; money; penny; nickel; dime; quarter; one-dollar bill; five-dollar bill; ten-dollar bill; twenty-dollar bill; dollar sign; $; cent sign; ¢; decimal point; cost; "How much does this cost?"

Materials: Activity Sheets 9–11A and 9–11B; Pencil; 1 of each: penny, quarter, nickel, dime, one-dollar bill; 1 sheet of lined paper for each student

Directions:

1. Give the student a copy of Activity Sheet 9–11A. Point to the illustrations of the coins and the bills and tell the student that this is called *money*. Ask the student to repeat. Next, ask the student to brainstorm ideas of what money is used for, e.g., to buy things, to pay bills, to save, allowance, salary, etc. Discuss.

2. Point to the coins on Activity Sheet 9–11A and say, "These are called *coins*. They are round and are made from metal." Begin with the penny. Show the student a real penny and let him/her touch it and examine it, front and back. Then tell the student that this coin is called a *penny and it is worth one cent*. Explain that *worth* means "value" or "how much." Write **1¢** on the board and ask the student to copy. Explain that **¢** is called a *cent sign*. Now point to the penny and ask, "What is this called?" (**Response:** "A penny.") Ask, "What is it worth?" (**Response:** "It is worth one cent.")

3. Continue with the same procedure for the nickel, dime, and quarter.

4. Next, point to the bills. Explain that these are called *bills* and are made from paper. Begin with the *one-dollar bill*. Show the student a real one-dollar bill and let him/her touch it and examine it. Point out the numeral one on the corner of the bill. Explain that this numeral tells us how many dollars the bill is worth. We say "one dollar bill." Student repeats. Tell the student that one dollar is worth 100 cents. Point to the dollar and ask, "What is this called?" (**Response:** "One dollar.") Ask, "How much is it worth?" (**Response:** "One hundred cents.") Next, name the five-, ten-, and twenty-dollar bills. Student repeats.

5. Write **$1.50** on the board. Explain that the *dollar sign* shows the dollar amount and that a *decimal point* is placed before the cent value. Model how to say the amount and have student repeat. Write various amounts on the board. Ask the student to copy and say the amount, e.g., $1.25, $5.50, $10.75, etc. Next, just say an amount and ask the student to write it.

6. Continue with the same procedure for the five-, ten-, and twenty-dollar bills.

7. Explain that the cents can be written with a dollar sign. Write **$.50** on the board. Explain that this is fifty cents. Tell the student that the two places to the right of the decimal point mean cents. Write other examples on the board. Ask the student to copy and say the amount.

8. Give the student a copy of Activity Sheet 9–11B. The student will be asked to write cent and dollar amounts. The student will also be asked to write the correct word for each coin and dollar. **Answer Key:** (*Part One*) dime 10¢, penny 1¢, quarter 25¢, nickel 5¢, dollar $1.00 100¢; (*Part Two*) $10.35, $.10, $5.50, $.40; (*Part Three*) 15¢, 6¢, 21¢

Extension Activities:

1. Cut out various coins and bills from Activity Sheet 9–11A. Make various combinations and ask the student to say the amount. *Variation*: Say an amount. The student must choose the correct coins and bills and write the amount.

2. Write various amounts on index cards. The student must say the amount.

3. Buy play money and call it "ESL money." The student can earn the ESL money by accomplishing various tasks or jobs in the classroom. Have a supply of candy bars, pencils, pens, small toys, etc., and place a money value on each one. The students can use their ESL money to buy these items.

4. Purchase paper price tags from an office supply store. Write various amounts on the tags and put the tags in a bag. The student picks a tag from the bag and says the price. A point is scored for each correct answer. (The student tries to get a certain number of points for a treat or privilege.)

Name_____ Date_____

Money! Money! Money!

Penny	Nickel	Dime	Quarter
1¢	5¢	10¢	25¢
one cent	five cents	ten cents	twenty-five cents

One Dollar

$1.00

one hundred cents

Five Dollars

$5.00

Ten Dollars

$10.00

Twenty Dollars

$20.00

Name_____ Date_____

Money! Money! Money!

Part One: Write the correct word next to the coins. Then write the amount using the ¢ sign.

| quarter | dollar | penny | nickel | dime |

_____   _____   _____

_____   _____   _____

Write the correct word. Then use the $ sign and the ¢ sign.

_____

_____

_____

Part Two: Add the money. Then write the amount using $ and a decimal point.

_____   _____

_____   _____

Part Three: Add the coins. Write the amount using a ¢ sign.

_____   _____   _____

Lesson 9-12: Standard Measurement (U.S.)

Objective: The student will learn the vocabulary and understand the concept of inch, foot, and yard.

Vocabulary: measure; inch; foot; yard; yardstick; length; width; height

Materials: Activity Sheet 9–12; Pencil; 1 12-inch ruler for each student; Yardstick; 1 sheet of 8½ × 11 lined paper for each student; Tape or overhead projector

Teaching Note: This lesson lends itself to working with a partner. You may want to do this lesson over several days.

Directions:

1. Tell the student that today he/she is going to learn to *measure*. Explain that to measure means to find out the size of something. Give the student a 12-inch ruler. Point to the inch marks and tell the student that this ruler is divided into twelve small parts. Each part is called an *inch*. Write the word **inch** on the board. Ask the student to repeat. Now ask the student to count the inches aloud while pointing to each one.

2. Place your finger at the beginning line of the ruler and move to the numeral 1. Tell the student that this distance equals one inch. Ask the student to move his/her finger in the same manner and repeat "one inch." Repeat this procedure from 1–12 inches (e.g., one inch, two inches, three inches, etc.).

3. On the board, show the student how to begin at the starting point of the ruler and draw a line one inch long. Write **1″ or 1 in.** next to the line. Explain that ″ and in. are both short ways (abbreviations) to write *inch*. Say, "Draw a one-inch line." Student draws a one-inch line on his/her paper and writes 1 inch. Then ask, "How long is the line?" (**Response:** "The line is one-inch long.") Continue with this procedure for 2–12 inches.

4. Give the student a sheet of lined paper. Present it lengthwise (11 inches from top to bottom). Tape a piece of paper to the board. (This could also be done on the overhead.) Tell the student that you are going to *measure* the *length* of the paper. Run your finger along the paper's length. Explain that *length* means from end to end. Model how to measure the length of the paper. The student then measures his/her paper. Ask, "How *long* is the paper?" (**Response:** "The paper is eleven inches long.") Student writes the length on the paper.

5. Tell the student that you are going to measure the *width* of the paper. Model how to measure the width of the paper. Show the student the 1/2-inch marks and how to read them. The student then measures his/her paper. Ask, "How wide is the paper?" The student replies, "The paper is 8-1/2 inches wide."

476

Student writes the width on the paper. (For the older student, you may want to continue with 1/4 in. and 1/8 in.)

6. Write **12 inches = 1 foot** on the board. Read this and have the student repeat. Explain that *12 inches* equal *one foot*. Draw a line one foot long on the board. Write **1′** and **1 ft.** Explain that ′ and ft. are both short ways (abbreviations) to write *foot*. Ask the student to come to the board and draw a line 12 inches long. Student repeats and writes.

7. Next, show the student a *yardstick*. Say the name and ask the student to repeat. Tell the student that the yardstick measures one yard. Write *yard* and *yd.* on the board. Explain that yd. is a short way (abbreviation) to write *yard*. Trace the yardstick and draw a line 36 inches long on the board. Explain that *one yard* equals *36 inches* and count with the student (point to the inch marks). Ask a student to come to the board and—with a 12-inch ruler—measure the line in one-foot sections. The student should draw a line at each foot. Then together count the three sections. Ask, "How many feet equal one yard?" (**Response:** "Three feet equal one yard.")

8. Explain that we measure a person's *height* by using *feet and inches*. Explain that height means from the bottom of the foot to the top of the head. (**Gesture:** While standing, point to the bottom of your foot and then to the top of your head.) Ask student to stand by a wall. Place a sticker on the wall to show his/her height. Model how to measure a person's height by using the yardstick including both feet and inches. Then ask the students to work with partners and measure each other's height. Then they record the height, write, and read the sentence: <u>name</u> is _____ feet _____ inches tall.

9. Ask the student to take other measurements in the classroom and write them, e.g., the length and width of the classroom, the length of a window, the width of the door, etc. When done, ask, "What is the length of the room?" (**Reply:** "The room is _____ feet ____ inches long.") Continue with the question–answer activity.

10. Give the student a copy of Activity Sheet 9–12. The student will be asked to match vocabulary, measure, and write measurements. **Answer Key:** (*Part One*) 1. 6; 2. comb, 4; 3. rope, 5 inches long; (*Part Two*) Answers will vary; (*Part Three*) Inch—in., Foot—ft., Yard—yd.; (*Part Four*) 12 inches = 1 foot, 3 feet = 1 yard, 36 inches = 1 yard.

Extension Activities:

1. For homework, give the student a list of objects to measure in the home.

2. Ask the student to estimate length. Say, "Find objects in the room that are about an inch long, or a foot, or a yard, etc." The student then measures the objects to see how close the estimate came to the original estimate.

Name_____ Date_____

Inch, Foot, Yard

Part One: Measure the following objects. Write the correct words and numbers on the line.

How long is it?

1. The pencil is _____ inches long.

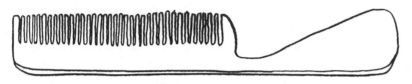

2. The _____ is _____ inches long.

3. The _____ is _____ _____ _____.

Part Two: Measure these items in your classroom. Write the length on the line.

Your teacher's desk _____   A crayon _____

A map _____   The computer mouse_____

Your index finger _____   A board eraser _____

Part Three: Draw a line from the word to the matching abbreviation. Write each one on the line.

Inch   yd.   _____   _____

Foot   in.   _____   _____

Yard   ft.   _____   _____

Part Four: Write the correct information on the line.

_____ inches = _____ foot   _____ inches = _____ yard

_____ feet = _____ yard

Lesson 9-13: The Metric System

Objectives: The student will learn the vocabulary for the basic units associated with the metric system. The student will learn the relationship between the metric system and the standard system of measurement.

Vocabulary: metric; standard; kilometer; meter; millimeter; centimeter

Materials: Activity Sheet 9–13; Pencil; 1 sheet of plain paper for each student; Yardstick; 1 ruler showing inches on one side and cm on the other side for each student

Teaching Note: Many ESL students will be familiar with the metric system. The United States is the only country in the world not totally committed to adopting this system. It is a simpler form of measurement and is based on the decimal system. The conversion table and visual representations will help the student make comparisons between the metric system and standard system of measurement. This lesson should be presented after Lesson 9–12.

Directions:

1. Give each student a ruler. Explain that there are two ways to measure things: One is called the *metric* system and the other, the *standard* system of measurement. Explain that the standard system is used in the United States.

2. Give the student a copy of Activity Sheet 9–13. Point to the conversion chart at the top of the page. Explain that 1 *meter* equals 1.1 yards or 3.3 feet. On the board, draw a line $39\frac{1}{2}$ inches long. Tell the student that this line is approximately 1 meter long. Write **1 meter** next to the line. Ask a student to hold the yardstick under the line and draw a line 1 yard long. Write **one yard**. Compare the meter to the yard. Ask, "Which one is longer?" (**Response:** "The meter is longer.") Then ask, "Is the meter a lot longer or just a little longer than the yard?" (**Response:** "The meter is a little longer than the yard.") Explain to the student that *m* is a short way (abbreviation) to write meter.

3. Point to the centimeter side of the ruler. Explain to the student that *cm* is a short way to write centimeter. Point to the table and show the student that 2.5 cm = 1 inch. Explain that .5 means $\frac{1}{2}$. Show the student the $\frac{1}{2}$ line for the centimeter. Ask the student to draw a line 1 inch long on a sheet of paper and write 1 inch next to it. Then under that line draw a line 2.5 cm long. Write 2.5 centimeters next to it. Ask the student to compare the two lines. Ask, "What do you notice about the two lines?" (**Response:** "The lines are equal.") Ask the student to draw and label a line 4 inches long on a sheet of paper. Now ask the student to measure the line in cm. Ask, "How many cm is it?" (10 cm) The student replies: "The line is 10 cm long."

4. Point to the standard side of the ruler and say, "12 inches equals one foot." Point to the cm side of the ruler and ask, "How many cm equal one foot?" Student responds: "30 centimeters equal one foot." Ask the student to draw two lines: one one foot long and one 30 cm long. Then compare.

5. Point to the *millimeters* on the ruler. Explain that *mm* is a short way (abbreviation) to write millimeter. (If the ruler does not show mm, see the ruler on Activity Sheet 9–13.) Tell the student that ten millimeters equal 1 centimeter. Point out the small size of the mm. Ask the student to draw a line 10 millimeters long and next to it write 10 millimeters. Now under it draw a line 1 cm long. Write 1 centimeter next to the line. Compare the two lines. Ask the student, "What do you notice about the two lines?" (**Response:** "The lines are equal.") (Or "This line is 10 millimeters. This line is 2.5 centimeters. The lines are equal.")

6. Choose a location that is approximately $\frac{1}{2}$ mile from your school. Say, "_____ is about one-half mile from school. That is about 1 kilometer." Explain that a short way (abbreviation) to write kilometer is *km*. (Walking the distance would be an excellent reinforcement activity.)

7. Ask the student to complete the rest of the questions on Activity Sheet 9–13. **Answer Key:** (*Part One*) 100 mm, 60 mm; (*Part Two*) 14 cm, 8 cm; (*Part Three*) Centimeter—cm, Millimeter—mm, Meter—m, 30 cm = 1 foot, 1 meter = 3.3 feet, 2.5 cm = 1 inch.

Extension Activity: Give the student a list of classroom objects and ask him/her to measure them in m, mm, cm. The student then writes the measurement and says, "The desk is _____ cm long." (For the more advanced student, ask him/her to convert metric to standard and standard to metric.)

Name_____ Date_____

The Metric System

Metric Conversion Table
1 meter = 3.3 feet or 1.1 yards   1 kilometer = 0.6 miles
2.5 centimeters = 1 inch   30 centimeters = 1 foot
10 millimeters = 1 centimeter

Part One: Cut out the ruler at the side of the page. Measure these objects in millimeters (mm).

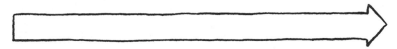

The arrow is _____ millimeters long.

The nail is _____ millimeters long.

Part Two: Measure these objects in centimeters (cm).

The line is _____ centimeters long.

The gum is _____ centimeters long.

Part Three: Match the word to its abbreviation. Then write the correct information on the line.

Centimeter	mm	_____ centimeters = 1 foot
Millimeter	m	_____ meter = 3.3 feet
Meter	cm	_____ centimeters = 1 inch

Lesson 9-14: Standard (U.S.) Liquid Measure

· ·

Objective: The student will learn the vocabulary and capacity of Standard Liquid Measurement.

Vocabulary: liquid; ounce; cup; pint; quart; gallon

Materials: Activity Sheet 9–14; Glass measuring cup; Pint container; Quart container; Gallon container; Food coloring; Large pitcher; Pencil

Teaching Note: It is helpful if the containers can be clear or semi-clear plastic. Plastic milk containers make excellent visuals.

Directions:

Before beginning the lesson, ask a student to fill a large pitcher with water and add a few drops of food coloring. This may need refilling.

1. Begin the lesson by discussing *liquids*. Give examples of different kinds of liquids. Ask the student to brainstorm more examples. Then ask, "What would be a problem when we measure liquid?" (**Response:** "Something must hold it.") (Or "It runs all over.")

2. Give the student a copy of Activity Sheet 9–14. Tell the student that this chart gives the units that measure liquid. Read the units (ounce, cup, pint, quart, gallon) and have the student repeat.

3. Begin with the *ounce*. Point to the ounce marks on the glass measuring cup. Tell the students that these measure ounces. Student repeats. Using the colored water in the pitcher, ask a student to fill the cup to the one-ounce mark. Give others an opportunity to do so. Ask, "How much water is in the cup?" (**Response:** "There is one ounce in the cup.") Write **oz.** on the board and tell the student that this is the short way (abbreviation) to write *ounce*. Give different amounts of ounces and ask the student to fill the measuring cup (5 oz., 3 oz., etc.).

4. Ask the student to fill the cup to the 8-ounce mark. Tell the student that 8 ounces equal *one cup*. Student repeats. Give other students an opportunity to pour 8 oz. of water in the cup. Ask, "How many cups is this?" (**Response:** "This is one cup of water.") Explain that the abbreviation **c.** is used for *cup*.

5. Show the student the *one pint* container. Tell the student that this container holds one pint. Student repeats. Explain that 2 cups equal one pint. Ask a student to measure one cup and pour it in the pint container. Ask a second student to do the same. Say, "This is one pint." Ask, "How many cups are in one pint?" (**Response:** "There are two cups in one pint.") Explain that the abbreviation **pt.** is used for *pint*.

6. Show the student the *quart* container and tell him/her that this container holds *one quart* of liquid. Student repeats. Tell the student that two pints equal one quart. Ask one student to fill a one-pint container and pour it into the quart container. Ask a second student to do so also. Say, "This is one quart." Now ask, "How many pints are in one quart?" (**Response:** "There are two pints in one quart.") Explain that the abbreviation **qt.** is used for *quart*. (You may want to extend this section to 4 cups = 1 quart.)

7. Show the student the *gallon* container and tell him/her that this container holds *one gallon* of liquid. Student repeats. Tell the student that four quarts equal one gallon. Ask one student to fill the quart container with liquid and pour it into the gallon container. Ask three more students to do so. Now say, "This is one gallon of liquid." Student repeats. Then ask, "How many quarts equal one gallon?" (**Response:** "There are four quarts in one gallon.") Explain that the abbreviation **gal.** is used for *gallon*.

8. Ask the student to complete Activity Sheet 9–14. The student will be asked to identify and compare liquid units of measure. **Answer Key:** (*Part One*) 8 ounces = 1 cup, 2 pints = 1 quart, 2 cups = 1 pint, 4 quarts = 1 gallon; (*Part Two*) Ounce—oz., Cup—c., Pint—pt., Quart—qt., Gallon—gal.;

(*Part Three*)

(*Part Four*) 6 cups = 3 pints, 8 quarts = 2 gallons, 16 ounces = 2 cups, 4 pints = 2 quarts.

Extension Activities:

1. Collect plastic containers of different varieties that hold a cup, pint, quart, gallon. Compare and ask the student to guess how much each holds.

2. Collect several of the same kind of container in different sizes (e.g., milk). Ask the students to put equal amounts together in groups (e.g., 4 quart containers = 1 gallon container, 2 cups = 1 pint, etc.).

3. For the more advanced student, ask him/her to solve more difficult problems. How many pints are in two gallons? How many cups are in one gallon? How many quarts are in two gallons? etc.

Name_____ Date_____

Standard Liquid Measure

ounces (oz.)	8 ounces = 1 cup
cup (c.)	2 cups = 1 pint
pint (pt.)	2 pints = 1 quart
quart (qt.)	4 quarts = 1 gallon
gallon (gal.)	

Part One: Look at the chart above. Write the correct information on the line.

_____ ounces = 1 _____   2 pints = 1 _____

2 _____ = 1 pint   4 _____ = 1 gallon

Part Two: Match the word to the correct abbreviation.

Ounce   gal.

Cup   pt.

Pint   qt.

Quart   oz.

Gallon   c.

Part Three: Color 6 ounces in the cup.

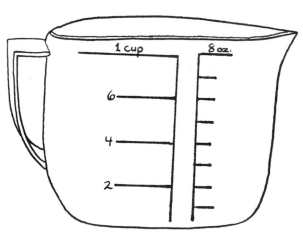

Part Four: Use the chart to help you solve these problems. Work with a partner.

_____ cups = 3 pints   _____ quarts = 2 gallons

_____ ounces = 2 cups   _____ pints = 2 quarts

Lesson 9-15: Graphs

• • • • • • • • • • • • • • • • •

- **Line Graph**
- **Bar Graph**
- **Pie Graph**

Objectives: The student will understand that a graph is a visual representation of information. The student will learn to read and to make a line graph, a bar graph, and a pie graph.

Vocabulary: bar graph, line graph, pie graph, label

Materials: Activity Sheets 9–15A and 9–15B; Pencil; Colored pencils

Directions:

1. Give the student a copy of Activity Sheet 9–15A. Point to the examples of the graphs and tell the student that both of these illustrations are called *graphs*. Explain that graphs are a way of showing information. Graphs help us "see" the information. Also explain that a graph helps *compare* information between two or more things. Tell the student that *compare* means to look at what is the same and what is different for each item.

2. Begin with Graph 1. Explain to the student that this type of graph is called a *line graph*. Point to the line. Ask the student to point to the line. Explain that the position of the line on the graph shows the information.

3. Point to the title of the graph. Ask the student to read it. Supply help, if necessary. Explain that the title tells what information the graph is giving. Ask, "What information is this graph going to show?" (**Response:** The amount of rainfall for the week of April 10) (or How much rain fell during the week of April 10)

4. Point to the labels across the top of the line graph. Ask, "What information is given along this part of the graph?" (**Response:** The days of the week or days)

5. Now, point to the labels along the side of the graph. Ask, "What information is given here?" (**Response:** Inches of rainfall)

6. Ask, "What was the amount of rain on Sunday?" Show the student how to "read" the graph by locating Sunday and then moving down the row of inches to the number indicated for that day. (**Response:** It rained two inches on Sunday.)

7. Read the questions for Graph 1 on Activity Sheet 9–15A. The student should first answer verbally, then write the answer. The answer should be in a complete sentence, e.g., Thursday had the most rain.

8. Point to the *bar graph*. Explain that this kind of graph is called a bar graph. Ask the student, "How is this graph different from the line graph?" (**Response:** It uses bars instead of lines) Ask the student to read the title, "Second-Grade Candy Sales." Ask, "What information is the graph going to give?" (**Response:** How much candy the second grades sold) Ask the student to read the label on the top line of the graph (classroom numbers). Then ask, "What information does this give you?" (**Response:** Identifies the second-grade classes)

9. Ask the student to read the label at the side of the graph (Boxes of Candy Sold). Ask the student, "What information does this give you?" (**Response:** How many boxes of candy were sold)

10. Next, ask the questions from Activity Sheet 9–15A. The student should answer verbally and then write the answer. **Answer Key:** (*Part One*) 1. Thursday; 2. Saturday; 3. Monday and Tuesday; 4. 4 inches; 5. 1 inch; (*Part Two*) 1. 214; 2. 213; 3. No; 4. 50 boxes; 5. 70 boxes.

11. Now, ask the student to look at the *pie graph* on Activity Sheet 9–15B. Explain that a pie graph gives information in parts that look like pieces of a pie. The bigger the part, the larger the amount.

12. Have the student look at the title of the pie graph and ask, "What does this pie graph show?" (**Response:** The languages spoken by students in Mrs. Shaya's ESL class) Ask the questions written for the pie graph and ask the student to answer verbally and then write the answer in a complete sentence.

13. Ask the student to complete Example 2 on the activity sheet. The student will be given specific information and asked to draw a graph to represent the information. **Answer Key:** 1. Five languages; 2. Spanish; 3. Vietnamese; 4. Arabic.

Extension Activities:

1. Ask the student to find different kinds of graphs in newspapers and magazines. Discuss the type of graph and the information it gives.

2. Ask the student to graph his/her scores on spelling tests for a month.

Name_____ Date_____

Line Graph and Bar Graph

Graph 1: Line Graph
The Amount of Rainfall
for the Week of April 10

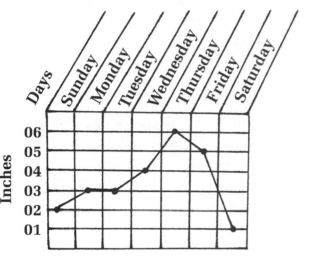

Part One: Read the graph and answer the questions.

1. What day had the *most* rain?

   _____

2. What day had the *least* amount of rain?

   _____

3. What days had *equal* amounts of rain?

   _____

4. How much rain fell on Wednesday?

   _____

5. How much rain fell on Saturday?

   _____

Graph 2: Bar Graph
Second-Grade Candy Sales

Room	#212	#213	#214	#215
100				
90			▨	
80			▨	
70			▨	▨
60			▨	▨
50	▨		▨	▨
40	▨		▨	▨
30	▨	▨	▨	▨
20	▨	▨	▨	▨
10	▨	▨	▨	▨
0	▨	▨	▨	▨

Boxes of candy sold

Part Two: Read the graph and answer the questions.

1. What room sold the *most* candy?

   _____

2. What room sold the *least* amount of candy?

   _____

3. Did any rooms sell *equal* amounts of candy?

   _____

4. How much candy did Room 212 sell?

   _____

5. How much candy did Room 215 sell?

   _____

Name_____ Date_____

Pie Graph

Part One: Read the graph and answer the questions.

The kinds of languages spoken in Mrs. Shaya's ESL class.

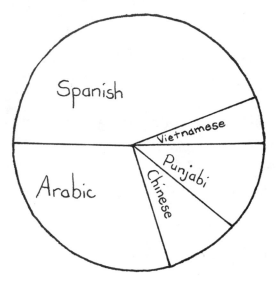

1. How many languages are spoken?
   _____

2. Which language is spoken by the most students?
   _____

3. Which language is spoken by the least number of students?
   _____

4. What language is the second largest group?
   _____

Part Two: Read the homerun results for the Cardinal baseball team. Make a graph to show the results. Don't forget the labels.

Player	Homeruns
Sam	2
Sophia	4
Luis	6
Kristie	8
Don	1

Lesson 9-16: Story Problems

• •

Objective: The student will learn the vocabulary commonly associated with story problems, how to decide what operation is required, and how to draw a picture to help solve the problem.

Vocabulary: story problem; How many are left?; How many in all?; How many more?; What is the total number?

Materials: Activity Sheet 9–16; Pencil; 1 sheet of plain white paper for each student

Teaching Note: Story problems can be a challenge for the ESL student, particularly because of the vocabulary involved. This lesson teaches the student a strategy called RADS that can help him/her understand and solve the story problem.

Directions:

1. Give the student a copy of Activity Sheet 9–16. Explain that a math story problem is written with words and not equations (numbers). A story problem tells the information in a story form and then asks a question. Write the following example on the board: "**I was bringing my groceries into the house. I had six oranges in a bag. I dropped the bag and four oranges fell out. How many oranges were left in the bag?**"

2. Tell the student that there is a way to help him/her solve a story problem. Point to the strategy RADS at the top of Activity Sheet 9–16. Explain the steps as follows:

   R—Read. Read the story problem from beginning to end.

   A—Ask. What is the question asking? Is there a clue word? Underline the question at the end of the problem.

   D—Draw. Reread and draw each step.

   S—Solve. Look at the drawing. Think about the question and write an equation. Solve the equation.

3. Give the student a piece of plain white paper. Using the RADS strategy, model on the board how to solve the problem that was given in step 1. The student should copy on his/her paper.

4. Explain to the student that key words in the question can help him/her decide how to solve it. Tell the student that "How many are *left*?" and "How many *more*?" usually mean subtraction. "How many *in all*?" or "What is the *total number*?" usually mean addition.

5. Explain that in story problems the answer should be labeled with a word identifying it, e.g., 2 oranges.

6. Ask the student to complete Activity Sheet 9–16. This can be done as either a directed or independent activity. Ask the student to solve the story problems using the RADS strategy. **Answer Key:** 1. 7 pieces of candy; 2. 21 homeruns; 3. 17 students; 4. 5 candy bars; 5. 26 teams.

Extension Activities:

1. Ask the student to work with a partner and write story problems. These problems are then shared and solved by other classmates. (Writing story problems gives excellent practice in using the language and understanding the analytical approach to the problem.)

2. For the more advanced student, you may want to expand to two-operation story problems. *Example*: Susie has pet cats. Three of them are white. Three are gray. Last night, two of the gray cats ran away. How many cats does she have now?

Name_____ Date_____

Story Problems

R—**Read.** Read the problem from the beginning to the end.

A—**Ask.** What is the question asking? Is there a clue word? Underline the question at the end of the problem.

D—**Draw.** Reread and draw each step.

S—**Solve.** Look at the drawing. Think about the question and write an equation. Solve the equation.

Directions: Solve each story problem using the RADS strategy.

1. Susan has ten pieces of candy. She gives three pieces to her friends. How many pieces does she have left?

2. Luis hit ten homeruns this baseball season. Sarah hit five home-runs and Jatin hit six. How many homeruns did they hit in all?

3. There are twenty-two students in Mrs. Sill's class. Five students went home sick. How many students are left?

4. There are fifteen students in Louisa's Math Club. She brings ten candy bars for treats. How many more candy bars does she need?

5. There are ten teams in the Red League, ten teams in the Blue League, and six teams in the Yellow League. What is the total number of teams altogether?

Lesson 9-17: Patterns

• • • • • • • • • • • • • • • •

Objectives: The student will understand what a pattern is and how to recognize one. The student will be able to create a pattern.

Vocabulary: pattern; repeat

Materials: Activity Sheet 9–17; Pencil; Colored pencils or crayons; 9 sheets of $8\frac{1}{2} \times 11$ construction paper—3 yellow, 3 red, 3 blue; Yellow, red, and blue construction paper cut in small squares—each student should have 3 squares of each color; Tape

Teaching Note: Recognizing patterns is a very important cognitive skill for the student to develop. It is used in many areas of the curriculum, in concrete and abstract ways.

Directions:

1. (*For a group*) Begin by asking the students to stand in a line at the front of the room. Place them in an alternating boy–girl pattern. Ask, "Do you see anything special about the line?" (**Response:** "It is boy–girl, boy–girl.") (You can use other patterns, such as blond hair, dark hair, etc.)

2. Place construction paper on the board in this pattern: yellow, red, blue, yellow, red, blue. Ask the student to say the colors with you. Then explain that this is called a *pattern*. It *repeats* over and over. (**Gesture:** Make a continuous arching movement with your hand to indicate again and again.)

3. Ask a student to come to the board and continue the pattern with the paper.

4. Give each student 3 small squares of yellow, red, and blue construction paper. Ask the students to copy the pattern at their desk or table.

5. Now, make other patterns with the colors and ask the student to copy them, e.g., 2 red, 2 blue, 2 yellow. Ask the student to identify the pattern, "What is the pattern?" (**Response:** "The pattern is two red, two blue, two yellow.")

6. Ask various students to make patterns and have the class identify and copy them.

7. Explain to the student that numbers can be put in patterns. Write the pattern 1, 3, 5, 7 on the board. Ask a student to identify the pattern and come to the board to continue writing it. Put other examples on the board and ask other students to identify and continue the pattern. Then ask students to create other patterns, and have other students come to the board to continue them.

8. Give the student a copy of Activity Sheet 9–17. The student will be asked to identify and continue patterns. They will also be asked to create patterns.

Answer Key: (*Part One*) Pattern of circle, triangle square; pattern of heart, heart, star; (*Part Two*) 40, 50, 60, 70, 80, 90, 100; 6, 5, 4, 3, 2, 1, 0; 1234567; (*Part Three*) Patterns will vary.

Extension Activities:

1. Give the student a piece of graph paper. Ask him/her to create a patterned design and color it in a pattern. See the sample shown here.

2. Give the student manipulatives and ask him/her to create a pattern (by color, number, etc.).

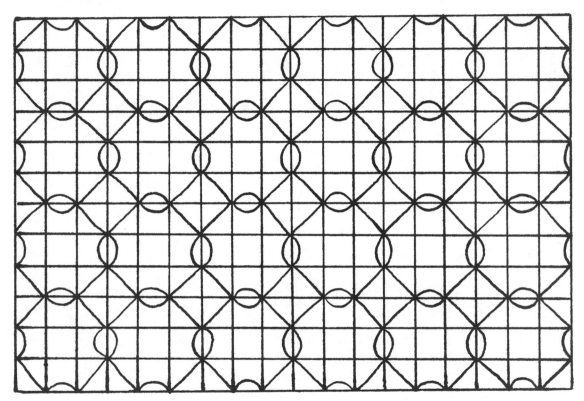

Name_____ Date_____

Patterns

Part One: Continue the pattern in each box. Then color it in a pattern.

Part Two: Continue each pattern. Write the number on the line.

10, 20, 30, _____, _____, _____, _____, _____, _____, _____

10, 9, 8, 7, _____, _____, _____, _____ , _____, _____, _____

1 2 3 4   1 2 3 4 5   1 2 3 4 5 6   __ __ __ __ __ __

Part Three: Draw a picture pattern. Then write a number pattern. Give your paper to a friend and ask him/her to identify and continue the patterns.

Section 10

Time, Calendar, and Weather

The information presented in this section is knowledge that the ESL student will use daily and will last for a lifetime. The ability to tell time is imperative in all walks of life and vital to a person's success in a new culture. Missed opportunities and negative reaction can occur from tardiness or missed appointments.

In some instances, the ESL student may be asked to supply the time, date, or weather conditions. It is always gratifying to be able to understand a question such as, "What time is it?" or "What's the date?" and to answer with a correct response.

Knowing weather conditions can be an issue of health and safety. Section 10 presents the ESL student with various kinds of weather and weather conditions. Dressing for the weather and weather information sources are described.

Calendar time is an excellent opportunity for language development and informing the student about upcoming events and important holidays. No student wants to show up for school when it's a day off! Discussing the date and the weather on a daily basis will aid the mastery of this life skill information and improve the student's quality of life.

Time, Calendar, Weather Pretest-Posttest

Student:_____   Date:_____

Class: _____

1. Ask the student to count to 60.

2. Ask the student to count by 5's to 60.

3. Ask the student to tell you the time on the clocks below.

4. On the clock below, ask the student to identify the hour hand, the minute hand, and the second hand.

5. Ask the student to tell you what he/she does in the morning, afternoon, evening, and night.

6. Ask the student to give you two names for 12 o'clock. (noon and midnight)

7. Ask the student to explain A.M. and P.M.

8. Ask the student to recite the days of the week in order.

9. Ask the student to read the names of these days:

Monday   Thursday   Sunday   Friday   Saturday

Tuesday   Wednesday

10. Ask the student to recite the months of the year in order.

11. Ask the student to tell you today's date. (month, day, year)

12. Ask the student to write today's date.

Time, Calendar, Weather Pretest-Posttest (continued)

13. Ask the student to write today's numerical date.

14. Ask the student to name the four seasons.

15. Ask the student to identify the following kinds of weather.

Notes:

_____

_____

_____

_____

_____

_____

_____

Lesson 10-1: Analog Teaching Clock

Objective: The student will make a clock to be used as a teaching aid and to identify the parts of a clock.

Vocabulary: clock; face/dial; minute hand; hour hand; wristwatch

Materials: Activity Sheet 10–1; Scissors; 1 brass fastener for each student

Teaching Note: It would be very helpful to make an analog teaching clock for yourself to use as a demonstration tool. You might also want to laminate the clocks.

Directions:

1. Point to the clock on the classroom wall (if possible) and say, "This is called a *clock*. Clocks show time." Ask, "What is this called?" (**Response:** "A clock") Ask, "What do clocks do?" (**Response:** "Clocks show the time.")

2. Give the student a copy of Activity Sheet 10–1. Tell the student that he/she is going to make a clock.

3. Point to your face and say, "This is my face. What do you see on my face?" (**Response:** "Eyes, nose, mouth") Next, trace the circumference of the clock with your finger and say, "This is called the *face* of the clock." Ask, "What is this called?" (**Response:** "The face of the clock") "We also call this the *dial*. What do you see on the face of the clock?" (**Response:** "Numbers" ["Numerals"])

4. Hold up your hands and ask the student to do so also. Ask, "What are these called?" (**Response:** "Hands") Tell the student that you are going to ask him/her to point at objects in the classroom. (Model: Point to the door, point to the board, etc.) Ask, "What am I doing?" (**Response:** "Pointing")

5. Point to the hands of the clock on Activity Sheet 10–1. Say, "These are the *hands* of the clock." Explain that the hands of the clock also point. Point to the classroom clock and ask, "What do the hands of the clock point to?" (**Response:** "Numbers")

6. Ask the student to cut out the face and the hands of the analog clock on the activity sheet. Place the hour hand and the minute hand next to each other. Point to the hour hand and ask the student to do so. Say, "This is called the *hour hand*." Ask, "What is this called?" (**Response:** "The hour hand") Follow the same procedure for the *minute hand*.

7. Ask the student to put the minute hand directly under the hour hand. Say, "The hour hand is short. The minute hand is long." (**Gesture:** Hold your index finger and thumb slightly apart for short, and move them farther apart for

long.) Ask the student to repeat. Now ask the student to point to the minute hand and then the hour hand. Student points.

8. Model for the student how to push the brass fastener through the designated holes, first in the hour hand and then in the minute hand. Then push it through the hole in the face of the clock. Ask the student to describe what he/she is doing and identify the parts as he/she is using them. (It may be helpful to poke a small hole in the paper before putting the fastener through.) Now show the student how to push the prongs of the fastener apart to secure the hands and clock.

9. Show the student how the hands move around the clock. Ask the student to do so. Then ask, "What do the hands do?" (**Response:** "They move around the clock.")

10. If the clock in your classroom has a second hand, explain that it is another hand of the clock and is called the *second hand.*

11. Point to the face and the hands of the analog clock and say, "The face and the hands make a clock. "

12. Review. Ask the student to identify the parts of the clock: face/dial, hour hand, minute hand, clock, (second hand on classroom clock).

13. Show the student a *wristwatch.* Explain that this is called a wristwatch, but usually we say "watch." Discuss the differences and similarities between a clock and a wristwatch.

Extension Activity: Ask the student to look through magazines and catalogs for different kinds of clocks.

Name_____ Date_____

Analog Teaching Clock

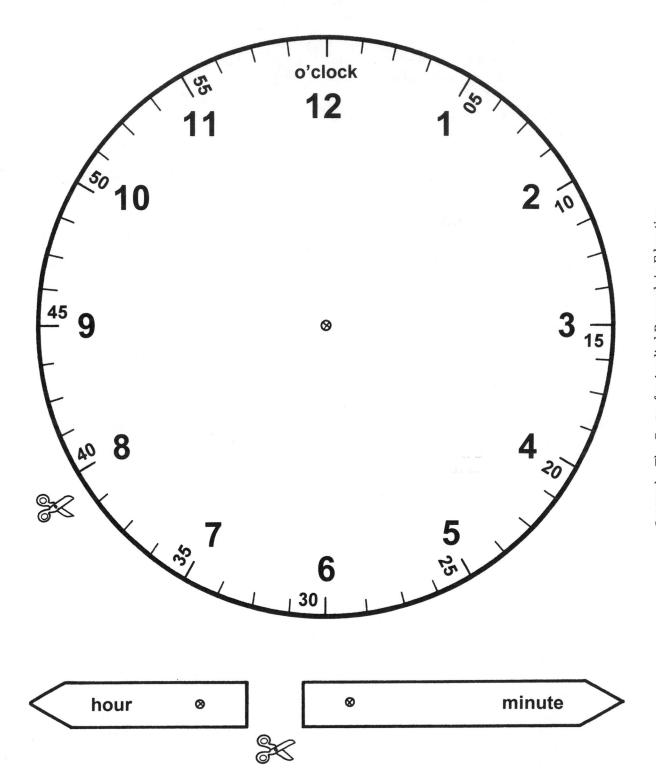

Lesson 10-2: Telling Time: o'clock

Objectives: The student will learn the concepts hour/first, minute/last, and also visually recognize and verbalize the term "o'clock." The student will understand and respond to the term "tell time" and the questions "What time is it?" and "Do you have the time?"

Vocabulary: o'clock; hour/first; minute/last; "tell time"; "What time is it?"; "Do you have the time?"

Materials: 1 analog teaching clock for each student; Activity Sheet 10–2; Pencil

Directions:

1. Say, "Today you are going to learn to *tell time.* 'Tell time' means that you 'know' and can 'say' the correct time." (**Gesture:** Point to your head for 'know' and to your mouth for 'say.')

2. Point to the hour hand on the analog teaching clock and say, "The hour hand points to the hour. We say the hour first." (**Gesture:** Hold up your finger to indicate first.) Next, explain that the large numerals 1 through 12 show the hours. Move the hour hand around the face of the clock and say each number as you come to it. Ask the student to say them with you.

3. Point to the minute hand and say, "The minute hand points to the minutes. We say the minutes last." Ask the student to supply the correct word: "Hours (first), minutes (last)."

4. Ask, "Where is the number 12?" (**Response:** "At the top of the clock") Ask the student to point the minute hand to the number 12. Point to the minute hand and the 12 and say, "When the minute hand points to the twelve, it is called *o'clock.*" Ask, "What is this called?" (**Response:** "o'clock")

5. Keep the minute hand on the 12 and move the hour hand to the numeral 1. Ask the student to do so. Point to the hour hand and say, "One." Student points and repeats. Then point to the minute hand and say, "O'clock." Student points and repeats. Then say, "One o'clock." Student repeats.

6. Keep the minute hand on the 12 but move the hour hand to the other numerals in succession and say "two o'clock, three o'clock, etc." Student moves hands and repeats the time.

7. Tell the student there are two questions that are used to ask for the time: "What time is it?" and "Do you have the time?" Point to the analog teaching clock and ask, "What time is it?" (**Response:** "One o'clock") Again point to the analog teaching clock and ask, "Do you have the time?" (**Response:** "One o'clock")

8. For practice keep the minute hand on the 12 but move the hour hand to random numerals. Ask the student to tell you the correct time. Alternate using the questions "What time is it?" and "Do you have the time?" You may want to switch roles, giving the student an opportunity to choose the hour and ask for the time using the questions.

9. Give the student a copy of Activity Sheet 10–2. The student will be asked to write the correct numeral before o'clock, and to draw the hands of the clock in the correct positions. **Answer Key:** (across) 1. 8 o'clock, 1 o'clock, 4 o'clock, 2 o'clock, 3 o'clock, 6 o'clock; 2. Check to see that the student's times are correct.

10. After the activity sheet is completed, ask the student to work with a partner, each one taking turns "telling" the time.

Name_____ Date_____

Telling Time: o'clock

1. **Write the correct time on the line below each clock.**

_____ o'clock   _____ o'clock   _____ o'clock

_____ o'clock   _____ o'clock   _____ o'clock

2. **Draw the hour hand and the minute hand to show the correct time on each clock.**

9 o'clock   3 o'clock   11 o'clock

5 o'clock   10 o'clock   7 o'clock

Lesson 10-3: Telling Time–Hours and Minutes

. . . .

Objective: The student will learn how to tell time using both hours and minutes (in increments of five).

Vocabulary: hour; minute; "o'five"

Materials: Activity Sheet 10–3; Pencil

Teaching Note: It is helpful for the student to be able to count by 5's to the number 55.

Directions:

1. Say to the students, "Today we are going to learn to tell time using all of the numbers on the clock for hour and minute."

2. Tell the student that there is a way to say the numbers when the minute hand points to them. Place the minute hand on the 12 and say "o'clock," then move it around the face of the clock counting by 5's. Ask the student to repeat the process.

3. Place the hour hand at any number and keep it there. Remind the student that we say the hour first, then the minute. Again move the minute hand around the face of the clock, only this time say the hour first, then the minute; e.g., 9:05 (o'five), 9:10, 9:15, etc. (You may want to point to the hour hand as you say the hour and to the minute hand as you say the minute.) Ask the student to move the minute hand on his/her clock as you do so and repeat the time.

4. Explain to the student that as the minute hand moves closer to the 12, the hour hand moves closer to the next hour. Model with the hour hand on the analog teaching clock; e.g., 9:40, 9:45, 9:50, 9:55.)

5. For practice, verbally give the student random times to demonstrate on his/her clock. Then show random times on your clock and ask the student to say the correct times. This activity can be done with learning partners as well.

6. Give the student a copy of Activity Sheet 10–3. Explain to the student that the time is written with the hour first, then two dots, and the minutes last. Point to the times underneath each clock. Read each time and ask the student to repeat.

7. Say various times and ask the student to write them on the board.

8. Ask the student to complete the activity sheet. He/she will be asked to draw the correct time on blank clocks and to write the time.

9. Ask the student to share his/her responses for #2.

Extension Activity: Ask the student to show and verbally share various times during the day when he/she has special classes, e.g., Art, Gym, ESL.

Name_____ Date_____

Telling Time—Hours and Minutes

1. **Read the time below each clock. Then draw the hour hand and the minute hand to show that time.**

9:20

10:10

2:35

1:30

10:15

7:05

5:45

3:40

6:55

2. **Read the sentence and write the time on the line.**

I wake up at _____.

School begins at _____.

School ends at _____.

I go to bed at _____.

Lesson 10-4: Digital Clock

Objectives: The student will learn to visually recognize and verbalize the time using a digital clock. The student will learn that 00 means o'clock.

Vocabulary: digital; 00

Materials: Activity Sheet 10–4; Scissors; Digital alarm clock (realia)

Directions:

1. Say, "Today we are going to learn to tell time using a different kind of clock. It is called a *digital clock*." Show the student the digital alarm clock. Ask, "Where have you seen this kind of clock?" (**Response**: In the bedroom, at home, in the car) This may be a good opportunity to demonstrate how the alarm clock works and what it is used for.

2. Point to the analog clock in the classroom (or use the analog teaching clock) and discuss the similarities and differences between the two kinds of clocks.

3. Turn on the digital clock and set the time to 1:00. Explain to the student that 00 on a digital clock means o'clock. Point to the one and say, "One." Point to the 00 and say, "O'clock." Ask the student, "What time is it?" (**Response**: "One o'clock")

4. Give the student a copy of Activity Sheet 10–4. Ask the student to cut out the clock and the number strips.

5. Show the student how to insert the number strips into the clock (hour first, then minute).

6. Put the hour strip at any hour and the minute strip at 00. Ask the student to do so also. Ask, "What time is it?" (**Response**: "_____ o'clock")

7. Now choose other hour-and-minute combinations and ask the student, "What time is it?" Student responds.

8. Say a time and ask the student to show it on the digital clock.

Extension Activity: Ask the students to work in pairs and show different times, e.g., What time do you wake up? start school? end school? go to bed? etc.

Digital Clock

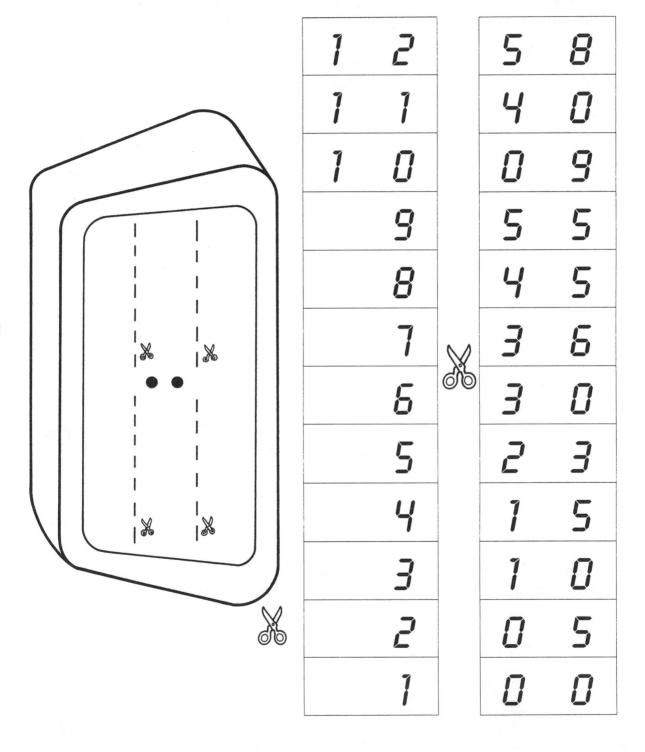

1 2	5 8
1 1	4 0
1 0	0 9
9	5 5
8	4 5
7	3 6
6	3 0
5	2 3
4	1 5
3	1 0
2	0 5
1	0 0

Lesson 10-5: Noon and Midnight

• •

Objective: The student will visually recognize and verbalize the concepts of noon and midnight.

Vocabulary: noon; midnight

Materials: Activity Sheet 10–5; Pencil

Directions:

1. Say, "Today you are going to learn two different names for 12 o'clock."

2. Give the student a copy of Activity Sheet 10–5. Point to the illustration of the first clock and ask the student, "What time is it?" (**Response**: "Twelve o'clock")

3. Then tell the student that twelve o'clock (point to the hands of the clock) during the day (point to the sun) is called *noon*. Ask, "What do we call twelve o'clock during the day?" (**Response**: "Noon")

4. Ask the student, "What do you usually do at noon?" (**Response**: Eat lunch, go to recess, have a class, etc.) For a prompt, point to the illustrations.

5. Say, "Twelve o'clock during the day is called noon." Ask the student to repeat.

6. Next, point to the second clock and ask the student, "What time is it?" (**Response**: "Twelve o'clock")

7. Explain that twelve o'clock (point to the hands of the clock) at night (point to the moon) is called *midnight*. Ask, "What is twelve o'clock at night called?" (**Response**: "*Midnight*")

8. Discuss what we usually do at midnight. (**Response**: "Sleep")

9. Ask the student to complete Activity Sheet 10–5. The student will be asked to identify and write *noon* and *midnight*.

Extension Activity: Draw a picture of a sun and a moon. Hold up the sun and the student replies, "Noon." Hold up the moon and the student replies, "Midnight."

Name_____ Date_____

Noon and Midnight

12 o'clock = "noon"

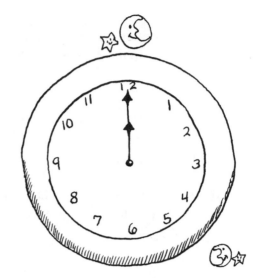

12 o'clock = "midnight"

day

night

1. Look at the pictures. Draw a line to noon or midnight.

Noon

Midnight

2. Read the sentence. Write noon or midnight on the line after it.

I am asleep at _____.

I eat lunch at _____.

Lesson 10-6: A.M. and P.M.

• •

Objectives: (*For older students, grades 4+*) The student will understand the concept of A.M. and its relationship to midnight and noon. The student will also learn that A.M. and P.M. each consist of twelve hours.

Vocabulary: A.M.; P.M.; noon; midnight

Materials: Activity Sheets 10–6A and 10–6B; Transparency of Activity Sheet 10–6A; Pencil; 24 manipulatives (tokens, dried beans, macaroni, etc.) for each student and one set for demonstration; Paper; Overhead projector

Teaching Note: The concepts of noon and midnight should be understood before this lesson is presented.

Directions:

1. Say, "Today you are going to learn that the day is divided into two parts called A.M. and P.M."

2. Give each student 24 manipulatives and one plain sheet of paper. Ask the student to place the manipulatives on the paper. Next, place 24 manipulatives on the overhead. Say, "One day has twenty-four hours." Ask, "How many hours are in one day?" (**Response:** "Twenty-four")

3. Point to the manipulatives and say, "Each of these (manipulatives) is one hour. Altogether they equal one day." Draw a circle around the 24 manipulatives. Ask the student to do so.

4. Tell the student that you are going to make two equal groups from the 24 manipulatives. Draw a line down the middle of the circle and make two groups of 12. Ask the student to do so on his/her paper. Ask, "How many are in each group?" (**Response:** "Twelve")

5. Write A.M. over one group and ask the student to do so. Say, "We will call this group A.M." Ask, "What is this group called?" (**Response:** "A.M.") Ask, "How many hours are in A.M.?" (Student counts and responds, "There are twelve hours in A.M.")

6. Next write P.M. over the other group and ask the student to do so. Say, "We will call this group P.M." Ask, "What is this group called?" (**Response:** "P.M.") Ask, "How many hours are in P.M.?" (**Response:** "There are twelve hours in P.M.")

7. Give the student a copy of Activity Sheet 10–6A. Point to the A.M. clock and say, "This clock shows the A.M. hours. A.M. begins at midnight. Midnight is also called 12 A.M. A.M. has twelve hours and ends at noon." Trace the arrows on the clock with your finger. Ask the student to do so also.

8. Next, point to each number and say the time as you move around the clock: "12 A.M., 1 A.M., 2 A.M., etc." Ask the student to do this with you.

9. When you arrive at the number 12 again, say, "Noon." Say, "A.M. begins at midnight, and ends at noon." Ask the student to repeat.

10. Now point to the P.M. clock. Tell the student that noon is also called 12 P.M. Explain that P.M. has twelve hours. Trace your fingers around the clock following the arrows. Ask the student to do so also.

11. Next, begin counting 12 P.M., 1 P.M., 2 P.M., etc. Point to each number and ask the student to count with you. Continue until you reach the number 12 again and explain that you are back at midnight and the A.M. hours begin again. Tell the student "P.M. begins at noon, and ends at midnight."

12. Ask the student to complete Activity Sheet 10–6A. Then give the student a copy of Activity Sheet 10–6B to complete. The student will be asked to draw pictures of what he/she does at specific A.M. and P.M. hours. **Answer Key**: 1. P.M., A.M.; 2. A.M., P.M.

Extension Activity: Draw two long columns on the board. Write the headings A.M. and P.M. Then write a time with the same number in each column, e.g., 9 A.M., 9 P.M. Ask the student to write what he/she is doing at each time, e.g., in school, doing homework. This helps reinforce the time of the day when A.M. and P.M. occur. Choose other times and add to the list.

Name_____ Date_____

A.M. and P.M.

A.M.   P.M.

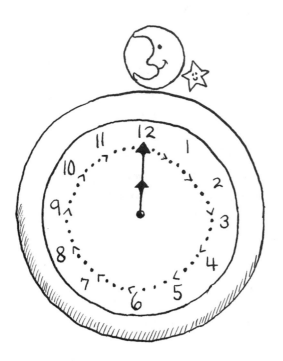   

Begins at midnight,   ends at noon.   Begins at noon,   ends at midnight.

1. Circle A.M. or P.M.

A.M./P.M.   A.M./P.M.

2. Write A.M. or P.M. on the line.

Begins at midnight,
ends at noon.   _____

Begins at noon,
ends at midnight. _____

Name_____ Date_____

A.M. and P.M.

Draw a picture in each box to show what you do at the time.

7:30 A.M.	9:00 A.M.
12:00 P.M.	**3:00 P.M.**
6:00 P.M.	**10:00 P.M.**

Lesson 10-7: Morning, Afternoon, Evening, Night

Objective: The student will learn the meaning of morning, afternoon, evening, and night as specific times of the day related to the position of the sun and behavior.

Vocabulary: rising, morning, afternoon, evening, night

Materials: Activity Sheet 10–7; Scissors; Pencil

Teaching Note: This is an excellent lesson in which the student can use gestures to learn vocabulary. For example, *stretching*, *yawning*, *getting dressed*, and *eating breakfast* can be used for the morning.

Directions:

1. Say, "Today you are going to learn the names of certain times of the day."

2. Give the student a copy of Activity Sheet 10–7. Begin with the word *morning*. Say the word and ask the student to repeat. Then point to the illustration of morning and ask the student to describe what is happening. (**Response:** Someone is waking up, getting out of bed, stretching, etc.) (**Suggested gestures:** Waking up—close, then open your eyes widely; Stretch—everyone stretches with arms above the head.) Next, note the position of the sun. Say, "The sun is *rising*." Ask the student to repeat. (**Gesture:** Move your hand in an arching motion as if rising.) Ask, "What do you do in the morning?" The student should respond in a complete sentence; e.g., "I get up. I get dressed. I take a shower." For the more advanced student, show the hours of the morning on the analog teaching clock. Explain early morning and late morning.

3. Continue with the same procedure for afternoon, evening, and night.

4. Ask the student to cut out the pictures and the word cards from Activity Sheet 10–7. Then have him/her mix them up and put them back in correct pairs.

5. Keep the picture cards face up. Turn the word cards face down. Mix up the word cards. Ask the student to choose a word card, read it, and match it to the correct picture. *Variation:* Turn the word cards and the picture cards face down and mix them up. The student then turns over a word card, reads it, and then turns over a picture card to try to make a match. If it matches, he/she keeps it. If not, the cards are turned over and returned to the pile. This activity can be done with a partner.

6. If the student is unable to read the words, play the game with the picture cards only and accept a verbal response.

Extension Activities:

1. Ask the student to write Morning, Afternoon, Evening, Night on the back of Activity Sheet 10–7. Then under those words, he/she makes a list of things he/she does at that time of day.

2. Ask the student to choose a time of the day (morning, afternoon, evening, or night) and then pantomime an action for that time, e.g., stretch, sleep, etc. Then the other students try to guess the time of day.

Morning, Afternoon, Evening, Night

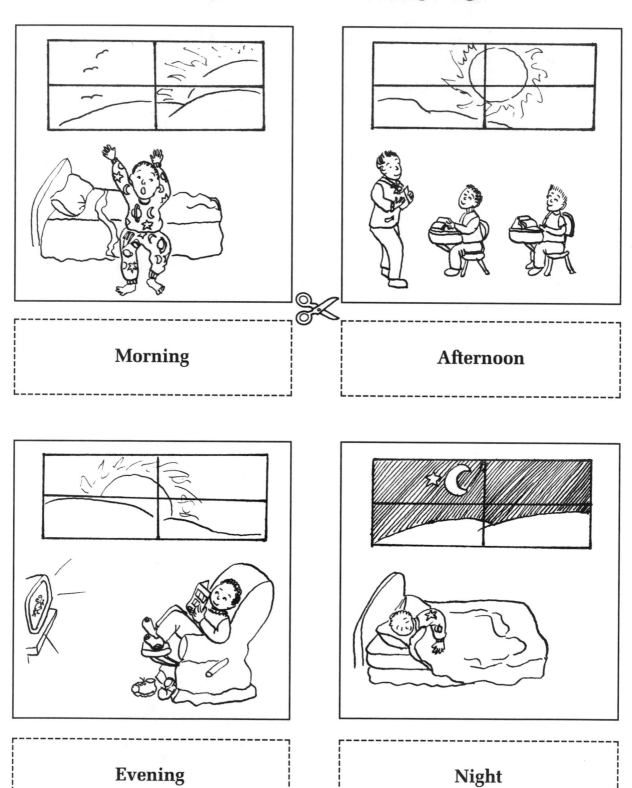

Morning

Afternoon

Evening

Night

Lesson 10-8: Time Change–Daylight Saving Time

Objective: The student will understand that in the spring the time changes and the clocks are set one hour forward; in fall the time changes and the clocks are set one hour back. The reason for this is to provide more hours of sunlight.

Vocabulary: time change, Daylight Saving Time, spring, fall, forward, back

Materials: Activity Sheet 10–8; Analog teaching clock (1 for demonstration or one for each student)

Teaching Note: This is an excellent lesson to present just prior to a time change. The student can then take the activity sheet home and remind his/her parents to change the clocks.

Directions:

1. Say, "Today you are going to learn about Daylight Saving Time. In spring and in fall, we change the time on our clocks."

2. Give the student a copy of Activity Sheet 10–8. Explain that in order to have more hours of sunlight (point to the sun) twice a year (point to the calendars), we change the time (point to the clocks). Now say, "This is called Daylight Saving Time." (At present, the changes take place for spring on the first Sunday in April; for fall, the last Sunday in October.)

3. Point to the first Sunday in April that is indicated on the calendar. Explain that on that day, the first Sunday in April, we move the time *one hour forward*. Trace the illustration of the arrow and move your finger forward. Ask the student to do so also while repeating the word "forward." Ask: "In spring, when do we change the time?" (**Response:** "The first Sunday in April") Ask, "How do we change the time?" (**Response:** "One hour forward")

4. Put your finger on the clock and trace one hour forward. Tell the student that this clock shows how to move the time one hour forward. Ask the student to trace one hour forward.

5. Next, demonstrate on the analog teaching clock how to move the *hour hand* one hour forward. Ask the student to repeat and change the time on the clock moving the hour hand one hour forward.

6. Next, teach the time change for fall. Repeat the same procedure as above.

7. Teach the student the saying "Spring forward! Fall back!" Point to the illustrations on the activity sheet. Say the saying and ask the student to repeat. Then ask the student to stand, say "Spring forward," and jump. Then say "Fall back" and the student gently falls back.

517

8. The actual time changes at 2 A.M., Sunday morning. Ask the student why this could be a problem when changing the clocks. (Most people are asleep.) Inform them that most people change the time before they go to bed on Saturday night.

Extension Activity: Say a season (fall, spring) and an hour. Ask the student to change the time accordingly on a teaching clock.

Name_____ Date_____

Daylight Saving Time

April

Sunday	Monday	Tuesday	Wednesday	Thursday	Friday	Saturday
●						

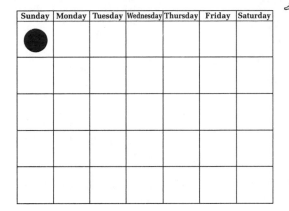

October

Sunday	Monday	Tuesday	Wednesday	Thursday	Friday	Saturday
●						

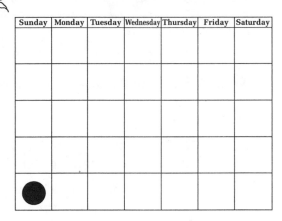

The first Sunday in April

The last Sunday in October

Spring—1 hour **forward**

Fall—1 hour **back**

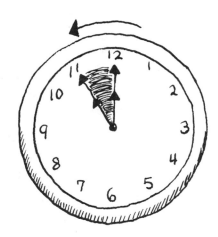

"Catchy Reminder"

Spring forward!

Fall back!

Lesson 10-9: Quarter After; Half Past; Quarter to

● ●

Objective: (*For students grades 4+*) The student will learn alternative vocabulary used to describe specific times of the day.

Vocabulary: quarter after; half past; quarter to

Materials: Activity Sheet 10–9; Pencil; Analog teaching clock

Directions:

1. Give the student a copy of Activity Sheet 10–9. Tell the student that he/she is going to learn some different ways of saying certain times.

2. Point to the first clock and ask the student to tell you the time. (**Response**: "Five-fifteen.") Inform the student that there is another way to say five-fifteen: *quarter after* (or *past*) *five*. Explain that if the minute hand is pointing at the number 3 (15 minute position), then it is called *quarter after* that hour.

3. Practice with the analog teaching clock. Keep the minute hand at the quarter after position and choose various hours. Ask the student to say the time. Remind the student that quarter after is said first, followed by the number of the hour.

4. Use the same procedure as above to teach *half past* and *quarter to* (or *of*). You may want to inform the student that starting from half past 12 is actually halfway around the face of the clock.

5. For reinforcement, move the analog teaching clock to random hours and either quarter after, half past, or quarter to that hour. Ask the student to tell the time. Then give the student a time to show on the analog teaching clock.

6. Ask the student to complete Activity Sheet 10–9. **Answer Key**: 1. half past, quarter to, quarter after; 2. Check to be sure student's clocks show the correct times.

Name_____ Date_____

Quarter After; Half Past; Quarter to

Quarter after (past)

(5:15)

Half past

(5:30)

Quarter to (of)

(5:45)

1. Circle the correct time words under each clock.

quarter after (past)

quarter to (of)

half past

quarter after (past)

quarter to (of)

half past

quarter after (past)

quarter to (of)

half past

2. Draw the hour hand and the minute hand to show the correct time on each clock.

quarter to ten

half past two

quarter after six

Lesson 10-10: Time Equivalents

• •

Objective: (*For students grades 4+*) The student will learn the time equivalents for second, minute, hour, and day.

Vocabulary: second; minute; hour; day; equal

Materials: Activity Sheet 10–10; Colored pencils; Scissors

Directions:

1. Give the student a copy of Activity Sheet 10–10. Tell the student that he/she is going to learn about equal amounts of time using seconds, minutes, hours, and a day.

2. Point to the bars at the top of the activity sheet. Say, "These two bars are the same size. They are *equal*."

3. Ask, "What is different about the bars?" (**Response:** "One is divided into smaller parts.") Ask the student to color each part of the bar a different color.

4. Ask the student to cut out the smaller parts on the top bar and place them on top of the bottom bar. Ask, "When we put the smaller parts together, are the two bars still equal amounts?" (**Response:** "Yes.") Say, "We can put smaller parts together to equal one large unit."

5. Point to the illustration of the clock. Point to the second and minute lines around the face of the clock. Explain that these lines tell how many seconds and minutes have gone by. Ask the student to point and count them with you.

6. Point to the time equivalents on the activity sheet. Ask the student to read them with you.

7. Ask the student to complete the activity sheet. The student will be asked to supply the correct amount of time to equal a larger unit of time. **Answer Key:** 60 minutes = 1 hour; 24 hours = 1 day; 60 seconds = 1 minute. *Stumpers*: 48 hours; 240 minutes; 300 seconds.

Extension Activity: Ask the student to solve some equivalency math problems, such as:

Three hours = _____ minutes.
Two days = _____ hours.
120 seconds = _____ minutes.

Name_____ Date_____

Time Equivalents

Color each part of the top bar a different color. Cut out each part. Then put them on top of the bottom bar. Are the amounts still equal?

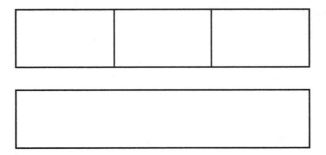

There are 60 second and minute marks on this clock.

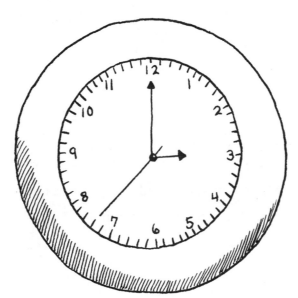

Time Equivalents

60 seconds = 1 minute
60 minutes = 1 hour
24 hours = 1 day

Fill in the blanks:

_____ minutes = _____ hour

_____ hours = _____ day

_____ seconds = _____ minute

Stumpers: _____ hours in 2 days? _____ minutes in 4 hours?

_____ seconds in 5 minutes?

Lesson 10-11: Time Zones

• •

Objectives: (*Students grades 4+*) The student will understand that the continental United States is divided into four time zones, with an hour difference between each one. The student will be able to identify in which time zone he/she resides. The student will learn that from the east to the west an hour is added between time zones, and from west to east an hour is taken away.

Vocabulary: time zone; Eastern Standard Time; Central Standard Time; Mountain Standard Time; Pacific Standard Time

Materials: Activity Sheet 10–11; 4 different highlighters or colored pencils (light colors) for each student; Analog teaching clock

Directions:

1. Give the student a copy of Activity Sheet 10–11. Say, "Today you are going to learn that the United States is divided into four different *time zones*. A time zone is a geographic part of the country that shares the same time." Point to the various time zones. (Explain that Alaska and Hawaii are not shown on the map because they are not in Pacific Standard Time.)

2. Give the student four different colored highlighters or light colored pencils. Begin with the *Eastern Standard Time Zone*. Ask the student to color (shade) that area on the map. Ask, "What time zone is this?" (**Response:** "Eastern Standard Time Zone") Next discuss the cities and states located in that time zone. Inform the student that this is the eastern part of the continental U.S.

3. Move to the other time zones and follow the same procedure as above.

4. Then locate your town or city on the map. (Or write it on the map.) Ask the student to identify the name of the time zone in which he/she lives.

5. Say the names of various cities and ask the student to identify in what time zone it is located.

6. Explain to the student that there is a one-hour difference between each time zone. As you go from east to west, the time is one hour less. As you go from west to east, the time is one hour more.

7. Point to the clocks at the bottom of the map. Begin with Eastern Standard Time. Ask the student, "What time is it?" (**Response:** 10 o'clock) Now, move to Central Standard Time and ask, "What time is it?" (**Response:** 9 o'clock) Point out to the student the time is one hour less. Continue through the different time zones.

8. Switch directions and begin with Pacific Standard Time. Follow the same procedure as above.

9. Ask the student to complete Activity Sheet 10–11. The student will be asked to give the time in different time zones.

10. Explain that the abbreviations for the time zones are: EST, CST, MST, PST.

11. You may want to inform the student that when a time is announced, it is wise to listen for the time zone. A TV program aired at 10:00 EST must be calculated as to what time it will be shown in another zone. **Answer Key**: (*Part Two*) 1. 9 o'clock; 2. 9 o'clock; 3. 12 o'clock; 4. 7 o'clock.

Extension Activity: Give the student a TV program guide to find his/her favorite program. Then ask the student what time the program would be on in the different time zones.

Name_____ Date_____

Time Zones

The continental United States (not including Alaska and Hawaii) has four different time zones. These time zones are Eastern Standard Time, Central Standard Time, Mountain Standard Time, and Pacific Standard Time.

Part One: Color each time zone a different color.

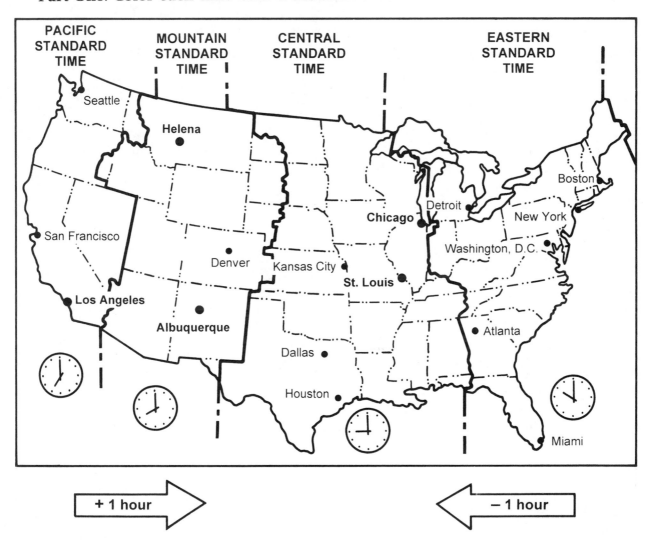

Part Two: Read the question and write the correct time on the line.

1. When it's 8 o'clock in Denver, what time is it in Chicago? _____

2. When it's 11 o'clock in Kansas City, what time is it in Los Angeles? _____

3. When it's ⸱ o'clock in New York, what time is it in Seattle?_____

4. When it's 6 o'clock in Dallas, what time is it in Boston? _____

Lesson 10-12: Calendar

• • • • • • • • • • • • • • • • • • • •

Objective: The student will learn the concepts associated with the calendar: days of the week, months of the year, date and numerical date, and year.

Vocabulary: days of the week; months of the year; date; numerical date; year

Materials: Activity Sheets 10–12A, 10–12B, 10–12C, 10–12D, 10–12E; 1 clear bingo chip for each student; Pencil

Teaching Notes:

1. This lesson plan is divided into five separate concepts, each pertaining to the calendar. The concept will be listed along with the accompanying activity sheet and suggestions for teaching.

2. It is important to set aside time each day for discussing the calendar. It is a language-rich opportunity and should include not only the date, but discussion of upcoming school events and holidays, and a daily weather report.

Directions:

1. *"Calendar," Activity Sheet 10–12A*. Give each student a copy of a monthly calendar. Ask the student to write the name of the month, the year, and the numbers of the days in the correct location. Note any special events, vacation days, or holidays on the calendar. It is important that the student realize that in the United States we say the *month*, *date*, *year*. In many other countries, the order is date, month, year. The concept of *today, tomorrow, yesterday, the day after tomorrow, the day before yesterday*, and *weekend* should be taught. Provide each student with one clear bingo chip to put on today's date, say the concept to be learned, and ask the student to put the chip on the correct day. (For example, say, "Yesterday." Student moves the chip to yesterday's date.) It is important for the student to use the correct form of the verb "to be" when saying "Today is, Tomorrow is, Yesterday was." Also point out that today is the present, tomorrow is the future, and yesterday was the past.

2. *"Days of the Week," Activity Sheet 10–12B*. Explain to the student that in the United States, Sunday is the first day of the week. (In many other countries, it is not.) Ask the student to say the days in order with you. Then ask the student to write the day and the abbreviation in the blank boxes provided on Activity Sheet 10–12B. Remind the student that the name of the day begins with a capital letter. Next, ask the student to cut out the boxes that contain the name of the day, mix them up, and put them in order again. *Variations*: (1) Cut out the number cards also. Put the number cards in order and the student must place the correct day next to it. (2) Turn over the number cards and the name cards, and mix them up. The student must turn over one name card

527

and one number card trying for a match. This continues until all matches are made.

3. *"Months of the Year," Activity Sheet 10–12C.* Give the student a copy of the two-page activity sheet. Together, read the months of the year. If needed, break the months into smaller units for memorization. Point to the numbers on the month cards and explain that January is the first month, and so on. This concept will be important to understand when the student writes the numerical date. Ask the student to write the name of the month and the abbreviation in the boxes provided. Remind the student that the name of the month begins with a capital letter. *Variations*: (1) Ask the student to cut out the month cards, mix them up, and put them back in order again. (2) Write a number from 1–12 on the board and ask the student to identify the name of the month that corresponds to it.

4. *"Date and Numerical Date," Activity Sheet 10–12D.* Give the student a copy of the activity sheet. Explain that there are two ways to write the date: write the whole date (March 25, 2002) or use a short way with numbers (3/25/02). Tell the student that there is a comma between the number of the day and the year. Explain how to write the numerical date. Ask the student to complete Activity Sheet 10–12D as a directed activity, with a partner, or independently. When completed, ask the student to read the dates. Check for accuracy. **Answer Key:** (*Part One*) 1. 3/30/00, 2. 4/10/94, 3. 1/5/05, 4. 10/7/06, 5. 6/15/02, 6. 11/26/04, 7. 7/14/01, 8. 2/6/99, 9. 8/17/03, 10. 5/1/98; (*Part Two*) 1. July 19, 2002, 2. June 26, 2001, 3. November 26, 1999, 4. September 3, 1998, 5. February 14, 2004, 6. May 30, 2003.

5. *"Calendar Equivalents," Activity Sheet 10–12E.* Give the student a copy of the activity sheet. Together, read the equivalents on the chart at the top of the page. Ask the student to complete the questions on the activity sheet. This is a good activity to do with a partner. **Answer Key:** (*Part One*) 1. 7, 2. 30 (31), 3. 1, 4. 12, 5. 52, 6. 365; (*Part Two*) 1. 2, 2. 21, 3. 2, 4. 3; (*Part Three*) 365 days = 1 year, 12 months = 1 year, 52 weeks = 1 year, 7 days = 1 week, 30 (31) days = 1 month, 4 weeks = 1 month.

Extension Activities:

1. Ask the student to investigate the traditional signs of the zodiac. He/she can then find his/her sign, the symbol that represents it, and the attributes that go along with it.

2. Ask the student to research Stonehenge, one of the oldest and heaviest calendars known to people.

3. Ask the student to research calendars from other countries.

4. Ask the student to bring a calendar from his/her native country to school and share it with the class. Make a bulletin board of the various calendars.

5. Ask the student to find out the meaning of the names of the days and months.

Calendar

Month _____

Year _____

Sunday	Monday	Tuesday	Wednesday	Thursday	Friday	Saturday

Name_____ Date_____

Days of the Week

1	**Sunday** **Sun.**	
2	**Monday** **Mon.**	
3	**Tuesday** **Tues.**	
4	**Wednesday** **Wed.**	
5	**Thursday** **Thurs.**	
6	**Friday** **Fri.**	
7	**Saturday** **Sat.**	

Name_____ Date_____

Months of the Year

1	**January** **Jan.**	
2	**February** **Feb.**	
3	**March** **Mar.**	
4	**April** **Apr.**	
5	**May**	
6	**June** **Jun.**	

Name_____ Date_____

Months of the Year

7	July Jul.	
8	August Aug.	
9	September Sept.	
10	October Oct.	
11	November Nov.	
12	December Dec.	

Name_____ Date_____

Date and Numerical Date

Part One: Say the date and then write the numerical date.

1. March 30, 2000   ____ / ____ / ____

2. April 10, 1994   ____ / ____ / ____

3. January 5, 2005   ____ / ____ / ____

4. October 7, 2006   ____ / ____ / ____

5. June 15, 2002   ____ / ____ / ____

6. November 26, 2004   ____ / ____ / ____

7. July 14, 2001   ____ / ____ / ____

8. February 6, 1999   ____ / ____ / ____

9. August 17, 2003   ____ / ____ / ____

10. May 1, 1998   ____ / ____ / ____

Part Two: Read the numerical date. Then say and write the whole date like this: March 8, 2002. Don't forget the capital letter and the comma!

1. 7/19/02 _____

2. 6/26/01 _____

3. 11/26/99 _____

4. 9/3/98 _____

5. 2/14/04 _____

6. 5/30/03 _____

Part Three: Say and write the whole date and the numerical date of your birthday.

_____   ____ / ____ / ____

Name_____ Date_____

Calendar Equivalents

7 days = 1 week	12 months = 1 year
4 weeks = 1 month	52 weeks = 1 year
30 (31) days = 1 month	365 days = 1 year

Part One: Look at the chart above. Then answer the following questions.

1. 1 week = _____ days

2. 1 month = _____ days

3. 4 weeks = _____ month

4. _____ months = 1 year

5. _____ weeks = 1 year

6. _____ days = 1 year

Part Two: Stumpers! Work with a partner and answer these questions.

1. 14 days = _____ weeks

2. 3 weeks = _____ days

3. 24 months = _____ years

4. 12 weeks = _____ months

Part Three: Draw a line to match the equal items.

365 days

12 months

52 weeks   1 year

7 days

30 (31) days   1 month

4 weeks   1 week

Lesson 10-13: How's the Weather?

Objective: The student will learn the vocabulary and meaning of the concepts associated with the weather.

Vocabulary: weather; outside; sunny; rainy; snowy; cloudy; partly cloudy; icy; windy; hot; warm; cold; cool; meteorologist; forecast; thermometer; degrees; Fahrenheit (F); Centigrade (Celsius) (C)

Materials: Activity Sheets 10–13A and 10–13B; Pencil; Indoor/outdoor thermometer, if possible; Current newspaper (with weather forecast)

Directions:

1. Ask, "Are we inside or outside?" (**Response:** "Inside.") Now bring the student to a window and point outside. Ask, "What is that called?" (**Response:** "Outside") With the student still standing at the window, discuss what is outside (e.g., houses, trees, birds, etc.).

2. Explain to the student that there is something else outside called the *weather*. It means what is happening in the air or the atmosphere. Weather happens outside.

3. Give the student a copy of Activity Sheet 10–13A. Read and say the weather terms with the student. Ask the student to complete the activity sheet.

4. Point to an illustration on Activity Sheet 10–13A and ask, "How's the weather?" (The student reads the weather words to describe the picture.) Provide help, if necessary. Choose different illustrations and continue. **Answer Key:** 1. It's windy; 2. It's rainy; 3. It's cloudy; 4. It's snowy; 5. It's icy; 6. It's sunny; 7. It's partly cloudy; 8. Thermometer; 9. Meteorologist.

5. Point to the *meteorologist* and explain that this is a person who studies the weather. Discuss the fact that most weather persons on TV are meteorologists.

6. Say, "Today it is (weather). What will the weather be tomorrow?" (Point to the calendar, if necessary.) Ask the student to predict. Tell the student that he/she is making a weather *forecast*. Discuss the fact that meteorologists study the weather and make weather forecasts from that information. Next ask, "Where can we get the weather forecast?" (**Response:** TV, newspaper, radio, etc.) Show the student a current weather forecast in the newspaper. Discuss the forecast for your region. Discuss why it is important to know the weather forecast (e.g., to know how to dress, make plans [outdoor], safety).

7. Point to the illustration of the *thermometer* on Activity Sheet 10–13A. Show the student a real thermometer and tell him/her that this is called a thermometer. Tell the student that *degrees* on the thermometer measure how hot

or cold it is outside. Show the student the degree marks on the thermometer and explain that there are two kinds of degrees: *Fahrenheit* (32° freezing, 212° boiling) and *Celsius* (0° freezing, 100° boiling). Tell the student that in America we use Fahrenheit degrees. Explain that a capital F and the degree mark ° mean Fahrenheit degrees. On the thermometer, read the Fahrenheit degree marks with the student. Next, explain that 32° is the freezing mark and means that it is *cold* outside. Move your finger down to show that the lower the degrees, the colder the temperature. (Pretend to shiver.) Tell the student that ice and snow form when it is cold. Discuss the type of clothing that is worn when it's cold.

8. Explain that the higher the temperature rises, the warmer the air around us feels. Move your finger up the thermometer and stop at 50°. Tell the student that at this mark it feels *cool* (a little cold). (**Gesture:** Hold your index finger and thumb a little apart.) Discuss the fact that we wear light jackets and sweaters when it is cool. Now move up to 70° and tell the student that now it will feel *warm*. Discuss the type of clothing that is worn when it is warm (short sleeves, no jacket, etc.). Now move up to 90° and tell the student that now the weather will feel *hot*. Discuss the type of clothing that is worn when it is hot (shorts, no sleeves).

9. Write various temperatures on the board and ask the student to identify them as *hot*, *warm*, *cool*, *cold*. Also ask the student to share what kind of clothing he/she should wear. Discuss the different activities that are done in different kinds of weather.

10. Ask the student to complete Activity Sheet 10–13B. The student will be asked to read and write the degrees, supply a weather word, and identify the correct clothing for different types of weather. **Answer Key**: (*Part One*) 70°F/warm; 10°F/cold; 50°F/cool; 100°/hot; (*Part Two*) Be sure student's matches are correct.

Extension Activities:

1. Ask the student to describe and draw rainbows. Ask the student to predict what causes rainbows. (Sunlight shining on raindrops.) Share the predictions. Read *A Rainbow of My Own* by Don Freeman.

2. Ask the students to take turns giving a daily weather report. The daily weather person is responsible for reporting the current temperature and the forecast for tomorrow. The following is an example: "Today was a (weather) day in (city or town). The temperature was _____. The weather forecast for tomorrow is _____." Show the student how to find the weather report in the newspaper, or calling for weather information on the telephone, or watching the weather report on TV.

3. Read *Cloudy With a Chance of Meatballs* by Judi Barrett. Ask the student to write what foods he/she would like to have as part of the weather.

4. Read *The Cloud Book* by Tomie de Paola. Take the student for a walk to observe clouds. Write descriptive words about the clouds. Ask the student to draw clouds with white paint on deep blue paper.

5. Investigate sayings about the weather. Ask the student to share sayings or weather myths from his/her native country.

6. Take a walk in the snow. Ask the student to describe what he/she sees.

7. Make a wind chime. Paint a small square of cardboard and punch holes in the top. Attach seashells or metal rings to string and put them through the holes. Hang outside.

8. Graph the weather for a month. Using the information from the graph, ask the student to make weather predictions.

Name_____ Date_____

How's the Weather?

Write the correct words under each picture.

It's rainy.	It's sunny.	It's windy.	It's cloudy.	It's partly cloudy.
It's snowy.	It's icy.	Meteorologist	Thermometer	

1. _____

2. _____

3. _____

4. _____

5. _____

6. _____

7. _____

8. _____

9. _____

Name_____ Date_____

How's the Weather?

Part One: Read the degrees on each thermometer. Then write the temperature in Fahrenheit degrees and the word that describes it on the line.

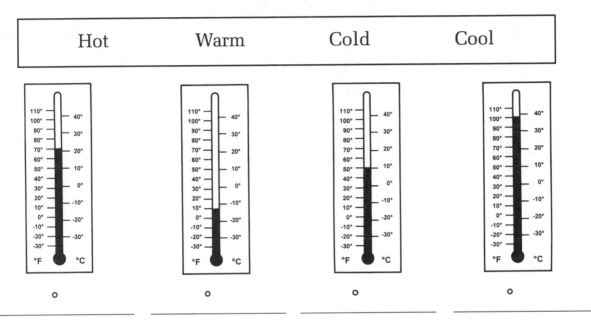

| Hot | Warm | Cold | Cool |

_____ _____ _____ _____

Part Two: Match the correct clothing to the weather.

Lesson 10-14: Weather Safety

● ●

Objective: The student will understand the safety rules to follow during dangerous weather situations.

Vocabulary: tornado; lightning; flood; heat; heatstroke; dehydrate; freeze; frostbite; thunderstorm; flashlight

Materials: Activity Sheet 10–14; Pencil; Flashlight; Hardcover book

Teaching Note: The ESL student may be unfamiliar with various weather conditions found in the United States and may not have experienced many of them. It is important for the student to know what to do if confronted with dangerous weather conditions.

Directions:

1. Give the student a copy of Activity Sheet 10–14. Tell the student that sometimes weather can be very dangerous and harmful. Explain that it is important to know how to stay safe during violent weather. Point to the illustrations at the top of the activity sheet. Discuss the different kinds of weather and what to do to keep safe. Use the following guidelines:

   - **Tornado.** A tornado is a funnel cloud that touches the Earth and destroys what it touches. It is strong enough to tear trees out of the ground, destroy houses, and pick up cars. *How to stay safe*: Obey the warning siren. Go to the lowest part of the house or building. Stay away from windows and outside walls. Cover your head or get under a table. (**Gesture:** Cover your head with the hardcover book.) Ask the student to do so. Practice the tornado drill in your building.

   - **Lightning.** Lightning is electricity made in the clouds that can come to Earth. It is bright flashes of light in the sky. Lightning is very dangerous to people and can kill. Lightning can travel through objects after it hits them. Tell the students that it does not have to be raining for lightning to occur. *How to stay safe:* Don't use the telephone, TV, or electric appliances. If you are outside, stay away from trees and get to the lowest level of ground and lie down. Stay away from metal objects when it is lightning.

   - **Heatwave.** When the temperatures become very high (90°+), people must be very careful not to stay outside in the heat for long periods of time. We can get heatstroke (high body temperature) and become very ill. Explain to the children that it is easy to get severe sunburn in hot weather. This can cause burning, blisters, and perhaps more serious diseases. Our bodies need water to live and when it is hot we perspire (lose water). If a person loses too much water, he/she can become dehydrated and very ill. *How to* *stay safe in severe heat*: Stay indoors, go out only for short periods of time, drink a lot of water, and put sunscreen on exposed skin before going outside. (Show the students a sample of sunscreen and how to use it.)

- **Freezing Cold.** When the temperature becomes very low (0° and lower), people must not stay outside for long periods of time. We can get frostbite. Explain that frostbite is when parts of the body get frozen. It is very painful and can become very serious. Discuss the fact that water freezes and ice forms in severe cold. Although lakes, ponds, and rivers can freeze, this does not mean that it is safe to walk or play on the ice. *How to stay safe*: It is important to wear winter clothing to cover their skin when it is very cold, especially feet, hands, and face. Discuss proper clothing for winter weather. Explain that an adult should be with them if they are playing on icy surfaces.

- **Severe Thunderstorm.** A severe thunderstorm has a lot of rain, lightning, thunder, and wind. Explain that severe thunderstorms can cause damage and can be frightening. Often, electricity goes out, and strong winds can cause damage to houses and trees. Severe thunderstorms can mean more dangerous weather is coming. Tell the students to listen for weather sirens and obey the warning. *How to stay safe*: Keep a flashlight where you can easily find it. Make sure it has fresh batteries. Listen for and obey warning sirens.

- **Hurricane.** This is a strong windstorm and rainstorm. Hurricanes always happen near the ocean. *How to stay safe*: Get away from the ocean and board up windows and doors.

- **Fog.** Fog is moisture in the air. It is like a cloud on the Earth. Fog makes it difficult to see. *How to stay safe*: Be very careful walking across the street because cars may not be able to see you. Wear light colored clothing, carry a flashlight, and have reflectors on your bike.

- **Flood.** A flood is when water overflows a river or stream bank. It can also occur when the ground can't hold any more water; then the water stays on the surface of the ground. *How to stay safe*: Go as high as you can, stay away from dirty water, and don't go near rivers or streams. If you live in an area where flash floods occur, this is very important information to give the student.

2. After discussing the types of dangerous weather situations and how to stay safe, cut out the weather cards on Activity Sheet 10–14. Give each student a card or divide into groups/partners. Each group then pantomimes the safety rules and the other groups must guess the kind of weather.

Extension Activity: Ask the student to watch the Weather Channel or view it in your classroom. Watch for severe weather in other parts of the country. Identify it and discuss the safety procedures involved.

Dangerous Weather

freezing cold 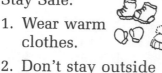	Stay Safe: 1. Wear warm clothes. 2. Don't stay outside for a long time. 3. Don't play on frozen lakes or ponds.	**lightning** 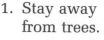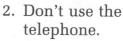	Stay Safe: 1. Stay away from trees. 2. Don't use the telephone. 3. Lie flat on low ground.
heatwave 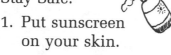	Stay Safe: 1. Put sunscreen on your skin. 2. Don't stay outside for a long time. 3. Drink a lot of water.	**flood** 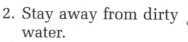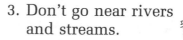	Stay Safe: 1. Go as high as you can. 2. Stay away from dirty water. 3. Don't go near rivers and streams.
hurricane 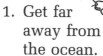	Stay Safe: 1. Get far away from the ocean. 2. Board up windows and doors. 3. Stay away from windows.	**tornado**	Stay Safe: 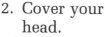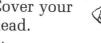 1. Go to the lowest floor. 2. Cover your head. 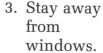 3. Stay away from windows.
fog	Stay Safe: 1. Shine a flashlight. 2. Wear light colored clothing and have reflectors on your bike. 	**thunderstorm**	Stay Safe: 1. Keep a flashlight handy. 2. Listen for any warning sirens.

Lesson 10-15: Seasons

. . . .

Objective: The student will learn the reason for the seasons, the names of the four seasons, and the weather associated with each season.

Vocabulary: season; summer; spring; winter; fall; autumn

Materials: Activity Sheet 10–15; Pencil; Calendar; Globe; Yellow ball or paper circle to represent the sun

Directions:

1. Give the student a copy of Activity Sheet 10–15. Tell the student that today he/she is going to learn about the four *seasons*. Explain that many parts of the United States have four different seasons of weather. This happens because the Earth is tilted as it circles around the sun. Point to the illustration for clarification. Next, ask a student to hold the "sun" (yellow ball or paper circle) as you rotate the globe around it. Explain that when parts of the Earth are closer to the sun, the weather is warmer; when farther away from the sun, the weather is cooler.

2. Point to the illustrations and discuss each season. Explain that the four seasons are called *fall* or *autumn*, *winter*, *spring*, and *summer*. Explain that fall or autumn is from September to December, and the weather is cool. The leaves fall from the trees. Winter is from December to March, and the weather is cold. It snows and can be icy. Spring is from March until June, and is rainy, warm, and windy. Plants and flowers begin to grow. Summer is from June until September, and is hot. Next, go back, point to each picture, and ask, "What is the season?" (Student responds.) "What is the weather?" (Student responds.) Follow the same procedure for the rest of the seasons.

3. Discuss the different types of clothing and activities for each season.

4. Ask the student to complete Activity Sheet 10–15. Depending upon the level of the student, this can be done as a directed activity or independently. Provide help with reading, if necessary. The student will be asked to answer questions about the seasons from looking at the illustrations. The student will be asked to draw a picture of each season and him-/herself doing an activity in that season.

Extension Activities:

1. Read *Red Leaf, Yellow Leaf* by Lois Ehlert.

2. Ask each student to choose his/her favorite season, and draw a picture of him-/herself doing a special activity in that season. The student then shares and tells why it is his/her favorite.

3. Take a class vote for the favorite season. Graph the results. (Summer usually wins!)

4. Ask students to describe and share the seasonal changes in their native countries. How is it the same and how is it different from America?

Name_____ Date_____

Seasons

Why do the seasons change?

Because the Earth is tilted as it circles the sun.

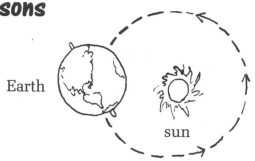

Earth

sun

fall or autumn  September to December	winter  December to March
spring  March to June	summer  June to September

Answer the questions on a separate sheet of paper. Then discuss them.

1. How many seasons are there? Name them. In what months is each one?

2. What season is it now?

3. Describe the weather for each season.

4. What are the birds doing in fall and spring? In winter? In summer?

5. What is the girl in the picture doing in each season?

6. What do you like to do in each season? Draw a picture for each one.

Section 11

Colors and Shapes

ESL students need to learn the basic information of colors and shapes. This information crosses all curricular areas and aspects of everyday life. A danger for the older ESL student is that in an effort to teach academic content, the basic concepts of color and shape can be overlooked.

The colors taught in this section are basic. Perhaps the art teacher would like to expand upon this and add colors or introduce the color wheel. Some ESL students have come from cultures where art supplies are scarce. These students particularly enjoy coloring and experimenting with color. Graphic shapes and design sheets are wonderful for this purpose. Coloring or drawing designs is a good activity for the first few days of school, especially for the newcomer. From a language perspective, the information is not difficult and the activities are enjoyable.

The information on shapes can be used for any-age ESL student. The more basic shapes can be introduced to the younger student and the more complicated shapes included for the older student. This lesson will be very helpful, particularly in the math curriculum.

The lessons in Section 11 provide an excellent starting point for the beginning language learner.

Colors and Shapes Pretest–Posttest

Student:_____   Date:_____

Class: _____

Before you begin, you will need examples of the following colors: orange, blue, green, red, white, black, brown, purple, pink, yellow.

1. Ask the student to identify each color by name.

2. Ask the student to read these color words:

   blue   **red**   **green**   **orange**   **white**

   black   **brown**   **purple**   **pink**   **yellow**

3. Ask the student to identify the following shapes (circle, square, rectangle, oval, star, triangle, heart, diamond, ring, crescent, cross, arrow, cone, cube, semi-circle, pentagon, hexagon, rhombus).

Lesson 11-1: Colors

● ● ● ● ● ● ● ● ● ● ● ● ● ● ● ● ●

Objective: The student will learn the vocabulary and identify visually the colors: red, yellow, green, orange, blue, brown, black, white, purple, pink.

Vocabulary: color; red; yellow; green; orange; blue; brown; black; white; purple; pink

Materials: Activity Sheets 11–1A and 11–1B; Enough crayons/colored pencils for each student to have one of each color listed above; Scissors; 1 piece of construction paper for each color listed above, with the name of the color printed on each; Tape

Teaching Note: You may want to divide this lesson into smaller units depending upon the age and level of the student. For the older student, five colors presented in one lesson is sufficient. For the younger student, one color per lesson is sufficient.

Directions:

1. Give the student a copy of Activity Sheet 11–1A. Secure the corresponding colors of construction paper to the board. Tell the student that he/she will be learning the names of *colors*. Point to the colors on the board and read the names of the colors. Ask the student to repeat.

2. Begin with the color *red*. Ask each student to find a red object in the classroom. Then ask each student, "What color is the (jacket)?" (**Response:** "The jacket is red.") Continue with the same question–response for each item found.

3. Next, ask the student to read and trace the color word *red* on Activity Sheet 11–1A. Then ask the student to color the corresponding picture of a red apple. Ask, "What color is the apple?" (**Response:** "The apple is red.")

4. Continue the same procedure as above with the rest of the colors on Activity Sheets 11–1A and 11–1B.

5. When all of the colors on the activity sheets have been introduced, review the color names again. Then ask the student to cut out the color word card and the corresponding picture card. Ask the student to mix the cards and match the color word to the correct color illustration. Then ask the student to name the color words again.

6. Give each student a different color card. (Some duplicates may occur.) Then ask the students to sit in a circle. Give directions such as *red* stand up, *green* stand up, *red* sit down, *yellow* stand up, *green* and *yellow* sit down. Choose other actions and colors and combinations of colors.

7. Continue with this procedure until all the colors on Activity Sheets 11–1A and 11–1B are learned.

Extension Activities:

1. Read *Brown Bear, Brown Bear, What Do You See?* by Bill Martin, Jr. For older students read *Hailstones and Halibut Bones* by Mary O'Neill.

2. Play "Color Memory." Turn the color words and color illustrations face down. The student tries to make a match of a color word and a color picture. If a match is made, the student keeps the pair. The student with the most matches wins.

3. Make a color collage. The student looks in magazines and catalogs and makes a specific color collage.

4. For the younger student, the board game "Candyland" is an excellent reinforcement for color.

Colors

red _____ - - - - - - - - - - - - _____	
blue _____ - - - - - - - - - - - - _____	
orange _____ - - - - - - - - - - - - _____	
yellow _____ - - - - - - - - - - - - _____	
green _____ - - - - - - - - - - - - _____	

Colors

purple	
—————— - - - - - - - - - - - ——————	
brown	
—————— - - - - - - - - - - - ——————	
black	
—————— - - - - - - - - - - - ——————	
white	
—————— - - - - - - - - - - - ——————	
pink	
—————— - - - - - - - - - - - ——————	

Lesson 11-2: Shapes

. . . .

Objective: The student will learn the names and be able to visually identify the following shapes: circle, square, triangle, rectangle, oval, heart, star, ring, crescent, diamond.

Vocabulary: circle; square; triangle; oval; heart; star; ring; crescent; diamond; arrow; cross; *more advanced:* cone; cube; semicircle; hexagon; pentagon; rhombus

Materials: Activity Sheets 11–2A, 11–2B, 11–2C; Pencil; Crayons or colored pencils; 1 construction paper shape of each listed above with the name of the shape on each one; Tape

Teaching Note: Present this lesson in several sessions, introducing five shapes in each one. The more advanced shapes are intended for the older student. Two spaces are provided for any shapes you might want to add to the activity sheet.

Directions:

1. Secure the paper shapes to the board and give the student a copy of Activity Sheets 11–1A and 11–1B. Tell the student that he/she is going to learn about *shapes.*

2. Begin with the first shape to be taught. Point to it on the board, say the name, and trace the perimeter of the shape. The student repeats the name and draws the shape with his/her finger in the air. Then ask the student to locate the shape on the activity sheet, say the name, trace the shape, and write the word. The student may color the shape.

3. Ask a student to come to the board and locate a specific shape; e.g., "(Student's name), find the square." (Student points.) Then ask, "What is the name of the shape?" (Student responds.) Ask the student to remove the shape and hold it. Continue the same procedure for the rest of the shapes, calling on different students. When all of the shapes are taken, ask the other students, "What shape does (Student's name) have?" (Students respond.) Continue through the rest of the shapes.

4. After all the shapes on Activity Sheets 11–2A and 11–2B have been introduced, ask the student to complete Activity Sheet 11–2C. The student will be asked to locate and count specific shapes.

Extension Activities:

1. Read *When a Line Bends . . . A Shape Begins* by Rhonda Gowler Greene.

2. Ask the student to find a specific shape in the classroom, identify it, and say (for example) "The flag is a rectangle." Ask the student to make a list of shapes and objects.

3. Provide shapes for the student to trace. The student then traces various shapes out of colored paper and makes a shape collage or picture. **Variation:** The student creates a design out of various shape pieces, placing them on a piece of white art paper. Then spray paint and take off the shapes.

4. Draw a shape picture. Give the student specific directions, such as, "Draw a triangle, then draw a line at the top point of the triangle. What did you make?" (a teeter-totter) "Draw a circle. Draw two triangles inside the circle at each side. Draw a triangle in the center of the circle. Draw a half circle at the bottom. What did you draw?" (a jack-o'-lantern face)

5. Ask the student to find specific shapes in magazines or catalogs and then write a sentence describing it; e.g., The doughnut is a ring. The wallet is a rectangle. The cookie is round.

Name_____ Date_____

Shapes

circle	**triangle**
square	**heart**
rectangle	**diamond**
oval	**ring**
star	**crescent**

Name_____ Date_____

Shapes

	cross
	_____ - - - - - - - - - - _____

	arrow
	_____ - - - - - - - - - - _____

	cone
	_____ - - - - - - - - - - _____

	cube
	_____ - - - - - - - - - - _____

	semicircle
	_____ - - - - - - - - - - _____

	hexagon
	_____ - - - - - - - - - - _____

	pentagon
	_____ - - - - - - - - - - _____

	rhombus
	_____ - - - - - - - - - - _____

| _____
 - - - - - - - - - -
 _____ | _____
 - - - - - - - - - -
 _____ |

Name_____ Date_____

Shapes

Find 5 triangles. Color them green.

Find 4 squares. Color them yellow.

Find 6 circles. Color them red.

Find 2 stars. Color them blue.

Find 3 hearts. Color them red.

Find 4 rings. Color them purple.

Find 1 crescent. Color it black.

Find 3 diamonds. Color them pink.

Find 2 ovals. Color them white.

Find 4 rectangles. Color them gray.

Section 12

Spatial Concepts, Direction, & World Geography

This section introduces the student to the concepts of position and his/her location in the world. It is of particular importance for the ESL student to master this information because direction words are used in all areas of everyday life, and must be understood to insure the ability to function successfully.

Trying to navigate and find your way in a new and strange environment can be a confusing and frightening experience for anyone. The lessons in Section 12 present the new student with an opportunity to learn and practice direction skills in a safe location. The ESL student often finds him-/herself in a situation where he/she must find various places in the school or the community. Knowing how to ask for directions and follow them is an important life skill for the newcomer to develop. Also, the ability to give directions will help the student develop a sense of confidence and positive self-esteem.

The ability to identify and locate his/her native country is comforting and provides the student with an opportunity to share part of his/her knowledge with others. It is essential that the ESL student be able to "place" him-/herself in the world physically as well as emotionally.

Spatial Concepts, Direction, & World Geography
Pretest–Posttest

Student:_____   Grade:_____

Date: _____

- **A plastic cup and a pencil will be needed for question 2.**
- **Put a ✓ on those items that are correct.**

1. Ask the student to identify his/her right hand and left hand.

2. Give the student a pencil and a plastic cup. Ask the student to place the pencil in the following positions in relation to the cup: in the cup; out of the cup; beside the cup; next to the cup; behind the cup; over the cup; under the cup; in front of the cup; between the cup and self.

3. Point to the compass rose and say, "This is a direction finder called a compass rose. Point to these directions on the compass rose: North, South, East, West."

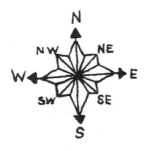

4. Ask the student to identify the in-between directions of northeast, southeast, southwest, and northwest.

5. Ask the student to look at the world map and identify: North Pole; South Pole; equator; prime meridian; lines of latitude; lines of longitude; Atlantic Ocean; Pacific Ocean; Arctic Ocean; Indian Ocean; North America; South America; Asia; Europe; Australia; Africa; Antarctica.

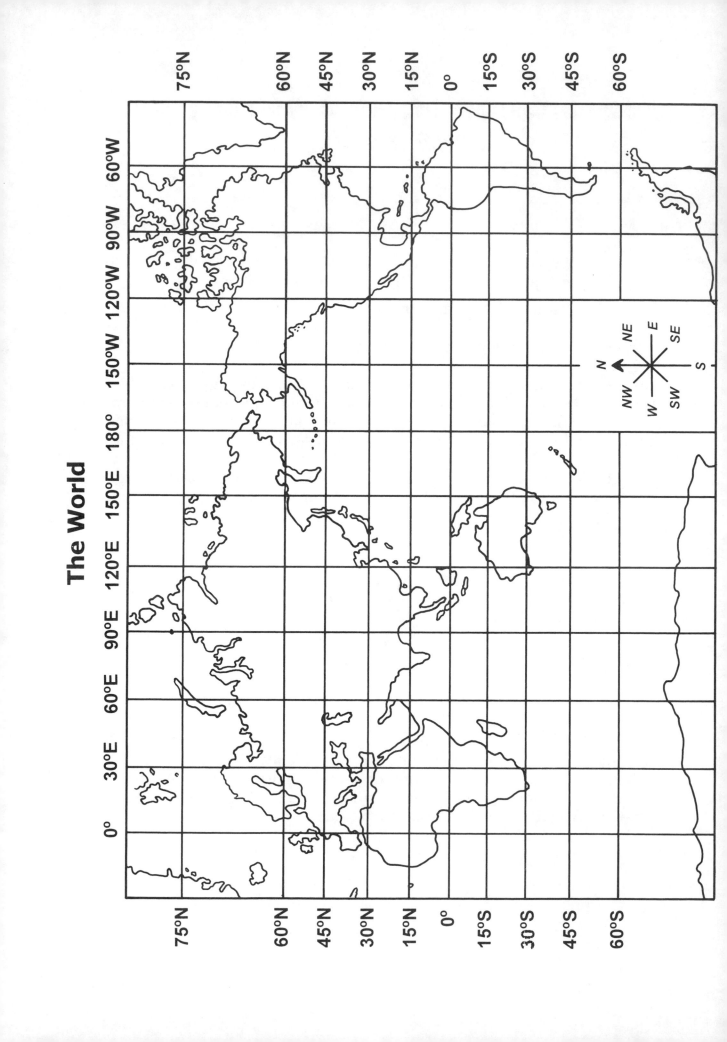

The World

Lesson 12-1: Spatial Concepts

Objective: The student will learn the vocabulary for and demonstrate the spatial concepts of in, outside, next to, beside, across, under, between, in front, behind, over, on top of.

Vocabulary: in; out; next to; beside; across; under; between; in front; behind; over; on top of

Materials: Activity Sheet 12–1; Pencil; One beanbag or ball for each student (you may use any soft item that can be tossed; a stuffed sock that is tied also works well); Empty trash can

Teaching Note: This is an excellent lesson to coordinate with the physical education teacher, who may also be a good resource for obtaining the beanbags, balls, etc.

Directions:

1. Tell the student that today he/she is going to learn words that tell where something is. Give each student a beanbag and model the following statements. (The student performs the same action and responds to the question.)

   - "The beanbag is *in front*." (Place the beanbag in front of your feet; student puts a beanbag in front of his/her feet.) Ask, "Where is the beanbag?" (**Response:** In front)

   - "The beanbag is *behind*." (Place the beanbag behind your feet; student follows.) Ask, "Where is the beanbag?" (**Response:** Behind)

   - "The beanbag is *between*." (Place the beanbag between your feet; student follows.) Ask, "Where is the beanbag?" (**Response:** Between)

   - "The beanbag is *beside*." (Place the beanbag beside your feet; student follows.) Ask, "Where is the beanbag?" (**Response:** Beside)

   - "The beanbag is *next to*." (Place the beanbag next to your feet, only this time on the other side; student follows.) Ask, "Where is the beanbag?" (**Response:** Next to) Indicate that *beside* and *next to* have the same meaning.

   - "The beanbag is *under*." (Place the beanbag under your foot; student follows.) Ask, "Where is the beanbag?" (**Response:** Under)

   - "The beanbag is *on top*." (Place the beanbag on top of your head; student follows.) Ask, "Where is the beanbag?" (**Response:** On top)

   - "The beanbag is *over*." (Hold the beanbag over your head; student follows.) Ask, "Where is the beanbag?" (**Response:** Over) Emphasize the space between your head and the beanbag, as opposed to "on top of" where it rests on the head.

- "The beanbag is *in*." (Toss the beanbag in the trash can; student follows.) Ask, "Where is the beanbag?" (**Response:** In)

- "The beanbag is *out*." (Take the beanbag out of the trash can; student follows.) Ask, "Where is the beanbag?" (**Response:** Out)

- Ask the students to form two lines facing each other. Then say, "Toss the beanbag *across*." Student tosses the beanbag to the person across from him/her. Ask, "Where did you toss the beanbag?" (**Response:** Across)

2. Give the positions in random order and ask the student to place or toss the beanbag accordingly. Then let the student give positions and others follow. This is a good opportunity to play the game "Simon Says."

3. Give the student a copy of Activity Sheet 12–1. He/she will be asked to look at a picture and write the correct position word. Help with reading may be necessary. **Answer Key:** 1. Between; 2. In; 3. Over; 4. In front; 5. Under; 6. On top; 7. Out; 8. Beside; 9. Behind.

Extension Activities:

1. This is a list of other spatial concepts that are important for the student to learn. Suggested activities follow:

   - Nearest—Farthest: Have a beanbag toss. Identify the nearest and the farthest.

   - Up—Down: Pick the beanbag up, then put it down. Toss the beanbag in the air; it goes up and comes down.

   - Top—Bottom: Stack the beanbags and indicate which one is on the top and which one is on the bottom.

   - Below—Above: Stack the beanbags and indicate one that is above and one that is below.

2. Give one direction for placing the beanbag, e.g., "Put the beanbag between your feet." Then give two directions, e.g., "Put the beanbag between your feet and on top of your head." Keep adding directions until a fun chaos ensues.

3. Read the book *We're Going on a Bear Hunt* by Michael Rosen and Helen Oxenbury. This is a wonderful story with many spatial concepts incorporated within the text. The story is read in rhythm, accompanied by actions. As the student becomes familiar with the text, he/she can say it along with you and perform the actions.

Name_____ Date_____

Where's the Soccer Ball?

Look at the word box. Then look for the soccer ball in each picture. Write the correct word on the line.

in	out	beside	under	between	in front	over	on top of	behind

1.

2.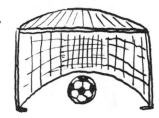

3.

_____   _____   _____

4.

5.

6.

_____   _____   _____

7.

8.

9.

_____   _____   _____

Name_____ Date_____

Where's the Soccer Ball?

Look at the word box. Then look for the soccer ball in each picture. Write the correct word on the line.

in	out	beside	under	between	in front	over	on top of	behind

1.

_____

2.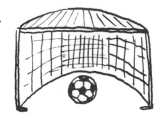

_____

3.

_____

4.

_____

5.

_____

6.

_____

7.

_____

8.

_____

9.

_____

Name_____ Date_____

Listen and Do

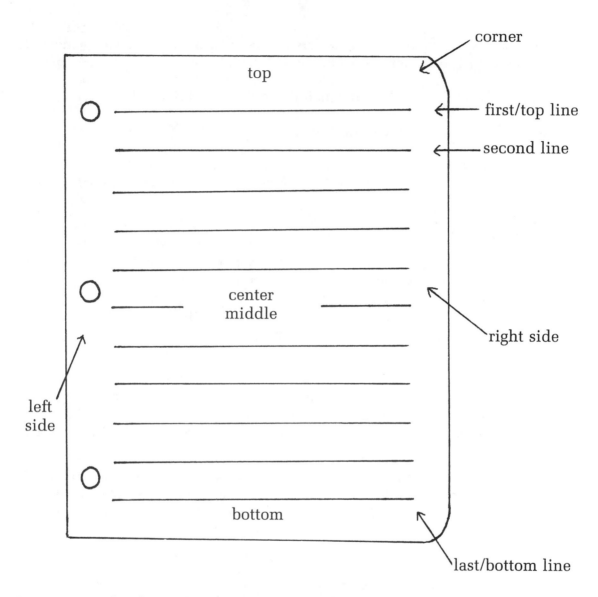

Directions: Listen for directions, then do what they say.

- Print your name in the top right corner.
- Print the date in the top left corner.
- Print your birthday on the first line.
- Print your age on the second line.
- Draw an X in the center of the paper.
- Sign your name at the bottom.
- Draw a straight line down the right side.
- Draw a curved line down the left side.

Lesson 12-3: Side–Right and Left

· ·

Objectives: The student will understand the concept of side. The student will learn to distinguish between the right side and the left side.

Vocabulary: side; right; left; "high-five right"; "high-five left"

Materials: Activity Sheet 12–3; Pencil

Teaching Note: The concept of "side" will be introduced and then the terms "right side" and "left side." This is a good opportunity to reinforce the irregular plural of foot (feet).

Directions:

1. Give the student a copy of Activity Sheet 12–3. Point to the illustration in Part One. Explain that if we draw a line down the middle of a person, there are two parts. Each part is called a *side*. (**Gesture:** With your finger draw an imaginary line from the top of your head to the bottom of your torso.) Ask the student to stand and do the same.

2. Tell the student that each side has a name. Face the same way as the students and say, "This is the right side." Next, ask the students to stand and—facing the same way (forming a line is a good way to model this)—say, "This is my right side." (**Gesture:** Run your hand from your head to your toes. Ask the student to do the same.) Then ask, "What side is this?" (**Response:** The right side.)

3. Then point to your eye and say, "This is my right eye." Continue with other body parts on the right side (ear, arm, hand, leg, foot). Then give the students the following commands: "Point to your right eye, right ear. Raise your right arm. Wave your right hand. Lift your right leg. Stomp your right foot."

4. Use the same procedure as above for the left side.

5. Next, ask the student to hold a pencil/pen in the hand in which he/she writes. Then inform the student that this is called right-handed or left-handed. Ask each student to identify the correct term for him-/herself and say "I'm right/left handed."

6. Ask the student to complete the activity sheet. The student will be asked to trace a line down a body and draw identical sides. The student will be asked to identify right and left hand, right and left foot, and place utensils on the right or left of a plate.

7. The concept of opposite sides when facing another person is always a challenging concept to teach. The game "High-Five Right, High-Five Left" can

help clarify this in the student's mind. To begin, ask a student to be your partner. Stand facing one another. Point to your right side and say, "My right side." Then draw a diagonal line in the air to the student's right side and say, "Your right side." Next, hold up your right hand, palm facing the student and say, "This is my right hand. Raise your right hand." (Student raises right hand.) Now say, "High-five right!" and slap right hands (with the student) using the "high-five" action. Follow the same procedure for the left side. Divide the students into pairs and say "High-five right, high-five left" in an alternating fashion. *Variation*: Add "Low-five right, low-five left." Students slap hands held low.

Extension Activities:

1. Teach the students the words and motions to the song "The Hokey Pokey."

2. Play "Simon Says." Give various commands alternating between the left and right sides, e.g., "Raise your left leg. Wiggle your right ear. Wink your left eye." Each command must be preceded by "Simon Says." If the command is not preceded by "Simon Says," the players do not do the command. Players who do must sit down. Let the students take turns being "Simon."

3. Play "Sleight of Hand." You will need two small paper cups and a small piece of candy. Place the candy under one cup and move the cups around, changing positions very quickly. Stop and ask the student to guess under which cup the candy is hidden. The student must say, "It is on the (right/left) side."

4. Ask the student to trace his/her hand and label it either as the right hand or left hand.

5. Ask the student to trace his/her feet on paper and cut them out. Label the feet right or left. Secure the paper feet along the wall in the hallway going to the classroom door and display the sign "This way to ESL!"

Name_____ Date_____

Left and Right

Part One: Trace the line down the middle of this body. Make each side look the same. Then write or tell what is on each side.

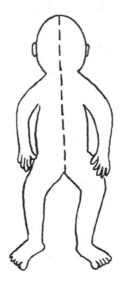

Part Two: Circle the correct side, right or left. Use your hands and feet to help you.

left or right

left or right

left or right

left or right

Part Three:

I write with my _____ hand.

I am right-handed.

I am left-handed.

I kick the soccer ball with my _____ foot.

Part Four: Draw a knife **and a spoon** **on the right side. Draw a fork**  **on the left side.**

Lesson 12-4: Directions: Turn Right, Turn Left, Go Straight

Objectives: The student will understand the directions of turn right, turn left, go straight. The student will be able to give directions to a specific location using the phrases: turn right, turn left, go straight.

Vocabulary: directions; turn right; turn left; go straight; on the left; on the right; across from; corner; "Where's the . . ."; "How do I get to the . . ."

Materials: Activity Sheet 12–4; Pencil

Teaching Note: The ability to ask for, understand, follow, and give simple directions is a very valuable life skill for the ESL student to develop. There will be many new locations for which the student will need directions. This lesson plan teaches these directions in regard to the school building, and allows the student to practice this knowledge in a safe environment.

Directions: This lesson requires enough space for the student to walk a short distance (large classroom, gym, cafeteria, etc.).

1. Write the word *Directions* on the board. Under this word write *Turn right*, *Turn left*, *Go straight*. Explain to the student that *Directions* means which way to go to get somewhere. Explain that when a person wants to know how to get somewhere, he/she usually asks, "Where's the (restroom, office, etc.)?" or "How do I get to the (restroom, office, etc.)?" Ask the student to repeat the questions using a specific location.

2. Then discuss the simple directions of turn right, turn left, go straight.

   - *Turn right*: Draw an arrow similar to this on the board ↱. Say, "Turn right." Point and turn your body to the right. Ask the student to repeat and perform the action.

   - *Turn left*: Draw an arrow similar to this on the board ↰. Say "Turn left." Point and turn your body to the left. Ask the student to repeat and perform the action.

   - *Go straight*: Draw an arrow similar to this on the board ↑. Point straight ahead in front of yourself. Ask the student to point and repeat.

3. Next, ask the student to stand. Stand in front of the student and say, "We're going to play 'Follow the Leader.' I'm going to be the leader. I'll give you directions and motions, and you must say and do the same things I do." Begin by giving these directions, if space permits; otherwise, create your own pattern:

- *Go straight* (motion, then walk). *Turn right* (motion, then turn). *Go straight* (motion, then walk). *Turn left* (motion, then turn). *Go straight* (motion, then walk). *Stop.*

- Next, give the directions but stand on the side. The student must follow the verbal directions, repeating them and the gestures.

- Finally, ask a student to be the leader and give directions; the others follow and repeat.

4. Make the directions more specific and to a specific location; for example: (Location: teacher's desk) "Go straight. Turn right at the (flag). Go straight. Turn left at the (bookcase). Go straight. The teacher's desk is on the right." Student follows and repeats the directions. Explain to the student that *on the right* means that the chosen spot will be on his/her right side.

5. Choose a location where the ending direction is "on the left." Explain that the chosen spot will be on the student's left side.

6. Next, draw this illustration on the board: ⌐. Explain that this is called a corner. It is where two walls or hallways meet. Point to the corner in the classroom. Ask, "What is this called?" (**Response:** A corner)

7. Ask the student to stand across from another student, each facing the other. Explain that they are *across* from each other. Motion your hand back and forth. Ask, "Who is across from you?" Student responds.

8. Now choose a place outside the classroom. Lead the student(s) to a specific location in the school by giving directions as before. Begin these directions by saying, "Go out the door . . ."

9. As you walk to the location, ask the student to identify corners and rooms that are across from each other; e.g., "The restroom is *across from* the gym." Ask the student to repeat. Give other examples as you walk around the school; e.g., "What room is across from the office?" Student responds.

10. Remind the student that after he/she has received directions, it is a good idea to repeat those directions to the person giving them. Practice the following role-play:

    STUDENT: "Where's the Office?"
    TEACHER: (Give the directions to the Office)
    STUDENT: (Repeats directions to teacher. Then says) "Thank you."

11. Give the student a copy of Activity Sheet 12–4. The student will be asked to trace a way to two locations and put the directions in order. **Answer Key:** (*Jose*) 3 (or 5), 1, 4, 2, 5 (or 3), 6; (*Rita*) 4, 5 (or 3), 1, 2, 3 (or 5), 6.

Extension Activities:

1. Hide an object or treats in a specific location in the school. Write the directions using words and arrows. The student(s) must find the hidden item. *Variation*: Ask a student or staff person to hide. Give the student(s) directions to find that person. (The principal is a fun choice. When found, the principal reads the student[s] a story.)

2. Give each student a specific place in the school to which he/she must write directions using arrows and words.

Name_____ Date_____

Directions: Turn right, Turn left, Go straight

Jose and Rita are both in Room 103. They each need directions. Can you help them?

Jose needs directions to the **Office**. Use your pencil and trace the way. Then read the directions and put them in the correct order from 1 to 6.

Rita needs directions to the **Restroom**. Use your pencil and trace the way. Then read the directions and put them in the correct order from 1 to 6.

Jose: Directions to the Office

↑
_____ Go straight down the hall.

⤵
_____ Go out the door.

↰
_____ Turn left at the drinking fountain.

↱
_____ Turn right.

↑
_____ Go straight down the hall.

_____ The Office is on the right.

Rita: Directions to the Restroom

↱
_____ Turn right at the corner.

↑
_____ Go straight down the hall.

⤵
_____ Go out the door.

↰
_____ Turn left.

↑
_____ Go straight down the hall.

_____ The girls' restroom is across from the gym.

Lesson 12-5: Reading a Grid

Objective: The student will learn how to read a grid using the coordinates given.

Vocabulary: grid; coordinates

Materials: Activity Sheet 12–5; Pencil; Colored pencils/crayons; Scissors; Glue

Teaching Note: This is a good lesson to present before introducing map skills. It is a skill for locating intersecting lines of latitude and longitude.

Directions:

1. Give the student a copy of Activity Sheet 12–5. Tell him/her that this is a map of a new sports store called Sportsland. Explain that this map uses a *grid* to show where things are located. Explain that a grid is a set of lines, with the lines usually going across the top and down the side of the map. Trace across the top of the grid and read the numbers 1, 2, 3, 4, 5, 6, 7, 8. Ask the student to trace and repeat. Next, trace along the side of the grid and read the letters A, B, C, D, E. Ask the student to trace and repeat.

2. Explain that the numbers and letters are called *coordinates*. Ask, "What are the numbers and letters called?" (**Response:** Coordinates) Explain that these letters and numbers *name* each square.

3. Now say, "Let's find square B4." Model how to put a finger on B and move across to 4. Ask the student to do the same and ask, "What is in square B4?" (**Response:** You)

4. Name various coordinates and ask the student to locate each one.

5. Ask the student to look at the squares at the bottom of the activity sheet. Ask him/her to read the coordinates and what is in each one. Next, ask the student to cut out and glue the squares onto the correct location on the grid.

6. After Activity Sheet 12–5 is completed, ask the student to locate various items by identifying the coordinates; e.g., "Where can I find soccer balls?" (**Response:** C6) This can be done with a partner. *Variation:* Identify coordinates and ask the student to say where you are located; e.g., "I'm in square B6. Where am I?" (**Response:** By the vitamins)

Extension Activity: Ask the student to make a grid of the classroom. *Variation:* Ask the student to make a grid of his/her bedroom.

Name_____ Date_____

Reading a Grid

A new sports store called SPORTSLAND has opened in your town. Cut out the squares below the grid map. Read the coordinates and glue them onto the correct squares in the grid map.

Sportsland Grid Map

	1	2	3	4	5	6	7	8
A								
B				☺ YOU!				
C								
D								
E								

✂

A-2 cashier	B-8 basketball	D-2 golf	C-4 swimwear	E-6 shoes	D-5 weights	E-4 clothes	E-8 shoes
E-1 men's restroom	C-6 soccer ball	C-8 basketball hoops	A-4 cashier	C-2 hockey	A-8 ice skates	E-5 clothes	D-7 games
B-1 bikes	E-7 shoes	E-3 clothes	E-2 women's restroom	B-5 sports drinks	B-2 helmets	A-6 cashier	B-6 vitamins

Lesson 12-6: Directions: North, South, East, West

• •

Objectives: The student will learn how to recognize the directions of north, south, east, and west on a map. The student will learn the abbreviations N, S, E, W. The student will learn that a direction finder (compass rose) on a map will show where each direction is located.

Vocabulary: map; direction; north; south; east; west; N S E W; compass rose

Materials: Activity Sheet 12–6A (for the older student, grades 3 and up); Activity Sheet 12–6B (for the younger student, grades 2 and below); Pencil; 4 sheets of different colored paper with North, South, East, and West written on a different sheet; Classroom map of the U.S.; Tape

Directions:

1. Secure the direction words to the wall or board (next to the map) using this configuration:

   North

   West   East

   South

   Tell the student that he/she is going to learn about direction words. Explain that *north*, *south*, *east*, and *west* are direction words and tell us how to find places. Point to and read the direction words. Ask the student to repeat.

2. Point to the classroom map and say, "This is a *map*. It is a flat picture of the Earth. Maps show us where places are on the Earth. Most maps show us land and water." Point to the various pieces of land and bodies of water. Ask, "What is this?" (**Response:** A map)

3. Explain that most maps have a direction finder called a *compass rose*. Point to the compass rose on the classroom map or the one on the activity sheet. Ask, "What is this called?" (**Response:** A compass rose) Next, show the student how the compass rose points to the directions. Explain that *North* is the direction toward the top of the map (point). Ask, "What direction is this?" (**Response:** North) Say, "*South* is the direction toward the bottom of the map" (move your finger down and point). Ask, "What direction is this?" (**Response:** South) Then say, "*East* is the direction to the right." (point with right hand) Ask, "What direction is this?" (**Response:** East) Say, "*West* is the direction to the left." (point with left hand) Ask, "What direction is this?" (**Response:** West)

4. Ask the student to look at the map and point to the directions as you say them: *North* (student points up toward the top of the map); *South* (student points down toward the bottom of the map); *East* (student points to the right

with right hand); *West* (student points to the left with left hand). Next, mix the order of the directions and ask the student to point in the correct direction.

5. Take the papers on which the direction words are written and hand each of them to a different student. Ask the student to place his/her direction word in the correct position on the map. Continue until each student has had a turn.

6. Remove the direction words from the map. Then point to the north, south, east, and west parts of the map and ask the student to say the direction. Next, point to the directions in random order and have the student respond with the correct direction.

7. Write **North–N, South–S, East–E, West–W** on the board. Explain to the student that the abbreviations for north, south, east, and west are: N, S, E, W.

8. Give the student a copy of either Activity Sheet 12–6A or 12–6B depending on grade level. The student will be asked to identify the directions north, south, east, and west in reference to a map of the United States and the map of a playground.

Answer Key for Activity Sheet 12–6A: 2. North–N , South–S, East–E, West–W;

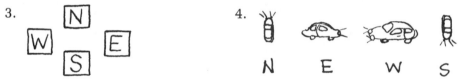

Answer Key for Activity Sheet 12–6B:

1.   N
     W North E
     West   East
            S
          South

2. N, E, W, S.

Extension Activities:

1. Ask the student to find his/her native country on a world map. Discuss what is north, south, east, and west of it.

2. *For the older student:* Place cards with north, south, east, and west on the appropriate wall of the classroom. Show the student how to "face" north in the classroom. Ask the student to identify south, west, and east. Then ask the student to face east and to identify north, south, and west in the classroom. Continue in this manner with south and west. This will give the student a "feel" for directions. Then ask the student questions regarding directions; e.g., "If I'm traveling east, what way do I turn to go north?"

3. Ask the student to face different directions and then walk several steps in another direction; e.g., face east and walk three steps north. Continue and vary directions to face and to walk.

Name_____ Date_____

North, South, East, West

1. **Look at the compass rose. Write the correct direction on each line.**

_____

_____

_____

_____

2. **Match the direction to the correct abbreviation.**

North	E
South	W
East	S
West	N

3. **Write N, S, E, W in the correct box.**

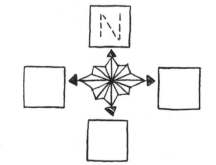

4. **Look at the cars. In what direction is each traveling? Circle the correct direction underneath each car.**

N S E W   N S E W   N S E W   N S E W

Name_____ Date_____

North, South, East, West

1. Print the name of each direction and its abbreviation.

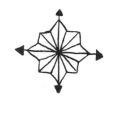

2. Read each sentence about this map. Circle the letter for the correct direction word. Then print it on the line.

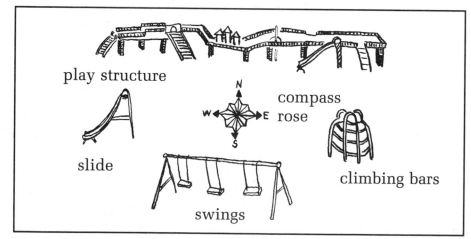

 The play structure is _____.   N   S   E   W

 The bars are _____.   N   S   E   W

The slide is _____.   N   S   E   W

The swings are _____.   N   S   E   W

Lesson 12-7: Directions: Northwest, Northeast, Southwest, Southeast

•••

This lesson is designed for the older student, grades 4+.

Objective: The student will learn to identify the in-between directions: northwest, northeast, southwest, and southeast.

Vocabulary: in between; northwest; northeast; southwest; southeast

Materials: Activity Sheet 12–7; Pencil; Marker/highlighter; Classroom map of the U.S.; 4 pieces of different colored paper with the words North, South, East, and West written on a separate sheet; Tape

Teaching Note: This lesson should be presented after the student has completed Lesson 12–6.

Directions:

1. Give the student a copy of Activity Sheet 12–7 and use the classroom map to illustrate. Point to the compass rose on the activity sheet and explain that directions are not always directly north, south, east, or west. Sometimes, places are *in between*. Point to each direction on the compass rose and read it, asking the student to point too and repeat. Explain that northeast is between north and east, southeast is between south and east, southwest is between south and west, and northwest is between north and west. Then ask the student to repeat and tell you the in-between directions and what directions they are between.

2. Place the four direction words on the appropriate walls of the classroom (North on the north wall, etc.). Give the student the following commands: "Walk three steps *northwest.*" (Student walks three steps northwest.) "Walk two steps *southeast.*" (Student walks two steps southeast.) Continue with the other directions. Next, ask the student to give the commands for others to follow.

3. Point to Colorado on the classroom map and say, "Colorado is *northeast* of Arizona." Then tell the student that if you drove your car from Arizona to Colorado, you would be traveling northeast. Draw a line with your finger going in a northeasterly direction from Arizona to Colorado. Ask the student to draw a line (with a marker/highlighter) on the activity sheet from Arizona to Colorado, going in a northeasterly direction. The student repeats, "Colorado is northeast of Arizona."

4. Continue with the same procedure and use the following examples: Kansas is *southeast* of Wyoming. Texas is *southwest* of Illinois. Maine is *northeast* of New York.

5. Continue with other examples. Ask the student to also contribute other examples.

6. Explain to the student that the abbreviation or short way to write each direction is (write on the board) **Northeast–NE, Southeast–SE, Southwest–SW, Northwest–NW.**

7. Have the student complete Activity Sheet 12–7. The student will be asked to identify northeast, southeast, southwest, and northwest, and define various locations using these directions. The student can use his/her highlighter to mark the directions.

Answer Key:

(*Part One*)

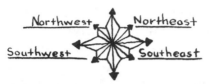

(*Part Two*) Northeast–NE, Southeast–SE, Southwest–SW, Northwest–NW
(*Part Three*) 1. NE, 2. NW, 3. SW, 4. SE, 5. NE, 6. SE

Extension Activities:

1. Ask the student to locate states that are NE, SE, SW, and NW of his/her home state.

2. Play "Uncle Louie's Trip." Begin the game by saying, "Uncle Louie lives in Kansas. He wants to visit Cousin Homer in Michigan. In what direction will he have to travel?" Divide the class into teams. A point is scored for each correct answer. *Variation*: Each team makes up a place for Uncle Louie to visit. The other team must tell the direction he must travel. This is also an opportunity for the students to become acquainted with the geography of the U.S. You may want to say, "Uncle Louie wants to visit the Capitol of the United States. Where is it?" (**Response:** "Washington, D.C.") Then say, "In what direction will he travel?"

Name_____ Date_____

Northeast, Southeast, Southwest, Northwest

Part One: Write the correct direction on the line: northeast, southeast, southwest, northwest.

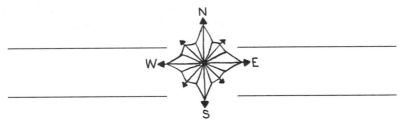

_____   _____

_____   _____

Part Two: Circle the correct abbreviation.

Northeast — NE   SE   SW   NW   Southwest — NE   SE   SW   NW

Southeast — NE   SE   SW   NW   Northwest — NE   SE   SW   NW

Part Three: Look at the map and answer the following questions. Write NE, SE, SW, NW on the line.

1. Virginia is _____ of Tennessee.   4. Kentucky is _____ of Iowa.

2. Oregon is _____ of Utah   5. Michigan is _____ of Illinois.

3. California is _____ of Wyoming.   6. Florida is _____ of Missouri.

Lesson 12-8: Reading a City Map

• •

Objective: The student will understand how to read and locate specific places on a city map.

Vocabulary: map; corner; block; in between; next to; across from; on; symbols; key

Materials: Activity Sheet 12–8; Pencil

Teaching Note: An excellent source from which to obtain local city maps is a car rental agency. Most agencies are very cooperative and will generally donate maps to teachers. These concise and easy-to-read maps provide an excellent reference for extension activities for the older student.

Directions:

1. Review the spatial concepts *in between*, *next to*, *across from*. Ask the students to make a line and identify who is standing next to them on each side. Then the students identify who is standing between two students. Ask the students to form two lines facing one another. The students identify who is standing across from each other. If further clarification is needed, see Lesson 12–1.

2. Give the student a copy of Activity Sheet 12–8. Explain that this is a map of a city and shows the locations of places and streets. Ask, "What is the name of the city?" (**Response:** Red Rock) Trace along the various streets with your finger and read the street names. Ask the student to trace along and repeat the name of the street.

3. Point to the map *key* and tell the student that a map key has pictures called *symbols*. Explain that the key tells what the symbols mean. Point to each symbol, read, and describe/discuss what it means. Ask the student to point and repeat.

4. Next, tell the student that a city or town is divided into *blocks*. Point to the blocks. Ask, "How many blocks are on the map?" (*Student counts and responds:* Six blocks are on the map.) Tell the student that blocks can be different sizes.

5. Tell the student that a *corner* is made when two streets cross each other. Point to a corner of Pine and First Streets and trace the lines of the corner with your finger. Say, "This is the *corner of* Pine and First Streets." Ask the student to trace and repeat. Then say, "The school is *on* the corner of Pine and First Streets." Ask, "Where is the school?" (**Response:** On the corner of Pine and First Streets) Now point to the corner of Second Street and Lake Road. Ask, "Where is the grocery store?" (**Response:** On the corner of Second Street and Lake Road)

6. Ask the student to identify what is *on* each street. Ask, "What is on Pine Street?" Provide help when needed. This is an excellent opportunity to discuss what is found and what people do at each location.

7. Ask the student the following questions. Provide help when necessary.

   • Where is Burger Barn? (On the corner of Second Street and Pine Street)

   • Where is the hair salon? (Between the bank and the post office on First Street)

   • Where is the zoo? (On the corner of Pine Street and Second Street)

   • What is next to the fire station? (The gas station)

   • What street is the school on? (First Street)

   • What is across from the grocery store? (The shopping mall)

   Continue with these kinds of questions using *between*, *on*, *on the corner of*, *across from*.

   For the older student you may also want to ask direction questions; e.g., "If you are at the park, in what direction do you walk to get to the police station?" Continue with other situations.

8. Have the student complete Activity Sheet 12–8. The student will be asked to look at the map, use the key, and answer questions regarding the location of various places and their location to each other. **Answer Key:** (*Part One*) 1. on the corner of, 2. next to, 3. between, 4. on, 5. across from; (*Part Two*) 1. No, 2. Yes, 3. No.

Extension Activities:

1. For older students obtain local city maps from a car rental agency. Design activities for the student to become familiar with major roads and important locations.

2. Ask the student to draw a map of the area surrounding the school.

3. Ask the student to draw a map of his/her neighborhood.

Name_____ Date_____

City Map

Red Rock City Map

Part One: Choose words from the word box and complete each statement.

next to	across from	on the corner of	between	on

1. Burger Barn is _____ Pine Street and Second Street.

2. The gas station is _____ fire station.

3. The hair salon is _____ the post office and the bank.

4. The school is _____ First Street.

5. The bank is _____ the park.

Part Two: Look at the map. Read each sentence and answer yes or no.

1. The zoo is on the corner of Pine Street and First Street. _____

2. The grocery store is across from the shopping mall. _____

3. The police station is on Lake Road. _____

Lesson 12-9: Reading a Map to Scale

• •

Objectives: The student will learn that a scale on a map represents a certain distance. The student will calculate the distance on a map using a bar scale.

Vocabulary: scale; measure; distance; far

Materials: Activity Sheet 12–9; Pencil; 1 sheet of plain white paper for each student; Yardstick

Teaching Note: A ruler is not used in this lesson to measure distance; instead, a strategy using a sheet of paper is used. This is a useful life skill for future situations when the student may need to measure distance but does not have a ruler in his/her possession.

Directions:

1. Ask the student to stand. Walk to the student and place one end of the yardstick by the student's foot. Then you stand at the other end of the yardstick. Say, "You are three feet away from me." Point back and forth along the yardstick. "That is called *distance*. Distance tells how *far* something is." Ask, "How far is it from you to me?" (**Response:** Three feet) Ask the student to use the yardstick and stand three feet away from other objects or other students in the room. Then ask, "How much distance is there between you and _____?" (**Response:** Three feet)

2. Give the student a copy of Activity Sheet 12–9. Say, "A small distance on a map is usually a much larger distance on the ground." (**Gesture:** Hold your hands apart indicating a small distance and point to the map, then move them apart farther to indicate a larger distance and point to the ground.)

3. Explain that maps use a *scale* to show distance. Point to the scale on the activity sheet. Explain that one inch equals five miles. Ask the student to trace along the inch line with his/her finger and say, "One inch equals (is) five miles." Ask, "How much is one inch on the map?" (**Response:** Five miles)

4. Give the student a piece of plain white paper. Ask him/her to place the edge of the paper underneath the scale and mark the point at the beginning of the inch line and the end.

5. Show the student how to measure the distance between two points using the inch marks on the paper. For example, "How far is it from Green Mountain to Fish Lake?" (**Response:** Fifteen miles)

6. Ask the student to answer the remaining questions on the activity sheet. The student will be asked to measure distances between specific places using the inch scale. **Answer Key:** 1. 15 miles, 2. 10 miles, 3. 20 miles, 4. 15 miles, 5. 5 miles, 6. 10 miles, 7. 15 miles.

Extension Activities:

1. Ask the student to measure the classroom and draw a map to scale.

2. Ask the student to draw a map of his/her route to and from school. Design a scale to show the distance.

3. Ask the student to identify the location on the activity sheet by direction and miles; e.g., Redwood Forest is 10 miles west of Bear Cave. Continue with other locations.

Name_____ Date_____

Going the Distance

Look at the map. Place the edge of a piece of paper under the scale. Draw two points. Measure the distance and answer the questions.

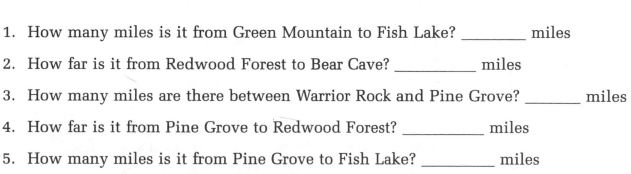

1. How many miles is it from Green Mountain to Fish Lake? _____ miles

2. How far is it from Redwood Forest to Bear Cave? _____ miles

3. How many miles are there between Warrior Rock and Pine Grove? _____ miles

4. How far is it from Pine Grove to Redwood Forest? _____ miles

5. How many miles is it from Pine Grove to Fish Lake? _____ miles

6. How far is it from Warrior Rock to Bear Cave? _____ miles

7. How many miles are there between the tent and Bear Cave? _____ miles

Lesson 12-10: Using a Globe: Continents and Oceans

Objectives: The student will understand that a globe is a model of the Earth. The student will learn the names of the seven continents and how to locate them on a globe. The student will learn the names of the four main oceans and how to locate them on the globe.

Vocabulary: globe; continent; Asia; Africa; Europe; Australia; North America; South America; Antarctica; ocean; Pacific Ocean; Atlantic Ocean; Indian Ocean; Arctic Ocean

Materials: Activity Sheets 12–10A and 12–10B; Pencil; 1 yellow and 1 blue crayon/colored pencil for each student; Globe; Picture of an ocean scene

Directions:

1. Show the student the globe. Tell the student that this is called a *globe* and is a map of the world that is shaped like a ball. Ask, "Why is it shaped like a ball?" (**Response:** The Earth is shaped like a ball.) Explain that a globe shows all the land and water that is on the Earth. Ask, "What is this called?" (**Response:** A globe) "What does it show?" (**Response:** All the land and water on Earth)

2. Give the student a copy of Activity Sheet 12–10A. Explain that there are seven large pieces of land on the Earth. These are called *continents*. Point to the names of the continents, read each one, and point to it on the illustration as you read it. Ask the student to repeat and point to the continent.

3. Now ask the student to find each continent on the globe and say the name as he/she locates it. Provide help when necessary. Ask the student to identify the continent on which his/her native country is located. Ask the student to identify the continent on which the United States is located. Provide help when necessary.

4. Explain that there are four large bodies of water on the Earth called *oceans*. Show the student a picture of an ocean scene to clarify. Ask, "What is this called?" (**Response:** An ocean)

5. Read the name of each ocean on Activity Sheet 12–10A. Point to the ocean on the illustration as you read it. Ask the student to repeat and point.

6. Now ask the student to find each ocean on the globe and say the name when he/she locates it.

7. Finally, ask the student to complete Activity Sheet 12–10B. The student will be asked to locate and write the name of each continent and ocean. The student can use the globe or Activity Sheet 12–10A for reference.

Extension Activities:

1. Play "What Continent Am I?" Give descriptions of the locations of different continents and ask the student to identify each continent. *Examples:* "I am between the Indian Ocean and the Atlantic Ocean. What continent am I?" (**Answer:** Africa) "I am an island southeast of Asia. What continent am I?" (**Answer:** Australia) *Variation:* Divide the students into teams. The team that says the correct answer first scores a point.

2. Draw a large globe of the world. Ask each student to locate the continent on which his/her native land is located and write his/her name on the continent. Display as a bulletin board.

3. Show the student a flat map of the world and ask him/her to identify the continents and oceans.

Name_____ Date_____

Oceans and Continents

Continents

North America
South America
Europe
Africa
Antarctica
Asia
Australia

Oceans

Pacific Ocean
Atlantic Ocean
Indian Ocean
Arctic Ocean

Name_____ Date_____

Oceans and Continents

Directions: Find the continents and oceans. Write the name of each one in the correct place on the maps. Then color the continents yellow and the oceans blue.

Continents

North America

South America

Europe

Africa

Antarctica

Asia

Australia

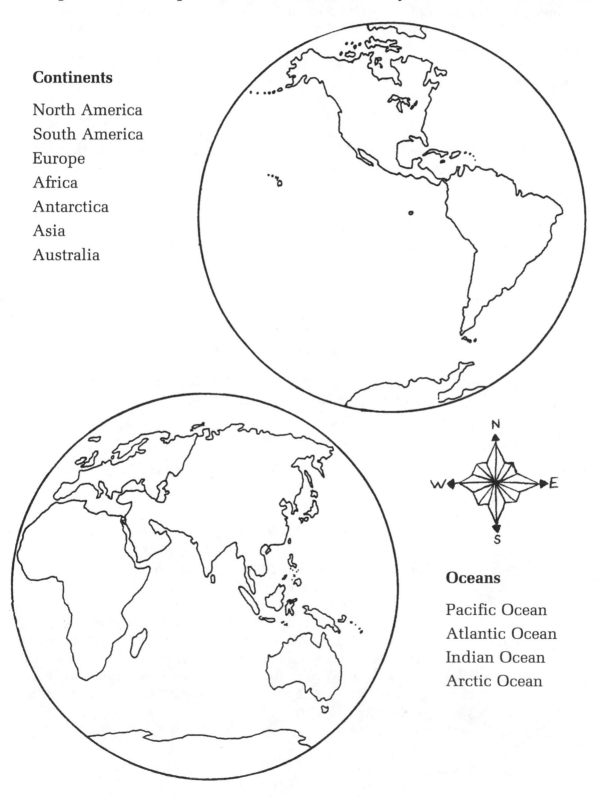

Oceans

Pacific Ocean

Atlantic Ocean

Indian Ocean

Arctic Ocean

Lesson 12-11: Latitude and Longitude

• •

This lesson is designed for the older student grades 4+.

Objective: The student will understand the terms latitude and longitude and how to find specific locations using latitude and longitude.

Vocabulary: North Pole; South Pole; latitude; longitude; parallel; meridian; equator; prime meridian; degree; global address

Materials: Activity Sheet 12–11; Pencil; Map; Globe

Teaching Note: It would be helpful for the student to have done Lesson 12–5 as practice for locating places that intersect by degrees of latitude and longitude.

Directions:

1. Place the globe in front of you and the students. Say, "This globe shows the Earth. It is a map of the world that is shaped like a ball. The very top of the Earth is called the *North Pole*." (Point to the North Pole.) Ask, "What is the top of the Earth called? (**Response:** The North Pole) Trace your finger down from the North Pole to the bottom of the globe and say, "The bottom tip of the Earth is called the *South Pole*." Ask, "What is the bottom tip of the Earth called?" (**Response:** The South Pole) Now ask the student to trace his/her finger from the North Pole to the South Pole and identify each one.

2. Explain to the student that it is easy to find directions on a globe because north is always toward the North Pole and south is toward the South Pole.

3. Explain that every place on the Earth has a *global address*. Ask, "Why does your home have an address?" (**Response:** "It tells where to find it.")

4. Tell the student that there are two numbers in a global address: a number for *latitude* and a number for *longitude*. These numbers are called *degrees*.

5. Point to the *equator* and tell the student that this is an imaginary line that divides the Earth in the middle. It divides the Earth into two parts: *north* and *south*. Ask the student to trace the equator with his/her finger around the globe. Ask, "What is this line called?" (**Response:** The equator) Explain that the equator is 0 degrees. Show the student how to write 0°, using the symbol for degrees. Explain that other lines that run the same direction as the equator are called *parallels*. Parallels are north and south of the equator. Each parallel has a number north or south of the equator. Explain that the parallels above the equator are called *north latitude* and the parallels below are called *south latitude*. Ask the student to find parallels and their numbers, north or south of the equator. Remind the student to say 20 degrees north or south when identifying a line of latitude.

6. Next, point to the North Pole and the South Pole. Tell the student that imaginary lines called *meridians* divide the Earth into east and west and go from the North Pole to the South Pole. The *prime meridian* is 0° and goes through Greenwich, England. Ask the student to trace his/her finger along the prime meridian from the North Pole to the South Pole. Ask, "What is this called?" (**Response:** The Prime Meridian) The other lines of longitude run east or west of this meridian to 180°. Explain that the meridians to the right of the prime meridian are *east longitude* and the meridians to the left of the prime meridian are *west longitude*. Ask the student to find other lines of longitude and their degrees east or west of the prime meridian.

7. Give the student various degrees of latitude and longitude and ask him/her to locate the place on a map or globe; e.g., 106° W 28°N—Chihuahua, Mexico. Next, give the student a name of a city or location and ask him/her to give the global address of this spot: degrees of latitude and longitude; e.g., Denver—40°N 105°W.

8. Give the student a copy of Activity Sheet 12–11. The student will be asked to identify the equator, prime meridian, lines of latitude, and lines of longitude. The student will be asked to locate places using their global address of latitude and longitude. **Answer Key:** (*Part Two*) 1. meridians, 2. parallels, 3. 0°, 4. 0°, 5. north, 6. south, 7. east and west.

Extension Activity: Play "Where in the World Is . . ." Each student chooses a city in the world and identifies it by latitude and longitude. The other students try to guess where each student is located. *Variation:* Each student gives the latitude and longitude of the city and the others have one minute to find the student. If they are incorrect, that student scores a point. The student then gets another turn to choose a city and stump his/her classmates again. The player with the most points wins.

Name_____ Date_____

Latitude and Longitude

Part One: Look at the globes. Trace the equator and the prime meridian. Then write the name on the line.

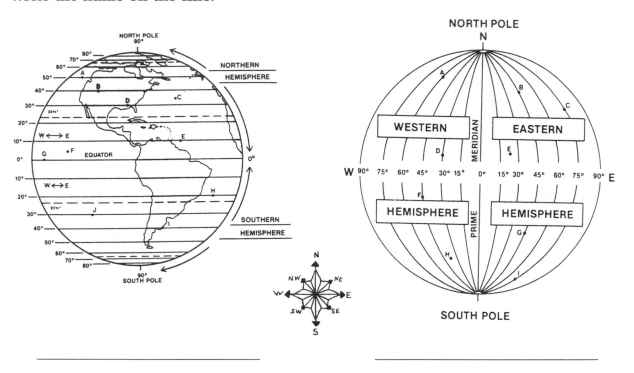

_____   _____

Part Two: Choose words from the word box and write the answer on the line.

parallels	meridians ‖	0°	east →	west ←	north ↑	south ↓

1. Lines of longitude are called _____.

2. Lines of latitude are called _____.

3. The equator is _____.

4. The prime meridian is _____.

5. Above the equator the parallels are _____.

6. Below the equator the parallels are _____.

7. Meridians show the directions _____ and _____.

Lesson 12-12: Poles and Hemispheres

• •

This lesson is designed for the older student grades 4+.

Objective: The student will learn the locations and names of the four hemispheres.

Vocabulary: North Pole; South Pole; equator; prime meridian; Southern Hemisphere; Northern Hemisphere; Eastern Hemisphere; Western Hemisphere

Materials: Activity Sheet 12–12; 2 oranges (or any other round fruit that is easy to cut); Knife to cut fruit; Pencil; Marker; 1 green, yellow, blue, and red crayon for each student; Globe

Directions:

1. Place the globe in front of you. Then say, "This globe shows the Earth. It is a round map. The very top of the Earth is called the *North Pole*." Ask the student to put his/her finger on the North Pole. Ask, "What is the top of the Earth called?" (**Response:** The North Pole) Now move your finger from the North Pole south to the South Pole. Tell the student that the bottom tip of the Earth is called the *South Pole*. Ask, "What is the bottom of the Earth called?" (**Response:** The South Pole) Ask the student to trace his/her finger down the globe from the North Pole to the South Pole and identify each one.

2. Explain to the student that it is easy to find directions on a globe because north is always the direction of the North Pole and South is always the direction of the South Pole. Now ask the student to point to north and south on the globe.

3. Tell the student that the Earth is a big ball (sphere). Show the student the orange. Say, "Imagine that this orange is the Earth. I can cut the Earth in two and make two parts." Draw a line around the middle of the orange with a marker. Say, "This line is an imaginary line called the *equator*. It goes around the middle of the Earth." Ask, "What is this line called?" (**Response:** The equator) Now cut the orange. Explain that the two parts of the Earth are called *hemispheres* (half ball). Separate the parts and hold the top part next to the North Pole and the bottom part next to the South Pole. Tell the student that the top part is called the *Northern Hemisphere* and the bottom part is the *Southern Hemisphere*. Ask the student to repeat.

4. Put the orange together again and give each student an opportunity to separate the pieces and hold one to the north and one to the south of the globe and name each hemisphere. Ask the student to name countries in each hemisphere. Provide help when necessary. Ask the student to identify in which hemisphere the U.S. and his/her native country are located.

5. Explain that we can make two different parts of the Earth if we cut it another way. Tell the student to pretend that the (new) orange is the Earth. Point to the

top of the orange and say, "This is the North Pole." Then point to the bottom of the orange and identify it as the South Pole. Begin at the top of the orange and draw a line down to the bottom of the orange. Tell the student that this is an imaginary line called the *prime meridian*. Put the orange together and hold it in front of the globe. Cut the orange along the line and separate each part. Hold one to the east and one to the west. Explain that these two parts of the Earth are called the *Eastern* and *Western Hemispheres*.

6. Give each student an opportunity to hold the orange in front of the globe and separate it into the Eastern and Western Hemispheres. The student should name each hemisphere. Ask the student to name countries that are found in each hemisphere. Provide help when necessary. Ask the student to identify the hemisphere in which the U.S. and his/her country are located.

7. Give the student a copy of Activity Sheet 12–12. The student will be asked to identify the North and South Poles, and the Northern, Southern, Eastern, and Western Hemispheres.

Extension Activities:

1. Say the names of various countries and ask the student to say if they are located in the Northern or Southern, and Eastern or Western Hemispheres.

2. Give the names of two hemispheres and ask the student to locate a country that is in each one; e.g., Northern and Western Hemispheres. (**Answer:** The United States)

Name_____ Date_____

Poles and Hemispheres

Part One: Trace the lines. Then read the words and put the correct number by the location on the Earth.

1. North Pole
2. South Pole
3. Northern Hemisphere

4. Eastern Hemisphere
5. Western Hemisphere
6. Southern Hemisphere

Part Two: Color the Northern Hemisphere green. Color the Southern Hemisphere yellow.

Part Three: Color the Eastern Hemisphere blue. Color the Western Hemisphere red.

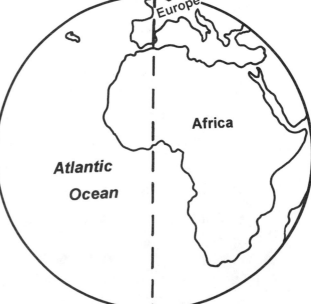

Section 13

Technology and Sources of Information

The world is truly a much smaller place with the continuing growth of technology. The World Wide Web has made it possible to connect to the far corners of the Earth in just minutes/seconds. Every day new technology and ways to use existing technology are developed. In order to function successfully in our technological world, the ESL student will need to understand not only computer language, but also how to access the information and services that are available to us.

Some ESL students may have prior knowledge of computers and how to use them; others may have had little or no exposure. However, in both cases, the student will need to comprehend the language of technology and the direction words needed to perform the functions. Because of the importance of technology in our classrooms today, teaching the ESL student how to access the school computer system should be a priority. Children love working on the computer, and with the many wonderful software programs and websites available, learning can be greatly enhanced and supported.

The lessons in Section 13 are designed to teach the student basic computer language and functions. As the new student progresses, more complicated tasks can be introduced.

Other sources of information are also included in this section. The dictionary, newspaper, encyclopedia, and the electronic encyclopedia are a few of the references presented. Knowing where to get information is the first step in broadening the student's knowledge base and expanding his/her world.

Useful Software and Websites: Many useful software programs and websites for ESL students are available. Here are some suggestions to help you get started.

- *Subject*: Geography; *Software*: "See the USA"; *Publisher*: Compu-Teach
- *Subject*: Time Lines; *Software*: "TimeLiner"; *Publisher*: Tom Synder Productions
- *Subject*: Social Studies; *Software*: "Discovering America"; *Publisher*: Lawrence
- *Subject*: ESL (Spanish); *Software*: "All About Me!"; *Publisher*: Creative Pursuits
- *Subject*: ESL; *Software*: "Annabel's Dream"; *Publisher*: Texas Caviar

- *Subject*: ESL; *Software*: "ESL Companion"; *Publisher*: Creative Pursuits
- *Subject*: ESL; *Software*: "The Bilingual Writing Center"; *Publisher*: The Learning Company
- *Subject*: ESL; *Software*: "The Writing Journal"; *Publisher*: Creative Pursuits
- *Subject*: Animals; *Website*: "Zoo Net"; http://www.mindspring.com/~zoonet/
- *Subject*: Rainforest; *Website*: "Rainforest Action Network"; http://www.ran.org/
- *Subject*: Ecology; *Website*: "Good Green Fun"; http://www.efn.org/~dharmika/
- *Subject*: Writing; *Website*: "World Writers"; http://wwwbir.bham.wednet.edu/wws/wws.htm

Technology and Sources of Information Pretest–Posttest

Student:_____   Grade:_____

Date: _____

1. Show the student the picture of the computer components and ask him/her to identify each one.

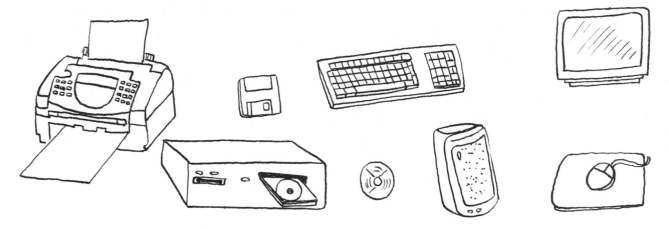

2. Give the student a dictionary. Ask him/her to find the word *tiger*. Then point to and ask the student to identify the following items: guide words, entry word, pronunciation, definition, part of speech, word forms, illustration.

3. Ask the student to identify the name of your hometown newspaper. Then show him/her a copy of the newspaper and ask him/her to identify the following items: headline, front page, sections, advertisements, classified ads, obituaries, comics, weather, puzzles, news article.

Lesson 13-1: Know Your Computer

• •

Objective: The student will learn the names of the basic component parts of a computer.

Vocabulary: computer; monitor; keyboard; CPU; printer; mouse; mouse pad; floppy disk; disk drive; CD; CD-ROM; speaker

Materials: Activity Sheets 13–1A and 13–1B; Pencil; Scissors; Glue; 1 sheet of white paper for each student; Classroom computer; CD in a hard case

Teaching Notes:

1. Each brand of computer has some differences in style and placement of component parts. Also, each school district has its own method of service. This lesson discusses the basic, generic computer and its component parts. Please accommodate on the activity sheets for any differences in appearance or alternative component parts.

2. If you haven't put labels on the classroom computer, you can do this as part of this lesson. The boxes on Activity Sheet 13–1A were designed for this use.

Directions: Present this lesson in close proximity to a computer. This lesson is generic in nature because computers and systems differ. Ask the student to come to the computer. Give the student a copy of Activity Sheet 13–1A. Point to the computer (all the components) and say, "This machine is called a *computer*. A computer is a machine that can do many things." If possible, brainstorm what people can do on a computer (get information/ideas, communicate with others by e-mail, write stories, draw pictures, listen to music, etc.).

1. Explain that the computer has different parts with different names. Point to each component part and explain as follows. (Ask the student to repeat and point to the correct component.) If you have not done so, this is a good opportunity to label the component parts of the computer. Ask the student to place the correct word on the component as you read and explain it. Use the boxes from Activity Sheet 13–1A as labels.

   Monitor: Is like a TV screen.

   Keyboard: Has many letters and numbers on it. Lets you "talk" to the computer. When we push the buttons, we call it keyboarding or typing.

   Mouse: A small object that you roll with your hand. It moves the cursor on the screen. It is attached to the keyboard.

   Mouse Pad: A small pad that is under the mouse when you roll it.

   Printer: Prints the information given from a computer onto paper.

Hard Drive—CPU (*Central Processing Unit*): Directs the functions of the computer.

CD-ROM: Allows the computer to show information, movies, or play the music on a CD disk.

CD: A disk that contains information, music, movies, etc. It is round and is kept in a hard case. (Show the student how to open the CD case and touch the CD on the edge only. Allow the student to perform the action.)

Disk: A thin, usually square, disk that stores computer information.

Disk Drive: The disk goes into this part of the computer. It transfers information to and from the disk.

2. Now give the following commands: "Touch the keyboard, touch the mouse, touch the monitor." Continue with the rest of the components.

3. Ask the student to complete Activity Sheet 13–1A. The student will be asked to read and write the name of each component part.

4. Give the student a copy of Activity Sheet 13–1B. The student will be asked to identify the component parts of the computer, cut them out, and glue them together in a logical configuration. The student will be asked to write the name of each component by the part. After the computer is glued, you may want to ask the student to draw wires from each component part to the CPU. A separate sheet of plain white paper will be needed for this.

Extension Activity: Ask the student to cut out the boxes from Activity Sheet 13–1A. Then cut out the words that were printed. Mix them up and have the student match them.

Name_____ Date_____

Computer Labels and Visuals

Read		**Write**

computer ⟶ _____

monitor ⟶ _____

keyboard  ⟶ _____

mouse ⟶ _____

mouse pad ⟶ _____ _____

disk drive 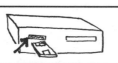 ⟶ _____ _____

printer ⟶ _____

CD-ROM 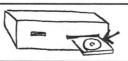 ⟶ ___ ___ ___

speaker ⟶ _____

CPU ⟶ ___ ___ ___

floppy disk ⟶ _____ _____

CD ⟶ ___ ___

Computer Components

The computer was delivered to your classroom in separate parts! Say the name of each component. Cut out the pictures. On a separate sheet of paper, put the components in place. Then glue them. Write the name next to each one.

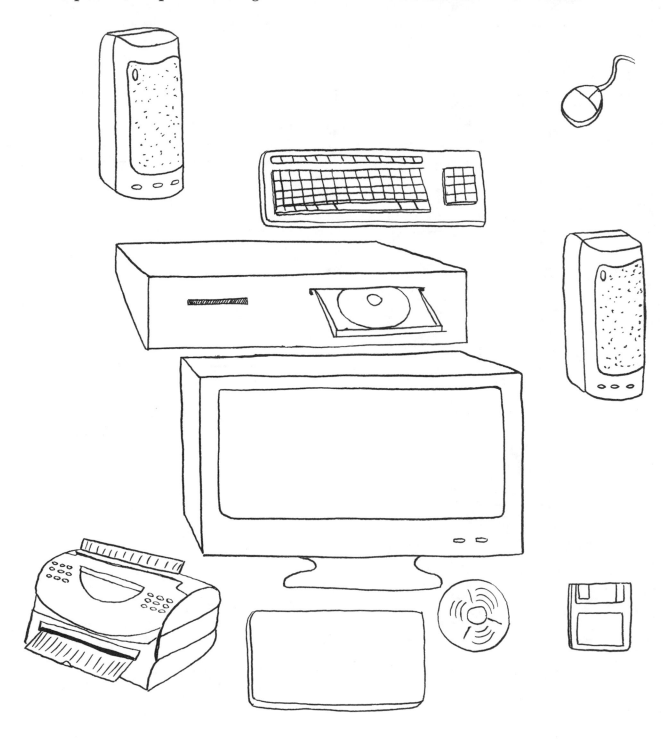

Lesson 13-2: Knock! Knock! How Do I Get In?

● ●

Objective: The student will learn the computer language involved in operating a computer. The student will learn the names of the various items on a computer screen. The student will perform basic functions on the computer.

Vocabulary: log on; log off; user name; toolbar; menu; password; cursor; click; double click; right click; icon; mouse pointer

Materials: Activity Sheets 13–2A and 13–2B: Pencil; Computer

Teaching Note: This lesson presents the basic vocabulary and actions for operating a computer. Your system may differ somewhat, so accommodate when needed. Choose the vocabulary and activities that are relevant to your student's computer situation. Activity Sheet 13–2A provides illustrations of items found on the computer screen. You may wish to teach vocabulary before presenting this lesson at the computer. Activity Sheet 13–2B will serve as a checklist. After each function is performed, the student can check it off on his/her activity sheet. This can also serve as an evaluation tool.

Directions:

1. *User Name*: Give the student a copy of Activity Sheet 13–2A. Inform the student of his/her User Name and explain that this is a special computer name that he/she will use. Ask the student to write it on the Computer ID Card provided on the activity sheet.

2. *Password*: Inform the student of his/her password. Tell the student that this is a secret name/number and should not be told to anyone else. (**Gesture:** Put your finger to your mouth in a quiet sign.) *Optional*: Ask the student to write his/her password in the space provided on the Computer ID Card. The student can keep this sheet for reference until the User Name and Password are memorized. Space has also been provided for the student's e-mail address.

3. *Click/Double Click/Right Click*: To click, push the left button on the mouse once, then let go. To double click, quickly push the left button on the mouse twice, then let go. To right click, push the right button on the mouse once, then let go. Ask the student to perform these functions.

4. *Log On*: Show the student the process for logging onto your computer system. Explain that "log on" is the same as telling the computer your name and that you want to use it. Ask the student to log on to the computer. Next, explain that the computer will ask for the student's password. Explain that this tells the computer that it is really you at the computer asking for access to (to look at) your information.

603

5. *Screen*: Next, bring up examples of the following items that are found on the computer screen. Describe and explain each one. Ask the student to point to, repeat the name, and (if applicable) perform the function.

   • *Icon*: A small picture on the screen that means a computer program or what the computer will do. Point to and explain the meanings and functions of the various icons on your classroom computer.

   • *Mouse Pointer*: A little arrow that is moved by the mouse. It puts the cursor where you want it to be. Ask the student to move the mouse pointer.

   • *Cursor*: A straight line on the computer that tells where you are on the screen. Sometimes, it blinks on and off.

   • *Menu:* A list of commands or programs. Point to, identify, and explain the items on the menu. Model and then ask the student to open a program.

   • *Toolbar*: A set of icons you click to perform tasks. Usually found at the top of the screen. Show the student how to click onto various toolbars and explain their functions.

6. *Log Off*: This process tells the computer you are done. Model and ask the student to perform the function.

7. Ask the student to complete Activity Sheet 13–2A. The student will be asked to identify various items on the computer screen. This can be done independently or with a computer buddy. Older students from other classrooms can help in this capacity.

8. Give the student a copy of Activity Sheet 13–2B. After the student has performed the task, he/she may check it off. A computer certificate is included. This can be done with a computer buddy.

Name_____ Date_____

Knock! Knock! How Do I Get In?

Computer ID Card

User Name ☺

Password 🤫 shh!

E-mail Address 🏠

Screen

Internet Explorer — ⯀ ✕

File Edit View Go Favorites Help 🅔

Back Forward Stop Refresh Home Search Favorites History Channels Mail

Address 📄 http://www.spacetravel.org ▽

New Document

Open Document

Programs ← e

Documents

Settings ← Word

Find ← netscape

Help

Run

Shut Down

User Name : _ _ _ _ _ _ _ _ _ _ _

Password: * * * * * * *

Find each item. Then write the word next to it.

menu, icon, toolbar, mouse pointer, cursor, user name, password, click, double click, right click

Name_____ Date_____

My Computer Checklist

Put a √ in the box after you have performed each activity.

I can:

☐ Log on to the computer—User name and password

☐ Click, Double Click, Right Click

☐ Move the mouse pointer

☐ Locate the cursor

☐ Insert a disk in the disk drive

☐ Insert a CD in the CD-ROM

☐ Access the Internet   www.spaceman.com

☐ Send an e-mail   e-

☐ Check my e-mail   √ e-

☐ Log off   Good-bye

User Name ------------------
Password: * * * * * * *

© 2001 by The Center for Applied Research in Education

Certificate of Merit

This certifies that _____

successfully completed all of the functions on the Computer Checklist.

_____   _____
Date   Signature

Lesson 13-3: Using E-Mail

• •

Objective: The student will learn the purpose of e-mail, the vocabulary associated with e-mail, and how to send an e-mail message.

Vocabulary: Internet; e-mail; electronic mail; e-mail address; New Message; To; From; Subject; Message; Send; New Mail

Materials: Activity Sheet 13–3; Pencil; Computer; Envelope/letter that was delivered through the Post Office; Samples of e-mail

Teaching Note: Before beginning the lesson, it would be helpful to have a person and his/her e-mail address to whom the student can send a message.

Directions:

1. Show the student the envelope and say, "This is mail. It is a message that was delivered to me by the mail carrier." Ask, "What is on the envelope?" (**Response:** name and address/return address and postmark) (Point to each.) Ask, "What does the name tell the mail carrier?" (**Response:** who gets the mail) Ask, "What does the address tell the mail carrier?" (**Response:** where to deliver the mail) Ask, "What does the return address tell the mail carrier?" (**Response:** who sent the mail and the address) Ask, "What does the postmark tell?" (**Response:** the date the mail was sent) Ask, "What is inside the envelope?" (**Response:** the message/letter, what the person wants you to know)

2. Now explain that there is a way to send mail with a computer. It is called *electronic mail* or *e-mail*. It is much faster than regular mail. The person can get your message in minutes. Show the student various samples of e-mail. Point to, identify, and describe these items:

   From: return e-mail address (name and address of sender)

   To: your e-mail address

   Date: when it was sent

   Subject: what the message is about

   Message: what the person wants you to know

   Compare each item to a regular piece of mail sent through the Post Office.

3. Explain that e-mail is sent on the *Internet*. It is a network of computer networks that are all connected. The Internet is like the mail carrier. Conduct the following exercise to explain the Internet. (You may want to make visuals to accompany the exercise.) See Activity Sheet 13–3, Part One.

   • Choose four students to participate: two are computers and two are networks. Make two pairs, each with a computer/network (pair #1 and pair #2).

- Write a simple *message* on a piece of paper, e.g., "Hi, how are you?" Give it to computer #1.

- Now tell the students that computer #1 wants to send this message to computer #2. Tell the students that the computer needs a network (is like the mail carrier) to do that. The student who is computer #1 gives the message to network #1.

- Explain that computer #2 needs his/her network to deliver the message. So network #1 gives the message to network #2.

- Network #2 gives the message to computer #2.

4. Tell the student his/her e-mail address. If you have not done so, ask the student to write his/her e-mail address on the Computer ID Card (refer to Activity Sheet 13–2A).

5. Model how to open your e-mail software program. Explain and model the following steps:

- Select *New Message*. Explain that this tells the computer that you want to send a new message to someone.

- Select *To*. Explain that this is where you type the person's e-mail address.

- Select *Subject*. Explain that this tells the person what the e-mail is about.

- Select *Main Text Area*. Explain that this is where to write your message.

- Select *Send*. Explain that this sends the message to the person's computer.

6. Next show the student how to check his/her e-mail for messages. Explain that this is usually called the *Mailbox*. Select *New Messages*.

7. Give the student a copy of Activity Sheet 13–3. The student will be asked to trace the route of an e-mail on the Internet, write information on an e-mail form, and then send it to the recipient.

Extension Activity: Arrange e-mail pen pals with other students in your district or a neighboring school district. This is fun when a party is planned and the student meets his/her e-mail pen pal.

Name_____ Date_____

E-Mail

Part One: This is what happens when you send an e-mail message on the Internet. Trace the dotted lines to see where the e-mail goes. Begin with Computer #1.

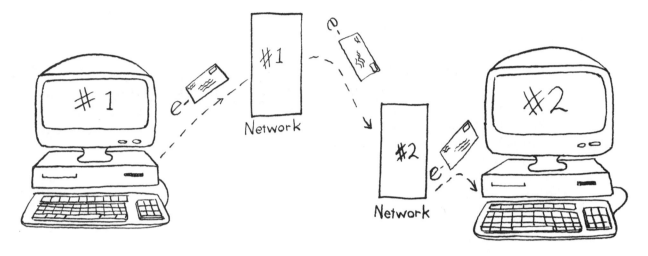

Part Two: Write the information in the e-mail box. Then input it on the computer and send your e-mail.

Send					

New Message:

To:

Subject

CC

BC

Lesson 13-4: Playing It Safe on the Net

Objective: The student will learn the safety rules associated with using the Internet.

Vocabulary: safety; Internet

Materials: Activity Sheets 13–4A and 13–4B; Pencil

Teaching Note: Internet safety rules are a very important part of the student's computer education. Many children are unaware of the dangers of giving information to strangers over the Internet and in chat rooms. It is much easier to give information when the stranger is not visible, and ESL children can be particularly vulnerable in this regard. The excitement of using a computer can often mask the dangers that lurk within. It is also a good idea to inform parents of the safety rules.

Directions:

1. Give the student a copy of Activity Sheet 13–4A. Read and discuss the Internet Safety Rules.

   - Never give your real name, address, or telephone number to someone you meet on the Internet.

   - Be careful. Not all people on the Internet are honest.

   - Never meet an online friend unless you check with an adult.

   - Tell an adult if you see anything that makes you uneasy or is not for kids.

   - Do not respond to "bad" messages.

2. Ask the student to complete Activity Sheet 13–4B. The student will be asked to decide if an item is safe or unsafe computer behavior. Help with reading, if necessary. **Answer Key:** 1. 0; 2. +; 3. 0; 4. +; 5. 0; 6. +; 7. 0; 8. 0.

Extension Activities:

1. Design a Computer Safety Contract. Explain and ask each student to sign the contract that promises he/she will obey the safety rules.

2. Write computer messages on pieces of paper and role-play. The student responds with an appropriate "safe" answer. *Example*: "Hi, what is your name?" (**Response:** Anything that isn't the student's real name. Initials like C.F. [for Computer Friend] is a good example. Or just the first initial of your name, such as M.)

Name_____ Date_____

Internet Safety Rules for Kids

Read the Safety Rules for the Internet. The pictures will help you. Discuss them with your teacher and classmates. Then follow them.

1. Never give your real name, address, or phone number to someone you meet on the Internet.

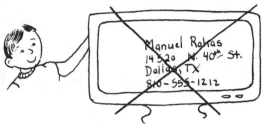

2. Be careful. Not all people on the Internet are honest.

3. Never meet an online friend unless you check with an adult.

4. Tell an adult if you see anything that makes you uneasy or is not for kids.

5. Do not respond to "bad" messages.

Name_____ Date_____

Playing It Safe on the Internet

Read the statements. Put a + on the line if it shows good computer safety. Put a 0 if it shows poor safety.

_____ 1. Juan sent this message to his computer friend:

> Hi, I'm Juan.
> I live at 667 Avon Ln. Detroit, MI.
> My phone # is 662-5550 - Come see me!

_____ 2. Sally asked her mom if she could meet her online friend at the movie theater.

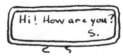

_____ 3. Jason got a bad message on his computer. It made him angry so he wrote a bad message back.

> I hate you!
>
> I hate you, too!

_____ 4. Anna saw an "Adult Only" picture. She got an uneasy feeling and told her teacher.

_____ 5. Huong says his computer friend always tells the truth.

> I'm 10 years old.
>
> My computer friend is ten years old and likes everything I do. He never lies. I trust him.

_____ 6. Sarah uses only her first initial to sign her messages.

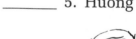

> Hi! How are you?
> S.

_____ 7. Caleb's computer buddy asks him to keep secrets. Caleb never tells anyone.

> My friend and I robbed a store. Don't tell.
>
> You can trust me. I'll never tell.

_____ 8. Toni used her mom's credit card number and bought something online. Her mom doesn't know.

> $25.99
> your credit card

Lesson 13-5: Using the Dictionary

• •

Objective: The student will learn how to locate a word in the dictionary. The student will identify the parts of a dictionary entry.

Vocabulary: dictionary; alphabetical order; entry word; guide words; pronunciation; definition; part of speech; word forms; illustration

Materials: Activity Sheet 13–5; Pencil; Dictionary (one for each student, if possible)

Teaching Notes:

1. The student should know how to alphabetize before you present this lesson. (See Lesson 7–3.)

2. Before beginning the lesson, choose a simple word to use as an example, such as *lion*.

Directions:

1. Give the student a dictionary and a copy of Activity Sheet 13–5. (You may want to use the activity sheet as a reference during the lesson.) Explain that this book is called a dictionary and gives a lot of information about words. Tell the student that the words in the dictionary are in alphabetical order.

2. Explain the following items found in a dictionary entry:

   • *entry word*: Explain that an entry word is a word that is listed in the dictionary. Tell the student the entry word you have chosen for him/her to "look up." Tell the student that to "look up" means to find the word in the dictionary. Explain that the entry word is divided into syllables or parts when it is written in the dictionary. A dot or a space separates the syllables.

   • *guide words*: Explain that guide words help you find the page your word is on. Ask the student to turn to the page your chosen entry word is on. Point to the guide words at the top of the page. Ask the student to point to them and read them. Explain that the first guide word is the first word on the page and the second guide word is the last word on the page. Ask the student to point to these two words on the page. Explain that (your entry word) will be located alphabetically between these two words. Ask, "What are these words called?" (**Response**: Guide words)

   • *pronunciation*: Explain that this tells you how to say the word. Point to the pronunciation of your chosen word. Then say it and ask the student to repeat.

   • *part of speech*: Explain that this tells you what kind of word it is (noun, verb, adjective, adverb). Tell the student that some words can be used as different parts of speech.

- *definition*: Explain that this tells the meaning of the word. Read the definition with the student. Point out that some words have more than one meaning. (You may want to use an example such as the word "safe." Ask the student to look it up. Then count and discuss the various definitions.)

- *illustration*: Explain that some entry words have a picture to show what they look like. This is called an illustration. Point to the illustration.

- *word form*: Explain that this shows how to make different forms of the word (plural form, adjective/adverb form, verb form, etc.).

3. Give the student various words to look up in the dictionary. Ask students to generate words for the class to look up.

4. Ask the student to complete Activity Sheet 13–5. He/she will be asked to identify the various parts of a dictionary entry. The student will be asked to find a word in the dictionary and identify the various parts.

Extension Activities:

1. *Bilingual Dictionary.* Teach the student how to use a bilingual dictionary from native language to English and also English to native language.

2. *Bilingual Electronic Dictionary.* Many new forms of electronic bilingual dictionaries are available. If your budget allows, invest in a few and teach the student how to use it.

3. *Play "Beat the Clock."* Give the class a word to look up. The students must find it in 30 seconds. Those who find it get a point. (*Variations*: [a] The first person to find it gets a point. [b] Student must identify the guide words.)

Name_____ Date_____

Using the Dictionary

Part One: Look at the dictionary entry below. Read the directions and do what they tell you.

linger   lip

li·on (lī′ən) *noun* 1. A large grayish–tan cat found in Africa and Asia. The male usually has a mane. *plural form*: lions

1. Put a ✓ by the **guide words**.
2. Circle the **entry word**.
3. Draw an X over the **pronunciation**.
4. Draw an arrow over the **part of speech**.

5. Underline the **definition**.
6. Draw a box around the **word form**.
7. Color the **illustration**.
8. Draw a line between the **syllables**.

Part Two: Look up the word <u>lobster</u> in the dictionary. Then write the correct information on the line.

1. The guide words are:_____

2. The entry word is: _____

3. The pronunciation is: _____

4. The part of speech is: _____

5. The definition is: _____

6. The word form is:_____

7. The illustration looks like this:

Lesson 13-6: Reading the Newspaper

• •

Objective: The student will learn how the newspaper is organized and how to find information in the newspaper.

Vocabulary: newspaper; headline; front page; international (world) news; national news; local news; business; classified ads; comics; obituaries; editorials; weather; lottery numbers; movies; TV; sports; puzzles; advertisement; stock market; reporter; news article

Materials: Activity Sheets 13–6A and 13–6B; Pencil, markers, or highlighters; 1 newspaper for each child

Teaching Note: This lesson is designed to introduce the student to the information in the newspaper and how it is organized. Newspapers may vary somewhat in organization or name of a section but most have similar elements. Add any information that is shown in your newspaper but may not have been included in this lesson plan. Although some students may not have achieved a reading level high enough to read the paper, they should still be exposed to what the newspaper has to offer.

Directions:

1. Give each student (or group) a newspaper. Say, "This is called a *newspaper*. It gives us the news. News is what is happening in our world, our city, our neighborhood. It also tells us many other things." If possible, ask the students to brainstorm other information that is in the newspaper. (Many students will have prior knowledge of newspapers in their native country.)

2. Explain the various parts of your newspaper. Ask the student to locate, circle the item, and repeat.

   • *The name*: Ask the student to repeat the name of your newspaper.

   • *Front Page*: The first page of the newspaper. It contains the most important information and an index.

   • *Headline*: The most important news of the day. Point to the headlines and ask the student to repeat.

   • *News Article*: The story that comes after the headline.

   • *Index*: This is located on the front page and tells what is in the paper and where to look (sections, weather, etc.) Locate the items listed in the index.

   • *Section*: Contains specific types of news and information. Read through the sections your paper offers. Usually, sections are given letter names.

   • *Classified Ads*: Advertisements for jobs, homes, apartments, selling items, etc.

   • *Personal Ads*: Messages for people.

   • *Editorials*: The editor's opinion about a subject.

616

- *Advertisement*: Tells about goods or services for sale.
- *Comics*: Funny drawings with humor.
- *Obituaries*: Lists who recently died.
- *Movies*: Tells the name of the movie, where it is playing, and what time(s).
- *Puzzles*: Crossword puzzles, word games.
- *Weather*: The local and national forecasts.
- *Sports*: Gives the scores of games, tells about games, articles about sports teams and athletes.
- *TV–Radio*: Lists the TV and radio shows for the day.
- *Stock Market*: Shows the price of stocks.
- *Local News*: Your city news.
- *National News*: News around the U.S.
- *International News:* News around the world.
- *Reporter*: The person who gets the news and writes about it.

3. After you have located and discussed these elements, give the student a copy of either Activity Sheet 13–6A or 13–6B. (Activity Sheet 13–6A is designed for the older, more advanced student, while 13–6B is for the beginner or younger student.) The student will need a copy of your local newspaper to complete the information on the activity sheet.

Extension Activities:

1. Assign a different student to be the news reporter for the day. Each morning this student will report on the news/current events.
2. Visit a news website on the Internet and discuss the differences between it and a newspaper.
3. Ask the student to bring in a newspaper from his/her native country. Make a reading corner or display in the school library.
4. Begin a classroom ESL newspaper.
5. Ask the students to bring in a cartoon to share. Make a bulletin board.
6. Underline or highlight quotations found in articles.
7. Write an advertisement for a favorite restaurant, store, etc.
8. Create an ESL comic strip.
9. Report on a sports team or game.
10. Ask the student to bring advertisements of things that appeal to him/her.

Name_____ Date_____

What's in the News?

Directions: Look at a copy of your local newspaper and answer these questions.

1. What is the name of the paper? _____

2. How many sections does the paper have? _____

3. What is the headline on the front page? _____

   _____

4. What is the weather report? _____

5. Write the name of a movie that is playing _____

   _____

6. Write the name of a person who died._____

7. In what section are the comics?_____

8. Write the name of a comic strip._____

9. Give the name of a hometown sports team. _____

10. Write the score of a game._____

11. What is the name of the section where you can find a job? _____

    _____

12. What were the winning lottery numbers? _____

13. In what section are the Editorials? _____

14. Write the name of a reporter. _____

15. On what page can you find an apartment?_____

16. Find a quote and write it here. _____

    _____

17. Write the name of one person who was in the news. _____

18. On what page is the stock market listed? _____

19. Write the make, model, and price of a new car. _____

    _____

20. In what section are the puzzles found?_____

Name_____ Date_____

What's in the News?

Directions: Read the words (the pictures will help you). Find the item in the newspaper and write the section number and page number where you found it.

Headline  Section _____ Page _____

Comics Section _____ Page _____

Sports Section _____ Page _____

Puzzles   Section _____ Page _____

Obituaries Section _____ Page _____

Weather Section _____ Page _____

Movies Section _____ Page _____

Classified Ads  Section _____ Page _____

TV Section _____ Page _____

Editorials 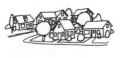 Section _____ Page _____

Local News Section _____ Page _____

National News Section _____ Page _____

World News Section _____ Page _____

Lesson 13-7: Reference Sources

Objective: The student will learn the various reference sources available in the library and on the computer.

Vocabulary: facts; encyclopedia; electronic encyclopedia; atlas; dictionary; World Wide Web—Internet website

Materials: Activity Sheet 13–7; Pencil

Teaching Note: This lesson should be taught in the school library or in a location where the reference material can be found.

Directions:

1. Take the student to the school library or a place where reference sources can be found. Explain that reference books are books of *facts*. Tell the student that a fact is information that is true.

2. Show the student the following reference materials, what each one contains, and how to use them.

   - *Encyclopedia.* Usually a set of books that gives facts about many different subjects. Explain that the encyclopedia is organized alphabetically.

   - *Dictionary.* Gives information about words.

   - *Atlas.* A book of maps.

   - *Electronic Encyclopedia.* An encyclopedia that is available on the computer. Many times this is on a CD and can be accessed by the CD-ROM.

   - *World Wide Web—Internet website.* Information that can be found on the Internet. Show the student how to conduct a search using the Internet service for your school.

3. Give the student a copy of Activity Sheet 13–7. The student will be asked to find facts relating to his/her native country from each type of reference material.

Extension Activities:

1. Give the student several subjects to investigate. He/she must find one fact from each type of reference resource.

2. Assign a written report. The student must use at least three different sources of reference.

Name_____ Date_____

Finding the Facts

Part One: Draw a line from the word to the correct picture.

Encyclopedia

Dictionary

Atlas

Electronic Encyclopedia

World Wide Web—Internet Website

Part Two: Find two facts about your native country in each of the references below. Write the name of the reference book and then the facts.

My Native Country: _____

Encyclopedia: _____ Facts: _____

_____

Dictionary: _____ Facts: _____

_____

Atlas: _____ Facts: _____

_____

Electronic Computer: _____ Facts: _____

_____

World Wide Web—Internet Website: (Address) _____

Facts:_____

_____

Notes

Notes

Notes